Why am I sick?

What's <u>really</u> wrong and how you can solve it using META-Medicine®

Revised
FIRST EDITION
First Published in Great Britain in 2009
Re-printed in 5 different countries
7th Printing 2010

Richard Flook

with
Rob van Overbruggen Ph.D

ISBN: 1-4392-4290-9

Contents

About this book and a note to you the reader

This book is about medicine and a new approach to how we go about healing ourselves called META-Medicine®.

The information in this book goes completely against the present thinking of traditional medicine. Throughout the book I have tried to be open and give you reasons as to why the present system is I believe flawed. I have endeavoured to give you evidence to prove each point as I go through it. However the information is controversial and is designed to make you think differently about disease, why we get it and how to solve it using approaches which integrates traditional, alternative, energetic and complementary therapies.

If you are suffering from a disease of any sort, and you are reading this book to find a solution to your problem, I implore you to get a medical diagnosis first. If you already have a diagnosis and you are thinking about certain therapies whether traditional, complementary, energetic or alternative, then this book will open your eyes as to why you have your disease and the symptoms you may be experiencing. However if you act upon any of the information in this book you do so at your own risk. Instead, please contact a Licensed META-Medicine® Health Coach, who will work with you and alongside your medical practitioner to find the right integrative solution to solve your issue. There is a growing database of them on www.metamedicine.com.

If you are therapist, then it is equally important to get a medical diagnosis for your client before you work on any disease issue. A licensed META-Medicine® Health Coach can assist you by answering why your client has their issue. They will design a therapy plan that is integrative in its approach to solving their underlying problem. This will mean working alongside their medical practitioner.

If the issue is not life-threatening, then you can get a quick consultation from my website www.meta-medicine.com. If you need more information, then contact one of the licensed META-Medicine® Health Coaches on www.metamedicine.com.

This book describes some of the models of META-Medicine® which we believe explain how disease works. These models are NOT a therapy. If you want to learn more about META-Medicine® we have many programmes available for download or a list of live trainings. Please go to my website www.meta-medicine.com or www.whyamisick.org.

NEW TECHNIQUE and internet based training courses
Since writing this book I have discovered so much more about how we heal. To learn about my new techniques and other developments as well as internet based trainings in META-Medicine®, visit www.whyamisick.org

Richard Flook
Head of International Training META-Medicine®

Acknowledgments

Whenever I look through acknowledgements in books I find them dull and boring. This is why I wanted to tell you why the people I want to acknowledge are here, so that you can fully understand the journey that I have been on and then better understand how significant these individuals have been for me in writing this book. This is a book that I am certain will change how you view disease, forever.

When I was aged six my mother left my father. She moved hundreds of miles away north from where I lived in the south-west of England in Bristol. By the time I was twelve she had died of cancer. It was this event that ultimately led to my writing this book. I hope that the death of my mother, Anne Richardson (Flook), has not been in vain. I wish that she could be here, reading this book. I am proud that my father, Julian Flook, will see the fruits of my labours, as he has supported me through my pursuit of understanding this material. I grew up having a difficult time with the relationships he had following his divorce; it took a long time for me to forgive him. I realise, now that I have a son of my own, how challenging being a parent is. We all make mistakes - after all, we are all human. He has had his fair share of illnesses and issues. His support has been inspiring, and without him you would not be reading this book.

My incredible wife Kristin Watson-Flook has patiently observed and assisted me in this book. Little does she know how her stability and groundedness has made this book a reality. When we decided to change our business from an NLP training company to META-Medicine® we both knew it would be challenging, and Kristin has stuck by me through thick and thin. My learning and regular free consultations as I strived to fully understand how META-Medicine® works for people in real life, meant we stopped earning by two-thirds what we were previously earning from NLP. I am certain that it will pay off; this information is so valuable for everyone.

Johannes Fisslinger is an amazing man; I love his passion and also his solid character. He opened the door to make META-Medicine® possible for everyone to use. He has been a friend, a mentor and a fantastic colleague.

Dr Anton Bader my mentor and friend; he has taught me so much, especially about Brain CT reading, META-Medicine® and has always been there when I needed a consultation, even if it was at two o'clock in the morning.

Christa Uricher is such a special person; her love and genuine heart for healing people with cancer is incredible. She has always been there helping and assisting me whenever I got stuck with the really difficult client cases.

Dr Kwesi Anan Odum; another great friend who is a medical doctor and who has shown me so many different developments in healing from Germany that whenever I speak to him there is always something new and exciting to discover.

Rob van Overbruggen; for his work on chapter 13, on psychological issues. Without him that chapter would not have happened. We worked and worked on that chapter to make sure it was correct, because this information alone is going change the world of psychology forever.

Birgitte Bakke; a very close and dear friend of mine who told me that what I do as a practitioner and a trainer is truly magnificent. I needed that recognition. I have been in the dark searching for many years to make all the therapies and application of META-Medicine®

theory really work, so that I could teach it. When someone I really respect acknowledged that what I was doing was truly special, I realised I had to raise my game and step up to the mark. Many parts of this book come as a result of her inspiration.

Professor Peter Fraser has been an inspiration; always challenging me to think differently about what is really happening, never to be stuck in a status quo because it has always been that way. Without him many of the emotional discoveries I made and the link between the energetic body and META-Medicine® would not have happened.

Harry Massey; for getting this information out into the world, and allowing me to be a part of his vision.

Karl Dawson; who was on my first 2-day introduction. He has remained a great friend ever since. Without him, so many doors would not have opened. He has told so many people about META-Medicine®.

Dr Khaled Al-Damallawy for assisting me with many aspects of what it is like to be a doctor in Egypt and getting META-Medicine® into the Arabic countries.

Karin Gustafson; even though I have only recently met her, I know she will be a friend for life. She helped me find the title for the book, and she has pointed me in the right direction as to how to market and develop META-Medicine® worldwide. You will see a lot more of her behind the scenes work, as she and I get this incredible information out into the world.

Lucille White; who was so downtrodden by life yet so full of it at the same time, she has pushed me and become what she is today. She will tell the world about this stuff.

Robert Waghmare; whose ideas are always inspiring. He was one of the first people to show me that META-Medicine® could really be applied in a coaching setting. Along with his partner Joanne Ross they are doing great work in spreading the word of META-Medicine®

Hannah Jane Wood; who painstakingly did the first proof read and edit of the book, which was no mean feat. Her patience and fun and continuous 'Oh my God! Is that true?' made me realise that what I have written could be something special.

Sue Waudby Smith who did the final edit. She is an Aunt of mine and her great work at turning the manuscript into a final readable version was so important to me.

Malou Laureys would always be there when I had a question about certain conflict shocks that I could not understand. She is a little gem of a person, who does not want to make a song and dance about her talent but she truly knows so much about this field, I feel in awe of her knowledge.

Susie Shelmerdine; for showing me a way to be able to clear the Kidney Collecting Tubule Syndrome, something that has plagued me and everyone in this field. Finally we have an answer.

Tim Harnden; who has remained a friend and has embraced personal development, sometimes finding it so difficult that it hurt. His continued journey to resolve his late onset diabetes where he has to inject insulin has changed his life.

Lothar Hirneise and his amazing book on chemotherapy woke me up to traditional cancer therapies and why they don't work.

Susanne Billander; for teaching me that love is the real healer. She was instrumental in Terry and myself talking again after many years of silence.

Terry Elston; for being a friend who pushed me to do what I have always wanted to do. Little did I know that it would cause so much friction at the time, but because of this book we are friends once more.

Tad James; who first introduced me to this work in a tape set training NLP. It was also through Tad that I met Johannes Fisslinger. Tad has been a pioneer of emotional clearing techniques.

Anne Sweet; whose grace and passion in explaining so much about what really goes on in cancer wards, and for her continuously asking, "How's the book coming along?"

Jenny Bourne; for embracing change and still working through her stuff and letting me share her story about her breast cancer.

Adam Sprackling; for showing me that META-Medicine® could be used in coaching to transform lives. His story about his life not moving forward was the catalyst for me to rethink how we can apply META-Medicine® in everyday lives.

Georgie Atkinson; whose bravery and determination are an inspiration to any women discovering they have breast cancer but are not willing to accept the traditional way of healing through chemotherapy and radiotherapy.

Kim Roberts; for letting me use her letter and to her son who could have been me.

To all my clients; those that are living and well and enjoying life to the full and those who have passed on. Without you all, this book would just be theory.

Frances Gard who is a personal friend and who took the pictures of me for the front cover and inside the book. She is truly an inspiring photographer who captures the real you. You can contact Frances through www.francesgard.com.

Sheena for letting me use her pictures showing the results of Kidney Collecting Tubule syndrome.

Dorothy wood for assisting me in my healing my right foot in 2010 by using homeopathy and B.Polaris (a natural antibiotic made by bees)

Martin Möhrke for his passion in spreading the word regarding healing devices such as the NES system and the PDT (Personal therapy device).

Dr Geerd Hamer, the brilliance of whose work is the backbone to many of the disease theories in this book. What he has painstakingly pieced together is truly the work of a genius. Without his work this book would not have been possible.

And of course all my students and clients who have shown me the way to challenge and open up this work, so it can be made available internationally. Without their enthusiasm and encouragement I personally would have given up the journey to spread this incredible paradigm shift in our thinking of how disease is created and wellness is our right.

Front cover picture, which is of the author and the inside cover of the author (Richard Flook) were photographed by Frances Gard. www.francesgard.com

Introduction

by Karl Dawson

As an Emotional Freedom Techniques (EFT)* Master, I've been on the cutting-edge of the personal development industry for a number of years. Like many, this particular journey started with my own health issues. 2001/2002, I had become increasingly ill with chronic fatigue, multiple allergies, inflammation, metabolism and blood sugar regulation issues.

Whilst recovering from these conditions I was drawn to EFT, and I soon became a therapist, a trainer and eventually EFT Master. In this time I drew a disproportionate amount of clients and trainees who were themselves overcoming serious illness and disease. The universe has a way of sending not only those who are on a similar path but also, if we pay attention, the solutions to our problems. So while I looked for the answers to help myself and my clients heal, I was lucky enough to find wonderful teachers from around the world. Gary Craig, the creator of EFT, was one such teacher. Donna Gates, the founder of the Body Ecology Diet, and cellular biologist Dr Bruce Lipton were other pioneering and inspiring teachers, whose incredible knowledge helped me make sense and understand the conditions I and others were experiencing. Health conditions for which the modern medical model had no solution.

Armed with a wealth of information from these great people, I developed my own EFT for Serious Disease Training, which has been popular with medical professionals, therapists and lay-people alike. My training explains how eventually as we age our early traumas and childhood experiences, if left unresolved, often manifest as a myriad of diseases as the body tries to adapt the subconscious mind's mistaken perceptions of self and the environment. As well as identifying the problem, my training helped to address the solution, showing how these conditions can be resolved with EFT.

On my journey I was fortunate to meet and train with Richard Flook, and to learn the invaluable diagnostic system, META-Medicine®. Time and again, I have been able to help my clients, trainees and workshop attendees, locate the underlying emotional cause of disease with pinpoint accuracy, and resolve it with EFT. I have seen great results working with Chronic Fatigue Syndrome, rheumatoid arthritis, Multiple Scherosis, Irriatble Bowel Syndrome, diabetes, asthma, cancer, Crohns disease, colitis, vitaligo, alopecia, hypothyroidism, anxiety, panic attacks, stress and depression amongst many other physical and emotional conditions. These results have been greatly accelarated thanks to META-Medicine®.

Several years ago I developed my own advancement on EFT, a technique which I named Matrix Reimprinting. Combining EFT with quantum physics and the developments in the New Sciences, Matrix Reimprinting is a powerful tool for personal transformation. Richard fondly refers to Matrix Reimprinting and META-Medicine® as a match made in heaven! The reason being is that with Matrix Reimprinting you can work directly with parts of yourself that have split off due to previous life-traumas, and with META-Medicine® you can identify which traumas have specifically caused which disease. So with careful diagnosis you can quickly get to the route of any disease condition using META-Medicine®, and resolve it using Matrix Reimprinting.

In 2008, with our shared passion to unite these two techniques, Richard and I created and filmed a three day training, entitled *EFT and META-Medicine®*. On the training we combined our knowledge. Richard skilfully questioned workshop participants about their existing medical conditions identifying which life trauma or traumas triggered them, whilst I helped them to resolve the stress and energetic disruption around the memory, and install more supportive memories using Matrix Reimprinting.

The results of the three day training where phenomenal. We worked with one workshop attendee, helping her to resolve bipolar affective disorder in the space of fifty minutes. With the accuracy of META-Medicine® we were able to identify the root cause of the condition - three early life traumas, and with Matrix Reimprinting we were able to reprogramme these traumas. Of course, we may have eventually resolved this condition with Matrix Reimprinting alone, but without META-Medicine®, it would have taken endless months of systematically working on different life traumas, in the hope of stumbling across the ones that caused the condition. Also, some of the traumas that people have experienced are not available to them consciously, so the ones which caused the disease may remain hidden. But with META-Medicine® conditions can be diagnosed accurately and precisely, enabling outstanding results.

I am, therefore, very pleased that Richard has written this book. There is, of course, much more to META-Medicine® than just resolving trauma, and Richard's book explains this very accurately. This book is a wealth of resources for doctors, medical professionals, psychotherapists, holistic therapists, nutritionists, as well as lay people who are looking to identify the root cause of their health conditions. It is the much-needed missing link between therapeutic practice, and the science behind sickness and disease. It is my hope that this book finds itself on the shelf of every practitioner who is serious about helping their clients to recover. It will certainly be top of the recommended reading list on my Matrix Reimprinting trainings.

Karl Dawson,
EFT Master,
Creator of Matrix Reimprinting.

*EFT is a self-help tool, based on the Chinese meridian system (the same system used in acupuncture). It involves tapping on meridian end points in the body whilst tuning into and verbalising a specific health or emotional issue. This helps to clear disruption from the body's energy system and restore health and emotional balance.

Chapter 1

The beginning of META-Medicine®

The greatest mistake in the treatment of diseases is that there are physicians for the body and physicians for the soul, although the two cannot be separated.
~Plato

There is no education like adversity - Disraeli

My Mum was Dead. It was 10.30 in the morning on a cold winter's day in late 1976. I was twelve years old and walking up a small hill to a classroom in the school I attended in Bath, England. Tears were flowing down my cheeks uncontrollably. I couldn't stop them, but I sobbed silently. I didn't want any of my school friends to see me - boys don't cry. I walked alone. It was a horrible, horrible day. However, in hindsight, it was an important one. It was the day I was to make one of the most fundamental decisions of my life, a decision that was to shape me and take me on an incredible journey that, until that time, I had not foreseen in any way, a decision the importance of which I would not realise until twenty-eight years later.

My father had awakened me as usual that morning but instead of popping his head around the door in his usual jovial manner, he walked silently into my room. His head was lowered hiding his eyes as he sat down on the end of my bed. I could feel something was wrong, as he was so obviously different. There was an air of deep anguish about him and as he looked at me I could see his eyes were red and bloodshot and I could tell he was in shock. I knew then that something awful had happened but I had no idea what. He sat for a moment, looking at me and shaking his head slowly from side to side. I can still see his saddened face. He looked away as he spoke, his words full of grief: "I don't know how to tell you, you know your Mum was very ill and I'm so sorry Richard but she died late last night."

My parents had divorced six years earlier and my mother had noticed lumps in her left breast eighteen months later. She had remarried and had moved a ten hour car journey away from where my father, my two brothers and I lived, in Bath in the south of England. We saw her infrequently and it was an extremely traumatic time for my brothers and myself - we missed her terribly. Little did I know at the time that this separation and worry about her three boys would be the cause of her breast cancer, the subsequent complications and her eventual death.

That was where and how my journey began; many years later, after trying in vain to find out <u>why</u> she died so tragically and so young, an unusual meeting of minds caused me to become part of META-Medicine®.

In 2003 I was reviewing an advanced emotional clearing technique called Time-Line Therapy® with Dr Tad James (the inventor) in Los Angeles, USA. I was asked to stand up and explain, as one of the few master trainers in this field, how I use and want to work with this material. I mentioned a German Doctor whose basic principles are both discussed in Time-Line Therapy® and make up some of the foundations behind META-Medicine®. Sitting right behind me was a man called Johannes Fisslinger and after I had spoken he tapped me on the shoulder and said: "I'm into the same work, we should talk". Johannes was just setting up the International META-Medicine® Association at that time and since then we have remained good friends and, together with other great people, we have developed META-Medicine® into what it is today.

What is META-Medicine® and what it is not?

So what is META-Medicine®? It is not a therapy or therapeutic intervention, but a model for diagnosing disease that is based on how the body reacts to a significant stressful event which affects the body, mind, spirit, social and environmental balance of a person or animal. Unlike a traditional medical diagnosis which diagnoses a symptom, META-Medicine® looks at the whole human being; how a disease affects us in all areas of our lives and is truly holistic in its approach to solving problems. Traditional medicine can accurately diagnose a person's symptoms whether it is heart disease, a cancer, the flu, a syndrome or any multitude of issues. From that information doctors will treat the symptom with the aim of getting rid of it by using drugs, surgery, heating, freezing or other therapies to make the symptoms disappear.

A META-Medicine® diagnosis is different from a traditional medical diagnosis because, although we use that information, we aim to go to the root cause of the disease, which we believe is a highly significant stressful event. This method then establishes a person's symptoms within what we believe to be the process a disease goes through.

This then allows us to explain how a disease and the symptoms move from the effect on the body caused by the ongoing stress, followed by how the body repairs itself after the stressful event has been resolved. From this information a META-Medicine® Health Coach puts together a whole therapy plan that involves the body, mind, spirit, social and environmental solutions, focussed around solving the stressful event that caused the disease to occur in the first place and then supporting the body through the disease process.

Traditional Medicine's whole premise seems to be based on one major factor - that a disease is a mistake of the body and that somehow we have caught or created this issue, growth or problem. Our body has gone wrong, it is not functioning properly, it is not our fault and therefore the issue/problem has nothing to do with us. That's why you hear people say: 'Doctor cure me, make me well again, get rid of this thing inside me, cut it out, zap it out, give me drugs to kill the germs, do whatever you want to do to me, just get rid of this thing'.

This approach has worked for many years and certainly modern medical techniques have had a profound effect on the world for the last one hundred years. The promise of being able to pop a pill to solve any issue has driven the pharmaceutical industry relentlessly to develop newer, better and more dynamic interventions, some of them brilliant. Plus it is what we as a society want: 'Give me a pill to make me better'. Until recently there has been a lack of proof that the mind is connected to the body, so who can blame the general public, the doctors or the pharmaceutical industry for this behaviour.

We may well ask the question though: why doesn't this system of 'curing' people work all the time? In recent years the truth has come out and in fact the massive growth of energy medicine is probably going to change health care worldwide. One such method is Nutri Energetics System - NES (www.neshealth.com) which is the brilliant work of Professor

Peter Fraser. NES works by correcting the balance of energy in the Human Body Field. It is an advance combination of acupuncture and homeopathy.

Time and time again I come across people who are not happy with the cripplingly expensive chemical pill popping culture, because it often only masks the symptoms and the drugs can create more side effects than the original issue gave the person in the first place. It is also strange that in the last twenty years I have found that doctors are no longer at the top of the social ladder. Honoured in the past for their magical abilities to cure every ailment they are now more likely to be sued for mal-practice than hailed as healers.

This, plus the fact that we have an enormous pharmaceutical industry, which interestingly remains totally un-policed worldwide and plays such a massive part in our society by keeping government health policy focussed on only one system of healing – that of using a chemical resolution for a disease, when clearly there is a wealth of evidence proving that this chemical approach accounts for only a small part of the disease jigsaw puzzle. So what has gone wrong?

I can only speculate because the facts are not available but I have some thoughts on this matter and when you have finished this book I believe you may think the same way. I will give you an example: are you aware that sixty years ago the intervention for cancer was chemotherapy, radiation and surgery? It was all experimental.

Today the intervention for cancer has remained practically the same: chemotherapy, radiation and surgery with a tiny little bit of hormone therapy. The survival rate for many cancers has remained the same despite reported improvements in the effectiveness of chemotherapies. Ralph Moss PhD, in his book Questioning Chemotherapy, (www.cancerdecsions.com) talks about how many doctors explain to the few clients who ask them, after they have received a cancer diagnoses, that having chemotherapy will improve their chances by 30%. Sounds good. But what does that 30% mean? Do people live longer and without reoccurrence? How are these statistics compiled? By personal supervision? Or by carefully controlled clinical trials?

Ralph Moss explains that the 30% often quoted tells a person how long they will live without signs of the disease, but does not tell them if they will actually live any longer if they had not had chemotherapy. He illustrates this point by mentioning that ten randomized trials of chemotherapy for node-negative breast cancer did reduce the rate of recurrence by about one-third, but had no visible effect on survival. (An example of the 30% improvement often mentioned.)

This may surprise you as everyday we are told about the dramatic improvements in cancer treatments. However it seems that the truth is not as good as we are led to believe. Yes, breast cancer reoccurrence rates are down by 50% over the past 30 years, which implies survival rates are up by 50%.

Reading through the literature most of these efforts are put down to better screening, smoking reduction and education.

As regards many chemotherapies, they have been proven unable to cure certain cancers. A person can take a test to determine whether a certain chemotherapy will have the effect that the doctor says it will on their cancer[1] but it is seldom used because it is costly.

It is also surprising to find that my native Britain lags behind the rest of Europe in cancer survival rates for lung, breast, colorectal and prostate cancer[2]. It has been suggested that over 25,000 lives could be saved per year if Britain performed as well as the some of the top performing countries.

It pains me to say that when one considers the trillions of pounds, dollars and Euros, often donated by charities, that have been spent on the so called 'War Against Cancer', these improvements don't add up. How many more people have to die before they start to look elsewhere other than in the bottom of a Petri-dish to establish that disease is a process that is triggered by changes in environmental conditions in a 'live' human being and not something that a single isolated defective cell decides to do with no cause, no reason, no explanation. Even a person with a defective gene who suddenly develops a disease after being healthy must have had something happen to trigger that gene to change so it expresses itself.

We think that the basic treatment and philosophies for most diseases are the same worldwide. However, every country has a different approach to treating disease. As an example; a diabetic friend of mine called Tim Harnden found that worldwide there are four separate philosophies as to the cause of diabetes and therefore where the focus of research and treatment is. In the UK it is believed that diabetes is hereditary and genetic, hence a lot of money is being put into stem cell research. In other parts of the western world it is believed that it's caused by a virus. In Israel they are researching how the beta islet cells (the ones in the pancreas that produce insulin) communicate with each other. They have found that these cells build tubes that talk with each other and in diabetes these cells are too busy chatting amongst themselves to do what the body wants them to do. Another belief that comes from the east says that it may be down to trace elements being out of balance in the body; if there is too much of one specific element, the insulin molecules clump together in sixes and are ineffective.

This gives us four completely different explanations as to what is the cause of diabetes and that seems to happen with practically all diseases. Undoubtedly all of them could be right. However, the money goes into what is in vogue at the time in that country. So the whole thing becomes a lottery based on who has the cash, who thinks they might be able to prove something is happening and what drug can be developed from this research. The sales from the drug then pays for the investment in research and what is leftover is profit for the company. I do not think anyone is conspiring to do anything wrong here but the process of the development of a wonder cure is not as idealistic as we may think.

In the last 50 years we have put a man on the moon, we have built wonderful new structures and buildings and other astounding engineering projects. We can do things with technology that were pure science fiction in the 1950's. Quantum Physics has told us that we are not who we think we are, and that matter is just pure energy. Find out more by watching 'What the bleep do we know' www.whatthebleep.com.

Quantum mechanics has been able to explain some of the world's most incredible phenomena, such as the weather, making faster computer processors and the World Wide Web. We can blow up the world a thousand times over with nuclear weapons (a direct result from splitting the atom). We are able to see things at a million times magnification through electron microscopes and through genetics we can determine so much of the imprints that make up the biological blue-print of our bodies.

Epigenetics – The new science of the genes

The point I am making is that wonderful things have been happening in science, as it evolves and challenges our current paradigms of thinking. But when it comes to medicine, these changes have not been acknowledged or even considered. Take, for example, the implications of Epigenetics; the new science born out of genetic research that is challenging the very philosophies of modern medicine in how many diseases are created.

Epigenetics is a science that finally proves that our DNA is not static and that genes can switch on and off, thereby expressing different traits based on specific events in our lives or changes in our environment.

4

Professor Wolf Reik at the Babraham Institute in Cambridge, has spent years studying this hidden ghost world of DNA and Epigenetics. He has found that merely manipulating the embryos of mice, without changing the DNA in any way, is enough to set off 'switches' that turn a gene's expression on or off. [3]

Professor Wolf Riek's work [4] has shown that these switches can be inherited. This means that a shocking 'memory' of an event could be passed down through generations. A simple environmental effect can switch a gene's expression on or off and this change has been found to be inherited. As an example, a great grandparent who went through a famine, almost dying from the effects, passes on an expression of a gene that tells the body to gorge when it can, and store excessive food so it won't starve to death in the future. A grandchild whose parents limit the intake of food, for health reasons, could be causing the grandchild's body to trigger this inherited gene's expression and the child ends up becoming clinically obese.

What we are saying is that a shocking experience suffered by a great grandparent is remembered and can be passed down intelligently through the gene pool to a grandchild. If that grandchild experiences something environmentally similar to that experienced by the great grandparent, then that triggers the same learnt pattern; it causes that key specific gene, with the memory stored in it, to alter its expression (not create a new gene or change its coding) but to switch on how that gene behaves in the body.

This goes a long way to prove that genes and the environment are not mutually exclusive but are inextricably intertwined; the environment affects the gene.

To back this up there have been discoveries showing that it is the cell membrane and not the DNA that is responsible for determining how the DNA switches itself on and off. Cells change their structure and function based on their environment. [5]

Our thoughts also affect our body. It has now been categorically proven through Neuropeptide research that the mind and body are connected as one. There have been many research papers concluding this. This means that as you think, you affect the whole of your neurology; this forms the basis behind Applied Kinesiology (which uses muscle testing to find the cause of disease). We now know so much more about our body and what it is doing than we did in the 1950's, when medicine promised us a pill that could cure everything.

This then begs me to ask the question - what has happened to the medical fraternity who, seemingly, have not learnt from these breakthroughs? It is as if they are unknowingly burying their heads in the sand and ignoring what has been going on around them in the last fifty to sixty years. A simple example of this is that if you give someone a drug that is supposed to solve a complex issue, that drug has been tested using Newtonian physics but we now know the body works in a Quantum mechanical way.

Every part of the body is affected by a drug, not just the organ it is designed to work on. Subsequently you get side effects. In this instance the medical fraternity is using science based on a system which is over two hundred years old. The literature explaining quantum biology is available but it seems as if the medical fraternity refuses to listen. Bruce Lipton's book 'Biology of Belief' covers this whole premise very well.

There are many more examples of this ostrich head burying phenomena, some of which I will mention later in this book but one of the craziest is that the cause of practically every illness, disease, pain or disorder, is not known. It is true, your doctor and all the medical scientists out in the world don't know what is causing ninety-nine percent or more of all the diseases people have. Look in any medical dictionary or the web and time and time again you will find 'the cause of this disease is not known'. There are hypothesises as to what may cause a disease but they remain hypothesises and cannot be categorically proven. The medical fraternity have no finite models they can follow; it is all guess work as to what is going on inside a person when they have a disease. That is akin to building a house with no foundation, along with having no knowledge whatsoever of the ground on which you are building.

We will find out more about this when I explain metastasis, (secondary cancers) in Chapter 14. It seems the medical fraternity are not really interested in the cause of a disease; why a lump appears in a breast, why someone gets eczema, why a person suffers horrendously with irritable bowel syndrome, why a cyst appears. What causes any of these issues cannot be explained, so the cause is ignored, as is the patient who asks why is their disease there, and why at this moment in their life? The doctor cannot tell them because, simply, they don't know.

It poses a real question that no-one has asked of the medical fraternity; 'How can you claim to cure a disease (and doctors are the only people who can claim to cure someone) if you don't know what caused it to occur in the first place?'

Please understand me, I believe the medical fraternity and doctors do a magnificent job; they are fantastic diagnosticians. When it comes to breaking a limb or in an emergency situation for example, then the 'Accident and Emergency' (A&E) or the 'Emergency Rescue' (ER) is the place to go. Plastic surgery is incredible and many drugs are lifesavers. It is just the flawed way of approaching disease that I believe must change.

As a youngster I would listen, with baited breath, as the next cure for cancer was announced, my interest spurred on as a result of my mother's death. Thirty years on I am still waiting. In fact I have given up. Finding a pill, drug, serum or treatment to stop this disease is not going to happen. We have thrown all the money we can possibly throw at cancer in this way to solve this issue, and we keep throwing more at it but where is the cure? When are all the people who dig their hands in their pockets to support a 'Cure for Cancer' charity going to stop and realise no 'Magic Drug' will ever be developed to 'cure' that disease? This way of looking at the body has not worked so far and I am going to say that this approach will not work in the future.

As I mentioned earlier, over the last 50 years many therapeutic interventions have remained the same. Those cancer research scientists are still looking inside the body for the wonder drug instead of looking outside at the bigger picture and at what has been going on in their own back yard. The attitude of the medical fraternity has not changed. The link between mind and body has not been acknowledged, DNA is still regarded as the culprit for all diseases and the medical fraternity has ignored all the biological breakthroughs since the 1980s which prove that it is the cell membrane that controls the switches of the DNA. This means that the environment, everything which is going on outside the cell, has a massive impact on how the cell reacts inside.

DNA is dumb. It can be compared to the hard drive of a computer; it does nothing until it is told what to do. That message comes from the CPU (Central Processing Unit - the main processing chip of a computer) that controls how the files are accessed and used. Why in modern medicine does consciousness, which is like the CPU, still play no part in telling the body what to do and what not to do, regardless of the undeniable evidence that proves that our thoughts affect our bodies? When it comes to so called 'modern' medicine, unfortunately I believe we are living in a bygone age.

So what is META-Medicine® again? First I can tell you what it is not. IT IS **NOT** A THERAPY. However it is a diagnostic system that uses conventional medical diagnosis, along with specifically targeted questions and other observations to establish the significant stressful event in our environment that we believe is the cause of a disease.

As I have just mentioned, it is important for me to say that META-Medicine® does not supersede a conventional medical diagnosis - we use conventional medical diagnosis as well. We also consider complementary, alternative or energetic viewpoints; all of these disciplines will have merit at some level. META-Medicine® works before any therapeutic intervention except emergency life threatening issues (which require immediate attention) and much of the rehabilitation work caused by accidents. However in this instance, knowledge of META-Medicine® can assist any medical practitioner in how they plan an intervention.

To sum up, the word 'Meta' means a level above or beyond, therefore META-Medicine® means medicine that describes medicine.

META-Medicine® can explain why a disease is there, what caused the disease in the first place, how long the disease has been there, what the disease cycle will be, where the person is within their disease cycle and what will be the next stage and therefore what symptoms to expect. It can predict to a degree the size of a conflict mass or the cell necrosis (cell loss) a person might experience. It also explains allergies, chronic diseases, reoccurring diseases, water retention, epileptic fits, migraines and heart attacks. Plus why we change our personality, our spiritual nature, our reaction to certain stimulus in the environment and why socially we change. Furthermore it predicts how long a disease will take to complete its cycle and what may cause a person to possibly die and why. All of these things can also be predicted with great accuracy.

In addition metastasis (the development of secondary cancers – therefore a cancer that travels through the system and attaches itself to another organ) can finally be correctly explained. The role of microbes, bacteria, virus and fungi can also be explained in this cycle and why they are not the evil, nasty villains of nature that should be eliminated at all cost in order for a person to survive. Additionally psychological issues such a depression, bulimia, bipolar, acute anxiety and other forms of neurosis and psychosis also have an answer.

META-Medicine® is really a way of turning someone's disease from something static back into an on-going process. By simply understanding what the body is doing, a person can complete the process and therefore return to health.

META-Medicine® is not a cure. I say to every client I meet that I have never cured anyone with META-Medicine® and I never will. (The only person I have ever cured of any ailment is myself). However META-Medicine® is a model of thinking about disease that a lot of recent traditional and medical scientific research is confirming. It uses medical systems to assist it in its diagnosis. It works before any traditional, complementary, alternative or energetic intervention. I also tell people that META-Medicine® is not the be all and end all. There may well be something else out there that could supersede it but until that time it is a fantastic model that explains so much.

I will guarantee you one thing: META-Medicine® will turn your world upside down and inside out when it comes to thinking about disease, pains, ailments, syndromes and psychological issues. However, as I say to all my students, 'A person who can hold two totally conflicting ideas in their heads and have them be okay is the sign of true genius'. META-Medicine® will raise many questions for you. It will turn your way of thinking about disease on its head. I guarantee you will be sceptical – I was until I tested it over and over again only to find out it always worked. There are no mistakes in the mind/body and therefore in META-Medicine® we believe that there is no mistake in a disease.

I meet many people who just want an answer to the question of their own disease. They want to know 'Why am I sick?' and in my quest for understanding my mother's death, I can now say I know what caused her breast cancer, I know what caused it to spread to her lymph glands, her liver, her bones. I know why she died and why at the time. I know why the chemotherapy, radiation and surgery did not work. Personally knowing that has given me a massive mental release and final closure on her tragic death.

People also ask me; "If META-Medicine® is so wonderful and can do what you say then why have I not heard of it before now?" To answer that question I need to explain the history of META-Medicine®, where it originates and who discovered some of the basic principles that are the backbone of the models. I shall also explain more about my beliefs regarding what the medical fraternity has done to stop you from learning this information and why.

The History and future of META-Medicine®

In 1978, an 18 year old son of Dr Geerd Hamer, a German doctor was holidaying in the Mediterranean when he was tragically shot, whilst sleeping on the yacht he was chartering with friends. He died four months later. The person who shot him was strangely only found guilty of possession of a firearm.

The German doctor, whose son died, had designed a knife that could cut through flesh without causing bleeding plus other advanced medical instruments and he had plans to retire early from the proceeds of this and the other medical patents.

Unfortunately the German doctor developed testicular cancer shortly after his son's death and he then postulated that there must be a link between the death of his son and his cancer. He successfully had the cancer removed and found a job working in a gynaecological surgery in Germany. He knew that ovaries have a similar biological makeup to testicles and they come from the same embryological layer. So he started interviewing every woman who had ovarian cysts and asking them if they had had some form of traumatic loss before the onset of the cysts. Without fail every women had experienced an unexpected, traumatic loss of a loved one, whether it was a child, partner, close friend or a pet, which left them feeling as if they needed to replace that loved person in some way because of their loss.

He carried out other work and submitted his discovery to a University in 1981, as a post-doctorate thesis for qualification as a University Lecturer. In 1982 this was rejected without even testing if what he was saying was true or not. Later on, in 2000, strangely this thesis was accepted.

The German doctor went onto work in other clinics in Germany and Austria, carrying out further research. During this time he made many discoveries: that a significant stressful event seems to be the start of a disease, that all diseases have a biological meaning and that disease has a process. This disease process can also be seen in the brain, through a brain CT, as well as in the organ. (CT stands for computer tomography, a complex x-ray machine that generates three dimensional images so a person can literally see slices of the inside of themselves.)

During this time he also found that there is a direct link between microbes, fungi, bacteria and viruses and the disease process. Each conflict shock shows up in a specific area of the brain based on an elegant system of embryology and the organs of the body react according to the same embryonic makeup (meaning the brain is connected to each organ). This system explains certain symptoms during a disease process and that each disease has a biological meaningful reaction based on surviving more effectively in our environment.

The German doctor has written many books (most of them are only available in German) and has taught thousands of people his ideas and ways of carrying out therapy. However, that is where META-Medicine® and this doctor part company. Over the past 30 years the doctor's passion for his work has caused him a significant amount of anguish. Not only did he lose his son, he also lost his wife to cancer. He was ignored by the medical fraternity. His confrontational manner with the pharmaceutical bodies, the medical fraternity, complementary, alternative and energetic therapy practitioners resulted in him losing his friends and making many enemies. He believes that leaving a disease to take its course is also highly controversial and subsequently has cost him his Medical Doctor's licence and landed him in prison several times.

Before META-Medicine® was created Johannes R. Fisslinger, the president of the International META-Medicine® Association, approached the German doctor at a seminar in 2003 in Spain, with the suggestion of creating a University where the information could be taught to doctors and other interested practitioners. Together with a group of veterans in that field, the first steps to create such an educational entity were taken. But unfortunately the German doctor decided against the idea. Therefore the idea of the university did not flourish and was quickly abandoned.

After long discussions and the insight that this very important and revolutionary new model of how we think and approach disease and wellness needs to be taught to health professionals, Johannes R Fisslinger and Dr Bader (the vice president of International META-Medicine® Association - IMMA) decided to create the International META-Medicine® Association and to formulate a healing paradigm called META-Medicine® based on a biopsychosocial model of integrative medicine. Using NLP modelling techniques the essence of the German doctor's findings were integrated into a professional structured training process, ongoing development of resources and medical research projects.

Since that time we have gone way further in our thinking in META-Medicine than the original approach this German doctor's ideas had given us. Our new methodology also incorporates the latest thinking about disease, as an example we incorporate energetic medicine and nutrition when working with a client. This allows us to put together an integrative therapy plan for a client that integrates medical practices, alternative approaches, complementary methods and energetic applications in a truly focussed and never before seen accurate way. Taking away guesswork and hypothesis which many of these therapeutic practices have but at the same time not conflicting with their core theories or disciplines. In my thinking this is the true sign of a paradigm shift.

Even though some of the basic models used in META-Medicine® have a background from the original work, we have evolved it and how we use the information is very different in our approach and application; META-Medicine® is a stress based diagnostic process and not a therapy. We don't heal anyone and we make no claims to do so. Instead we use medical diagnosis and psychological questioning to develop an integrative therapy plan with the client. This plan encompasses their mind through psychological intervention, their body through surgery, drugs (homeopathic or allopathic) and nutrition, their spirit through understanding the reason on a grander scale as to why they created the issue and their place in the world with regards to the disease. As well, we take into consideration their overall vitality as a human to deal with the disease. We also look at the social aspects of the issue the person is going through such as how that person interacts with friends/enemies, family, colleagues or people generally and how the person interacts with their environment; we look at where the person lives, where they work, the type of work they are involved in and what changes need to be taken into consideration environmentally so the person does not trigger off the same associations that could be causing the disease to reoccur.

In addition we focus on the wellness of the person, not the disease. Doctors, on the whole, will often dismiss a person because their disease has progressed too far or because they are focussing only on the disease and not the whole person. However this attitude towards people and focus on disease can have the effect of shutting the person down and causing them to switch off their reasons to live. As an example one of the exercises we ask cancer patients to do is to write down one hundred different reasons as to why they want to live. Some clients find this incredibly difficult while others love it. The medical diagnosis of a client who is told they have a specific illness can also cause what is called the 'nocebo' effect which is the opposite of the placebo effect. A placebo is a sham medical intervention intended to lead the recipient to believe that the intervention may improve his/her condition.[6]

As an example of the nocebo effect in action, a woman went into hospital because of Crohn's disease, a chronic form of Irritable Bowel Syndrome, unpleasant but not fatal and something she had been living with for many years. The x-rays showed some dark spots in her lymph which her doctors told her 'could' be CANCER, but they were not sure and further tests should to be done. She immediately had a conflict shock causing fear of death which, following the principles of META-Medicine® resulted in her starting a vigorous emergency programme at a deep survival level in order to fight to save her life. She developed a small cell carcinoma, a virulent form of lung cancer with the prognosis of death within six months with chemotherapy or two months without. She was a spiritual person but all her life she had feared dying of cancer, because her mother had died of cancer. This fear of death, from the medical diagnosis, caused a shock in META-Medicine® terms which cost her life.

For fear of being sued, the doctors had to tell her that she may have lymph cancer. From a META-Medicine® point of view however, a lymphoma of this sort is a minor self worth issue and the lymphoma was in the regeneration phase - the second part of the disease programme – and was therefore resolving itself. She had recently worked with one of the top alternative practitioners in the world, clearing up some deep issues to do with her self esteem; that equates exactly to resolution of a minor self-worth conflict. This would have caused her lymph to swell as it healed and would have shown up as looking like a dark spot on an X-ray. If she had not focussed on the word CANCER, she may not have had the diagnosistic shock and maybe, I can only speculate, she would be alive today.

So the META-Medicine® approach is different. It looks at a disease as an opportunity to literally re-programme the whole person, so they can evolve. Jenny Bourne, a lovely woman who I have had the pleasure of assisting has had her life completely turned around since she developed breast cancer.

We also know that this way of thinking is not a mistake or some fancy new age idea. As I explained earlier, Epigenetics proves the theory that, as we go through a conflict shock we literally switch 'on' or 'off' certain genetic programmes, therefore causing us to alter our whole make-up and how we interact with the environment. We are literally changing by learning to adapt more creatively to our surroundings, so we can survive and pass on those lessons to our offspring. Any person who has been through a horrific disease will tell you that their issue taught them so much. As a friend and META-Medicine® colleague of mine, Christa Uricher, says: "Terminal illness is not a death sentence, but our approach to dealing with it is".

In the next chapter we will explore how the present approach to healing is costing us our evolvement and health. We shall look at what happens to someone when they become sick and how we traditionally treat illness by separating the mind from the body. We shall explore the whole notion that disease and especially 'cancer' is a mistake of the body and what the survival rate of a person with cancer is. From my point of view, cancer is worth discussing because I believe it to be the ultimate disease programme. Therefore understanding cancer allows us to better understand any disease, whether chronic or minor.

Chapter 2

The State of health in the world

Healthcare should be a right for every American. In a country as wealthy as ours, for us to have people who are going bankrupt because they can't pay their medical bills--for my mother to die of cancer at the age of 53 and have to spend the last months of her life in the hospital room arguing with insurance companies because they're saying that this may be a pre-existing condition and they don't have to pay her treatment, there's something fundamentally wrong about that.

President Barack Obama

A decision that affected every part of my life

The hill up to my next class was really long that day. Bath is built on hills and my school happened to have been built on one of the steepest. Normally the walk was an annoying inconvenience as every pupil had to walk from one class to another up and down these hills everyday. This day was different. I did not care about the hill; it gave me extra time to think. I found myself, like any person who has lost a loved one, obsessing about what they should have done, what they could have done. Why did it happen? Why did she die? Why could I not do something about it? Why didn't I see her before she died? Why? Bloody why?

I had not seen my mother for over six months. I had not heard from her either. This was unusual but I had not realised how long it had been until that day. The last time I saw her she had told me that she was going to die. I did not accept what she had said but she had desperately tried to explain what was going on in her life regarding the cancer. She had had a full mastectomy (removal of her breast). I remember asking if I could see it and she did show me the scar. Little did I know how traumatic that event must have been for her. She cried and cried openly in front of my brothers and me as she explained that she was dying. I was strong and in denial. She would not die; she was my mother! Mothers don't die. She will get better-the cancer had been chopped off. She had the best medical care, she had chemotherapy and radiation, she had experimental chemotherapy – the best - she wasn't going to die and I was going to make sure that she knew it.

Earlier that day she had driven her car at great speed through the lanes close to where she then lived in Northampton. I remember she was exhausted after what seemed like a normal fun drive. She had to use a wheelchair and be pushed around because she was so weak and she slept a lot. We had been to see a new friend of hers, a vicar. My mother was not a religious person but in the last year I noticed that, strangely, she carried around a bible and had met up with this vicar several times.

The day my mother died, as I was walking up the hill to my next class, I decided I would do something about her death. She would not die in vain. I personally would find a solution to why people die of cancer. I would devote my whole life to this quest. I would study to become a doctor, a research scientist, a surgeon, a chemist – I would find a cure. That was it, obsession over. I felt better. Little did I know that the simple decision I made that day would have a profound effect on my life and the course I would take. I was only twelve years old and I really had no right to make those types of decisions but, on reflection, it was truly a momentous day.

Cancer affects 6-7 million people worldwide and it is on the increase according to the World Health Organisation (WHO)[7]. It is the third biggest killer after heart disease and death through medical intervention. Yes, you did read it correctly; medical intervention that goes wrong is either the first or second biggest killer of people. The figures are rarely mentioned and seem to be a closely guarded secret, but you can find them.[8]

Needless to say that without medical care many unnecessary deaths would also occur. It is a catch 22. If modern medicine goes into a developing country, the survival rate increases dramatically. People's lives get better; they don't die of cholera, malaria, or other horrific diseases such as small pox. They can have cheap cataract operations, whereas in the past blindness was commonplace. Modern surgical techniques applied in the third world countries save many more lives. Drugs have and do solve many problems and some of the interventions are truly amazing and are definitely lifesavers.

The same can be said for modern medical practices in the western world. To say that everything is wrong in modern medicine would be heresy but, as I touched upon in the previous chapter, there needs to be a review of modern medical practices and the foundations on which they are built.

I think it's also worthwhile mentioning some figures about the cost of keeping us healthy. I do this so that you may realise how much money is spent keeping disease at bay. In the UK, where I come from our healthcare system is free. You don't have to pay anything at all when you go and see a General Practitioner (GP). If you find yourself with something more challenging than a verruca (a wart), your General Practitioner can and does refer you to a consultant. They will see you and explain what procedure you are to have whether it be surgery, drugs or some other form of treatment.

But there is a catch to this, and that is efficiency. British governments over the last thirty years have been trying to reduce the costs of what is the biggest employer in Europe. The National Health Service employs over 1.3 million people (figures from 2006)[9] at a cost of £3 billion a year. Each GP (family doctor) is paid between £80,000 and £120,000 a year before tax. Each consultant can earn up to £170,000 depending on their length of service. The higher you go up the ladder the more specific the consultant's knowledge and so obviously the more difficult it becomes to get seen by a consultant.[10] The figures seem on a par with the USA, except private physicians in the USA can earn staggering amounts of money.[11]

Like any large organisation, efficiency is the biggest problem. Money is spent without any regard for how wisely it is spent. There was a fascinating programme where a business trouble shooter called Sir Gerry Robinson[12], went into an English hospital and was filmed over 6 months trying, and I do mean trying, to make the whole system work more effectively. Doctors and consultants are not business people. If they realised that the majority of their clients earned only £25,000 a year, I think they would have a massive shock.[13]

Doctors are not interested in business and why should they be? They are there to 'cure' us. How efficient they are is of no interest to them. They want to be seeing and 'curing' people not running a budget. If they need a new, special surgical tool to do a specific job, they need it. It is not whether it is going to make them more efficient or more effective; it is because they have a client who would benefit from the treatment.

Money is scarce in the National Health Service in the UK. However, you could pour billions more into it and it would not change anything. In the last five years another 30,000 employees have been added to the NHS. The problem is the attitude, which was highlighted time and time again by Sir Gerry Robinson's programme. Doctors that won't speak to nurses, nurses that won't deal with certain hospital staff, hospital staff who don't do their jobs correctly or to the required standard, not because they don't know how but purely because of the system.

In the UK each person pays 11% or more of their earnings into the National Health Service. For an average wage of £25,000 that is £2,750. People have no idea that each month they pay on average £229 per month into this pot. It covers many things not just health but people in general are oblivious to the fact that the National Health Service is not free. In America people have to pay a fortune for health insurance. They know it is not free.

The question I want to address is that of stress and disease. If stress causes disease then why don't doctors diagnose this? Why do they still prescribe drugs that they know only mask symptoms? When they know a combination of drugs can cause serious problems, why do they carry on administering them?

I spoke in depth to a doctor friend of mine about stress and the META-Medicine® approach and his comment was "I could not use it, nor could I recommend anyone to you." I was flabbergasted by his statement. He went onto say, "I have on average seven minutes per patient to diagnose and then treat them, usually with a drug, which is how I am measured performance-wise, on whether I prescribe or not. So I could not spend the time analysing each client for the stressful event that caused their disease," though he liked the idea behind what I was saying. More importantly, he told me that clients in the UK just would not pay.

"When they walk into see me," he said, "they know it's FREE - and doctor, it is your job to cure me." He went on to point out that clients believe that the doctor is responsible for their health and that telling them a stressful event in their life has caused their problem is too big a leap for them.

Another doctor who is a trained in META-Medicine® also told me "Richard, there are three reasons why META-Medicine® will not work within the medical system.

1. Where is the proof? - Research papers.
2. Who is going to treat the client?
3. Who is going to pay for that treatment?"

She also said to me, "It's easy with drugs, a client comes to see you, you prescribe a drug and the client goes away happy."

However the problem is that in many cases the clients don't take the drugs or the drugs don't work or the side effects can be horrible. Doctors are at a loss, they don't know why a disease is there and they can't explain side effects of the drugs they prescribe.

You don't have to look further than your next door neighbour to find a story of just how difficult the whole problem is for doctors. Claire (name changed) is in her seventies. She lost her husband in 2006; he was walking up the hill I lived on when he suddenly collapsed and died of a heart attack. Claire, who is a lovely lady, has not really been right since that day and she has been taking medication for her heart. Over the past six months however, her problems have become worse. She collapsed at home and broke her nose - not because she was frail but because of the side effects of the drugs she has been taking. She has been in and out of hospital because of these side effects. She has had a group of consultants at various times see her and prescribe certain drugs only to find her next week in the hospital not feeling well due to those new drugs.

My wife and I know all of this because we have had to rush Claire to see a doctor. Over the past six months I have seen this lady go from being a strong healthy seventy year old into a frail skinny lady. However in late 2008, I saw her and I asked her how she was. She said that the doctors have taken her off of all her medication bar one, of which she now only takes half a dose. The real surprise was how she looked to me. Colour was back in her face again, and she looked and told me she felt well.

Over and over again I find this to be the case. I was sitting next to a girl on a flight to Australia to teach META-Medicine®. When she asked me what I did, I explained. She said, "OK, it sounds as if you know what you are talking about. Explain why I have this skin problem all over my neck, and chest/belly area". I asked her what separation issues had been going on in her life four weeks ago, which was when the issue appeared. She told me her fiancé decided to go to Australia to set up a business (she was on a trip out to see him) and she knew she would be separated from him. She went red and her eyes became watery. I then said, "Why don't you pack in your job and move over to Australia with him?" She went bright red again and tears welled up in her eyes. Clearly she was under a lot of stress. She told me that she could cope with him being away but she admitted to me that it was a lot tougher than she thought. This was because she could not bear to be away from her family.

Why is this story so significant? Randomly I happened to sit next to someone on a plane who was young and healthy (so it seemed) and then I do a quick five minute diagnosis only to find out that the doctors had no idea what the issue was or why it started. It was obvious to her when I pointed it out and I showed her the reason for the skin issue; which is so you don't feel the separation (you literally don't feel the skin in what is called the first phase. More of that later.) It's the doctor who was at a loss; he prescribed her a steroid cream but he did not tell her of the long term side effects of this cream on the body. (It thins the skin - and we can explain why this is the case using META-Medicine®).

Another case is the one of META–Medicine® Health Coach, Robert Waghmare. His father had a heart attack. He received CPR from Robert and his close family for thirty minutes before the ambulance arrived and rushed him to hospital. In hospital he was given further drugs followed by an operation. He was not in good health with his heart before this heart attack.

Robert knows a lot about medicine as he comes from a family with a medical background. He told me that the doctors did not know what the problem was. He spoke to a friend of mine called Dr Kwesi Anan Odum (who is a Doctor trained in META-Medicine®). Contrary to what the doctors had told Robert, Dr Kwesi diagnosed (over the phone) that the problem had to do with the musculature of the heart and not the veins or the arteries. The medical symptoms did not fit coronary heart disease. Robert was brushed aside when he explained what he thought was wrong with his father. Remember, Robert knows his stuff. This was his father and he had spent practically every day him for the last month, so he knew the symptoms that his father had been experiencing.

Unfortunately his father died but his death was not due to his heart condition but from pneumonia that had not been diagnosed correctly by the doctors whilst he was in hospital.

Robert was furious because this was a simple diagnosis and a totally solvable problem.

My issue here is that the doctors have a very difficult time. They are guessing all the time as to what is causing the problems they are dealing with. They have only drug therapies, surgery or removal as solutions. There is no link between the mind and the body as to why a disease is there and what might be the next set of symptoms and why. The drugs they prescribe have one side effect followed by another, the explanation of which is based on old science but this is not how the body behaves. The system they work in is archaic, with poor management when compared to modern businesses such as Virgin, Microsoft, and GE. The structure stops anyone from being allowed to explore areas of research other than drug trials.

Those doctors who are dissatisfied with simply being drug pushers have to reinvent themselves and pursue a career in a different way. Three people come to mind who have successfully achieved that; Deepak Chopra www.chopra.com who wrote a book called 'Quantum Healing', Dr Christiane Northrup www.drnorthrup.com who has written many books including 'Women's Bodies and Women's Wisdom', and Dr Karl Simonton www.simontoncenter.com, one of the forefathers in this modern approach where mind and the body are totally linked. He wrote an amazing book called 'Getting Well Again.'

Doctors, stuck in their modern practices, are not allowed to look at other possible causes of a problem. This means that even in a modern hospital the consultant deals only with their speciality and none of them speak to each other. They often have very little regard for each other. Certainly the psychologists rarely mix with the medical doctors. If you don't believe me go to your local hospital and ask where each area of specialisation is situated. You will often find psychiatry in a small building sometimes miles away from the rest of the complex. The mind has no connection with disease even in the one place it should – your hospital.

This is crazy. Even more stupid is the amount of research that proves categorically that 'Almost every major illness that people acquire is linked to chronic stress[14] [Segerstrom and Miller 2004, Kopp and Rethelyl 2004, McEwen and Lasky 2002, Mcewen and Seeman 1999.] These are research papers that prove there is a link. Many doctors sign people off as sick because of stress. But have they not made a link? I personally find it ridiculous that if these research papers are correct, then the way in which we treat illness needs to be re-thought.

So why is this not happening?

We all assume that every doctor is as good as the next but we never think that of a business owner or designer. Each doctor has a different character and, since conventional medicine is based on hypothesis with no real science to back up why something works or not, they can be easily led. This is where business does come into the equation - in the form of drug companies.

Drug company turnover is massive. The investment they have put into finding new drugs is staggering. It takes years to get approval for a new drug, so the money involved is astronomical. So, imagine if someone like me was to say that the drugs that are being produced don't do what they are supposed to do. That the solution to a client's problem may not be to take that expensive drug treatment because the results from the drug trials don't really prove you will live longer or that your symptoms will disappear. If I was to say this then the drug companies would hound me down.

The simple reason for this is money and investment. If I was the CEO of Pfizer or Bayer and my business was threatened then I would fight. It would be a one sided battle as well. The pharmaceutical industry has fingers in every pie: politically, in the medical profession, in charities, in big businesses, and in the World Health Organisation (WHO). This is understandable given the nature of the business. However, the pharmaceutical industry is ungovernable. It is now so large and powerful it seems it can do what it likes.

If you don't believe the power of the pharmaceutical industry then fully consider this. Why is it that many vitamin supplements are being banned in the EU? Well, because many of them are not tested in the conventional pharmaceutical way, which costs approximately £250,000.00 per supplement and may also require testing on animals (something many of the people who take these pills would find intolerable).[15]

Why inexpensive supplements will never become mainstream prescriptions

To explain this further let us consider a study carried out at Harvard University concerning arthritis which showed categorically that chicken cartilage in high dosages has an incredible effect on relieving and sometimes reversing the pain of Arthritis. You can buy this supplement as Chondroitin Sulphate and Glucosamine Sulphate - Type II Collagen (both inactive supplements with no side effects), but can these people market this wonder drug and teach people the right quantities to take? The right quantity has to be high in order to get the right effect.[16]

Have the doctors been told of the power of Type II Collagen, this 'wonder drug', and the reason it works? Probably not. The simple reason for this is you may think that the pharmaceutical industry have said "Where are the drug trials? You cannot prescribe something that has no drug trials?" But in this case there are drug trials, which were carried out by Harvard University. Put simply, the reason why you don't hear about these types of interventions is straightforward - marketing. Anyone can make this product. It is cheap. It does not have to be prescribed, therefore you don't get it from your doctor but from a health food store. In fact many doctors have never heard of it, or if they have they may tell you they are not sure if it works. Well, it does work in the right quantities.

Unfortunately these cheap drugs have no chance of becoming mainstream. To understand this in more detail, let me explain what happens in a doctor surgery. Imagine you were a doctor and you had a marketing representative from a pharmaceutical giant, coming to your surgery to 'educate you' about their new arthritis drug. Imagine for the moment you do recommend to your patients to buy over the counter Type II Collagen. As the representative explains their new drug and its side effects, plus clinical trials, they would not be able to convince you that their drug was as good as Type II Collagen – you know this because you have read that Type II Collagen has few if any side effects and also has double blind, placebo clinical trials to prove that it works.

But here's the problem, as a doctor your performance is measured on what you prescribe; Type II Collagen is not something that is on your list of recommended prescription drugs for arthritis. So your practice manager will question your reason for recommending this non-prescription drug. Even if Type II Collagen was on your list of recommended prescribed drugs, because it is so cheap to make and there is little money to market it, the other more expensive drugs that are heavily promoted will come to your attention first, so you end up prescribing those. As a doctor you will want to do right for the patient however you will probably end up prescribing what is at the forefront of your mind at the time of diagnosis.

The conclusion is, it is money that drives this skewed business of disease. As an example in America some of the TV stations are backed by pharmaceutical giants. That means these pharmaceutical giants have carte blanche to advertise their products every 15 minutes to an unsuspecting public.

As an example, in the UK the pharmaceutical industry has almost successfully lobbied government to make Statins (anti cholesterol drugs) an over-the-counter drug.[17] 'That's a good thing', you may say. Yes and no. Statins are drugs that are designed to reduce cholesterol in the blood system. The counts go down, that is true. However the studies that showed the wondrous effects of these drugs seem to be flawed.[18] The death rates attributed to these studies were very biased.

What they also don't tell you is the long-term side effects of these drugs. Lipitor, one of the common Statins, has been linked to Neuromuscular degeneration (brain and muscles cell decrease) as a side effect. This is probably because your brain is 60% fat. Diseases such as Multiple Sclerosis or losing muscular control of the body have been reported. My thoughts

16

are if you reduce the natural production of cholesterol in your system, you will affect brain function. This has yet to be proven. But hey, who cares? The psychologists don't talk to the doctors who don't talk to the neurologists. There is no joined-up thinking in the medical profession so nothing will change.[19]

Statins are being introduced worldwide and are said to be the next aspirin. Doctors are handing out Statins like candy with three month prescriptions becoming normal. Most men and women over fifty will do as they are told. The educated few will do the research and discover what I have told you. There will be an outcry in twenty years time as many people will find that their brains and nervous systems are not functioning as well as they should, but by that time they will be too old to be taken seriously. It will take a few more years before someone might make a link between Statins and brain health. People will die early but who will care because another drug will be introduced to combat the side effects of the Statins and the whole mess will go around in circles again.

Money rules when it comes to disease

Money is the driving force behind the pharmaceutical industry. If I was in the pharmaceutical industry, I would be rubbing my hands together because I know my job would have been done; billions of pounds of tax payers and medical insurance money going right into my pockets. It is driven by money and if you know how to play the game you can win the jackpot regularly.

This issue with the pharmaceutical industry, the medical profession and the political situation is unlikely to change. The only thing that will effect change will be public awareness. I liken this whole situation to Communism and the Berlin Wall in Germany. Before the Wall came down, people's lives were governed by the secret police. They could not think, speak out or say anything against the regime. Freedom of speech was banned. Movement from one country to another was banned. People lived in constant fear for their lives if they were doing something they should not be doing. If your face did not fit then you were in trouble. The government and its henchmen controlled everything - business, health education, everything. Life was okay if you did not want to excel at anything. Only those chosen by the state to do so could excel. You did as you were told.

Then people became frustrated en masse and they rebelled en masse. We watched it from the West and we saw things change dramatically overnight. I remember seeing people smashing down parts of the Berlin Wall - a friend of mine sent me a piece in the post. It was an incredible time. I never thought that it would happen in my lifetime but it did.

I believe that the same will happen in the medical profession; people are becoming more aware that the doctors don't have the answers. They are going to alternative practitioners in droves. Sometimes with good results, sometimes not.

I believe that people will start asking the really challenging questions after they have been diagnosed with a disease. They will start to ask the doctors questions such as; 'What caused my disease? Why don't you know? You are saying my body has made a mistake but why has it done this to me? I don't believe you when you say my body has made a mistake. Why do you always have to remove the affected part? Have you ever thought it might be there for a reason? What makes you so sure that my stressful life has not caused this disease and why can't you prove it? How do you know I will die if I don't have this treatment and on what basis can you say that? What is the life expectancy for people who do not take this drug? Why do these drugs' side effects seem worse than the disease the drugs were supposed to get rid of? Over the last fifty years how successful has this type of drug regime been? How do you know that the mind is not directly connected to the body? Prove it! Why don't you have connected thinking in the medical profession?

People haven't started asking these questions yet. But they will and when they do, the Berlin Wall of the Medical profession will come tumbling down. I predict that the doctors who have been keeping this status quo will be left standing with nothing on except their white coats, saying 'Oops! We made a mistake.' The information in this book is too challenging for them to admit they have made a mistake but ultimately, they will.

In the META-Medicine® association we believe that change will not come through the medical profession. We have given up trying to persuade them that this material is true, even though the wealth of information is conclusive. You can show them the research but their minds are stuck in an old paradigm whereby admitting they are wrong they will have to acknowledge change. Institutions based on outdated belief systems such as Apartheid and Communism fall, not because the people who control the system have changed their minds, but because pressure is brought to bear by those who are affected by the repressive system.

So change will happen but this will not be because the medical profession realise that the body has made a mistake or that the mind and body are interlinked. The change will happen through political and economic forces and through millions of people and the media asking the questions I mentioned earlier, only to be given answers that consistently don't add up. So the change in attitude will come about through the general public.

But what of the infrastructure? If what I am saying is true, then what will happen to the hospitals, to the medical profession and to the drug companies? It is possible that they will collapse. Yes, there will have to be some serious rethinking about the approach to disease and procedures will have to be rethought. But that's not the point. More elegant procedures will be developed - ones that will make sense because they follow the process a disease goes through based on its cause and the reason for it being there, rather than cutting, burning or drugging it.

The good news is that the infrastructure is already there. This change in how we approach disease will cause doctors to talk to the complementary, alternative and energetic practitioners. They will have to have joined-up thinking. The pharmaceutical industry will have to rethink their approach to the drugs they develop. Like all businesses they will change and adapt to new ways of looking at drugs.

Governments will also change their attitude as to how we treat disease; they will simply fall in line with what is going on in order to keep their particular party in power. So the prognosis is not one of disaster, as the medical profession and the drug companies would probably lead us to believe. They have campaigned against, blocked and ignored so much of this research because it did not fit with their beliefs. This is also why they have shied away from the evidence. What it will do will change everything as far as disease is concerned, and it will welcome a new dawn on a fantastic journey into amazing new cures that were considered impossible before META-Medicine® came about.

In the next chapter we will explore why diseases happen. We will also take a look at our present way of thinking about disease; is it caused by a mistake of the body, a gene that has miraculously mutated, a poison, radiation, or could it be something else?

Chapter 3

Why do diseases, pains or cancers happen?
Are they a mistake or is it there for a reason

"When you treat a disease, first treat the mind."
Taoist teaching

"Nature does not make errors or mistakes. Our organism is a highly intelligent, orderly and sophisticated system with biological meaningful and intelligent reactions which we have labelled diseases or illness. Rather every disease process can be understood as a biological, spiritually meaningful event of nature with the goal of survival, resolution and awareness of a conflict, evolution and the self healing of our organism."
One of the ten META-Medicine® Models

How a shock caused a herniated disc

The following story is about what happened to me, why I got into META-Medicine® and what drove me to find a solution to an issue that left me practically unable to walk without being in excruciating pain. There are many messages in this story, as well as the reason for the issue in the first place, which took me a year and a half to discover; the stress I went through, why the issue did not disappear, what I did to solve it and how it affected me in all aspects of my life.

I was on a roll; you may know the feeling when everything comes out of your mouth and what you are saying is being listened to attentively and people are in awe of your every word. As well as being trained in META-Medicine®, I am a trainer of NLP (Neuro Linguistic Programming). If you have not heard of NLP, it is an amazing set of techniques that work at the deepest level to get rid of unwanted emotions, beliefs and events that are either affecting your health or your vision of your future. I am trained in Time Line Therapy™ (TLT) which goes hand in hand with NLP. With TLT you can get rid of a phobia in under an hour or an emotion that has been plaguing you for the whole of your life. Either way, these are some of the techniques I use to assist people when doing therapy in META-Medicine ®.

I was co-training a seven day NLP Practitioner course in Brighton in the UK and every word that was coming out of my mouth was, I thought, magical. There was a buzz in the air because my future wife (my girlfriend of over five months) was watching me do what I think I do best – assist others in letting go of problems, whether they are health issues or business situations.

It was also amazing because it was the first NLP Practitioner training that I was running with my friend Terry. We had set up a business together and this was what we had been aiming for.

I was unhappy with the company I had been working for and this was the opportunity for me to really show my expertise in training and do something special. I was really stepping up to the mark and becoming a professional NLP trainer with my own company. Also there was an unwritten contract between Terry and myself that I was the lead trainer. Due to my background, I had more experience in training, more knowledge and I knew my stuff better than he did, something he acknowledged at the time. So a scene was set.

I was on a roll, it was the first day of the training and I could see the eyes of the audience light up. I could feel the energy in my body giving every word a true meaning. I looked out at everyone and I could see them all taking in what I was saying. I saw in the corner of my eye Terry's hand and body come over to whisper some great feedback in my ear. And I was ready for it. We'd had our differences on the lead up to the training. Two alpha males in the same room can cause some challenges, but I knew he was going to say something really motivating.

As he leaned over, I smiled and he said "Fucking hurry up".

I was dumbfounded, shocked. I did not expect that. I did not know what to do, what to say, it felt like my whole world had suddenly collapsed in front of me. My whole energy went inside, I felt isolated. I dried up, stopped what I was saying and looked at the audience. Having been full of words I was suddenly at a total loss for words. My sentence came to a stop and I said "Over to you, Terry".

This was a shock but it did not end there. Things had changed, my personality changed, how I interacted with Terry changed. I was no longer the lead trainer who knew how to make these specialised seven day trainings work. Instead I was second in command and what ever Terry said, I agreed. I was afraid he would chew my ear off again; I was really scared of him. So I did everything I could to avoid any confrontation and as a consequence I let him walk all over me.

After that first day of the course I was exhausted, and so was Kristin, my partner. I wanted to say something to her but I knew that she had enough on her plate so I did not want to trouble her too much. I did say something had happened and she gave me some advice but I remember being very closed and thinking to myself, 'I am a professional and it will all be okay tomorrow'. What was playing continuously on my mind was that I was going into business with Terry. Was this the right thing to do? I thought, 'I am an NLP trainer and I can sort anything out'. So even though I was totally afraid of what Terry might do and say, I persevered.

That night and every night of the training I did not sleep well. I would find myself fully awake at night obsessing about what had gone on. Why was I not standing up for myself? I wanted to challenge Terry but I didn't. Inside I remember feeling devalued.

Something strange happened to me when we got home. The non sleeping I had experienced in the hotel, the insomnia, carried on. So I utilised it to work. I would wake up at 4 a.m. having gone to bed at 12.30. This carried on for many months.

I decided to set up a training company of my own to get away from this situation. By this time Kristin had started working with me and she helped us to set up on our own. We were commissioned to deliver a special two day business-refocusing training for a company in the North of Wales. I was delighted and so was Kristin. Other things were going well too. Business was flying in and I was really happy.

I remember that training in Wales very well. Kristin and I had travelled to Manchester so we were close to the venue. However, we had travelled up there on my birthday; the 23rd of September and we did not really celebrate. It was a horrible hotel but we did at least have a good meal with one of my best friends.

The next day, on the 24th, we both set up the training room. I was so excited, this was our first training together and it meant a totally fresh start for both Kristin and me. I was dreaming of all the wonderful things we would get up to in our new business together. I was happy. Happy to my core.

It was during this special training for the company in Wales that something major happened in my life; something that was so challenging it changed everything. That first day was so exciting, I was so happy inside; nothing could touch me. I got up and I knew I could really help this company turn things around in their business. Well, I was on a roll again. The situation sounded very familiar.

Sitting next to me was Kristin, taking notes. I looked around and saw our first training together, our first business together. It was truly fantastic. I saw, out of the corner of my eye, Kristin looking at me, happy and content. I looked at the audience; they seemed excited by what I was saying, and I said to myself, 'I LIKE THIS, I'M THE BOSS HERE'.

It was a few minutes later that I got out of my seat ripped off a flip chart that I had been writing on, put some blue-tack on the back of it and placed it on the wall behind us. This meant that I had to lean over to the left a little bit, not an unusual manoeuvre but one that was a little tricky. Then IT happened. A small pain crept across my lower back, focussed on the left hand side. It became worse and I became worried.

I quickly got back into my seat and sat down; by this time I was very worried. The pain became even worse. I leaned over and whispered in Kristin's ear and said 'My back's gone'. She said 'You're a professional. Carry on and put them into an exercise as soon as possible. We will have a break and I'll do some hypnosis with you, and massage your back so you can get through today'.

However even with these words of persuasion I knew something was not right. Why was I sick? Why now, when everything was going so well. Why did my back go? I was hoping that it was only a muscle that I had pulled and that, I knew, was easily corrected. But this pain was horrendous. I had pulled a muscle before and this was different. It felt like the same pain I had had when I had a rugby accident when I was eighteen. That pain lasted ten years. I got rid of it when I did an NLP training at the age of twenty-eight. I was damned if I was going to go through that again.

Twenty years after the rugby accident and ten years on from when I resolved the pain, I was thirty-eight. I was also confused. I kept asking myself, 'Why was I sick?' I was very worried. Why did my back give out at that time? What had my body done wrong? This pain was a mistake? I was angry with my body. Everything was finally going really well for me. I had broken away from Terry. Kristin and I were being really successful. I did not need this, not now, not at this time in my life. I had my own business. How the hell was I supposed to run the business as the main bread-winner with this debilitating back problem?

I also felt that I had let myself down; I am an NLP trainer and NLP trainers don't get sick. They are the epitome of great health and success. Not only did it hurt so much that I couldn't walk more than ten metres without being in horrific tear jerking pain, but all my dreams with Kristin and our new business together seemed a long way away. This was truly a disaster for me. What was I going to do?

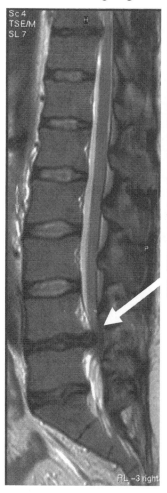 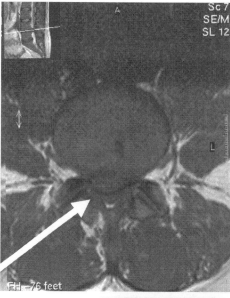

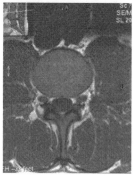

The herniated disc in my lower back. You can see from these MRI pictures how the disc is pushing up against the nerves, hence the horrendous pain

A normal disc

I remember that night though. Kristin gave my back a massage, which helped a little. She also did some more hypnosis and the pain disappeared somewhat so I slept through the whole night. I woke up feeling very good but as soon as I walked, I felt the pain again.

So why did I have this problem? Was there a reason for my back pain? Why was it there? Why did it happen to me at that exact time? I remember thinking about this at length because I knew, through NLP (META-Medicine® was not set up then), that the mind was connected to the body. I asked this question over and over again. Why me and why then? What was the purpose for such a debilitating issue to happen to me at that specific time, especially since everything was going so well. I searched and searched for the answer (it took one and a half years of searching before I finally worked it out). It became apparent that this pain was not the reason; it was the second part of a very precise process that the body goes through.

So what did cause my back to give out in the way that it did? Well, after I finished the two days of training, I travelled down to London and delivered a further two days of training for an international bank; it was presentation skills training which I had to deliver sitting down. I did not get my usual excellent feedback but that was only to be expected due to the circumstances. As I ran my own company, unlike many other people who work for a large corporation, I could not sign myself off sick. So I had to work throughout the whole of the time I had this issue. Let me remind you; I could walk ten metres, and then I would have to go down on my haunches and wait for the pain to subside before I could continue walking. As soon as I got back to Bristol I booked into see a chiropractor and that visit started a whole new chapter in my life.

In my case the chiropractor told me that I was relaxed and had pulled a muscle because I suddenly got up and that muscle was weak. He did a quick five minute history and that satisfied me at the time (remember - I had a history of lower back pain). However, I had not got up suddenly, the strain was nothing that I had put myself under. I had not been lifting anything heavy beforehand. I had not been doing anything unusual. My muscles in my back did not feel weak. On reflection, this diagnosis was flawed.

So did my body make a mistake or not? There are two schools of thought about disease. The first is that of conventional medicine, (and many alternative and complementary medicines) which says that the body had made a mistake. If you go to a doctor or a professional such as a chiropractor, acupuncturist, hypnotherapist, or the majority of therapy practitioners out in the world, then they say that your disease is a mistake. Something happened to you and the disease developed because your body was weak or out of balance and, as a result of this, the disease attacked your body in that place.

The next school of thought is that of META-Medicine®; the body has NOT made a mistake. If that is the case then what caused the issue to occur? The previous answers from the chiropractor didn't add up. Everything was going well in my life when I got the problem but what caused the issue to occur remained a mystery. I have also found out in my trainings and lectures that many others have found the same thing, life was finally working out, after a rough time and then they got sick.

They tell me "Everything in my life was finally going well and life was good before I got the problem, cancer or debilitating pain. I had been under a lot of pressure before then, and just as things were getting back to normal, wham, I got sick".

As an example; you go on holiday, with the chance to really enjoy yourself and then you go down with the flu or gastroenteritis within days of arriving at your resort. Why?

Why does the body make a disease happen? Is it because the body has done something evil? Has God suddenly struck us down from afar because we swore, under our breath, at our parents when we were seventeen and now, aged thirty-five, we have to pay the price? Is it because our genetics are at fault, or are we such highly developed organisms that we are more susceptible to diseases? So therefore our bodies give out on us, and we are prone to diseases because our lives are so stressful now that the body can't cope and it creates a disease to punish us?

Or is there another reason? Has the body NOT made a mistake after all?

Medical science says that disease is a mistake. So the therapy you receive is either to get rid of it, suppress, kill or shrink the issue. How they do this, is they use heat in the form of radiation or other therapies. Or the problem is removed with surgery. The other option, which I come across time and time again, is either you live with the problem for the rest of your life and take drugs to suppress the issue or you die. The prognosis is simple; because the body has made a mistake, drugs are used to cure the problem and the problem may go away.

However this may sound as though I am having a go at the medical profession. I am not. I have already mentioned in chapter 1 how the medical profession does incredible work and saves millions of lives, so it is the belief system I am challenging. However could the medical profession be barking up the wrong tree? Could the 'mistake' theory be costing more lives that it presently saves? Could medical science be mistaken? Let us explore the medical arguments for thinking this way by starting with Genes.

Do Genes Cause Disease? Are all diseases inherited?

Can defective genes cause disease? Gene research does not give us all the answers we thought it would. As an example, a gene was found that caused breast cancer. The laboratory that found it was naturally ecstatic and patented the genes BRAC1 and BRAC2 so they could develop therapies to 'cure' breast cancer. However, only five percent of women with breast cancer have these defective genes or one of the two hundred mutations.[20] Unfortunately, like many of these promises, gene research is not the answer.[21]

The truth seems to be that the environment controls how a gene expresses itself. In experiments carried out in the lab on human cells, it has been shown that if you provide a healthy environment for cells to grow, they multiply happily. Provide a less than optimal environment and they stop multiplying and show signs of sickness. 'Cells change their structure and function based on their environment.'[22] According to research carried out by Bruce Lipton – cellular biologist and author.

In the past this was not apparent because most cell biologists did not take into consideration the tissue cultures in which they grew their cells (their environment). The affect that the environment has on our lives and therefore our cells has seemingly been ignored after DNA's genetic code was discovered in 1959.

Even Darwin regretted omitting the environment and the direct affect that food, climate, social interactions and place have on individuals, independent of natural selection.[23]

So can we say that disease is caused by the environment? Well yes, the theories all point towards this being true and there seems to be a wealth of evidence to prove this.[24]

However, more research needs to be done to confirm this fact for certain. But if this fact has been all but proven, why do the conventional medical professions (your doctor), your well trained complementary practitioner or alternative practitioner still believe that the body has made a mistake? Genetics can not all be wrong, it is very confusing.

There are diseases that are caused by genetics. Cystic fibrosis, Huntington's chorea and beta thalassemia can all be blamed on genetic disorders but single genetic disorders affect less than two percent of the population. Why is it that someone who is completely healthy suddenly develops these diseases later on in life whilst others who have the defective gene never develop the disease?

Here's another puzzling thought; diseases such as heart disease, breast cancer and diabetes are said to be the result of complex interactions of multiple genes and environmental factors. That is the latest thought behind these biggest killers in our western civilization. Consider this strange fact - only five percent of cardiovascular and cancer patients can attribute their disease to heredity.[25] The BRAC1 and BRAC2 Breast cancer genes affect only five percent of women, and the other ninety-five percent of breast cancers are not hereditary. So, as far as hereditary diseases are concerned, the evidence does not look good for the 'the body has made a mistake' fraternity.

Were you aware that scientists have seldom found that one gene causes a trait or a disease? So what switches on these genes?

Do genes control the body? Or is this a hypothesis, not a truth, as was pointed out in a paper called 'Metaphor and the roles of genes and development.'[26] Did you know that there are NO scientific facts to prove that genes control the body? If it is not the genes, could the environment be the cause? We have to ask the question; could cells change, as the environment changes? Could genes switch on and off based on the environmental conditions? Even though science has successfully proven that the body has not made a mistake, practically all medical research done today still focuses on the premise that the body is, or has, done something wrong. As an example most cancer research is still trying to find the defective element or gene in the body, or studying the effects of killing a cancer cell using chemotherapy.[27]

'Defective' genes have nothing to do with the rapid growth of breast or any other cancer. In breast cancer, "bad" genes are described as disrupted growth factor functions, yet no research has identified the source of the dysfunction. The normal way to designate genes is by chromosome 'number' and 'arm'. So-called 'defective' breast cancer genes do not have these proper designations and are just theoretical. No cancer gene has ever been located and identified according to the combination of genetic bases and amino acid fault.[28]

I have noticed that all the studies into disease start off with the illness and work back to 'how can we make the body well again?' Could the body already know what to do? Have the scientists been barking up the wrong tree? I personally think so. So does Dr L. Hashemzadeh-Boneh, a scientist who recently trained to become a META-Medicine® Health Coach. She explained to me that scientists are often twenty or so years ahead of medicine. Scientists know that the body responds to the environment. That's old thinking. But the medical researchers don't listen to scientists.

I think this can be well explained if we look at one of the most exciting areas of genetic research called Epigenetic – Epigenetic is the study of how genes are switched on to express themselves due to precise changes in our environment.

'The malignancy in a significant number of cancer patients is derived from environmental induced epigenetic alterations and not defective genes'.[29] As quoted from Bruce Lipton's book Biology of Belief. Put simply, genes don't cause disease. Changes in our environment cause the genes to switch on or off.

It has recently been established that over thirty genes are responsible for breast cancer. Those companies which patented the rights to a single specific gene, thinking that was the only gene to cause a cancer are not going to make any money. The 'Human Genome Project' where every gene in a human body has been mapped, has not produced the Holy Grail that everyone was expecting. Science is like that – no sooner do you discover something new than it delivers you the complete opposite as being true. Just look at Newtonian physics and Einstein's Theory of Relativity. Here you can find a great example of how science has changed the face of the earth as we know it.

I personally believe it is important that, whilst we explore what medicine has given us, we need to think again; we must ask some of the fundamental questions and not take what doctors tell us as being true. The science and therefore the treatments and the drugs used have been superseded, as with Newton followed by Einstein. In META-Medicine® we are certain that people can die from a doctor's diagnosis. Not because of the doctors who personally have the welfare of the client at heart but because of the way the client's body reacts to both what the doctor says and the tone of voice used to say it, which causes further shocks to the system. Therefore the environment changes in the cells, many genes switch on or off and disease occurs.

Doctors' beliefs' and disease

Doctor's words are very powerful - a lay person saying the same thing about a prognosis of a patient does not have the same effect. The assumption that 'doctor knows best' has been handed down to us over many years. However, the tide is turning, the evidence they are using to back up their beliefs is out of date. Many doctors know this and have written extensively about a different shift in how they approach disease.

A few examples of Doctors beliefs and disease

Dr Bernie Siegel, a medical doctor from the USA, wrote the ground-breaking book called 'Love, Medicine and Miracles'. In 1986 Bernie Siegel said that there was a direct link between how we perceive an illness, and our healing. He used art therapy to understand and explain to a patient how they were healing. This practice is still used today with great effect in places such as the Penny Brohn Cancer Care. (Formerly the Bristol Cancer Help Centre, which is in my home town in England.) www.pennybrohncancercare.org.

The following excerpt is taken from Dr Bernie Siegel's website in an article called 'Waging war against cancer, against healing you life'. He writes about a traditional doctor's approach to healing.[30]

"We (meaning doctors – Ed) are not killers, consciously or unconsciously, and yet when you listen to the language of medicine you hear words like; poison, blast, kill, amputate, destroy, eliminate, assault and more. Unfortunately doctors are not taught how to communicate with patients and so our words and the words given to patients to read induce negative side affects. The words are coming from an authority and have a hypnotic influence. They tell you all the things which can go wrong but do not tell you what can go right. So wordswordsword are swordsswordswords. Yes, they become swords which can kill or cure as a scalpel can. If we told patients that their treatment was therapeutic and then explained there were side effects, but they do not happen to every patient, you would go home with a different feeling and option than being told all the side effects and none of the benefits. When given placebos (Chemotherapy placebos – Ed) patients have had their hair fall out and tumours shrink because they were told that is what would happen."

What I have seen is that doctors who speak out in this way are ostracized. Their own medical profession stops them from practicing by hounding them out of their positions thereby making it impossible for them to practice inside the normal system. So doctors stick to their status quo, earn their money and say nothing. I mentioned earlier in chapter 1 how my doctor friend said to me, "I totally believe in META-Medicine® but I can't and won't recommend any clients to you". On further discussions he said: "I would not be able to justify my reason to my colleagues and peers without seriously jeopardizing my name, my job, my career and my family".

This came from a doctor who has spent the last ten years or more studying anthroposophy - the philosophy of Rudolph Steiner.[31] The Steiner system is different in comparison to META-Medicine® but it is accepted by some doctors. Doctors accept it can be practiced, merely because it is established. This seems to me to be hypocritical, but that's our modern medical profession for you. My friend also told me that in the new practice, which he has recently joined, he will not be able to do much anthroposophical work since his practice manager, who is not a doctor, does not understand it. So he will go back to prescribing drugs in the way that he was originally taught.

As you can probably guess, in most countries the medical profession can't move even if they want to. They are stuck in a system that won't budge. However, people are starting to answer back. They are looking for alternatives to what the doctor tells them and refusing to accept what the doctor says as true. People can question what the doctors say; all they have to do is log onto the internet and run a search. They will find a wealth of information; the same information that the doctor knows and much of what they don't know. Take a look at Lynn McTaggart's ground breaking website, 'What doctors don't tell you' www.wddty.com.

People quickly find out that the doctors do know a lot and that they are very knowledgeable people. Especially when it comes to emergency medicine, which saves many lives throughout the world.

Even so, doctors still cannot answer that elusive question; 'What causes disease?' They don't even know how placebos work. Yet they are totally aware of their presence. Drug companies are very perplexed that the mind (placebos via sugar pills) is as effective as the drugs in clinical trials.[32] Placebo is not only found in drugs but in also in surgery. This was demonstrated through a study into the effects of surgery on knees. Of three groups, one of the groups had no surgery yet the skin was cut but the patients had no incisions. This group recovered just as well as the other groups, which received surgery.[33]

Microbes and disease

You may be asking the question; 'Aren't diseases caused by fungus, bacteria and viruses - the microbes?' Here is something really fascinating; were you aware that before the infection expresses itself (e.g. you get a cold) the virus is present in the blood system, multiplying but not active? Bacteria are multiplying in the blood for a long time before the infection occurs. Before a fungal infection occurs the fungus is growing, but again is dormant in the blood ready to be used when it is required. (More on this in chapter 10).

If microbes are the causes of disease, why do people rush to buy pro-biotic products such as Yakult which contains Lactobacillus Casei Shirota? Why are these so called 'good' bacteria there? Surely we should kill all of them? They cause disease! Let us drink pure bleach, (the chemical we use to clean our toilets), so we can get rid of all these horrible bugs out of our system. Why don't we do that?

Yet we get food poisoning from bacteria, but why? Why is it that not everyone gets food poisoning from the same meal? Why doesn't everyone get the flu when the flu is going around? Why doesn't everyone get athletes foot, (a fungal infection of the skin of the feet usually appearing between the toes), when they go to the gym or swimming pool?

If these deadly microbes really did cause disease then we would all be dead by now, because these microbes are everywhere. So why aren't we all dead? You may say it is because you have a good immune system and you have the antibodies to deal with these bugs. Well, I know plenty of really healthy people who exercise, don't smoke, eat well, but at the first sight of a bug they become sick. There are also people who smoke, eat unhealthy food, don't exercise yet they never seem to get these infections. Why?

I have also met people who are at the pinnacle of health and fitness. They feel great, they look great, they exercise, they have great mental attitudes towards life, they eat all the right foods and yet they get cancer, the cause of which they are told was probably a virus, as in the cervical cancer - the Human Papillomavirus (HPV). Why? Has this got anything to do with immunity? No, in META-Medicine® we don't think it has.

Could viruses, bacteria and fungus work in homeostasis (side by side) with our whole system? Could they be the cleaners and the digesters? The workers of our body?

There is also some belief that the so-called viruses such as smallpox and AIDS don't exist. No one has ever found the AIDS virus. In order to see a virus you need an incredibly powerful microscope. Only since the mid 1990s has the technology been available to do that. So how do we know these specific human viruses exist? It gets worse; if these so called 'viruses' have been found and isolated so that vaccines can be developed, then how is it that no university in the world can prove these viruses exist by producing a picture of them or by separating the virus structure completely outside of a cell?

I will explore this whole concept further in chapter 10. The whole theory that microbes are the cause of disease, again, like the other theories we have been sold, seems to be flawed. There is way more going on in the body than the medical profession and the pharmaceutical industry would lead you to believe.

I will leave you with one simple thought about bugs causing disease. Have you ever noticed that after a prolonged stressful time, once you relax, as on holiday after a project is finished and the stressful situation is resolved, you catch something. You get a virus, an infection. You get sick. So what does cause disease? If I am saying that it is not caused by genetics, nor is it the body making a mistake, and if it is not microbes, bacteria, viruses and fungi either, then it has to be poisons, toxins, radiation.

Radiation, poison, toxins and disease

Let us look at radiation and we all probably know that radiation kills. In Chernobyl a nuclear reactor blew up and resulted in a forty km exclusion zone. Studies show that the closer animals, (mostly birds), who live close to the centre of the explosion, there are more mutations and birth rates are significantly depressed. Further out from the centre, animals are not as highly affected. However, the effects of the background radiation that fell from the skies internationally is thought to affect between 4,000-30,000 worldwide, depending on which reports you read.[34] From the figures and observations I think we can safely say that background radiation is not the cause of all disease. However, radiation in large dosages, as used in cancer treatments, can cause significant damage and even cancer (see chapter 14). But the background amounts that we receive daily, in most healthy human beings, is not the cause of disease.

What about poisons? Yes, poisons do kill people just as radiation does but the amount needs to be specific and the type of poison administered has to be in a certain quantity for it to have a damaging effect. Chemotherapy that is derived from mustard gas is happily injected into cancer patients. Despite these extremely cytotoxic (toxic to cells) chemicals being used, the body can and does deal with it. (See chapter 14).

Any toxin in large qualities will kill you. In fact, any substance in large enough quantities or in the wrong place will kill you. Drinking too much water will kill you.[35] Air injected into your veins will kill you.[36] However, some people smoke and others live in poisonous environments and some of these people survive with no side effects while others develop nasty diseases.

So the body can deal with a mass of toxins. The medical profession uses toxins and radiation to 'cure' cancer. Do toxins therefore cause disease? Yes, you can be poisoned. Yes, you can be exposed to a large amount of radiation and die from it. However, toxins are not the cause of all disease.

So what are we left with? The only thing that we have not explored is 'stress' within our environment. What I mean by 'the environment' is how we react to certain situations caused by our surroundings; certain people, changing circumstances, challenging situations that cause us either immediate or ongoing stress that we can't deal with.

In the next chapter we will explore this missing link in the cause of diseases. What causes disease, pains and ailments to occur and where is the proof that this could be the case?

Chapter 4

What causes a disease?

Every human being is the author of their own health or disease.
- Buddha

A disease process originates from a Significant Emotional Event, which we experience as unexpected, dramatic and isolative. It occurs simultaneously at all levels of our organism.
The way we unconsciously react and associate a conflict experience determines which disease process (which organ and brain relay) is affected.
The emotional intensity, conflict length and the tracks (Anchors) determine the conflict mass and therefore the course of the disease process.
One of the ten META-Medicine® Models

Jenny Bourne and her Breast Cancer

My mother probably died from the complications caused by the treatment of breast cancer. So when I met Jenny through Professor Peter Fraser of NES in 2006, I was keen to assist her as much as I could. Peter Fraser was working with her, using the NES system, to help with her breast cancer. The questions she wanted me to answer were why did she get it, what was the cause and why did it happen at that time in her life?

Jenny had been diagnosed with breast cancer two years before and had been fighting it ever since. She had received chemotherapy, (only one course), but she was so sick from it that it almost killed her. Her oncologist said he had never seen anyone react to chemotherapy in this way.

When she came to see me she seemed full of health, life and vitality. She refused anymore chemotherapy and had made a decision to try alternative approaches. She had been working with Peter, using the NES system and the therapeutic interventions that accompany it to energetically rebalance and reactivate the coding in her body that would allow her to heal.

Jenny is a NES trainer and practitioner and had been working with Peter and I on some new interventions based on the META-Medicine® principles with great success (See chapter 15). However Jenny and Peter agreed that we would work together to understand what caused the biological change in Jenny's body for her cancer to occur.

When she sent me her Time Line History, (which I get from every client I work with), I saw what might have caused her issue; it was a shock that was to do with her son. It wasn't until I was able to meet her face to face and find out about the issue and all the surrounding circumstances that it became apparent why this lovely person had found herself with the breast cancer.

Jenny's first husband was a very unpleasant man. She found herself pregnant and trapped in a relationship that caused her untold problems and heartache. It was so difficult that she made a massive sacrifice: to leave her husband and her children. This was at a time when the courts did not recognise the importance of mothers in the upbringing of their children. I personally recognise this since my father had custody of my two brothers and myself after my parents' divorce.

Jenny's life was difficult and she had many problems with her children. The main issue was that her son is a heroin addict. This was an ongoing issue that Jenny has little to do with and then one day out of the blue he called from prison, to say that he had been arrested for raping a girl. Jenny told me how the sound of his voice was so chilling that it still resonated deep inside her.

As I probed further into the circumstances around this phone call she went bright red and relived the shock. It was horrible to hear a mother, who still felt totally guilty for leaving her children, go through hearing his voice saying how helpless he was. He did not know what to do. He didn't even know if he had raped the girl. The police said he would be put away for a long time for this crime. She told me how she felt a massive fear that she may never see him again.

This event changed her whole life. She dropped everything she was doing and started a 'one women crusade' to clear her son's name. She spent every penny she had trying to do this. Eventually she succeeded and you could hear the relief in her voice as she recounted the verdict from the jury saying her son was 'not guilty'.

What was so sad was that her son could not have cared less. It was as if he was glad he had been arrested so that she had to save him. He did not care that she had spent all her money and every moment of her time to clear his name.

It was approximately one and a half years later that she was diagnosed with ductal breast cancer. (Ductal carcinoma in situ). Why did she get the cancer? Could the stress caused by clearing her son's name be something to do with it?

We have already discussed many things to do with disease including the fact that modern medicine has no idea what causes a disease. This is rather alarming. How can you find a cure for something if you don't even know what caused it? To explain this I have written a small example of how not knowing the cause of a disease and therefore the belief system that 'the body has made a mistake' has an influence on how a doctor treats a patient.

You are not a doctor – what do you know? Part 1
The following story has been adapted from real life circumstances. Imagine a young girl who had a tumour that was growing on her head. She was only eight, a lovely, happy little girl, full of life and, apart from the tumour, was completely normal. Her parents took her to see a specialist doctor, and he was very concerned about the growth. The parents asked the doctor what had caused the growth. He could not answer and told them not to question him with such trivial matters; this young girl's life was in danger, and quick removal of the tumour was necessary. A brain CT was carried out and the parents insisted on having a copy. The doctor was very unhappy with this situation but reluctantly let them have a copy with the proviso that they write a letter stating that they would not sue the doctor based on the CT. They agreed. The CT obviously showed that the tumour was not connected to any part of the bone, nor was it invasive.

The girl had an operation and the tumour was removed. She was happy and the tumour did not re-grow. A month later a special scan (PET scan) was carried out to see if there were any other tumours present. There was a small marking on the oesophagus which the doctor said was a secondary tumour. The parents asked what had caused this and again the doctor told them not question him. Could it have been from the tube that was put down the child's throat they wondered, as she had been complaining of a pain in her lower throat ever since the operation? The doctor disagreed and refused to do more exploratory tests, believing the marking to be a secondary tumour.

He then insisted that the girl needed chemotherapy. He also insisted that he personally explain to the girl the reason why he wanted to use chemotherapy. When the parents disagreed, he insisted, replying that she was old enough to understand and he went ahead and told her. This shocked the child and the parents spent many hours consoling the girl back at home.

The parents asked for a second opinion. They took the girl to a different doctor, who looked at the scans and did not agree that the child needed chemotherapy. The original doctor became very angry and called the new doctor telling him to stop interfering with his patient. He also involved the authorities in the case who visited the parents saying that if they disagreed with the doctor's opinion, that she needed chemotherapy, then they would take their child away and give her chemotherapy.

The parents were horrified and got a third medical opinion. This doctor looked through all the facts, and told them that the child had no secondary cancers; the scan only showed a recent scar from the operation tube. He rang the original doctor and explained his findings. The original doctor disagreed and told the authorities that the girl needed chemotherapy. The child was taken away from the parents and given chemotherapy. She was very unhappy, she lost all her hair and was very, very sick from the treatment.

After the chemotherapy, which took nine months she slowly recovered. A few months later another scan was carried out. The same marking in the oesophagus was there and had not changed in size. The doctor ordered another round of chemotherapy. The child became very sick again. A few months later the next scan showed the same marking in the same place. It had not changed. He ordered exploratory surgery. They found scarring from the tube from the original surgery on the tumour.

The child was extremely ill. She was hospitalised for many months being weakened from the chemotherapy and the operation.

The parents could do nothing. Eventually the child recovered but was very traumatised by the whole experience and was no longer the happy, full of life little girl she had been. She unfortunately regressed into herself, becoming shy. Her health suffered with continuous infections and she developed an on-going bowel disorder.

I had a similar problem with the pain in my back, and unfortunately I can personally relate to this situation. I spent over £8,000 trying to solve my herniated disc problem over a year and a half. I went to everyone I could find, including some of the top back professionals in the UK. They could not tell me what had caused it to happen. By that time I did not care. All I wanted was for the pain to disappear and to be able to walk again. I had the foresight not to have surgery because I knew it would not help me in the long run. I had a lot of pressure from my doctor to have invasive treatments and to take pharmaceutical drugs. He diagnosed me incorrectly saying I had Ankylosing Spondylitis. He said it was hereditary. He could not tell me what caused it to occur and he questioned me saying I was not a doctor - what did I know? My brain CT which was read by Dr Bader, a META-Medicine® doctor, showed the trauma in my disc and corresponding cause of the problem, which was a self-worth issue to do with my personality as I have explained earlier.

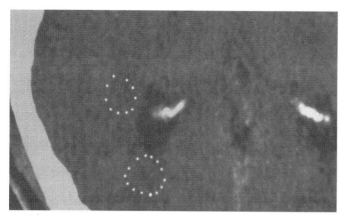

The section of my brain CT that shows the conflicts that I went through. The cause of the conflict was a deep personality self worth issue, where I let people walk all over me. This area is in the Medulla (Mid Brain) – See Chapter 9 for more information about the brain and other examples of brain CTs.

I have come across many people who have had the similar problems. My guess is that you have either been, know of someone or are going through the same experience yourself. The question is, if you don't know the cause of the problem then how can you solve it?

The cause of disease is not known

Did you know that modern medicine does not know what causes ninety-nine percent of all diseases? Please read this sentence again. It is profound. When I first heard this I ignored it until I realised what was being said. Modern medicine doesn't know what causes a disease. This is crazy.

The truth is that medical doctors can label a symptom very well. They are brilliant at emergency medicine but they can't tell you why a disease occurs. They don't know. Yes, you did hear me correctly. "The medical profession doesn't know what causes diseases to occur."

If this is the case then how can they claim to cure a disease? The truth is that often they don't. A good doctor friend of mine said to me, when I asked him how the drugs worked to cure a particularly unpleasant bout of gastric flu I had had: "The pills did not cure you, your body does that naturally, the drugs merely block you up. Most drugs just mask your symptoms whilst your body heals itself".

I was flabbergasted to hear this, especially from a medical doctor.

So how can a doctor work if they don't know what causes a disease to occur. To understand this we need to go back to the beginning of the medical profession.

Over two hundred years ago when doctors first started practising medicine, they were considered quacks. People believed in religion more than they did in doctors. Doctors were members of the Royal College of Barbers and Surgeons. In 1745 they broke away as they started to earn more money and gain more respect. Modern medicine only really started to make a difference in people's health after the introduction of the 'germ' theory, whereby it was understood that they thought that germs were the cause disease.

Germs do have a part to play in death. There is no doubt that cleanliness reduces the likelihood of dying from a horrible infection, but why? Could the germ theory be wrong? I will pose this question now and answer it a little later on in the book in Chapter 10, but here is food for thought. As we will discover later, these germs are already in our system and we live in symbiosis with them. They only become active during certain times and only for a reason.

From then on very little has changed. 'Germs cause disease' has been the major premise behind modern medicine's approach to healing, even with the introduction of new diagnostic machines which enable us to peep inside living people. Since the development of Computer Tomography (CT's, 1973), Ultrasound (1979) and Magnetic Resonance Imaging (MRI) (1977) very little has changed. Diagnosis is still a haphazard process. Dr Bader, the Vice President of the IMMA mentioned that even with these incredible machines, the amount of correct diagnosis has not increased.

What is also surprising is that according to a recent Bloomberg report the number one cause of death in the United States may be due to the medical system itself.

"A definitive review and close reading of medical peer-review journals, and government health statistics shows that American medicine frequently causes more harm than good. The number of people having in-hospital, adverse drug reactions (ADR) to prescribed medicine is 2.2 million. Dr. Richard Besser, of the Center for Disease Control (CDC), in 1995, said the number of unnecessary antibiotics prescribed annually for viral infections was 20 million. Dr. Besser, in 2003, now refers to tens of millions of unnecessary antibiotics. The number of unnecessary medical and surgical procedures performed annually is 7.5 million. The number of people exposed to unnecessary hospitalization annually is 8.9 million. The total number of iatrogenic deaths (deaths caused by medical interventions – Ed) is 783,936. It is evident that the American medical system is the leading cause of death and injury in the United States. The 2001 heart disease annual death rate is 699,697; the annual cancer death rate, 553,251." Death by Medicine - October 2003, released by the Nutritional Institute of America.[37]

Since Edward Jenner's discovery of the first vaccine, and Louis Pasteur's 'germ theory', modern medicine has seemingly remained unchanged concerning the cause of disease.

The germ theory has saved many lives with antibiotics by stopping bacterial infections. But the cause of many other diseases has not been established and only one hundred bacteria have a detrimental effect on our bodies. (See Chapter 10 on Microbes and Chapter 11 on Antibiotics and Vaccinations).

If you look up in any medical dictionary, on the web or in book form, you will find to your surprise, that modern medicine will say they don't know the cause of many diseases.

They have a guess but the research is inconclusive. So many thoughts from the medical profession as to what might cause disease are based on a hypothesis.

Take heart disease for example; the medical profession doesn't know what causes it but they do have risk factors. The main ones of which are high blood pressure, high cholesterol, diabetes, obesity, smoking, stress, alcohol and age.

Now I agree that those people who have these risk factors are more likely to develop some form of heart issue but what causes heart diseases to occur? There are people with one or all of these risk factors who never have heart problems and there are others who don't have any of these issues but who do have heart problem. Why? What caused them to get the problems? The medical profession cannot explain this.

What about cancer? What causes cancer? A defective gene? A virus? A bacteria? Old age? Your immune system? Diet? Carcinogens? Your environment? The medical profession does not know.

You can find a complete list of all the things, according to epidemiologists, that give you cancer. Looking through the list I realise I should not be alive. And neither should you.[38] Here's a shortened list:

alcohol, air pollution, baby food, barbequed meat, bottled water, bracken, bread, breasts, bus stations, casual sex, car fumes, celery, charred foods, chewing gum, Chinese food, chips, chlorinated water, cholesterol, low cholesterol, chromium, coal

33

tar, coffee, coke ovens, crackers, creosote, dairy products, deodorants, depression, diesel exhaust, diet soda, fat, fluoridation, flying, formaldehyde, french fries, fruit, gasoline, genes, gingerbread, global warming, granite, grilled meat, hair dyes, hamburgers, high bone mass, hydrogen peroxide, incense, infertility, jewellery, kissing, lack of exercise, laxatives, lead, left handedness, low fibre diet, magnetic fields, marijuana, microwave ovens, milk hormones, mixed spices, mobile phones, night lighting, night shifts, not breast feeding, not having a twin, nuclear power plants, NutraSweet, obesity, oestrogen, olestra, olive oil, orange juice, oyster sauce, ozone, ozone depletion, passive smoking, PCBs, peanuts, pesticides, pet birds, plastic IV bags, potato crisps (chips), power lines, proteins, PVC, radio masts, railway sleepers, red meat, saccharin, salt, semiconductor plants, shellfish, sick buildings, soy sauce, stress, styrene, sulphuric acid, sun beds, sunlight, sunscreen, talc, testosterone, tight bras, toast, toasters, tobacco, tooth fillings, toothpaste (with fluoride or bleach), train stations, under-arm shaving, unvented stoves, UV radiation, vegetables, vinyl toys, vitamins, wallpaper, welding fumes, well water, weight gain, winter, wood dust, work, x-rays.

I took out all the long unknown chemical names. Even with those gone the list is still ridiculous.

Let us delve even further into what the medical profession think is the cause for disease.

Multiple Sclerosis

"Doctors still don't understand what causes MS. However, there is interesting data that suggest that genetics, a person's environment, and possibly even a virus may play a role."(Source: WebMD.com).

Eczema

"Eczema is divided into a small number of subgroups based largely on the factors that may be most important in causing eczema in any one individual. But it is important to recognise that the symptoms and appearance of the skin in all these types can be exactly the same. Also, the classification system is far from perfect as it is often difficult or impossible to accurately say what causes eczema to occur in any one person." (Source: netdoctor.co.uk)

Irritable Bowel Syndrome (IBS)

"We don't know what causes IBS." (Source: netdoctor.co.uk).

Acne

"Acne is caused by the over activity of the sebaceous glands that secrete oily substances onto the skin." (Source www.bupa.co.uk). But what caused the over activity? They mention testosterone but they don't mention why there is excessive testosterone and what causes that to occur in men and women?

Depression

"Some depressions run in families. Researchers believe that it is possible to inherit a tendency to depression. This seems to be especially true for bipolar disorder (manic depression). Studies of families with several generations of bipolar disorder (BPD) found that those who develop the disorder have differences in their genes from most who don't develop BPD. However, some of the people with the genes for BPD don't actually develop the disorder. Other factors, such as stresses at home, work, or school, are also important." (Source www.mentalhealth.about.com).

"The causes of depression are many. Depression is a complex disease that can occur as a result of a multitude of factors. For some, depression occurs due to a loss of a loved one, a change in one's life, or after being diagnosed with a serious medical disease. For others, depression just happened, possibly due to their family history." (Source www.webmd.com).

Anxiety

"Anxiety is often triggered by stress in our lives. Some of us are more vulnerable to anxiety than others, but even those who become anxious can easily learn to cope with it. We can also make ourselves anxious with "negative self-talk" - a habit of always telling ourselves the worst will happen." (Source www.medicalnews.com).

Ovarian cysts

"A woman's ovaries normally grow cyst-like structures each month called 'follicles'. Follicles produce the hormones; 'oestrogen' and 'progesterone' and release an egg when during ovulation. Sometimes a normal monthly follicle just keeps growing. When that happens, it becomes known as a functional cyst. This means it started during the normal function of the menstrual cycle."[39] (Source www.mayoclinic.com). No reason is given as to what causes the follicle to keep growing.

Prostate cancer

"The exact causes of prostate cancer are unknown. However, research aimed at understanding how cancer cells start to grow and spread may indicate some contributing factors. These factors include: testosterone, age, heredity, genetics, and diet."[40] (Source www.ehealthmd.com).

Diabetes type II

"The exact causes of type 2 diabetes are not completely understood. However, it is known that the disease has a strong hereditary component. Individuals who have a parent or sibling with type 2 diabetes have a 10 to 15% chance of developing the disease (the risk is much higher if the sibling is an identical twin). Environmental factors like an inactive lifestyle or poor diet may act as a trigger for someone with a genetic tendency towards type 2 diabetes. Other potential causes of type 2 include: chronic stress, low birth weight (and associated foetal malnourishment), and gene mutations."[41] (Source www.dlife.com)

So, as you can see from this small snapshot of some of the most common diseases, the medical profession are in the dark when it comes to understanding what causes specific diseases. Look into this further yourself and you will find more of the same.

We do, however, know that stress does play a part in disease.

Almost every major illness that people acquire is linked to chronic stress.[42] The conclusion from a research paper by Segerstrom and Miller in 2004 and many others since 1999.

I mentioned this before but the question that arises from this finding is: "Which specific disease is caused by what type of stressful event?" That still remains a mystery.

In META-Medicine® we may have an answer to that question. When a person goes through a shocking experience that they cannot deal with, it causes the body to change, to fight or defend itself. The criteria of the shock must be as follows: -

Unexpected
Dramatic
Isolating
No Strategy

We call it UDIN, making it easier for you to remember the criteria. All of the criteria must be present for a disease to occur. Let me explain each one:

Unexpected

An **unexpected** shock is something that you just were not expecting to happen. Somebody who sees their mother being raped in front of them at age seven would be an example. On the other hand, if someone has heard their alcoholic parent say hundreds of times that they are going to kill themselves then, if they do although it is a horrific shock, it is not unexpected. There was an 'expectation' this could happen.

Dramatic

A **dramatic** shock is one where there is a lot of emotional energy involved in the event. An example would be someone leaving a person they love deeply because, as hard as they try, they could not be with that person. The shock is hearing the voice of their partner pleading with them not to go, in such an emotional way that it is heart wrenching and hurts them very deeply.

An incident which it is not dramatic is one where a daughter or son over hears their parents say that they don't want to spend Christmas with them. The parents have religiously spent Christmas with them and their family but the parents are difficult to get on with, cause many unpleasant arguments and so it is an unexpected shock but not that dramatic.

Isolating

An **isolating** shock is one that isolates us completely, meaning we feel totally alone after it happens. An example would be: The second wife of a man who has unfortunately died of cancer has to fight his children to stay in the marital home. Even though she was married to the man for fifteen years and had helped raise his children, they isolate her by taking her to court in order to get her to sell the marital home. She talks to no-one about her isolation.

An unexpected, dramatic shock that is not isolating could be a person suddenly hears that one of their best friends at school has been killed in a horrific car crash. The whole class rallies around to mourn the loss of their classmate. They talk openly about how sad a loss it was, even if they did not know that person as well as the person who has lost their closest friend.

No strategy

A shock where a person has **no strategy** is one where an incident happens but the person has no idea what to do. They are lost in the wilderness after the shock and they run over and over the whole event again and again trying to find a way out of it. An example would be a very strong-willed woman who is accused by her best friend, who happens to be married to her brother, that she must have known that her husband (the strong-willed woman's brother) had been having an affair. Even though the strong-willed woman denies any knowledge of what her brother had been doing, the best friend does not believe her. This is dramatic, unexpected, isolating and she has no strategy in being able to deal with this.

A situation which is unexpected, dramatic, isolating but where the person involved has a strategy to deal with the shock, would be a person is who is singled out and disliked by their manager and sacked from a job that they love for a misdemeanour they did not commit. It is unexpected, dramatic, isolating, but they have a strategy; they use the employment law to solve the problem. In the meantime they find another job and fight the issue in court, eventually winning the case. There is a strategy to deal with this type of problem.

META-Medicine® –What causes a disease

So from a META-Medicine® point of view the cause of disease is related to a specific type of stressful event, a UDIN moment and the fact that someone cannot deal with it causes the body to change, to fight or defend itself.

Now how can I say this is true? Bruce Lipton states in his book, 'The Biology of Belief' that a cell changes its constitution based on its surroundings. When under stressful situations, a cell is working. When there is no stress, the cell regenerates. There are two phases as to how a cell reacts (refer to Chapter 6). It cannot be in a stressed state and repairing itself at the same time.[43] What we are interested in, is the stress. If the event is unexpected, dramatic, isolating and there is no strategy to deal with the situation, then the cell remains in an ongoing stressful state. It does not have a chance to repair itself.

If our environment changes and we don't know what to do, we have a UDIN shock, where the cells in specific organs change their structure and function.

When a person gets an illness/disease, it does not affect every organ; a person gets breast cancer or cancer of the bowel, an eczema, muscle wastage, a cough. The illness/disease is localised.

As I have explained and is scientifically proven through research papers, that a cell changes its function and structure as a result of changes in environmental conditions. We are also aware that almost every major illness that people acquire is linked to chronic stress. If the illnesses/diseases are localised in one part of an organ in the body, then what are the cells in those organs changing for? For this we need to look at some basics to do with biology.

Basic biology and its link to disease

Let us look at some of the organs and their basic functions and how they relate to disease.

The digestive tract: A disease in this part of the body is because the person cannot digest something that has become stuck. If they cannot digest this stuck piece of food, then the food behind the stuck chunk will not be digested either because it cannot flow down the digestive tract. The functioning and possible survival of the organism is threatened. If it cannot eat it will starve. The cells in that part of the digestive tract change their structure and function so they more effectively digest the food that is stuck. This is what happens in worms. If a piece of food gets stuck in the digestive tract, more digestive tract is created around the area where the food is stuck. More digestive juices are produced from the new surrounding cells and the chunk of food is digested and then pushed up or out of the organism. As this happens the excess cells that were created are pushed out.

The stress created by the stuck piece of food, causes the specific localised cells to change so that the body can eliminate the problem and carry on digesting food and surviving. In humans information is food. Information affects our livelihood. Loosing ones life savings due to poor financial advice could be an example.

Cells change their function in the glands of the breasts. During pregnancy a woman's body knows she has to bring up a baby; the breasts grow bigger to produce milk to nurture the children. Any pregnant woman knows this because they have experienced this.

The stress of bringing up a baby, whose whole survival depends on the mother's milk in the first few months outside of the womb, causes the localised cells in the breast glands to multiply.

If a bone is broken then the body naturally mends it. Even in the wild I have seen foxes that have broken one of their back legs and within six weeks they are walking on the leg again, no plaster and the leg is fine. A strange phenomenon is that the rebuilt bone is stronger than the original bone in humans and animals alike.

After the stress of a bone being broken, the cells change to rebuild the bone. The cells organise themselves in an amazing way, rebuilding the bone in exactly the right amount in the right place and the place where the bone was broken is stronger than before the fracture. Any orthopaedic doctor will tell you that this is true.

37

When you tear a muscle through intense exercise it rebuilds itself to be stronger and bigger than before. Body-builders know this. Their whole profession is based on this natural fact.

During eczema there is a loss of skin followed by a rebuilding of skin. The way the medical profession treat eczema is by using steroid creams. Doctors tell a person not to use too much steroid cream because the skin becomes very thin; the cream is not a cure.

It is strange but the skin when it is thin (and I know this because I have had eczema) feels desensitised. The skin is our tactile sensory organ that connects us to the outside world. If you do feel that missing touch, you don't think about the person you have lost contact with. The rebuilding part is what we commonly call eczema but anyone who suffers from it will tell you there are two phases; the light, scaly, desensitised, cold skin and then a red, very sensitive, itchy, hot skin. Most women who stop breast feeding will have noticed that their baby will get eczema on the cheeks. The medical profession say it is an allergic reaction to the bottled milk. Could it instead be the loss of contact between the baby and the mother? I know women who use a machine to pump breast milk, feeding the baby with this breast milk via a bottle later on and the child still gets the eczema.

From what we know about stress causing disease, and the cells' function changing to adapt to the environmental conditions, eczema is caused by the loss of contact. This is a far more plausible answer to why our bodies react in the way they do, than an allergic reaction to powdered milk.

Especially when the medical profession cannot explain what causes an allergic reaction. However, META-Medicine® may have a very simple and plausible answer based on the shock/stress theory.

So, if organs change their function as a result based on changes in the environment and disease is caused by chronic stress, then what causes the chronic stress? Is the UDIN the beginning of chronic stress; the unexpected, dramatic, isolating event where the person has no strategy for dealing with what has happened?

Can we then say that the beginning of a disease has to start with an unexpected, dramatic, isolating event where there is no strategy for dealing with it? A biological conflict shock, a UDIN?

From a META-Medicine® point of view, this point when the shock happens causes many changes to take place. As the shock happens this then determines how we are going to react as an individual, organ-wise and personality-wise. As the shock occurs it seems that the body makes specific choices as to which organ will be affected. This is determined by the content of the shock and basic biology.

As I mentioned earlier, if the issue was one of inability to nurture, then it affects the breast. An issue concerning the skin would be the result of a loss of contact. A gut issue would be related to something that cannot be digested and an issue to do with the muscles would be because you are not strong enough, perhaps, to fight back.

So a shock does not affect every organ in the body, just the one that is connected to that specific type of shocking event. What is not apparent is that as a 'shock' occurs there is a corresponding reaction in the brain. We can see this 'shock' via a CT scan of the brain. Even more exciting is that each one of these 'shocks' shows up in a specific location in the brain that is directly related to the organ that is affected.

A good friend of mine, Professor Peter Fraser, has worked out that these shocks in the brain resonate at the same frequency as the waves used in CT scanning (i.e. X-rays). Therefore you can see these UDIN shocks stored in specific locations. He has discovered, (yet it is still to be proven in the laboratory), that these shocks, (which are seen as rings) are probably trapped emotion. This certainly fits with my experience as a therapy practitioner. When I work with resolving emotional conflicts, I find that people often get headaches at the exact point where the ring is, after they have released the issue.

More scientific work has to be carried out into this, but the rings are certainly there. Chapter 9 is dedicated to the brain and the location of these rings, along with many examples and pictures of CT scans.

Symptoms following a shock

As the shock happens, the body also changes its state from a normal everyday waking state into a state of stress. We have all experienced this at some point in our lives. It is typically called the fight, flight or freeze response.

Typical symptoms are cold extremities - your hands, feet and outer skin get cold. There is a rush of energy in the form of adrenaline to your heart, which beats faster. You feel wide awake, wired, full of energy. Your focus and attention is on one thing and one thing only - the stressful event you are going through and what you can do to solve it or get out of it.

Also during this time your personality changes. What you see, hear, feel, taste and smell are all affected. Your unconscious mind filters out what it does not need and draws attention to what it wants to focus on, often as an avoidance system. This avoidance system is called tracking and it can explain allergies and chronic diseases. (See Chapter 7).

Also our filters change and our personality is altered to solve the problem. The emotion is trapped in specific places in the corresponding brain and organ and it seems our bodies become obsessed, almost like a machine, with one aim - to solve the problem.

Take, for example, my client with breast cancer, Jenny; she became totally obsessed with clearing the name of her son.

She did not stop until her son's name was cleared, which was a year and a half later. Then after the conflict was complete she was diagnosed with ductal breast cancer.

The shock laid down the pattern. She told me about the sound of her son's voice, (that was the shock), and as a Mum she had no choice but to help him; it was an unexpected, dramatic, isolating shock where she had no strategy for solving the issue.

However, I do need to mention poisoning, accidents, malnutrition are shocks in their own right. Malnutrition, when it gets to a critical stage, causes a shock to the body and it starts to shut off specific organs one by one.

So, we understand that it is very likely that a specific type of shock is the cause of a disease. The evidence seems to point in that direction. This is also evident through our use of language. Here are some examples. You hear 'It hit me in the pit of my stomach' – stomach ulcer; 'it got stuck in my throat' – loosing your voice; 'it totally stank' - sinusitis; 'I was being attacked head on' – pleurisy; 'I felt powerless' – hypothyroidism; 'it broke my heart' - coronary heart disease; 'it was as if an arrow had pierced right through me' - melanoma; 'I was crippled by what was said' - herniated disc; 'I was so shocked I couldn't even come up for air' - bronchial asthma; 'I feel so totally disconnected from everyone' - eczema. 'The sweetness drained right out of my life' - diabetes. The statements and diseases listed are examples taken from my clients that had these issues.

In my work with clients, finding the shock that started the disease process is profound. It answers the question of why the disease is there and it explains the symptoms to the client. I can describe to them exactly how their personality changed, and how they reacted to other people and situations after the shock. It is as if I am reading their horoscope, only there is no guesswork, no hypothesis on my behalf. I am using theory to do this.

You are not a doctor – what do you know? Part 2

The parents of the lovely little girl who had a tumour removed from her head and were forced to have chemotherapy, contacted a META-Medicine® Health Coach.

The coach had her brain CT scan read by a META-Medicine® doctor (see chapter 9 for examples of brain CT markings) and no extra tumours were reported. The original conflict shock was found. The explanation for the tumour was explained to the parents; why it was there, why the tumour grew, what caused the issue in the first place, and why there were no metastasis; secondary cancers.

The trauma on the oesophagus was also spotted, which was probably caused by the tube going down the throat in the original operation. The META-Medicine® doctor was not aware of the history of the client until it was explained to him after he had read the brain CT. He remarked that if the child had been left alone after surgery, there would have been no extra growth of the original tumour on her head. He also mentioned that there were no metastasis and, in the long term, if nothing further had been done then she would have made a full recovery. When told about the chemotherapy he was horrified and said that this was completely unnecessary, even in normal medicine, especially after the PET scan had only shown the marking in the oesophagus.

The girl had 9 months of unnecessary chemotherapy. The side effects of this were horrendous. Many of the chemotherapies known side effects are that they cause cancer. Luckily her family supported the girl with homeopathy, nutritional changes, emotional support, EFT (Emotional Freedom Technique) everyday along with massive detoxification programmes after each treatment. We do not know of the long term consequences of this unnecessary treatment on the girl's long term growth – will she ever be able to conceive? Time will tell. Chemotherapy is known to destroy the reproductive organs, however young people's bodies are very resilient and she could be unaffected by this invasive treatment.

Since carrying out a review edition of the book, I unfortunately heard that Jenny Bourne passed away. She had a problem with swallowing and eventually she had to go to hospital to become rehydrated and get a tube put down her nose so she could get food into her. However whilst in hospital she had a full body CT to find the cause of her inability to swallow, an endoscopy showed no issues in her oesophagus but the CT showed that she had bone, liver and lung cancer. After hearing this news she very quickly gave up the fight to carry on, so her loving husband Brian told me. She was a fighter and I hope that her story will assist many others in our understanding as to what really causes a disease. Something I will explain in more detail in following chapters. She showed great resilience to do other forms of therapies after the failed chemotherapy that almost killed her. These other therapies such as NES (see chapter 15) and drastic dietary changes (see chapter 12) certainly kept her alive way beyond the medical prognosis. Here we can see how a diagnosis can have a negative effect on a person. I am very sad that she has passed away.

In conclusion the medical profession do not know what causes a disease and therefore the treatments they offer are based on guesswork and hypothesis. There is no theory behind the treatment they administer. Something I will discuss and prove in later chapters.

From a META-Medicine®'s point of view the UDIN, the shocking experience, is the key to unlocking a disease programme. In the next chapter we will discuss how, during this shock, the whole mind, body and spirit connection is affected as well as how that affects our whole environment and social interactions. This also explains so much about why our world changes after a conflict shock and how we also change personality, something I only touched upon in this chapter.

Chapter 5

Disease as a biological feedback monitor

"I would feel more optimistic about a bright future for man if he spent less time proving that he can outwit Nature and more time tasting her sweetness and respecting her seniority."
--E.B. White (American author)

"There is no separation between body, mind, spirit embedded in the environment. The process and development of a disease process is synchronous at all levels (organ, brain, environment, mind, behaviour).
Because all levels are synchronous and in phase with each other, we can use the data of one level to conclude the other levels. Every change at one level simultaneously affects and is visible on all other levels".
One of the ten META-Medicine® Models

Sam and his strange ear problems

Sam (name changed – Ed) is a great bloke. He works really hard travelling around the country putting up stages for large concerts. He does not like his job but he tolerates it. He is the main manager and, luckily for him, he is well liked by his workmates because he has a reputation for staying calm. Even when things are going completely wrong. People take orders from Sam and he is well respected.

When he came to see me it was because he wanted to be coached using NLP. He did not need or ask for META-Medicine®. I am a very experienced NLP coach and I like to think that I know my stuff. I train NLP up to Masters Level and have been doing so since 1993. Sam has a band that was doing okay but not going places. There was a lot going on in his life. He had a new 'so called' girlfriend, and he really liked her, but it was not really working out. His friends were also a problem. He had recently moved out from living with a female friend with whom he had been very close, as she had immense psychological problems. He moved in with a male friend.

I worked with him quite a few times over the space of three months. Unusually, we only made a little bit of progress, and things were not really getting much better. He was still not going anywhere in his life. Work was not good and his new relationship was breaking up. He was also having problems with all his friends, both old and new. Even after using all the NLP techniques I knew Sam's problems were not getting any better.

Throughout all of our meetings he kept complaining that he did not trust anyone. Neither did he trust himself. Eventually during one meeting, after an hour of me digging, I threw my NLP notebook down to the floor and said; "We are getting nowhere". I then told him that I was going to switch over to META-Medicine®. I quickly explained what META-Medicine® was - how stressful events are linked to disease and how, when an event occurs it affects us in every area of our life, both mind, body, spirit, socially and environmentally.

I looked Sam in the eye and asked him if he had had any illnesses in the past few months. He nonchalantly replied that he had ear infections in both ears. He was taking antibiotics which were having no effect whatsoever. One ear was worse than the other.

I looked through my notes because I had seen this combination of two separate illnesses occurring in opposite organs before and had in the last two weeks carried out a META-Medicine® diagnosis with a client with the same issue. The result of this was that the client thinks - 'I cannot believe what I am hearing.'

So I told Sam and he totally understood what I was saying but ironically he could not trust himself or me. I quizzed him even further about this and asked him "Don't you trust me at all?" To which he replied – "No, but I also don't trust myself either".

I asked him about what had been going on in his life a month prior to the ear infections. He told me that he had been in some very stressful situations with his female friend who he could not get through to; she had had an abortion and was in a complete mess because of it. He had tried to speak to her but she had told him to leave her alone in a way that was very alarming and upsetting for him. He decided he had to move out from that female friend's house. He moved into a flat with a friend, who he subsequently had a problem with. This friend had a massive argument with Sam, saying some really hurtful things to him.

All in all Sam had heard two very alarming things, all within the space of a few weeks. He told me that he had felt continuously stressed for a while and then he had settled down a bit but he had mood swings. Sometimes he felt really upbeat, more up beat than normal and then he would feel strange, he would crash and feel totally down. This was the real reason he started coming to see me.

He also said that during this time his calm personality had changed. He lost contact with his new girlfriend who he really wanted to be with. He could not trust her. He even accused her of being unfaithful. Band members were also a problem and everything was falling apart around him. His work was terrible, he kept arguing with everyone and subsequently he did not want to do it any longer.

He told me it was as if he could not live in the world - he trusted no one, not even himself and he did not trust anything that he heard. When I explained what had happened, it was so funny because he totally understood why he had the ear infections. He was in a really strange place, knowing why, believing it and recognising all the changes that had happened to him, yet not trusting me or himself. I even did a demonstration of how he would behave with other people and he confirmed that this was how he reacted. Knowing that he would never trust himself or me, I just got on and did the therapy.

The mind and the body are not linked in modern medicine

In modern medicine there is neither a link between the mind and the body, nor is there a connection to the environment. If there was, then doctors would not administer so many drugs because they would realise the effect the drugs have on the person's mind. Doctors would also pay a lot more attention to the effects of a diagnosis. Instead, this whole area is completely ignored by many, many doctors.

Also, doctors have no training in developing a good bedside manner. The doctors that I personally know are lovely, intelligent people but when it comes to understanding people and how fragile they are, they admit that they do not have time and neither are they trained to deal with an individual's emotional problems.

When a person is given a diagnosis, especially one that is life threatening, such as a prognosis of cancer, doctors can give people the facts but with such coldness it is frightening to hear. I personally have to coach my clients through every word a doctor has said. Clients react as if they are in a hypnotic trance when in front of a doctor. They often take every word a doctor says as the truth. I have met and heard of clients who have been given a prognosis and acted it out to the letter. I am certain most doctors have little or no idea how much of an influence they have on their clients.

I worked with a client who was told she had lymphatic cancer. Little did the oncologist know that this person had always thought that she would die of cancer. When I interviewed her, a few weeks after the diagnosis, she told me that she went white, and inside she said she knew she was going to die. The doctor had said that this type of cancer was treatable and the prognosis was good. She hadn't heard this. All she had heard was that she had cancer and thought that because her mother had died of cancer, she would too.

After a few weeks she was called into see the oncologist again for further tests. This time they found dark spots on her lungs, which had not been there before. Immediately they had said that the cancer has spread to her lungs; it was a single cell carcinoma, a very aggressive, inoperable bronchial lung cancer. They said that there was nothing they could do and that she would be dead within one month without chemotherapy. Six months with chemotherapy. She refused chemotherapy and she died a weird, morphine-induced death within one month of the diagnosis.

It appears that doctors are not taught that there is a link between the mind and the body. I have explained to the doctors I personally know, and other friends in the medical profession, that the words they use are *so* powerful. Dr Bernie Segal, the well known American oncologist who I mentioned earlier, explains in his famous book on cancer called 'Love, Medicine and Miracles' (1986).

"The way a doctor works with a client is vitally important. The clients are in a highly vulnerable state when they are presented with the information that could mean life or death, and that tells them how the symptoms of a disease are going to play out. Many doctors use statistics to explain a cancer prognosis. Telling the client that they have a one in five chance of surviving, (meaning their chances are very slim), is how they put the data across. However, who is to know that the client might not be in the twenty percent that survive? How a person hears the information is *so* important."

Any event that has a lot of stress behind it causes the body to react in a way to support it through the issue. We know this from the previous chapter. What is not clear is that when we experience a stressful event, an Unexpected, Dramatic, Isolating event where we have No strategy for dealing with the experience (UDIN), it affects us in many ways not just physically. Normally we are unaware as to what is happening to us physically after the stress hits but what we can notice are other effects, which show up on multiple levels. All together we see that the mind, body, spirit, social and environmental factors are affected by a UDIN.

Mind

Here we see that a ring appears in the brain at a specific location, observed via brain CT. This is relative to the type of shock that has occurred. It also relates to the organ that is designed to support the individual through that particular issue. What happens

43

in the brain can change brain chemistry, showing up as anxiety, paranoia, depression or mania. Other psychosomatic issues can also be shown to occur due to this imbalance. So we can also say that there is a personality change that occurs in the person, relative to the brain chemistry and the conflict shock.

Body

In the body, a specific organ reacts in line with the shock - e.g. part of the bowel grows (in the first phase – see chapter 6) so it can digest the chunk of food or information that has become stuck. Or there is a necrosis, as in muscle wastage. The organ changes to support the body through the disease process.

Spirit

The overall spirit of the person is affected; how they deal with the issue affects their personality at a very deep level. A simple way of explaining this would be if a woman who has been told she will lose a breast because it is cancerous, will think she is loosing part of her identity as a woman. They might think, 'What is the point of living if I have failed as a woman, I might as well die.'

Social

The person will change their way of behaving with other people so they can find a solution to the shock. If there is a specific individual who was there at the time of the original stressful event, then how that person reacts around that individual will change in accordance with the problem. (This could also be a group of individuals e.g. family or work colleagues).

Environment

The way a person reacts with regard to a specific space, place or item is also affected during the stressful event. e.g. if a person was shocked at their office desk at work, if that environment becomes linked at the unconscious level then going back to that place can retrigger the whole stressful feeling again. (This explains chronic diseases and allergies).

Let me give you an example. One of our META-Medicine® Health coaches, a funny and very lovable woman called Lucille, has suffered all of her life with anxiety. In META-Medicine® terms anxiety is caused by multiple shocks that affect the thyroid gland excretion and the pharyngeal gland.

I happened to be reading Lucille's brain CT and I noticed these two rings which appear in the forehead area of the brain, clearly visible to the trained eye. See chapter 13 for the picture. I telephoned Lucille and told her what I was looking at. She confirmed that throughout her life she had suffered from anxiety but she had no idea what the conflict shock was.

Whilst on an NLP Master Practitioner training in November 2007 she started to cry uncontrollably during a demonstration of how we as people have a strategy for being in love. It transpired that all her adult life she had been in abusive relationships, and the way she felt that she was loved was if a man aggressively took her and forced himself on her.

She had been out with drug addicts, alcoholics and violent men. She even married a man who fitted the bill exactly. He did a lot of drugs, was verbally abusive and was a horrible man altogether. She stayed with him for four years. If you met her, then you would have no idea how such a beautiful woman would be attracted to a man like this.

The original conflict shock that came up in my training was this: Her father, who was a jealous man, had left her mother with four children. Three years later he turned up, totally drunk, forced himself upon Lucille's mother and raped her in front of a five year old Lucille.

She remembered feeling totally powerless. She could do nothing. Her body reacted by altering the way the thyroid functions, as an endocrine gland. Under stress there is a cell necrosis (cell removal), this then causes the amount of thyroxin pumped into the blood to increase called hyperthyroidism. The body's reason for doing this is so that a person is better able to deal with the thing they feel powerless against, they can react faster. Ongoing excessive thyroxin in the system makes the person feel continuously anxious.

Technically there were two shocks: Lucille's violent father punching her mother in the womb whilst she was carrying Lucille, and then her father forcing himself upon her mother in a rage of drunken jealousy. These specific shocks affected the pharyngeal gland and the thyroid (thyroglossal ducts). These two cause a combination which results in anxiety and shows up as two rings in the frontal lobes on a brain CT. See chapter 13 for a picture of the CT.

What is so interesting is that Lucille's life had been affected by this major incident in the five different areas: -

Mind

Two rings appear in the frontal lobes of her brain CT scan (Cortex). This combination of thyroid (thyroglossal ducts) and pharyngeal gland is known to mean the person will suffer from ongoing anxiety. She also experiences tightness in the forehead and regular headaches in this area.

Body

Her body had too much thyroxin in it and she felt continuously anxious. There was more thyroxin into her blood than a normal person experiences. The ducts of the thyroid gland get bigger therefore allowing more thyroxin to be pumped into the blood quickly for a faster response.

Spirit

She was not attracted to any of the men she had had long term relationships with. Even with the man she married she was, at a very deep level, trying to solve the issue she had experienced as a child with her own father. The strange thing was she loved them all because every one of them had forced themselves upon her. That's how she experienced love and that's how the associations from childhood had become linked.

Social

She had rejected many other men that she had been attracted to because she never felt love towards them. She only went out with men in long term relationships that, unconsciously for her, had replayed the same original shock.

Environment

She moved to the UK to get away from her past associated with South Africa. She carried out meaningless jobs because she felt powerless to do anything that would put her in the spotlight. She is an intelligent woman but she put herself down in everything she did and attempted to do and she would take a lot of recreational drugs to alter her mood.

The really interesting thing with regard to this META-Medicine® model, is that if you only know certain specific symptoms from each one of these areas you can work back from these and determine what else is happening, everything is interlinked.

As an example, let's take a woman with eczema on both her inner arms. We can compile a lot of the detail relating to the other five areas:

Mind

There will be two rings in the outer cortex of the brain, near the centre of the top of the head. She will also feel a little bit down and a little manic from time to time. This will cause minor mood swings, depending on how the eczema is triggered. She will be a tactile person in nature and want to hold people close to her.

Body

The eczema will flare up <u>after</u> she has been through a stressful period. It will probably have shown up on the left and right arms in childhood whenever she experienced a separation issue with her parents. E.g. Her father being away a week for work.

Spirit

She would have an ongoing issue being separated from people to whom she feels connected. There would be problems with personal relationships. She would find it very difficult to let go of those she should let go of, and those where someone else wants to leave her would involve a lot of drama. Essentially in her life there would have been a conflict shock where the mother and father separated abruptly from the girl, perhaps a divorce or a forced separation.

Social

The faces of certain partners would trigger off the stress phase of the eczema; this would probably occur during arguments, or at times when the other party would be away for certain lengths of time. Most likely there would be a tone of voice that her partner would use that would trigger off the stress phase of the eczema. All her partners would be similar to her father; she would play her mother's role in the relationships. Each relationship would end up being in turmoil or with a break-up and her eczema would flare up regularly as and when these issues occurred.

Environmental

Specific things and pictures or places would trigger the stress phase of the eczema such as a ticking clock, a family picture, walking past the old family home or a previous ex-partner's house.

All of these areas are connected and one can lead to the other. Even though this example is made up, in my experience with working with eczema I have found this link between all the five areas to be so accurate, for my clients, they tell me, it feels as if I am reading their mind. When a conflict shock occurs it affects every part of the person – in a completely holistic way. We are not separate minds and bodies. Everything works as a whole integrated unit, everything is connected.

Knowing this means that we can no longer simply treat the body chemistry with a pill to solve a problem. We need to look at all the other aspects of a person in order to solve the root cause of an issue, if that person is to get well and stay that way.

The fact that the mind and body are connected is not new. It is well understood by scientists that Neurotransmitters (special chemicals that a neuron uses to communicate between each other) bathe every single cell in the body. When you have a thought, every cell in the body, from your big toe up to the cell in the end of you ear lobe, is aware of it. Our body communicates in a quantum mechanical way. In other words, imagine the nerve connections within a group of nerve cells in the body as the alphabet. We do not have a neat string of connections that follow each other - A then B then C then D then E etc, and so on. It does not work like that. Instead, ABCDE are all interconnected as one.

The Newtonian way - Linear

$$A \rightarrow B \rightarrow C \rightarrow D \rightarrow E$$

The Quantum way - Holistic

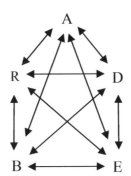

44

Not only is this example missing the rest of the alphabet, it is also only two dimensional. In reality so much more is going on. This model explains why many drugs do not work in the way they are expected to work. Although quantum physics has been around since the early part of the twentieth century, and every cell in the body works in a quantum way, the medical profession and the pharmaceutical industry have ignored the fact completely. They still have no idea why drugs have the side effects they do, or the fact that placebos can work as well as, and in some instances better than, the original drug. Candace Pert's book 'Molecules of Emotions' explains how thoughts and emotions affect our health. Are our bodies and minds distinct from one another or do they function together as part of an interconnected system?

I started with a story about Sam that explains how our minds and bodies are connected. What we can now see is that the shocks we go through not only affect our minds but they affect everything. Here is the end of Sam's story.

Sam's mind was in a spin. He could not trust what anyone said to him, nor could he trust what he said to himself. I had fully explained his behaviour to him. Everything fitted in with my diagnosis exactly. I could even show him how he would interact with people, how he was in this mess, the effect this was having on his relationships, his environment and his overall spirit as a person. He understood what I was saying, but he did not believe what he was hearing.

I then did the therapy. This involved my taking both the stressful incidents and the two people that had caused the issues in the first place, and placing them on opposite hands. I then spoke to each one of these people, and slowly each hand came together. There was a massive shift in Sam - he was lost for words and his body became really hot during this moment. After this his whole energy changed and after a few minutes he said to me: "That was very weird, but I feel different. I feel normal again", and I could see there was a calmness that came over him.

He said that he felt as if he trusted himself again, and that he trusted me. I sent him on his way. Two weeks later he told me that since that meeting everything had shifted. The situation with his work had returned to normal, he felt happier inside and was able to tell his workmates what to do, with no issues reoccurring from what he had said. The friend with

47

whom he lived apologised for being so unpleasant. But the best thing was that his 'so called' girlfriend became his official girlfriend and they moved in together. I have periodically met up with Sam and see him on odd occasions in Bristol when I visit. He's always happy and cheerful and life is treating him very well.

For me, the true significance and moral of this story was in the understanding of the massive effect that stressful events can have on everything in our lives. They don't just change the body; they also change the mind, the spirit, the environment and social aspects of our lives. All are altered and, by working back from one symptom, whether it is psychological, environmental or physical, we can determine which stressful event caused everything to change in the first place.

I have talked about serious diseases in much of this book. Sam's ear infections were not life threatening yet the effect that the issue had had on his life was overwhelming.

When you think about it, the whole concept that changes in the mind, body, spirit, social and environment plays in our lives after a shock, is mind-blowing. There is so much more going on than just the disease. What's more, if I had not had META-Medicine®, I would never have been able to help Sam. I was at a loss as to why he was in such a mess. It was a big realisation for me that I could use META-Medicine® so effectively in coaching that I now integrate it in all my therapy sessions.

The mind, body, spirit connection is amazing, and when we add social and environmental conditions we can see that everything is interlinked in one elegant, magnificent system. We can see that disease is not a mistake, but a fantastic massive programme, each part of which is linked to the original stressful event that caused the body to go into a spin.

In the next chapter we are going to explore this spin and how the mind/body works in an incredible way by showing symptoms at specific times, based on a programme that has two phases; a warm and a cold phase. These phases are undeniable when you see them in action, and their implications for all of medicine are profound. This next piece is fundamental to META-Medicine®.

Chapter 6

The two phases of a disease

"Sometimes, if you stand on the bottom rail of a bridge and lean over to watch the river slipping slowly away beneath you, you will suddenly know everything there is to be known."
- Winnie the Pooh

"Every illness goes through two phases; first, the conflict active phase and second, the ensuing phase. A complete progression from the beginning of a disease through to the healing is described as a disease process.
The typical symptoms of an illness, such as muscle pain, headache, running nose, ulcer, cancer or leukaemia are not the illnesses but a partial aspect of a comprehensive disease program.
The major points and phases of a disease process can be found by observing and specifically questioning the simultaneous changes that affect the mind, body, spirit, social and environmental conditions"
One of the ten META-Medicine® Models

This following story is made up but it explains the two phases of a disease process and also many other aspects of META-Medicine®. I tell it to many of my cancer clients because a story can explain so much more than just theory. You might want to make note of the UDIN and the changes a woman experiences throughout her whole life in her mind, body and spirit, socially and environmentally. You can also watch a recording of me telling this story on www.meta-medicine.com.

The META-Medicine® breast cancer story

Imagine a mother walking down the road holding onto her son or daughter's hand. Suddenly the child breaks away to chase after a ball that is rolling across the road, and around the corner comes a pink Bentley driven by a woman in a red trilby hat. The car hit the child and the mother goes into an Unexpected, Dramatic, Isolating shock where she has No strategy for dealing with the situation.

She either freezes, runs over to the child or freaks out trying to pick up the child to nurture it, i.e. fight, flight or freeze.

At exactly the moment when she saw the car hit the child, a switch in the brain changes in an exact location in the right hand side at the back of the brain (an area called the Cerebellum). This switch or relay is a 3 dimensional sphere but shows up as a 2 dimensional ring which we can see in a brain CT scan.

Simultaneously a sphere of trapped emotion and information would appear in the left breast, the brain being opposite wired, therefore an organ reaction of the left hand side of the body, shows up on the right hand side of the brain. We can also see a slice of this sphere as a two dimensional ring under a CT scan. (See chapter 7). Seeing these simultaneous rings is rare. (For examples of rings and their link to disease see chapter 9).

The breast gland cells would now start to voraciously reproduce, the reason being to produce more milk glands and subsequently milk so the woman can nurture the child back to health. This is different from when a woman gets pregnant because it is an emergency programme and thereby the cells multiply three times faster than normal. This is the biological reason for the body creating the extra breast gland milk producing cells.

For every extra breast gland cell produced there is also an equal 'dormant' bacteria cell. In this instance this bacteria cell is a tuberculosis cell. Often there are no tuberculosis cells in the body due to eradication via antibiotics. If this is the case then no tuberculosis cells will be produced. These tuberculosis cells are grown in the blood – one for every cancer cell that is produced. You can see this amazing phenomenon under dark field microscopy. NB. The dark field microscopy practitioner will say excessive bacteria in the blood is a bad thing. However, in META-Medicine® the body is producing these bacteria to complete the second regeneration phase.

Let us then imagine that the child is seriously ill in a coma in hospital, hooked up to a life support system.

Now this imaginary woman is in the media and she is very active socially. However, I am certain you can picture how, after the shock everything in her life will change. She will not sleep or eat, she will lose weight, her hands and feet will be cold, she will ignore her friends and her job will go to the bottom of the pile. Just as I described in chapter five, her whole spiritual focus will change to nurturing the child back to health; that will become her focus as a woman and nothing else in her world will matter.

Over the following months the tumour will carry on growing in just the same way breasts grow during pregnancy. Except it will grow three to four times faster and therefore bigger because it is an emergency programme. The size is determined by the depth of the conflict and, since this was a very deep conflict shock, the cancer will be large.

However, she will not really notice how her left breast would feel. She may notice that it is getting bigger and that it will be sore (similar to just before many woman have their period) so although there may be some symptoms she will probably ignore them because her mind is obsessed with nurturing the child back to health.

Everyday she will be with the child in the hospital. Her husband will probably be there too but since he did not see the accident it will most likely not affect him in the same way. (However, men can get glandular breast cancer as well but it is rare).

Then let us imagine that after many months the child comes out of the coma. She/he is not totally well yet but the consultant tells the mother that the child will make a full recovery.

Imagine the relief she would experience. She would feel totally relieved in her heart, mind and soul. The body would react as well, the ring in the brain would change; it would become less defined and start to break up. The breast would also react. The tuberculosis cells would be instructed, by the whole system, to eat away at the now redundant excessive glandular cells. They are no longer needed so the body gets rid of them. Her body would switch from a sympathetic nervous system to a parasympathetic nervous system; I explain what there nervous systems mean later on in this chapter. Hence her hands and feet would become hot as all the blood is directed to healing and not dealing with stress. She therefore would need to sleep and eventually (not straightway) her appetite would return and she would start to eat a lot more than she did before the stressful event.

During this time the tuberculosis cells that were in the blood arrange themselves around the tumour and, along with water which they need to multiply, they eat away at the excessive breast gland cells.

Sometimes this swelling breaks the skin. If you have ever been unfortunate enough to have been to a hospice where this has happened to a woman then you will agree that the smell is somewhat akin to rotting flesh.

So our woman will feel immense pressure in her left breast, and a swelling usually followed by redness around where the lump is. Naturally she would get concerned and go to see her doctor. Along with not feeling well, which she will certainly experience, and not having slept, she will find herself hardly able to keep her eyes open. Paying the doctor a visit seems like an obvious thing to do.

The doctor will examine her and very likely make a quick diagnosis of breast cancer. The doctor will immediately send her for a biopsy and arrange for further tests to be done. The woman will be told that if it is breast cancer (of which they will probably be totally sure) then the likely procedure is a radical mastectomy (removal of the breast), chemotherapy and radiotherapy.

All this because of what had happened to her son. Can you imagine, everything was going to be fine after he came out of the coma and now this? Although not obvious, what the doctor has told the woman about possible breast removal will have caused her to go into yet another shock, maybe several shocks. And the whole process starts again, only with a different organ or several other organs thus explaining the metastasis (secondary cancers).

I have listed these other possible metastasis this woman might get.

Cancer of the lymph glands (Lymphomas) under the breast plates and under the armpit
> This is caused by the diagnosis, usually a male doctor saying they had to remove the breast - the defining feature that makes the person a woman.

Liver cancer of the parenchyma - Metastatic Liver cancer of the meat of the liver, (not the mucous membranes known as the gall bladder ducts).
> Caused by the woman going through a mental starvation conflict; she cannot work so she will starve herself at a biological level, in order to put food on the plates of the rest of the family.

Lung Cancer in the alveolar (Adenocarcinoma) or bronchi as a single cell carcinoma
> Caused by a fear of death conflict from the diagnosis. Many clients hear the word cancer and it means death to them.

Bone cancer (sarcomas) - this could show up in many places but most probably in the breast plates.
> Caused by the self loathing of the person, often due to them not feeling like a woman – not being able to cope.

If stress causes disease, as we have discussed, then doesn't this explain metastasis? (Metastasis are secondary cancers.)

Cancer cells travelling through the body

The common notion that cancerous cells travel through the body and attach themselves to specific organs at random has never been proven. It is a hypothesis that has little or no scientific or medical grounding. NB. There have been some cells that do show up in certain places, such as with ovarian cancer cells showing up in other parts of the body, e.g. the lung but this is only in five percent or less of cases. The reason for this is a burst ovarian cyst (usually caused by a syndrome known as the Kidney collecting tubule syndrome* (see page 61), this is where excessive water collects around and in the organ making it swell). The burst tissue travels through the body and attaches itself to other organs which can give it a blood supply, where it grows. It is not life threatening unless it affects a person mechanically, because it will stop growing, in the case of ovarian cysts after nine months. The other ninety-five percent of secondary cancer cells are made up from the same cells in the organ itself. Therefore a secondary cancer in the lung will be made of lung cells.

The fact that stress causes disease has both scientific and medical grounding. A medical diagnosis of such magnitude as cancer and breast removal is an Unexpected, Dramatic, Isolating shock where there is No strategy for dealing with the conflict: a UDIN.

Georgie Atkinson and her ductal breast cancer

Georgie Atkinson lives in Australia and had heard about META-Medicine® from friends' who are NLP practitioners, having trained with Dr Tad James. Dr Tad James is one of my NLP trainers and also the inventor of Time Line Therapy®. Johannes Fisslinger, the President of the International META-Medicine® Association, taught the basics of META-Medicine® to Tad and some of his staff in a two day training session in 2005.

Georgie e-mailed me and ordered our two day META-Medicine® CD/DVD pack and was amazed, so much so that in August 2007 she invited me to train META-Medicine® in Canberra, Australia.

I knew she had ductal breast cancer but it was not until I arrived in Australia did it become clear to me how amazing Georgie was and what she was doing to solve her stressful conflict and the cancer.

Georgie had also discovered a medical intervention called Photo Dynamic Therapy or PDT. This had been around for some time and had not been that successful as a treatment for reducing tumour size. Georgie had one lot of Photo Dynamic Therapy treatment and her tumour shrunk but then it had reappeared.

When I met her she had just come back from Darwin where she had been receiving her second treatment of a trial of a new type of Photo Dynamic Therapy, (now in its third generation). Photo Dynamic Therapy works by injecting a special inert liquid into a tumour growth and then activating this substance by using light, which shines at a specific frequency. The liquid then becomes active and destroys the cells in and around the tumour. It has not been found to be successful with breast cancers as yet.

The key ingredient in Photo Dynamic Therapy is Psoralen, which is a plant-derived chemical that is unusual in that it is inactive until exposed to light. Psoralen is the active ingredient in a Nile-dwelling weed called ammi. This therapy was used by the ancient Egyptians, who noticed that people became prone to sunburn after eating this weed.

So when Georgie told me that the first treatment caused her tumour to shrink to nothing in a matter of weeks, I was amazed. Then I asked her why was she having further treatments, to which she replied that it was because the tumour had grown back bigger and larger. So the research scientist developed a new serum and also gave Georgie anti-rejection drugs, similar to the drugs transplant patients are given.

I said I knew why the tumour had grown back bigger and larger than before and I also went onto to explain why this and other therapeutic interventions such as Chemotherapy often fail. Georgie was all ears as I went onto explain the two phases of a disease.

The two phases of a disease

After a UDIN conflict shock occurs our body reacts to support us so that we can deal with the issue we were confronted with; it activates the 'Sympathetic' nervous system.

The classic symptoms of a Sympathetic nervous system appear as:

- Stress, tense body
- Obsessive thinking
- Sleeplessness
- Absence of appetite
- Loss of weight
- Cold body and extremities
- High blood pressure
- Contracted blood vessels
- Nervous and cold perspiration

We go into a flight or fight response; our body turns into a machine designed to solve the problem that we have just encountered. This is an activation of the 'Sympathetic nervous system'. This was discussed in Chapter 4 and is commonly experienced as feeling very stressed. Also, we know that the mind, body, spirit, social and environmental issues change as the person tries to solve the underlying problem (Chapter 5).

Obsessive thinking is really interesting because this, in my opinion, explains how stress affects us mentally. It also explains the erratic behaviour that we see in people who we would normally consider rational.

To explain this, imagine a loved one; a partner has just walked out on you with no explanation whatsoever. This was someone you loved dearly and you had no inclination that there was anything wrong. What would you be thinking? What would be going through your mind? You would be going crazy, asking yourself, 'Why did they leave? What did I do wrong? Are they seeing someone else?' You would then imagine them seeing someone else, which would send your head into a spin. You would be obsessed with trying to find out why this had happened. What is going on? Your work would suffer, you would not eat and you would not sleep. Your feet and hands would become cold as the blood in your system is directed to the muscles in order that you have the energy to solve the issue - a throw-back to the days when we were animals - the fight or flight response. Generally you would not feel any pain or discomfort.

What is not obvious is that specific organs change in order to support you through this process, as I discussed in Chapter 4. These organs change in alignment with their function. So the breast reacts with regard to nurturing, the gut to digestion, the skin to separation, the muscles to strength. Generally, the biological reason for all diseases is so you that are better equipped to fight or take flight if the event occurs again.

We are not programmed to live in this stressed way forever. After the stressful event, at some point we may resolve the problem. When we do, the body reacts by repairing or rebuilding the organ that was affected.

We then switch from the 'Sympathetic' nervous system, whose symptoms I have already explained to the 'Para-sympathetic' nervous system.

The Parasympathetic nervous system is the antithesis of the sympathetic nervous system. Whilst we are in this second repair phase, we generally feel very tired and if there is no pain, we mostly feel very relaxed.

The classic symptoms of a Parasympathetic nervous system appear as:
- Fatigue and tiredness
- Good appetite
- Weight gain
- Warm body and extremities
- Low blood pressure
- Slow heart rate
- Wide blood vessels
- Perspiration, hot skin and body
- Fever

If all diseases are caused by a stressful event which we know is supported by scientific data, then at some point after the stress we may solve the shocking issue that started us being stressed in the first place. I say 'may' because sometimes we never solve the stressful event and the body stays in a state of continuous stress.

In all my stress based diagnosing I have found that there are two phases to every disease cycle - the first stressful phase, followed by the repair phase. Biologists and the medical profession acknowledge there are two different states, the Sympathetic nervous system and the Para-sympathetic nervous system, but they have not made a connection between them.

Sympathetic	**Structure**	**Parasympathetic**
Rate increased	Heart	Rate decreased
Force increased	Heart	Force decreased
Bronchial muscle relaxed	Lungs	Bronchial muscle contracted
Pupil dilation	Eye	Pupil constriction
Motility reduced	Intestine	Digestion increased
Sphincter relaxes	Bladder	Sphincter relaxed
Decreased urine secretion	Kidneys	Increased urine secretion

The sympathetic and the parasympathetic nervous system are parts of what is commonly called the autonomic nervous system. (Autonomic = can not be controlled by the mind). You can say that these systems work in balance with each other and directly or indirectly affect almost every structure in the body.[45]

We actually experience these different states constantly. Our bodies are mostly in a Sympathetic state during the day and then at night we are in the Para-sympathetic state. However, after a shocking and stressful event, the body stays in the Sympathetic state until the issue is resolved. The body then goes into the Parasympathetic state.

At night, if we have experienced a shock earlier and we are in the Sympathetic state, we will find that we cannot sleep very well; we will toss and turn, and sleep lightly. In a worst case scenario a person will experience insomnia.

We probably have all experienced this at some time in our lives. Do you remember going for that important job interview? Or the night before an important exam? A sleepless night is not unusual in these situations. Following the resolution of the stress, finding whether or not you got the job, or passed or failed that exam, either meant the stress carried on until you did get what you wanted, or you gave up, or everything worked out fine for you. Once the stress has been resolved you would find that you need to rest. People often get colds or have a bout of mild diarrhoea. They feel hot and sweaty and out of sorts.

The same thing happens if you stress your body to the limit. For example running in a 10km marathon leaves you feeling exhausted and afterwards you need to rest.

These two phases are normal and well recognised in medical literature. However, what is not obvious is the long term effect an Unexpected, Dramatic, Isolating event has on a person, where they have No Strategy for dealing with the issue. If this is a deeply intense experience and carries on for a long time then a disease may appear, dependant on which organ is affected.

We all have shocks every day and some can be UDINs but often they are not very deep and they are quickly resolved. Take, for example, a friend of mine who was doing a project where she had to deal with some very challenging issues which caused her to have many heated discussions, some of them very stressful. She obsessed about one of these discussions: How she was going to deal with a specific woman at her school who was part of this project and had made life very difficult for her.

When she had resolved the issues, by finding out who was responsible for the glitch which was causing this woman to be so challenged in the first place, she went into resolution, (the parasympathetic state). She told me that as soon as the problem was resolved, she got a cold, a laryngeal cough and over the day she lost her voice. She had to go home, she felt terrible, she could not work and she slept very deeply. A few days later she woke up thinking she was better, she went to work but by midday the cold had returned and she was back at home tucked up in bed, feeling tired and exhausted.

The original stressful event had been a social one, where she was fearful of that person and it affected her identity in some way, (a common occurrence for women at work). During the stressful phase the larynx became ulcerated and widened, this went unnoticed but biologically it allows faster inhalation of air, and therefore more air is able to get into the lungs, so she had more energy to fight the problem. More air means more energy.

Then when she went into resolution the ulceration was repaired. This is a result of the body going into the second phase. A virus that had been collecting in the blood at the time, worked with the body in unison, helping to repair the laryngeal mucous membranes. She got hot, sweaty, tired, felt ill and ached. There was an increase of secretion from the repairing mucous membranes of the larynx and she started to cough, her energy reserves went into healing and the obsession about the lady, and how she was going to solve this problem stopped. The net result of this reaction is what we call 'the common cold or a cough.' NB Some of us get bronchial colds instead of laryngeal, therefore a chest cold instead of a cough. This happens to men more often than women and is due to how our brains are wired and the way men and women react to social and territorial shocks.

Half way through this second stage we also find a weird phenomenon. We wake up, sometimes very early in the morning, and we find ourselves feeling fine for a while but a little antsy and cold. We get out of bed thinking that we have beaten the cold, except for a slight headache, and get ready for work. We go to work telling everyone we feel fine. Then after a coughing fit, we quickly start to deteriorate only to find that by midday we are back where we started - the symptoms have reappeared. We go home to bed again and rest. This time we start to feel really hungry and want to eat good wholesome food. Fast food and coffee, which we were probably drinking in large quantities during the stress phase, is not what we want.

After a few days we come out of that state feeling totally well again and all that remains is a little coloured yellow/green mucous we cough up, which disappears within a few days.

Written below and also shown via a diagram is the process we believe a person goes through when they have a disease. We know in META-Medicine® that all diseases are caused by a significant emotional event followed by ongoing stress (COLD phase). If this is resolved, the body then goes into resolution (WARM phase). Half way through the WARM phase we have a biological test called the healing crisis. This point explains so many of the strange and dangerous symptoms people experience when sick. What also seems apparent is that all the symptoms that people go through can be explained by this disease process. Listed and shown below is each one of the nine points a disease process goes through:

Below is a diagram of these two phases and an explanation of each of the nine points:-

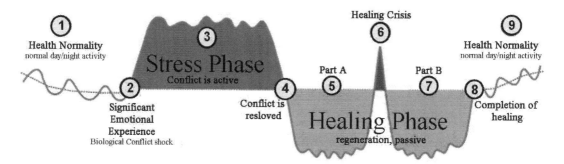

1) Health normality, normal day activity and night relaxation
2) Biological conflict shock – Significant Negative Emotional experience
3) Conflict phase – cold, sympathetic, conflict active
4) Conflict resolution or reversal (unconscious or conscious process)
5) Part A regeneration phase warm, parasympathetic, rest and recuperation
6) Healing Crisis – Short sympathetic, conflict active state, biological test
7) Part B regeneration phase warm, rebuilding of energy reserves
8) End of disease process
9) Normality, healthy return to normal day activity and night relaxation

(1) **Health, normality, normal day activity and night relaxation.** We feel fine, we are healthy. As you can see from the diagram there is a wiggly line that goes through a day/night rhythm. We are awake during the day and sleep at night. Notice that in this diagram the dotted line goes down. Let us imagine that we have been very busy at work; we have been pushing ourselves, sleeping less and working hard, eating fast foods, drinking a lot of coffee, drinking excessive amounts of alcohol and not exercising. Our vitality and reserves can become depleted. NB. we can still be totally healthy for a conflict shock to affect us but usually these events occur when our vitality or life force energy is reduced.

(2) **Biological conflict shock - Significant Negative Emotional Experiences.** We experience a Significant Emotional Experience (SEE) or a Biological Conflict shock which catches us completely off guard. This is the Unexpected Dramatic, Isolating shock where we have No Strategy for dealing with the issue. During this time everything that goes on is recorded; what we see, hear, feel, taste, smell and certain words are logged and stored. One of these senses has the most energy attached to it. Usually this is either the tone of a person's voice, or the look a person gives or something else visual, such as seeing a piece of jewellery. A sharp focussed sphere seen as a ring on a CT scan, appears in the brain at a specific location, corresponding to the organ that is able to deal with the issue most effectively. This sphere has all

the trapped energy that corresponds to the shock, which also sends a wave of energy through the whole body affecting mind, body, spirit, social and environment interactions.

(3) **Conflict phase - cold, sympathetic, conflict active.** Here we experience the first phase, what we would commonly call stress. Our hands and feet are cold; we eat little (the little we do eat is usually fast food and acidic foods). We can find ourselves eating sweets and drinking alcohol excessively during this time because we are trying to get away from the stress we feel. We skip meals, our blood pressure increases, we may have nervous and cold perspiration. Obsessive thinking takes over our whole lives. If this stressful phase carries on for any length of time we lose weight. The blood is directed from the digestive tract to the muscles and vital organs.

We have a high output of glucose and an increased secretion of adrenaline, making faster reactions possible. Plus, we sleep erratically and for short periods of time. Insomnia is common. The organ that is affected changes itself by necrosis (cell degradation), as in the widening of a tube such as a blood vessel or bronchial tube, allowing more fluid/air to travel down it. Or the body builds more cells as more intestine is produced to digest the issue, or more glands cells to produce milk to nurture a child back to health.

Depending on the type of organ and its arrangement in our body, there will be a growth of fungi, bacteria or a virus that will go unnoticed because it is in the blood. The microbes are dormant and the number of microbe cells produced are in direct proportion to the number of cells of the growth. For bacteria for every cell grown there is an equal cell of bacteria grown in the blood. Only, if you are exposed to, or have the bacteria in your system. Viruses are produced in the brain during this time in a measured amount in accordance with the cell growth. Sometimes we do not have the fungi, bacteria or virus in our system. If that is the case then the body will either find the fungi, bacteria or virus from outside in the environment or it will just not be produced.

Sometimes parasites collect in the body. These seem to be excellent at removing the heavy metals, such as mercury, in our system. The size of the parasite is also determined by the body, in the stress phase the parasite is multiplying, getting ready for the next phase. Antibiotics destroy the natural balance of the body and fungi, bacteria and viruses (the microbes). It is thought that parasites do the clean up work that could have been done by many of these microbes.

Typical symptoms of the first phase might be constipation, loss of strength in certain muscles, excessive energy, being able to breathe to the bottom of your lungs effortlessly with little or no mucous, flaking of the skin, increase in our nasal senses, sensitive to touch (as in breast glands), and thickening of the lower layer of the skin (dermis).

(4) **Conflict resolution or reversal (unconscious or conscious process).** The conflict is resolved; either we are consciously aware of this happening or completely unconscious of the resolution. Good examples of consciously being aware would be when we leave a very stressful relationship for good, or an argument gets completely resolved. Unconscious examples would be whilst we sleep a resolution happens. You wake up with a cold having gone to bed feeling fine. Or something triggers an association which unconsciously reminds you of a person. This happens with eczema. The resolution of the conflict happens in the same sense that triggered it but

57

is opposite to the trigger, therefore a different tone that resolves the issue or an opposite picture, e.g. a person looks at you with a genuine smile instead of the angry grimace that was in the original shock. At this point the symptoms start to appear and we will start to experience a feeling of the regeneration phase. An example would be when you feel like the weight of the world has been lifted off your shoulders.

(5) **Part A – Regeneration/Rebuild phase; warm, parasympathetic, rest and recuperation.** Part A of the regeneration/rebuild phase starts just after the conflict resolution and then the symptoms start to get worse. You feel the relief immediately in the conflict resolution or reversal but, depending on the background stress, the main symptoms may not appear until later on that day, e.g. you may have been in a meeting where you resolve something major, you get the first symptoms such as a runny nose, you feel tired so you stress yourself a little and drink some coffee. You have to go for a meal that night, the symptoms get even more intense, you take a cold remedy which probably contains caffeine and stresses your body a little more to fight off the symptoms. Eventually you get the cold.

During this time the organ that was under stress in the first phase goes into regeneration. If there had been a cell reduction, as in the widening of a blood vessel to allow more blood to flow, then this needs to be repaired. The cells that were taken away in the stress phase are replaced. In blood vessels this results in swelling and a restriction of the blood flow. In muscles, the muscle is rebuilt and grows. This is carried out by the body working in homeostasis with the fungi, bacteria or viruses that were produced in the stressful phase.

In organs where there was an increase in cells, (such as in the bowel or the breast glands), the extra cells are no longer required so they are eaten away by fungi or bacteria. If the bacteria are not in the system then the issue becomes encapsulated; a thin film of skin forms around the tumour where it lies dormant.

Extra water is used to support this process hence swelling is normal where the organ needs to be repaired. This is why we feel pain during this time. The body directs all the blood towards the digestive organs - we have warm hands and feet. Blood pressure is low and we usually have a fever. We perspire and feel hot. We feel tired and fatigued, our digestive organs receive more blood, our appetite comes back but not in the same way as Part B Point (7).

(6) **Healing Crisis - short sympathetic, conflict active state, biological test.** The healing crisis is one of the most important points in the disease process, so much so that I have dedicated a whole chapter to it (see chapter 8). This is where most people really think the issue is either reversing or getting significantly worse. The healing crisis is a biological test and it serves another purpose; that of squeezing out the water that was used in the first Part 'A' of the regeneration phase. It is a challenging time because the symptoms are so acute and in some instances can be fatal – as in a heart attack. Some of the typical symptoms are feeling antsy, having had no energy, anything from a mild headache up to a migraine, muscle cramps, muscle twitching, epileptic fits, coughing fits, sneezing fits and intense itching. Excessive urination is also a common factor during this time. People usually notice that they have to visit the bathroom/toilet a lot and the amount of water that is passed is significantly greater than the amount they have been drinking during the day. The healing crisis happens halfway between the start of the regeneration phase (4) and the end of the process (8) depending on the water storage.

(7) **Part B - Regeneration phase; warm, rebuilding of energy reserves.** After the healing crisis, we go into more of the regeneration phase. During this time we will still feel unwell but the main pain has disappeared. The infections we have had will have subsided but we are not back to normal yet. We eat more during this period and it is common to feel ravenously hungry. People tend to put on weight as the body builds up reserves. The main healing is basically done. Now that the repair is being completed, the affected organ is either being degraded by bacteria/fungi or rebuilt by bacteria and viruses, depending upon how the organ reacted in the first stressful phase. E.g. If there was cell growth as in an intestinal issue, then the excess intestine will be passed out during this stage. If there was cell degradation as in the common cold the larynx or bronchi cell wall is rebuilt; we feel breathless and spit out the excessive mucous that was required to repair the cell wall.

A good example of this excessive skin growth happens when we cut ourselves. A scab appears excessive to the repair which is happening underneath. This is the same for the bronchi mucosa and this is what we notice as we blow our nose or cough up phlegm. You will see it as yellow, brown or slightly bloody phlegm.

(8) **End of the disease process.** - As we complete the process of healing we start to feel better and our energy returns. This can take time, depending on the length of the second phase. The deeper the second phase, the longer this process will take. During this time there may be some remnants of the healing process. e.g. a scab may take a few more days after we feel better before it is ready to fall off. There may still be some old phlegm stuck in the bronchi which we eventually cough up or end up blowing out through the nose. The intestine stops being so sensitive to certain foods. Specific organ swelling decreases and returns to normality. Any pain subsides and eventually stops.

(9) **Normality - healthy return to normal day activity and night relaxation.** - We feel normal and all remnants of the two phases and symptoms have disappeared. Except for maybe a scar, encapsulated growths (a thin film of skin is built around the growth) or loose ends of old tissue that are doing nothing. Generally we feel good inside and normal bodily functions are resumed. The area that was affected usually has no excessive extra biological material around it. There may be some scarring (which tends to be stronger but less durable than the original tissue.) Sometimes the repair leaves an excessive amount of skin, bone or material that can be removed, as in a tumour that has been encapsulated. Or there is cell reduction, such as in a dimple with acne scarring. At this time we end up feeling good, and normal day/ night rhythm is resumed.

Something really fascinating about the two phases is that the length of time for the first phase (point (2) to point (4)) is often but not always equal to the length of point (4) to point (8). And the healing crisis often happens right in the middle, time-wise. This can mean that a META-Medicine® health coach with enough information is able to work out exactly when the start of the disease process occurred. I do this regularly with my clients. If I know a client has just come into the regeneration phase and I can determine the exact time of this phase and the conflict shock, I am able to tell the client exactly what time they will experience the next set of symptoms, and therefore I can prepare them so they need have no fear and they can go through the process in the knowledge that the body is doing what it is designed to do.

I have personally been through this myself. I recently had to complete a project for a META-Medicine® training. This involved listening to some recordings I had made of Dr

Bader – the vice president of the International META-Medicine® Association. I only had a limited time frame to complete this work and I was being continually interrupted by phone calls and other more urgent things. I reluctantly and angrily said to myself at midday, 'I will have to eat into my own personal time in order to complete the project'. This was something I could not digest but I knew I had to do. I worked through the evening and late into the night, finishing at 4.00 a.m. During this time I was stressed and anxious to complete the project, which I finally did.

I then went to bed totally relieved and slept well. I was hot in bed and remember sweating quite a lot. I started to feel a little 'out of sorts' in my belly area when I woke up at 11.00 a.m. I knew something was not right. I felt like eating, but I didn't because my belly felt strange. At 11.30 a.m. I started having an intense bout of diarrhoea that lasted until 1.00 p.m. I felt antsy and out of sorts during this time. After the diarrhoea finished I felt really tired again. I also felt really hungry so I ate some rye bread with hummus. I had a meeting in the afternoon at 5.00 p.m. which I attended. I was exhausted but I felt otherwise OK. After the meeting I slept until 8.00p.m. and when I awoke I felt absolutely fine. I went to bed at my normal time and slept well.

People I spoke to during this time told me that I must have eaten something that had gone off. I replied that I had eaten the same as my wife and she was one hundred percent symptom free. They said, "Then you must have caught it from someone". I explained that I had not gone out or done anything different from my wife, and she was fine.

What I want you, as a reader, to understand from this is that you don't catch a bug that causes diarrhoea; it is in your system anyway. Neither is the diarrhoea caused by the food you eat. Even with allergies to certain foods there is a reason (See Chapter 7). What was so amazing about this whole process was that before I really understood META-Medicine® I would have panicked and taken some form of pill to stop the diarrhoea, but because I was able to work out exactly what was going on in my body, and to what time, I could predict exactly to the hour, when I would be feeling well again. Which is exactly what happened. I did not use any drugs to make myself well again, something I would have done in the past. I explain this whole process and the reason for diarrhoea in more detail in Chapter 8 – The Healing Crisis.

Bacteria in your system

If you do not have the necessary bacteria in your system, because you have been taking antibiotics, then the body will take the bacteria that it finds from its surroundings to complete the second phase repair work. This is where we need to be careful if we are on holiday. Usually we rush around like idiots getting everything prepared before we leave. We are under stress; arguments are common (especially with our spouses). Our boss asks us to complete a complex project in two days, (something that would normally take a week), and we have no choice but to work really hard and late. We are frustrated and angry. Other stressful things happen that take up our precious time making it worse. This is a stress phase. Then we get to our holiday destination and eventually we relax. At that time we go into the reversal phase (Point 4). We make up with our partners. We forget about our boss and that project. All the anger and frustration is forgotten.

Now, because we live in such a sterile environment (due to antibacterial soaps and because we are super clean), and because we may have had antibiotics or have eaten food which contains antibiotics, we often do not have the necessary bacteria in our gut to heal ourselves. So the body uses the most appropriate bacteria it can get from the environment. This it gets from the local food. We then find that a few days into our holiday we end up with diarrhoea (the Healing Crisis - Point 6). It is not the due to the food, or the cooking process, which admittedly can be very unclean. It is because the body gets and uses whatever viruses, bacteria, fungi or parasites that it requires to complete the second phase - its healing process. In foreign countries these bacteria are a different strain from those we have grown up with in our normal environment, which is why the reaction can be quite violent in some instances.

Therefore if you go to a different country the microbes are different. The people from the local area don't get the same reaction from eating their food. A friend of mine from Egypt, Dr Khaled Al-Damallawy, told me that in Cairo the healthiest kids are from the poorest families. They have built up a stock of microbes from playing in the streets and even though they cannot afford to have antibiotics or vaccinations, they don't have anywhere near the same health issues as the children of wealthier families do, who are regularly unwell. No-one in Egypt could understand this but after he heard about the two phases and how microbes work in homeostasis with the body and the environment, he said it made more sense than other hypothesis's that have been banded around.

Going back to the two phases and how people react in most cases; a healthy person such as my friend with the common cold that I mentioned earlier, will experience a full disease process; a 'stress phase' followed by the 'reversal phase', including a healing crisis. But the elegant timing that I experienced with my diarrhoea can be interrupted by taking 'over the counter' drugs or any other type of pharmaceutical, recreational or stimulant such as coffee. What interrupts the process are things like pain killers such as aspirin, paracetomol, Tylenol, codeine, ibuprofen even coffee can stimulate the system or anti swelling* drugs can also elongate the disease process.

*IMPORTANT Note - Kidney collecting Tubule Syndrome

A word of caution, some swelling is caused by the Kidney Collecting Tubules which is a separate conflict related to an issue of abandonment/isolation that causes intense water retention in the regeneration/second phase. People often get a swelling in the abdomen or around the legs and ankles. The use of diuretics during this time is recommended to bring this excessive water retention down or to stop it getting any worse. However, I have worked successfully with clients in reducing this swelling by using other methods that did not involve drugs, just mental therapies such as hypnosis and EFT, I also need to mention it does take quite a few hours to do this type of therapy.

Many drugs and other therapies used by conventional medicine, plus other alternative and complementary therapies affect the two phases as well, usually causing stimulation of the body in the second phase, putting the client back into stress, therefore causing the pain to disappear and the symptoms subside.

People experience pain and illness in the second phase. Drugs and other therapies slow down the healing process and hinders the person from getting well. This can be a good thing since feeling so ill and being in excruciating pain can be soul destroying. However, we will need to complete the disease process at some time.

Don't get me wrong - I am not against drugs; there are times when the effects of these drugs are useful, as in the case of a client of mine with multiple brain tumours. She took a small dose of steroids and was able to function, having been bed-ridden for a month and unable to move her head because every time she did she would end up with a massive headache.

A small dosage of Aspirin is often prescribed for people who have experienced heart problems. This keeps them in a minor stress phase. My wife's father takes this small dose of Aspirin daily; he had a triple bypass surgery 14 years ago. He is constantly mildly stressed and also slightly anxious about everything. This is a good thing because if he went into regeneration he could suffer a heart attack in the healing crisis again which, at his age of seventy, would be very worrying for him. Therefore it is better to have the little bit of stress than to solve the problem completely. He can live with the anxiety although, personally, I would hate it.

This may sound as if causing stress is wrong. In my opinion, most people live in a stressful environment in our western society. Just drinking large amounts of tea and coffee everyday stresses your body. At one time I removed all stimulants from my life; tea, coffee, sugar and processed foods, in addition to red meat in order to experience what it is like to live a stress free lifestyle.

Why red meat? When an animal is killed in a slaughter house, the collective fear causes a rush of adrenalin that passes through the body, because the animal is stressed. e.g. If you don't eat steak that often and you have a rare piece of fillet steak, you can get a rush of energy from the meat as your body digests the adrenalin that was in the blood from the slaughtered animal.

The experience of living without the normal food-induced stress was so enjoyable that I have tried to maintain my diet in that way. I also got down to my optimum weight very quickly. However, in reality, travelling and staying with many friends around the world it is challenging to always stick to this diet. Plus, I love a good steak now and again and I believe, for my body, it is OK to do so.

I met up with Johannes Fisslinger (the head of META-Medicine®) in Los Angeles in 2007. We were having a conversation about META-Medicine® and the disease process, when he said, "We are healing machines; we go in and out of these two phases everyday in some form or fashion, and our bodies are easily capable of adapting to and dealing with these problems. We are designed to do it. It's when the shocks are so deep and intense as in a UDIN shock, that we have a problem."

Just to illustrate this point, I was delivering a training seminar on META-Medicine® in Bristol, UK and happened to be talking about the two phases. In the back of the room one of my assistants was typing on his computer, which really annoyed one of the delegates, John Blackett. He developed a tinnitus (the first phase of a hearing conflict). The tinnitus was at exactly the same frequency as the tapping of the keys. This is what happens with tinnitus; the frequency matches the tone that the person does not want to hear. After half an hour of this annoying typing, John spoke to the assistant and asked him politely to stop typing. He apologised and stopped. John then experienced a minor loss of hearing for half an hour, with a small thumping in his eardrums for one minute half-way through at about 15 minutes, as he went through the healing crisis. After this time the issue completely cleared up.

The majority of aches and pains and situations like this go unnoticed but we have found that these two phases seem to work so elegantly that, although there are as yet no research papers that I can find that confirm these two phases, the empirical evidence is undeniable. Time and time again without fail this process allows me and other people I have trained to establish exactly the root cause of a disease process by working back from the specific changes a client has gone through.

There is some evidence that points to the two phases of a disease process as being true and that, again, comes from Bruce Lipton, in his book 'Biology of Belief'. "Cells change their structure and function based on their environment." [46]

Cells, (we have fifty trillion of them), in our body work and repair themselves. It was thought that this process happened simultaneously. However, Lipton found out that this was not the case; a cell cannot be in a functioning (work) state, and be repairing itself at the same time. There seems to be one state followed by the other. We know this is the case because the Sympathetic nervous system and the Parasympathetic nervous system are two completely different states. What was not apparent, until Lipton's work, was that a cell cannot be in both states at the same time.

"The mechanisms that support growth and protection cannot operate simultaneously at the same time. Cells cannot simultaneously move backwards and forwards."[47] E.g. if you are running from a lion (e.g. a threat posed by a boss) your body is in fight or flight mode and it is not expounding energy or growth. The cells cannot be in both states at the same time, hence the two phases. The longer you stay in this flight or fight mode, protecting yourself from the attack, the more you compromise growth. Not all of our fifty trillion cells have to be in a growth or protection (fight or flight) phase at any one time.

There are other research papers that point to the two phases being true as well. In an article in Science Daily in the USA:

"Scientists from Wake Forest University School of Medicine are the first to report that the stress hormone epinephrine causes changes in prostate and breast cancer cells that may make them resistant to cell death. These data imply that emotional stress may contribute to the development of cancer and may also reduce the effectiveness of cancer treatments," said George Kulik, D.V.M. Ph.D. an assistant professor of cancer biology and senior researcher on the project.[48]

Certain cells grow in the stress phase. E.g. prostate cancer cells and glandular breast cancer cells will grow in the first phase of the disease process, hence the ineffectiveness of many cancer treatments to shrink a tumour because traditional cancer treatments such as chemotherapy and radiotherapy put the body under immense stress.

It is also interesting that scientists look at cells in Petri-dishes but have omitted to consider that stress is linked to disease, (most probably after a UDIN shock). Scientists don't talk to the people whose cells are being worked on. They know that the mind and body are linked but omit to include this vital fact when studying a group of cells in a Petri-dish. A fundamental flaw in all medical scientific research is that 'the mind' is not there to influence the cells.

Whilst we are on the subject of cancer, why chemotherapies and radiotherapies often don't have the desired effect with treating these diseases is because the medical profession don't yet know these two phases exist, meaning that they are all too often treating people for the wrong reasons, from the point of view of the mind and body.

The medical profession doesn't know why a cancer grows. They have no idea that some cancers grow after the stressful event has occurred (e.g. bowel and glandular breast cancer), and usually only really show as lumps one to three years later. Some grow in the second regeneration phase, such as leukaemia, which is the regeneration phase of the bones - the stress phase is osteoporosis therefore cell degradation. In the liver which has ducts that lead into the gall bladder -the first stress phase is cirrhosis, the second, regeneration phase is hepatoma or hepacellular carcinoma. Interesting recent discoveries say that the virus that is thought to cause this cancer is the Hepatitis A,B,C D, E and G virus. The medical profession tries to kill the virus and has not thought about why the virus appears at this time, in the repair phase.

As we delve deeper into the two phases I am certain that you will find, as I have and everyone I have taught and worked with, that these two phases are undeniable. Every disease, from a simple pimple on a face to a horrific cancer has their origin and explanation for growth and healing in the two phases. Even with every spontaneous remission, a person goes through these two phases. During these so called miracles, the person goes through a really hot, sweaty time where they almost die only to come out the other side healed.

Georgie and her breast cancer – the explanation

Georgie's cancer had re-grown, even after the advanced treatment of Photo Dynamic Therapy. The doctor who was working on the third generation of this incredibly inexpensive drug was adamant that he had found a cure for cancer - he had devoted his whole life to its development. The problem is, he is a very obnoxious man.

Georgie listened intently as I started to explain why the cancer had re-grown. I said her cancer was a ductal breast cancer, and that in the first stress phase of the cancer there is a necrosis of the ducts of the breast; the ducts get bigger by the wall getting thinner. Typical symptoms are the nipple inverts, which, she told me, was exactly what had happened.

Then in the second regeneration phase, the ducts rebuild themselves and that is when she would have felt a lump behind the nipple. Again, she said that was exactly what had happened. The Photo Dynamic Therapy stopped the body rebuilding the cells, it had destroyed the rebuilding cells.

Although the Photo Dynamic Therapy worked really well, as soon as the therapy was stopped, the body went straight back to rebuilding the cells again. Hence the cancer returned. I told Georgie that she needed to address the shock that caused the issue to occur in the first place, then the body would have a better chance of completing the process and she would stand a better chance of recovering. This we did, and I was able to tell her exactly at what point the whole disease started and the exact minute that she resolved the conflict. We worked late into the night and I took her on a journey where she cleared out mentally everything that had caused the original problem to occur. This was to do with a boss who shocked her by his behaviour and attitude towards certain business transactions. She could not nurture his response and felt brutally separated from her business, which was very much her baby.

I left the next day for meetings in Auckland, New Zealand and Los Angeles, USA, returning in early September 2007. In December 2007 I spoke to Georgie again and she told me this time that the cancer has not returned. She had a set of CT scans that confirmed that the cancer was not there. Georgie was overjoyed and so are the Photo Dynamic Therapy people. Georgie is a naturopath and is incredibly knowledgeable in many other disciplines, such as nutrition and dark field blood analysis. She also took many months off work in order to allow herself to heal. She has addressed other mental issues with other people that she knows, changed her diet, her social and environmental interactions, plus her body (using PDT). Along with solving the original conflict shock using NLP, Time Line Therapy, EFT and hypnotherapy through me, she has affected the massive shifts that she needed to make in her life in order to solve the diseases process.

However, I did explain to her that the man she was working with to develop the PDT had a similar character to her original boss who had triggered the problem in the first place. I explained that PDT was similar to the traditional medical attitude of disease. Tumour gone = cancer gone. I went on to explain that the disease process needs to go through its cycle. You cannot avoid it and I advised her to be beware of this man and to stop working with him. She did not and every time I spoke to her, the stress that she was enduring showed in her voice.

There is more to come from Georgie in this book; I believe that her courage and story could be integral in assisting many women with breast cancers.

Her spreading the knowledge of META-Medicine® and the possible use of this very inexpensive Photo Dynamic Therapy, instead of inordinately expensive and life threatening chemotherapies, I believe, could change many of the cancer treatments available. We shall see. However the approach needs to be an integrative one. The PDT will not cure cancer on its own. As you find out later, Georgie's cancer reappeared exactly as I explained it would.

The two phases are undeniable but as yet unproven, I want to reiterate that. However, in my dealings with hundreds of people personally and the thousands collectively, myself, my students and my colleagues will all know that following a shock, the body goes into the Sympathetic state. Once the stress has completed, the Parasympathetic state occurs. We have all seen these two phases showing up, time and time again.

META-Medicine® has a mountain of empirical evidence to back it up plus it can explain why the two phases work theoretically. There is also some scientific research that points in the direction of the two phases. As we delve further into the makeup of the brain and embryology in later chapters, we shall see how elegant the body is and why the two phases need to be there.

We have already discussed how META-Medicine® easily and elegantly explains the cause of disease, the reason why disease occurs, the stress and also the regeneration phase. We will be exploring why cells go through a necrosis and why they grow. We will also answer questions that the medical profession has nothing but hypothesis for. Such as Metastasis (secondary cancers), the cause of disease and cancer at a cellular level, why fungi, bacteria and virus' are present.

In the next chapter I will explain why certain symptoms appear and disappear and then reappear, why someone can be ill for ten years with chronic fatigue or with eczema, or suffer all their adult life with Irritable Bowel Syndrome (IBS) or acne. And why people with Multiple Sclerosis have attacks, why Parkinson's patients don't shake at night but do shake all day. We will take a look at allergies; why they suddenly start and what really triggers them off.

Chapter 7

Why diseases keep reoccurring – when does a disease becomes chronic and how do allergies start

The immune system didn't evolve for allergy. Why in a hundred billion years of evolution would we evolve a response for allergy?
Joel Weinstocs - Author

Eczema - the two phase repeating themselves

Katrina Brunsden came up on stage as a demonstration subject during a META-Medicine® Certification training with me in 2007. From the age of eleven she had suffered from eczema. It had covered her whole body from time to time but now it was only showing up on her right inner arms, around the elbow joint and on a few other areas here and there. She had worked on solving the issues without using steroid creams, during her adult life. She had tried every cream, medical, complementary and alternative solution. She had reduced the eczema, mainly to this area.

She thought it was food related therefore an allergic reaction to certain foods, she worked with a nutritionist and this did help, but it did not solve the problem and she spent a lot of her life eliminating and changing her diet to resolve the problem. Things had got better and, since she had been in the UK, it had improved dramatically because of the things she had been doing nutritionally but it would still flare up from time to time.

When I looked at the eczema it was red, hot and, she said, a little itchy. She showed the audience; the size of the eczema was similar to the size of the palm of my hand. Some of the delegates came up for a closer inspection. I told them to touch her skin and palms to feel how hot they were. She explained that this recent patch of eczema would come and go. She did not want to use creams on it but sometimes it would become hot, annoyingly itchy and red. The skin would crack and ooze and it would become very painful to the touch, just like it was at the moment.

She had been studying META-Medicine® for few months but she had never really got to the bottom of why the eczema was there. She knew it was a separation conflict and she had some idea that it had to do with being separated from her family. However, why had it not disappeared completely? What kept triggering it off and what was it that was doing the triggering? Katrina sat anxiously in the demonstration seat as I started to decipher the disease process with her.

I asked her to clap her hands and I established she was right-wired, from which I deduced that she felt separated from her father and she wanted to hold him close but she could not.

She looked at me as if I was onto something. I explained to the group that what can trigger a disease process off again, in my experience, is the sound of a person's voice, or the look of something or somebody. Katrina is a New Zealander and she had been in the UK for a few years.

So looking at her in a curious manner I asked her, "Do you speak to your father in New Zealand very often?" she replied "Yes, I love my father but I don't feel separated from him." "I sense that," I said, "You don't miss him then?" I asked "No" she said.

'So what is it that he says to you, where he uses that tone of voice that causes you to feel that you are not his little girl?" She said "Nothing" and gave me a strange look as if to say, "are you mad?" The audience laughed but I knew deep down this was probably the trigger. I asked her if she had spoken to him recently, in the last week. She said "Yes, and it was a normal conversation."

Now I know that what triggers off disease can be totally out of conscious awareness. So I probed again. 'Run the conversation through your mind again, was there ever a point in it where you felt separated, disconnected from him in some way? Where you wanted, so badly, to hold him close to you but you couldn't. Where the conversation was difficult and you felt cut off."

She stopped, looked away, ran the conversation through her mind and at one point she went bright red. I said "Stop there. What was he saying then?" I asked. She looked at me in amazement "He was talking about me and that I have always wanted to work with food, career wise and he has always disapproved of me doing the food stuff."

I asked her "How's the eczema now?" "The itching has gone!" She replied, "that's amazing." She was looking at her arm as all the redness disappeared, "it's completely stopped itching, it's cold and I feel cold. Have you turned the heating off?" "No," I replied. Everyone in the room laughed.

Members of the audience came up and looked at the skin again. They could see that it had changed dramatically in the space of a few minutes. They touched her palms and they were cold. The skin where the eczema had been was also cold to the touch, the redness had disappeared, the oozing has stopped, and Katrina said, "It feels desensitised, as if it is not my skin."

"There's more" I said. I drew a diagram of the two phases on a flip chart and said, "This is one of the trigger points to the disease process" as I pointed to the start of the disease process Point 2. I then explained that during the stress phase there is a reduction in cells in the epidermis of the skin, it feels cold, desensitised, there is no itching and often the skin flakes away, getting thinner. The problem is that you don't notice this period; there is no pain, you don't feel the missing touch of the other person, which is what she said - it felt desensitised.

This is the biological reason for the disease, so we don't notice the lack of touch, the separation from the person we are missing.

Katrina shook her head in disbelief. "There are times when I feel so in control of my life but disconnected at the same time. I don't need anyone and that is when the eczema disappears and I thought it was getting better. Then there are times when I miss my home and my family and then the eczema gets bad. Now I know that when it seemingly disappears, it is not getting better and instead I am stressed and in the first stress phase. Wow and bugger at the same time," She said.

"Yes but now listen to this." I said. 'Do you remember a time when you heard the opposite from your father, or his voice was missing from your inner conversation with yourself?" She looked at me again and then went to think. "Yes, there are times when I feel

67

totally connected to him, his voice is so nice when he is like that." I asked her to replay the sound of his voice in her head, just how he would say those words to her. She did and then everything changed.

She took a deep breath in and started to shake the jumper that she was wearing, to get some cool air circulating. She involuntarily started to scratch her right arm, you could see she felt uncomfortable, but what amazed me was that she started to perspire and she took off her jumper saying "I am boiling hot, are you sure you have not been playing with the heating?" I said "No" and we all laughed. Audience members came up to look at the skin again to find that it had gone bright red and Katrina's hands were hot to the touch. 'That's incredible' said Katrina, "Can you stop it again?" I said, 'Yes, hear the tone of your Dad's voice as he talks in the disapproving way about wanting to have a career in food."

She changed again, this time there were people holding her hands and they felt the heat drain right out of them. Katrina said "The itchiness has stopped, my skin feels desensitised again." The audience members by her side were looking in amazement as all the redness in the patch of eczema disappeared from her skin over thirty seconds right in front of their eyes.

She asked to stay in this stress phase because it felt better, at least until she could work out a solution with me or one of the trainees as to how she could solve the issue once and for all. I agreed but I also wanted to point out a few more things.

I said "Now do you believe that there are two phases to a disease process? And that it's not an allergy?" Katrina's jaw dropped. "The reason it has got better whilst you have been here is because you have not had so much contact with your father. Therefore the disease process is not being triggered so often. I bet it got better when you moved away from home as well." She nodded.

"I also believe that the nutrition will have helped dramatically in reducing the everyday stress you go through and keeping you mentally positive, but that's only part of the whole equation," I explained. "I have proven to you that the process is triggered by the tone of your father's voice; one part causes you the stress, putting you in the first phase, Point 2 - when he talks disapprovingly about your career, and the other puts you into the regeneration phase. The regeneration phase is Point 4 on our chart, which is when you feel totally connected with him. We have triggered off both points a couple of times and now you know that, we can start to work with the tracks and the triggers and remove them by changing your mind, body, spirit, social and environmental situation."

The demonstration finished, but it was not until months later when I saw Katrina again at a London 'Mind, Body and Spirit' show that she told me of the profound effect the demonstration had had on her.

The cause of allergies and chronic diseases

So what does cause allergies, chronic diseases, reoccurring issues and cancers to re-grow? Why do they do it? Do dust mites cause asthma? Why doesn't steroid cream cure eczema? Is washing powder responsible for skin rashes? Is Irritable Bowel Syndrome (IBS) caused just by food, and why do certain foods cause it to be worse whilst others are okay? Why doesn't anyone, medical, complementary or alternative, know how to cure these problems? They promise the earth but often they never fully deliver.

We know there are two phases of a disease process according to META-Medicine®, but there are people who seemingly have ongoing diseases. Do these people then go through the two phases as well? If they do then how does that happen?

To explain this we need to briefly visit the start of a disease again. We talked comprehensively about this event, which is Point 2 in our diagram. You may remember the special criteria that causes a conflict shock to get trapped in our neurological system; the Unexpected, Dramatic, Isolating shock with No strategy (the UDIN) and how, during this time our mind, body, spirit, social and environmental situations all change to support us through the disease process.

When a UDIN shock like this happens, all the information that was going on at that time gets trapped. The neurology seems to take each sense such as a the tone/sound of the voice of a person, the tone/sound of an object, the look of their face, the pictures of specific things, any external touch, any specific smell or taste (including any food that you may be eating at that time) and it holds this event so it can deal with it and resolve it at a later date.

We learn by association and this event is the same; two things get linked, such as when you hear that special tune that reminds you of that incredible moment. When you see a foreign word it is not until someone explains what it means that you learn.

The same is happening here in the UDIN. However, the event is challenging, unsolvable, a shock, you have no strategy for dealing with the event so the body takes the event and holds it in the neurology. We can see this trapped energy and information in the brain under a CT scan at exactly the location of where the organ in our body is located. This shows up as a ring.

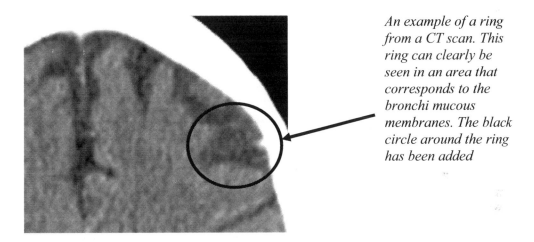

An example of a ring from a CT scan. This ring can clearly be seen in an area that corresponds to the bronchi mucous membranes. The black circle around the ring has been added

According to my friend, Professor Peter Fraser, this trapped energy is vibrating as a standing wave, at the same rate as the waves used in CT scanning. This also makes sense as regards quantum mechanics and the work of Milo Wolfe concerning the way energy in atoms move and work together to create patterns.

However, we know that these rings are not really rings, but balls of trapped energy. You can see this under specific types of CT scans slicing and it is possible to make out that the energy is not a two dimensional ring but a three dimensional ball. Another thing to note is that these balls of energy are not static; they do change over time. The brain is not a static organ, as a CT would portray but is changing from moment to moment.

The trapped energy and information in this ball holds the key to why a disease becomes chronic, or why an allergy to a specific substance appears. The energy ball seems to hold information in it, in order for the occurrence to be completely resolved. This information acts as a warning mechanism to prevent us from repeating the same mistake.

There is trapped energy inside the energy ball that is vibrating as a standing wave. The energy cannot escape. What we see in a brain CT is a slice through this sphere.

"Flashbacks in Post Traumatic Stress Disorder can give us an indication of what might be happening in our brains in these rings. Research on Post Traumatic Stress Disorder shows the state-dependent nature of its symptoms.[49] Sudden re-experiencing of a traumatic event (called a flashback) shows that the memory has trapped emotion in it."**

People with multiple personality disorder have also shown activity in certain areas of the brain.

Psychiatrist Don Condie and neurobiologist Guochuan Tsai used a MRI scanner to study the brain patterns of a woman with "multiple personality disorder". In this disorder, the woman switched regularly between her normal personality and an alter ego called 'Guardian'. The two personalities had separate memory systems and quite different strategies. The MRI*** brain scan showed that each of these two personalities used different neural networks (different areas of the brain lit up when each personality emerged)."**

** Parts Integration And Psychotherapy Excerpt taken from Richard Bolstad.
A Neurological Model For Understanding The Task Of Therapy.[50]

***fMRI refers to a functional Magnetic resonance Imaging scan. This type of scan measures the neural activity in the brain and spinal chord. It has been around since the early 1990's .

An example of how trapped energy can change everything in our lives

Let us take a real life example, for this I have to give you some background information in order for it to makes sense.

For seven years I suffered from a form of dermatitis on my left hand. The symptoms which appeared as very small blisters under the skin of my left hand could easily be seen when the skin was wet. There was little feeling during this time as the skin felt desensitised and foreign. I would often pop these small blisters in an attempt to feel the skin. This is the first phase of our disease process Point (3).

Then this was followed by a horrible itching and scratching session which would last a few minutes or more until the blisters popped, Point (4), then disappeared as the skin became hot, inflamed and very uncomfortable. The skin would peel and new skin would appear, replacing the old dead skin, Point (5). Sometimes I would be woken up in the middle of the night by how the skin felt, Point (6). The healing of the skin would complete and fully repair itself, Point (7), with no trace of there ever having been a problem. The whole cycle would take 2-4 weeks, depending on the size and clusters of the blisters. The dermatitis only showed up on the inside of my left hand and never anywhere else. It did spread over my palm from the centre through to the middle and bottom of certain fingers and my thumb.

It changed every time I started to explore the event that caused it to occur, sometimes the cycle would repeat itself in the same place and other times it would show up in different places. It did not disappear until I fully addressed the mind, body, spirit, social and environmental cause, Point (2), of the problem. Let me explain the journey and then the link between the skin's two phases.

The dermatitis first appeared when I left my ex-partner of nine years in August 2000. I had been in a very challenging relationship with her and I had tried to leave her many times in the last seven years of the relationship. The difficulties were two sided and it was equally as difficult for her as it was for me to be in the relationship.

I discovered the underlying issue in 2005, five years after we split up; she was like a daughter to me and I was like a son to her. Our relationship was not traditional but not unusual; I have come across couples in a similar situations. I remember now in hindsight how often I acted like as a father to her, and she like a mother to me. This dysfunctional relationship came about because we had both lost parents at important ages – she her father and me my mother. We both played out this partnership in a seemingly normal way and it worked to a degree. But I did not want to be in this type of relationship, as I discovered after doing a lot of personal development work on myself.

Eventually I plucked up the necessary courage to leave once and for all. It was one of the most challenging things I have ever done in my life. What you are unaware of is that this wonderful person who I was with, had a disability. It hardly affected her, no one really ever knew, except close friends, but I felt responsible 'as a father' to look after her and support her. So you can imagine that as a man, who wanted to be loved as a man and not as a father, I was deep in conflict inside myself on a daily basis.

In 2005, having worked out why I had the dermatitis on my hand, I vividly remember revisiting, inside my mind, the day I left. I did not understand how META-Medicine® really worked until that day, and it was at this time that I started to uncover the horrific event as to why I had the dermatitis.

How did I know that the issue was to do with me being a father figure? I am a right-wired person; this means that as I clap my hands my right hand goes over the left hand.

How we are wired relates to which side of our body will react to certain issues. If an issue shows up on the same hand that is the leading- hand, (in my case the right) then the problem will be to do with outside issues in our world, such as conflicts with our business, boss, friends or father.

If the issues show up on the opposite side (NON-Leading Hand) of our body then it has to do with our inner world; our children (if we have any), mother, anything we consider as a child such as a business that is our 'baby' or an animal that is our baby, such as a cat, dog or bird.

There is some proof about being left or right-wired; in identical twins one will be left-wired and the other right-wired. Nature has a way of ensuring we react differently to different shocks. There is also plenty of empirical evidence that we have found when carrying out a META-Medicine® diagnosis, the hand clapping and the content relating to a father or mother issue seems time and time again to bring up the cause of the disease.

However, there is research that concludes that the two brain hemispheres have different functions. Some says it is pseudoscience, others not. I think it is not that great a leap to conclude that there might be a link to how we react as humans to specific conflicts. As I mentioned earlier, the hand clap test seems very accurate.

71

Leading Hand

Father
Partner (male or
female)
Boss
Business/work
Anyone that is like a
person's father (e.g.
Sugar Daddy)
Outer world

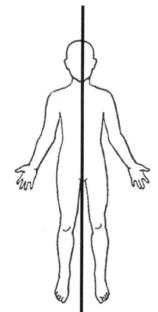

NON-Leading Hand

Mother
Child/Baby
Nest
Anyone/Anything
that is like a
person's
baby/mother
e.g. a business that
is a person's baby
Inner world

The dermatitis showed up on my inside of my Non-Leading hand (my left hand – I am right wired), so it was to do with an event that I considered to do with my inner world, or a 'mother issue'. It took me a long time to trace the event back to the time I left. What I did was to notice when the hand would become desensitised, then recall what I was thinking before the skin changed.

I discovered that there was a lot of emotion, such as guilt and desperation. It would have been triggered by my thinking, hearing or seeing something to do with my ex-partner.

One day I consciously triggered this horrible feeling and over the next twenty-four hours I watched as the blisters appeared. I repeated this experiment many times over several months.

Once I knew it was this emotion that triggered it, I followed the emotion back to its source. I did this by using META-Medicine® questioning, knowing the cause and my wiring, where the leading hand is right.

I started by eliminating certain things. By understanding that the issue was on my left hand, the NON-leading hand, I thought could it be something to do with my mother, who was dead and I had no emotion of either guilt or desperation attached to her, so I dismissed that. It could be something to do with a child but as my wife and I didn't have any children, I dismissed that too. I considered could it be someone acting like a mother to me or they are like a child to me, or perhaps something to do with my inner world? The issue being on the palm of hand, from a META-Medicine® point of view meant that I was trying to grab hold and pull a person close to me. I knew that the reason for the dermatitis was a separation issue. I also knew that the time when the issue had started was approximately five years ago.

I loaded a question for myself: From whom did I have a feeling of separation in the later part of 2000? Someone who was like a mother to me, or who I felt was like a child to me, someone I wanted to bring close to me, where there had been an unexpected, dramatic and isolating shock where I had no strategy to deal with the situation?

I have to admit that it took me a long time to put that question together. It now forms the basis of the META-Medicine® questioning technique. Through my NLP training I knew the unconscious mind would hold onto events until it found a resolution. Therefore if you ask the right question, the unconscious mind will give you the right answer. So I asked this question and I landed at the conflict shock. It was as if I had been transported right back to the point and I was right in it again. It felt horrific.

Let me explain: I finally decided to leave my partner of nine years. I had been planning to tell her for months. I had the support of my family and friends and I had met someone who I knew would also help me through the separation. Leaving someone you had been with for nine years is one heck of a challenge, especially when you loved them and had no hate for them and especially since you did not want to hurt them. You just knew you were in the wrong relationship.

She came home and as was normal, we started to argue. I told her calmly that I was leaving and it was final. She went upstairs and shouted "Go! Just bloody go!" I collected my things and went from the kitchen to the front door and as I was standing there she came down and sat on the bottom of the stairs, distraught. She knew I was finally serious. I said again in a calm voice I was leaving. Everything was fine up until the moment when she reached over with her right hand and touched my face and said "Don't go Flookie, don't go." Flookie was the endearing nickname she would use for me. She had never looked like this before. I had never seen this look of total fear and desperation in her before. Her voice was full of hopelessness. It was horrific and something I had not reckoned with. She had asked me to leave so many times before; I thought she would have been happy I was going.

At that point I remember my heart stopped, I felt a wrench inside, as if I was leaving a little child, a little girl who needed to be cared for. It caught me completely off guard. I had no idea what to do. I froze. I was stuck to the spot. Time stood still. I remember thinking, 'I will stay, I can't leave her, she needs me and perhaps she will change.'

These were the same patterns I had played over the last seven years knowing full well I was in the wrong relationship, not just for myself but also for her. I knew that the only way to stop hurting her and myself was to leave. So I did. I turned around and quietly said, "I have to go." I shut the front door and got into my pre-packed car with all my possessions and drove to my parents. I felt nothing but numbness. I also felt I had finally left.

I was strong and my whole family was very supportive. However, I am very sensitive to people's feelings. I always have been and I remember bawling my eyes out over this event for weeks, each time whilst seeing the desperate face of my ex-partner, feeling her hand on my cheek and hearing those gut wrenching words, "Flookie, don't go."

I never resolved this event, I just put it to one side, knowing that what I was left with was this ongoing dermatitis which showed up a few weeks later, when I moved in and started a new relationship, on the rebound, with the girl who had supported me through leaving. I now know this to be the resolution of the event.

I first noticed it on my face, and then my hands. It cleared from my face in a few months but my left hand did not clear up until 2007.

The issue affected me, as I said, in many ways which I shall go through in more detail.

Mind

After that incident I felt down and a little depressed. I masked these symptoms by feeling righteous and full of confidence in myself, as I knew that I had done the right thing. I felt no separation from my ex-partner. This was during the stress phase. Then I felt guilty during the regeneration phase. In the regeneration phase, on the right side of my brain I would feel a strange pulling around the top of my head. This corresponded with the feeling around Point (6), the healing crisis. You can see this point in the diagram of the brain and the mapping that comes from the work of the Dr Wilder Penfield Institute in Montreal, Canada. Dr Penfield found the outer cortex of the brain corresponded to the feeling sensations in our nerves relative to position of our body. The whole body is beautifully mapped, as you see from this diagram. Penfield called this mapping the Homunculus (little man).

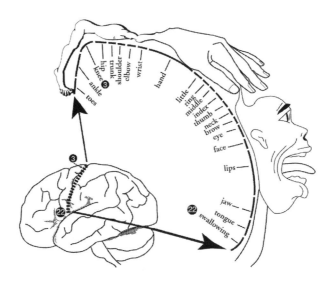

The body represented as a little man/woman or Homunculus in the windings of the cortex of our brain

Also psychologically, in the first phase I felt good. I had done the right thing. I felt full of confidence in myself and very righteous. Then, when I resolved the issue Point (4), I felt guilty. I had let this poor girl down. I had left her and I felt a wrench in my gut and in my heart letting go of someone I cared for. I hated what I had done but I knew deep down that she and I would never have a 'normal' relationship. I know this now because I am now married and in a 'normal' relationship.

Body

The body reacted to this issue by causing the epidermis (the top layer of skin) of the inside palm of my left hand and fingers (my NON-leading hand) to blister in the first phase Point (3), and then rebuild this blistering in the second phase, Points (5+7). This area of the body where the issue presented itself relates to wanting to hold onto a child, a daughter, to bring them close. The biological meaning in the first phase is such that you do not feel the separation from the person. This was certainly backed up by my MIND/ Psychological reaction.

This whole pattern repeated itself time and time again as I would trigger off the issue by seeing, thinking about, talking with or experiencing things that I had associated with my ex-partner. These would take me back unconsciously to the original cause, I would re-experience the shock, I would feel the emotions, then feel righteous that I had make the right decision and convince myself that I had done the right thing. The feelings of separation disappeared and the blistering would appear. The process would happen over and over again. Sometimes there could be several of these disease processes happening at the same time. The picture below shows my fingers at a time where my skin is in the first part of healing phase Point (5) on the middle finger and blistering on the ring finger Point (3).

Skin in second phase Point (5) as it is healing, it would flake or peel away. The skin would itch.

Newly repaired skin would be formed after the blisters had gone. This skin was smooth with no markings.

Blistering of skin Point (3), you can see the bubbling of skin underneath the top layer, no itching, the skin would feel desensitised and there would be no feeling when you touched this area.

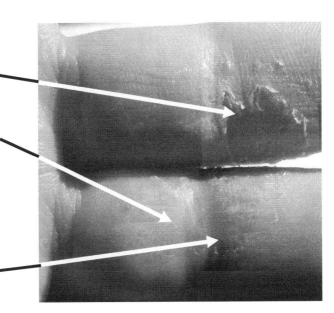

The next thing that would happen was that I would feel sorry for her and feel a sense of connection again. Here the blistering would disappear as the skin would start to rebuild. Interestingly the skin would itch directly after I resolved the problem, Point (4). This would often happen in the middle of the night when I would find myself scratching my left hand.

Spirit

My spirit as a human being was affected by the process. I felt that I was responsible for my ex-partner even after I had met my wife. It meant that three years later when my ex-partner was involved in a horrible car accident, although she was not hurt, I still felt responsible for making sure she was OK. I could not let myself go from her. I did not want to be with her in a relationship but I was compelled to care for her as a father would care for his daughter. When I told her, four years after we had split up, that I was getting married, it was a very traumatic time for both of us.

I am still very much in love with my wife, Kristin. The relationship with my ex-partner was completely different and the guilt I felt continued to affect me deeply until mid 2007 - seven years later!

The whole process brought me back to losing my connection with my own mother many years before. So spiritually, I was playing the same pattern and at some deep level I was wanting to solve a conflict that had plagued me since I was age six, when my mother left my brothers and me to be with another man. The same voice saying she was leaving had bothered me, only this time it was in reverse. I was the parent now leaving the child.

75

Social interaction

I noticed that I would want to call my ex-partner regularly to check that she was OK. In fact this interaction was what caused the 'rebound' relationship to fail. Once I left the 'rebound' relationship seven months after splitting up in the first place, I tried making up with my ex-partner. I felt the separation and wanted to heal it. The relationship between us was still the same and, as hard as I tried to heal the relationship, it was never going to be right. I had just met my future wife Kristin by this time. I remember telling my ex-partner, in a wine bar, that any form of reconciliation was pointless. I then remember her telling me that I had broken her heart twice. This hurt me greatly, and I felt the separation very deeply.

It also affected my relationship with my wife to a very small degree. Kristin noticed that I had a connection with my ex-partner but fortunately she is not a jealous person and let it go.

Environmental interaction

There were many triggers environmentally that I noticed. As I drove past the cottage we had lived in, in Bristol, I would feel the wrench in my gut. The village, called Clifton Village in Bristol brought back memories that again triggered off this feeling. Each time the place would remind me of my ex-partner, and I could see the desperation in her face from that night. The same would happen if I drove past the wine bar where we had sat.

The tick of any watch on a wooden surface also reminded me of her. I gave her a watch as a birthday present some years ago. I am particularly fond of watches. The ticking of her watch would sometimes keep me awake at night, and the ticking of my own watch reminded me of her again and that horrible night.

There were many other environmental triggers; clothes I owned which I had bought with her, presents that were given to me from her, pictures of the two of us, people with a similar problem to her (this happened sometimes when news or a documentary about the issue my ex-partner had would be talked about). Each time, it would take me back to the image of her desperate face and I would obsess about her in my mind, therefore starting the whole disease process off again. As you can see from the mind, body, spirit, social, and environmental situations that I went through, this whole disease process was not just to do with my skin. The disease affected me in every area of my life.

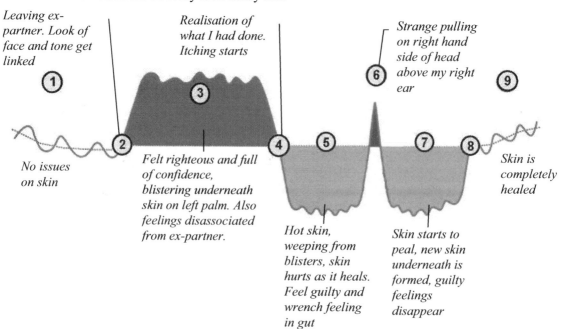

Leaving ex-partner. Look of face and tone get linked

(1)

No issues on skin

(2)

Felt righteous and full of confidence, blistering underneath skin on left palm. Also feelings disassociated from ex-partner.

Realisation of what I had done. Itching starts

(3)

(4)

(5)

Hot skin, weeping from blisters, skin hurts as it heals. Feel guilty and wrench feeling in gut

Strange pulling on right hand side of head above my right ear

(6)

(7)

Skin starts to peal, new skin underneath is formed, guilty feelings disappear

(8)

(9)

Skin is completely healed

Why the emotions, pictures, tones of voices of the conflict shock, Point (2), became trapped is thought to be as a warning signal. During the conflict shock, Point (2), all the pictures, sounds, feelings, tastes, smells and words were recorded and then stored. As I discussed earlier this, we believe, shows up as an emotional ball in the brain that corresponds to the location in the body. This emotional ball is similar to a PART that is spoken of in NLP, Hypnotherapy and in Cognitive Behavioural Therapy (CBT). CBT is used in the UK's National Health Service as a psychological treatment for dealing with mental health issues such as anxiety and depression.

The theory about PARTs is well understood and is based on the fact that when a trauma occurs, a PART of the unconscious mind becomes separated off from the rest of the nervous system. The reason for this is so that the person can carry on surviving without having to deal with the traumatic event. However, the unconscious mind knows that this event will need to be resolved at some time. When it thinks it is appropriate, it will bring up the emotion for re-evaluation by the conscious mind. This normally happens just before we are about to go to sleep, or when we are feeling relaxed.

We have all experienced this: Just think about the delayed shock you or other people you know have experienced after a traumatic experience. The basis behind the theory of the unconscious mind separating off from the whole comes from the teachings of an NLP trainer Dr Tad James. The notion of PARTs comes from Gestalt therapy which has many of its foundations in Freudian Psychoanalysis and was developed by Fritz Perls.

Parts are similar to trapped emotions or beliefs but, unlike these states of mind, Parts are completely separated from the rest of the unconscious mind and have their own personality, set of beliefs and values about life. They can sometimes believe that they separately control the whole of the body and the unconscious mind.

What I have noticed through the thousands of clients I have worked with since I trained in NLP in 1992 is that if someone has experienced an unpleasant event in their childhood, or earlier life, where a lot of emotion was trapped or we took on a belief which was untrue, then the issue will still need to be resolved.

For example: Imagine an experience where a young person goes through a trauma such as the loss of a parent, which results in a lot of trapped emotion. The emotion then needs to be resolved and a pattern is started. Even though later on in life we may consciously believe that we have dealt with the problem, it appears in our lives as a pattern that plays over and over again. We are unaware of it and unable to control the emotion. Carl Jung, founder of Analytical Psychology talked about this phenomenon in his book 'Psychological Types'.

This pattern then plays throughout the life of the person. The trapped emotion creates ongoing issues with relationships, such as being unnecessarily jealous or, as in my case, going out with a person who was like a mother to me. My younger brother also created a similar pattern in his life by marrying a woman who looked like our mother. They had a child and when their daughter was three, my brother's wife left him because she felt that she had not 'lived'. Our mother left my father for exactly the same reasons, and my younger brother was age three when it happened.

We attract into our lives similar situations that we need to resolve. This then causes us to recreate the whole problem again. It is as if the unconscious mind wants us to resolve the problem and puts us back into the same situation time and time again. This, from my experience, shows up as a minor ailment or a reoccurring pain that often goes unnoticed.

However, if an event is an Unexpected, Dramatic, Isolating event that catches us completely off guard, where there is No strategy to deal with it, then a 'Part' is created. This time this 'part' will create a disease.

Part is created

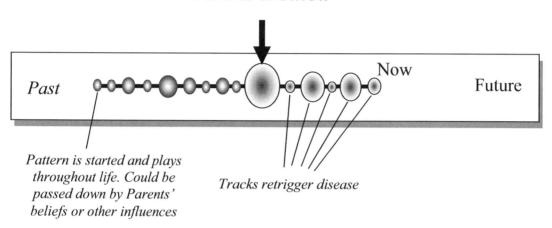

Past   Now   Future

Pattern is started and plays throughout life. Could be passed down by Parents' beliefs or other influences

Tracks retrigger disease

Another interesting phenomenon about 'parts' is that there is always an underlying positive intention as to why they are there. It is as if we have a positive built-in early warning system, so we avoid environmentally going back to the same place or socially interacting with the same person. However, if we do interact with the same environment/person then our body has already got the programme for all the necessary organ reactions and behavioural reactions to deal with the problem again.

This would explain why my dermatitis did not disappear after the very first time I experienced the dermatitis disease process. A 'part' became formed that was triggered off time and time again as an early warning signal. My brain was saying, 'Do not go near this person or return back to that environment again, stay away.' However, when I did reconnect with my ex-partner, the disease process was triggered off again. I would feel desensitised. Repeating the programme assisted me while I was in the environment that was linked to my ex-partner.

The triggers that would start the disease process off again were: Seeing my ex-partner walking down the street or in a bar in Clifton village, Bristol; a watch ticking on a wooden surface; going past the cottage we lived in; seeing a person who reminded me of the issue my ex-partner had; seeing old friends who had stayed loyal to my ex-partner; hearing her name; an old photograph with her in it or presents she had given me which I still kept. All of these would then remind me of the look on her face; I would hear her voice and experience the feelings of the horrific separation.

This would start me back on the disease process once again, as you can see from the following diagram. The first disease process ran its course. Then additional triggers happened, all interlinked into the 'Part' and all leading to the visual image and tone of my ex-partner's voice and ultimately the horrible gut wrenching feeling, and the whole process would start all over again.

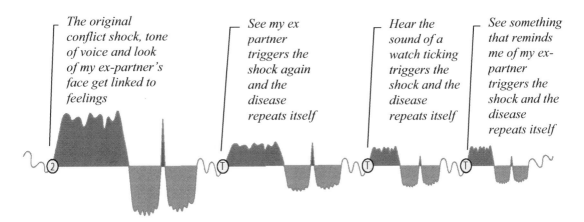

The original conflict shock, tone of voice and look of my ex-partner's face get linked to feelings

See my ex partner triggers the shock again and the disease repeats itself

Hear the sound of a watch ticking triggers the shock and the disease repeats itself

See something that reminds me of my ex-partner triggers the shock and the disease repeats itself

This notion also has its theory in Epigenetics (see Chapter 1). A traumatic event that affected our grandparents such as a drought, which meant the family almost starved to death, can have repercussions on our offspring or even our grandchildren, who can still be affected in generations further down the line. Once triggered by a new emotional event, a horrific situation such as a child screaming at the top of it's voice because it is denied certain food, which it loves and is smacked to shut up, could be the trigger that starts obesity or even early onset diabetes.

This is thought to explain why some children are found to be born with such diseases. If the event is traumatic enough, such as a mother starving herself in order to stay slim, or arguing continuously with the father whilst being pregnant, it could recreate a disease whose pattern is lying dormant and is then passed down through the generations.

Repeating the pattern similar to the grandparent's conflict shock, the DNA of the grandchildren will start to express itself with the same alterations in the body, e.g. to eat excessively, in order to put on enough weight to survive the impending drought.

You may think that this cannot be true. Then consider Afro-Caribbeans in America who, during slavery, experienced drought and a lack of food. Their great, great grandchildren's offspring now experience extreme obesity. The same generational line in Africa and the Caribbean did not have the same issues and even with the abundance of food now found in these regions, obesity is not an issue in the mother country. (See Chapter 1 - Epigenetics)

Allergies also seem to have their origin in this theory. If you can imagine that during a traumatic event, a UDIN, everything that was going on at that time becomes linked. So tastes and smells become linked to a disease process. If you were eating an orange at the time of the conflict shock then that can trigger off a disease process. I find that I cannot eat oranges, or drink orange juice. As soon as I do, literally within minutes, I get mouth ulcers. I do not know the shock that caused this to happen but I am not too bothered as I have never liked oranges or orange juice.

Commonly found nut and peanut allergies can come from the same source. These nut allergies can cause vomiting, mild stomach upsets, a rash and in rare cases anaphylactic reactions, the bronchial mucosa in the lungs contracts causing extreme issues with breathing and sometimes death if not treated immediately.

For more information on this amazing subject look at, 'Projected meaning' - Marc Frechet, 'Unconscious parental projections. Psycho-genealogy' - Anne Ancelin Schützenberger – "Transgenerational memories. Programming conflict – Conflicts caused by certain times of the year or combinations and dates and Memorised biological cycles - Christian Fleche – The cyclical appearance of stressful events."

Malou Laureys has recorded an excellent training on this subject matter. If you are interested please go to www.meta-medicine.com and look for a downloadable training on Psycho-genealogy - a therapeutic model which works by identifying and treating the negative effects of issues passed down from one generation to the next and then dealing with that in your present life.

An allergy can be started by earlier generations and then passed down to an individual. Or it could have been caused by a reaction to a shock whilst in the womb of the mother or, most likely, the reaction happened in childhood. Take nut allergies as an example; there will have been a conflict shock as the person was eating or swallowing nuts or a product that contained nuts, and the two became linked. The stress of a shock gets linked to the nuts by association.

Dr Kwesi Anan Odum, a colleague of mine in META-Medicine®, had an allergy to apples. He discovered that the problem occurred when his father left for Ghana from Germany when Kwesi was five. His father left him and his mother to fend for themselves. He said the intense realisation that his father had gone for good came about as he walked to school with his mother as a young boy.

Ever since then he was unable to eat an apple without having a minor, but discomforting reaction. During a META-Medicine® training he was used as a demonstration subject whereby the META-Medicine® consultant, a qualified Health Practitioner from Germany called Karen Seidel, worked with Kwesi to find the shock, and at the same time she resolved the issue by collapsing the emotion around the time when he felt the problem, using Kinesiology. Kwesi told me some time later that the street he walked down had apples trees lining it and there would have been apples growing in abundance at the time of year when his father had left. He was not eating an apple at the time of the conflict, as far as he could remember, but he reckoned that the apples and the emotions had become symbolically linked.

After clearing the emotion, Kwesi ate an apple in front of the audience and reported no ill effects, even days later. Several months after the therapy he reported that there were still no ill effects from eating apples and he was very pleased, as it had caused him some minor issues in the past.

I have worked with many allergy clients and found the same to be true. An UDIN shock causes certain allergens such as flower or grass pollen, fur or dust to become linked in the same strange way. Removing the original shock stops the client from experiencing the reaction again.

One of the first Time Line Therapy® therapeutic interventions I ever did was with a young woman, who suffered horrendously from hay fever. I distinctly remember that the issue would not disappear until I asked her to go back to before she was conceived and clear the issue from before her birth.

Once she did this, pollen did not affect her. I had her smelling roses and flowers in her back garden with no ill effects. She also went back to the family home later on that summer, during the grass-cutting season. Ironically her parents were farmers. Her mother was flabbergasted to see her as she came to the door during hay fever time. My client nonchalantly said that she had been to see some guy who cleared out an issue from Grandmamma thereby making the problem disappear. Her mother said, 'but Grandmamma is dead' to which she had replied, "Not in my body she wasn't."

I never had an explanation as to why these amazing phenomena occurred until now. With META-Medicine® we have a process as to why such normal everyday things such as pollens, nuts and fur become incorrectly linked for no apparent reason. No explanation has ever made sense to me until I came across META-Medicine® and Epigenetics.

Katrina and her Eczema

A month later at a 'Mind, Body, Spirit' event in London, where I was exhibiting META-Medicine®, Katrina came to meet me. I managed to break away from some of the clients to speak to her. She had been trying to talk to me for a couple of hours. She said that after the training the eczema had disappeared and she really understood why it had been there. However, she had a lot of eczema around both sides of her face and hands and I asked her what the reason was for this problem now.

She told me that she had always had a dream of owning her own specialist food restaurant, one that produced very special healing food made in a unique way, some of it raw, some of it specially cooked. As she spoke her eyes lit up. She said that although she did not want to be a META-Medicine® consultant, she did want to combine it with how she used food for healing.

I thought this goal was excellent but I was confused as to why she was telling me this right now. She told me that her New Zealand father had always criticised her obsession with cooking and her lack of ambition. A chef was not the career for his daughter. She had compromised her life to this belief and had felt not only separated from her father but, more importantly, from herself. This explained why the eczema was showing up on both hands and both sides of her face at this time. Her inner and outer worlds were being affected.

I was taken aback by this story, especially the deep meaning behind the process. I asked her when the eczema had showed up. She told me that it had appeared a few days before, after she had decided that she would now go and do the thing she had always dreamed of.

Here's what Katrina said when she wrote to me recently.

"The work with Richard Flook and META-Medicine® made a profound difference in the way I viewed my eczema. Before my healing with Richard I used to "hate" my eczema. But over the 2 years I have learned to be thankful whenever my eczema gets triggered. It guides me to keep doing what I love. Even today, if I let fearful thoughts enter my mind about not being able to do what I want with my life, my eczema can flare up. Fortunately, nowadays, thanks to Richard and the META-Medicine® healing modality, I'm always able to understand why it is happening and as such can quickly change my state so today the eczema rarely happens." Katrina Brunsden 2009.

In this chapter we have explored the significance of the UDIN and how what gets stored during this time plays an important role in causing a disease to become chronic. It also explains why allergies, to seemingly normal things, are created. In the next chapter we will explore another strange phenomenon that causes diseases to do a quick repeat of the original shock. It also explains why migraines happen and what causes asthma attacks, fits, and even a fatal heart attack. We will approach this in the strange world of Point (6) - The Healing Crisis.

Chapter 8

The Healing Crisis

The reason for heart attacks, migraines, headaches, epileptic fits, muscle cramps, asthma attacks, Parkinson's and Chronic Fatigue Syndrome (ME)

"Healing takes courage and we all have courage even if we have to dig a little to find it."
Tori Amos (Pop Rock Singer b 1963)

"In a prime-time address, President Bush said he backed limited federal funding for stem cell research. That's right, the President said, this is a quote, the research could help cure brain diseases like Alzheimer's, Parkinson's, and whatever it is I have."
- Conan O'Brien quotes (American Television talk show host (Late Night) and Writer, b.1963)

John and his Parkinson's disease

John (name changed – Ed) has Parkinson's disease and when John came to see me he had the intention of selling me his skills. We had been introduced by a friend who had asked me to talk to John, as a favour for her. I called him up and, during our preliminary conversations, I found he was more interested in persuading me to pay him for things he could do for me, skills unfortunately I did not need.

I was more interested in finding the cause of his Parkinson's disease and with this in mind we openly agreed to meet. The consultation was free, something I rarely do unless I am really intensely curious about something. In these circumstances my curiosity gets the better of me - I need to know. How does a person get them self into such a situation? Why is it that although these people come across as being perfectly normal over the phone, they secretly suffer. In John's case the Parkinson's disease affected two limbs - an arm and a leg. Why does the body create such a disease and for what purpose? Why has this issue not healed completely?

It took me a few hours before I really understood the answer to those questions. Although we had agreed just to meet and discuss his disease, John spent much of the time trying to persuade me to pay him to teach me how to write letters. Even though I know my written English could be improved, I rarely write letters, and prefer a quick e-mail instead. The way he kept pushing me to employ him came across in an unfortunate, pitiable way that made me question his abilities. It was as if he was stuck in the past. Letter writing is quaint but in my mind it's something from the last century. I was better able to understand his behaviour as the consultation carried on.

John was in his late sixties when I met him; slight in build and, overall, a charming man. He had been married for forty of those years to the same woman. I am always intrigued how people stay in partnerships for that length of time, having come from a family where my father had divorced twice, married three times; twice to my step mother. He also had several other serious relationships in between.

Being faithful and married to the same person either shows total commitment to one another or there is an underlying cultural or religious belief system running, that keeps two unhappy people together. I understood that quite well, having been stuck in a challenging nine year relationship myself.

As John sat across from me, telling me his life story, it gave me a chance to observe his symptoms. John's whole left arm would shake with the main spasm acting as if he wanted to pull something close to him, but he could not quite get hold of whatever it was. Drinking a cup of tea in the therapy room was a challenge for him. His right foot would also twitch involuntarily but not as much as the hand. It was as if he wanted to move that foot forward but he could not.

As the story of John's life started to unfold, I slowly got the answers to my questions as to why and how the hand and leg would shake, and why the way he presented himself was perceived as pitiable.

John genuinely loved children in a beautiful and innocent way. He told me so openly - he adored children and enjoyed their company. But sadly, he was in a childless marriage. I asked him why this was but he would repeatedly avoid answering the question.

I needed to find out if he was right or left-wired. By asking him to clap his hands I found out that he was right-wired. Therefore the left-hand jerking issue had to do with a mother/son, child or inner world conflict and his right foot had to do with an issue concerning his father, partner (his wife) or his outer world.

I then started to probe and found out that the Parkinson's started in August 2000, six years ago. Knowing that he had no children, I asked him if his mother died at that time, to which he replied, "No, she died in the mid-eighties." Next I asked whether something had shocked him that he could not get hold of in his personal, inner world. He said no, nothing had happened to him at that time.

I was drawing a blank but experience had taught me that the body never lies, there was a reason for John's symptoms and the symptoms are not a mistake. I excused myself from the room for a few minutes so I could think and I went to get a cup of tea. It was then that I got the question that I wanted to ask him.

I came back into the room and said, "I'm curious. What did your wife say to you in summer 2000 that caught you completely off guard? It was unexpected, dramatic, isolating, and you had no strategy to deal with it. Was it something to do with children and not being able to bring them close to you?"

John looked at me taken aback by the question. His face went bright red, tears welled up in his eyes, there was a long pause as the question he had been avoiding was answered for me. He said, "My wife told me she did not want children and she would never ever have children."

I was astounded. I asked him, "Do you ever have sex?" "No, never. We haven't for over thirty years," he replied. "How long have you wanted to have children?" I asked. "All my life," he said. "Then what changed on that day in summer 2000?"

"It was the way my wife told me. That day, after a wedding we had just been to, I knew then I would never have children, I knew there was no hope, but there is not a day that goes by without dreaming that I did." he said. I sat back in my chair shaking my head in disbelief, just thinking to myself how cruel the world can be.

The Healing Crisis

The healing crisis point (6) looks such an innocent part of the disease process. As you look at the spike in the middle of the second part of the two phases you wonder what on earth could 'mother nature' be doing by adding this little repeat of the first phase, exactly half-way between the resolution of the conflict Point (4) and the end of the conflict Point (8).

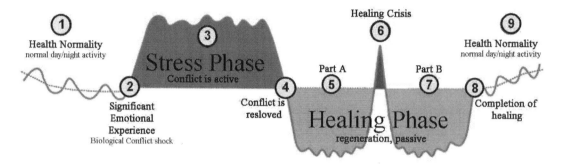

The two phases themselves are incredible enough, so what is the body doing by adding this little spike? This spike that is responsible for causing so many horrible acute symptoms, such as excruciating pain, fainting, fits and sometimes death. So what is the healing crisis and why is it there?

The healing crisis is thought to be a repeat of the original symptoms that started the whole issue off in the first place. From a META-Medicine® point of view it is an event that has the effect of checking if the person (or animal) is capable of being a useful member of the group or society. Have they got something to contribute that will enhance the survival or progression of their species? These are the questions that we believe are being asked during this time. This conclusion has been drawn from observations of the healing crisis in animals and humans alike.

The healing crisis also has another purpose on a biological level. During part 'A', Point (5) of the regeneration phase there is a build up of water in and around the organ and the brain relay. Once the first part of the healing has been done, the water is no longer required. Since the body needs to eliminate the water, it squeezes this water out from the organ and also out from the brain relay at the same time.

This gives rise to and explains the symptoms that we experience during the healing crisis. In the affected organ we experience cramping seizures of one sort or another in different organs - the obvious example would be muscle cramps. Other less obvious sorts are stomach cramps, which can often end in diarrhoea. During these times we often feel cold, anxious, and out of sorts. Comparing this to how we felt before this phase (hot and lethargic) it would appear that the stress phase is repeating itself.

Most people can remember a time when they had a bad bout of the influenza and even if you have been lucky enough not to have experienced the flu, I am sure you will recognise this story.

The flu and the healing crisis

I remember having a bout of influenza, five years ago. I was so unwell that I was confined to my bed all day, exhausted and aching all over. I was boiling hot, sweating and I could not move. I felt shattered and all I wanted to do was sleep.

Half-way through the afternoon I started to feel better. So much so that I got out of bed, showered and got dressed thinking 'this is over' and I went back to work. An hour later I was freezing and I felt really strange and full of excess energy. I went back to bed and wrapped myself in the bed covers, shivering with cold. My head was in a spin. I felt alert but at the same time uncomfortable. I really was under the weather. A headache started to develop on the right hand side of my head, just behind my right eye and ear.

Now I started to feel really worried. An hour ago I was laid up in bed with no energy, now I felt wired and had a thumping headache. Gradually I started to feel better; my headache subsided, the shivering ceased and my body temperature returned to normal. I also peed for England. Meaning more urine came out than the water I had drunk over the past few days and I brought up a large amount of phlegm in an uncomfortable coughing fit.

After this had passed I started to feel better and, thinking it was all over, I decided to get up and start work again. Within the hour I was back in bed, exhausted, feeling hot and out of sorts. I slept until the next day whereupon I awoke, feeling much better but a little fragile. The day after that I felt fine.

If you think back to your own experiences I am certain that you can recall having been through a healing crisis at some time during your life, even if it has only been diarrhoea, a coughing fit or a thumping headache. All of these are symptoms of the healing crisis.

What we have also noticed is that the location of the headache relates to the location of the brain relay that is affected. This is because the water is being squeezed out of the relay at the same time as it is being squeezed out of the organ. The brain is acting like a pump which literally squeezes the excess water that has collected in the relay in Point (5), 'Part A' of the regeneration phase and forces it out through the ventricles of the brain, back into the body, where it is passed out later through our urine. This action can feel like a thumping action from within. There are no pain receptors inside the brain so the thumping comes from the cramping and swelling of the brain, forcing certain other organs to feel the increased pressure.

Often we feel the excessive pressure behind the eyes, above the forehead, around the ears and at the back of the head near the neck. These symptoms also explain why migraine sufferers experience light spots behind the eyes before and after the pain. This could be explained by the pumping starting to occur. In a few interviews I have had with migraine sufferers, they have told me that they experience these symptoms time and time again, sometimes feeling so bad that they have to shut off all light and lie down in a darkened room until the migraine passes. What is interesting is that instead of feeling tired, they feel restless.

Other well known examples of the healing crisis are fainting, blacking out, epileptic fits, asthma attacks, diarrhoea, vomiting, coughing or sneezing fits, shaking or twitching of one muscle group, numbness, intense itching, panic attacks, heartburn and coughing up or passing blood through urine.

These symptoms can last seconds, minutes, hours or even days. They can also repeat themselves continuously during the day, but disappear at night as with Parkinson's disease.

(In Parkinson's disease the sufferer does not shake at night, or whilst in a trance, as I found out with John.)

Another interesting phenomenon is that after the healing crisis, water is released from the brain and from around the organ where the disease was, resulting in a person urinating excessively or passing the excessive water out through the easiest orifice possible. An example would be with a bowel issue where the healing crisis is diarrhoea.

Every person who has been through a spontaneous remission from a terminal illness goes through a time where symptoms similar to the stressful phase they experienced before the disease came about are repeated intensely. In other words they became very, very ill with massive acute symptoms before they got better.

They report that there was a time between life and death that, once it passed, they knew that they were on the road to recovery. I personally thought that spontaneous remissions meant that the person woke up and the disease had miraculously disappeared. It was only after doing some research that I discovered that every one of those people who had experienced spontaneous remission went through a second phase which involved an intense healing crisis.[51]

Although there seems to be no direct proof of a healing crisis, what it can explain however, is certain diseases such as asthma, headaches and death (caused by a heart attack). There is some clinical evidence that the healing crisis has been noted in homeopathy and in medical literature.

Observations of clients taking homeopathic treatment has frequently revealed that when the body releases toxins that have been stored, they are eliminated and symptoms are temporarily reversed. This lasts for several hours or sometimes two to three days, always passing as quickly as it came on. Those clients, who experience these symptoms, usually continue to heal completely. There is also some homeopathic literature that states that if a client does not experience the repeat of the original symptoms then they will not fully recover.

A homeopath called Constantine Hering discovered that there are three basic principles regarding these symptoms and these seem to fit with our observations in META-Medicine®;
1.   All cures come from the inside to the outside.
2.   They come from the head down.
3.   They are in reverse order, so they show up in the opposite way they started.

The symptoms of the healing crisis have also been noted in what has been recognised as the Herxheimer Reaction. Dr Adolf Jarisch (1860-1902) and Dr Karl Herxheimer (1861-1942) noticed that when treating syphilitic symptoms of the skin, they would often get worse before they got better. The patients would develop a fever, night sweats, nausea, and vomiting and the skin lesions would become larger and would swell before settling down and healing. These symptoms would last a few hours or two to three days before the lesions would resolve. The intensity of the reaction was reflected by the intensity of the inflammation in the first place.

The Herxheimer reaction (also known as the Jarisch-Herxheimer or Herx) is thought to occur when a large amount of toxins are released, due to the death of bacteria. This is often as a result of taking an antibiotic. Common symptoms are headaches, fever and myalgia. How typical symptoms that fit with the healing crisis in the second half of the two phases relate to excessive bacteria and the relationship between antibiotics are not understood in META-Medicine®. However, the Herx reaction could be the healing crisis, although the hypothesis that this is caused by the release of toxins is based on observations and not science.[52]

Related research seems to confirm that the healing crisis is linked to massive electrical changes in certain organs. Examples of this are the changes of electrical impulses in the brain that occur during an epileptic fit. This further confirms the brain organ link with META-Medicine®.

When someone goes through an epileptic fit there is a high amount of electrical activity which has been measured by EEG machines. There are also convulsions and violent shaking of the body, which occur suddenly and then disappear, which fit the symptoms of the healing crisis. These epileptic fits can be life threatening and can cause a stroke. After a fit, a person can lose their ability to speak, other bodily functions are severely impaired, limbs become temporarily paralysed, and involuntary passing of water is common. In my experience and in most cases when these symptoms have passed, the person quickly returns to normal which can take anything from a few hours to several days.[53]

Many of my serious cancer clients have told me that they have had an epileptic fit. Some have had severe reactions from it, some go through the cycle and fully recover. Others have no energy left in their bodies to complete the process and, unfortunately, die from lack of vitality and not from the cancer (all of these clients have had Chemotherapy and/or Radiotherapy). This is what I mean by the body testing to determine if the person is capable of being useful in the group and can contribute to society. Maybe 'mother nature' is questioning: 'Will the person assist the tribe in its long term survival?'

One of the strangest experiences I have come across happened to me when I was consulting a client who was terminally ill. She had to take morphine because of the pain she was in. She had had bowel cancer and a liver cancer. The last operation she had undergone had caused two satellite tumours to appear where the incisions for the key-hole surgery had been made. From a META-Medicine® point of view, this was an attack against the abdomen and it had caused a growth to protect the abdomen from further attacks. The thick skin wall lining of the abdomen called the peritoneum, grew massively at the exact points where the incisions had been made.

My client had never wanted that last operation and she was ice cold before she had it. She reported freezing up whilst on the operating table, just before she was put under the anaesthetic. This was the conflict shock for the peritoneum and the signal for it to grow.

What was so sad was that there was no evidence of the bowel cancer or the liver cancer during the operation. She was clear of all the cancers but she died because of the morphine from dealing with the pain that was related to the satellite tumours.

Before she passed away however, something very weird happened. In the last three weeks of her life she spent most of her time in a deep comatose sleep. She stopped eating and started to waste away. She was also boiling hot to the touch. After a couple of weeks she miraculously woke up. She came completely out of the deep, deep sleep and she stopped taking the morphine. She wanted to get up and get out of the bedroom she had been in but she had no energy to move. Her daughter told me that her mother had had long conversations with her family and she was able to say many things that were very special for everyone concerned. Three days later she went back into an even deeper sleep and sadly passed away a week later.

One of my students, Anne Sweet, and a META-Medicine® Health Coach who was one of the first hospice nurses in England, said she had seen this many times as a nurse. She could never explain it until she realised that it was the healing crisis. She even mentioned that a few terminally ill clients had been through the healing crisis, fallen back into a deep sleep, and had slowly come out of this state feeling better (Part B of the regeneration process), wanting to eat, and their cancers had eventually disappeared. This is a very rare occurrence but I have it on good authority from Anne that this does happen.

Muscles show a similar change in electrical activity when they cramp, which, again is the healing crisis. Whilst I was in Germany, attending a training seminar in META-Medicine® brain CT reading, I woke up at 5.00 a.m. screaming with pain from a cramp in my left calf muscle. The pain lasted ten minutes and then disappeared. There was no fitness reason for this muscles cramp. I regularly work out and nothing concerning my condition had changed. I had no injuries and I had never experienced this type of reaction before. So why did it occur and what could explain the symptoms? It was definitely the healing crisis of me solving a moving forward conflict between myself and what I really wanted to do in my life which was META-Medicine®.

Parkinson diseases and shaking

Muscles also go through involuntary twitching spasms and have the same electrical changes, as I mentioned earlier. Shaking during Parkinson's disease is thought to be incorrect nerve impulses firing off in the brain. There is obviously a lot of electrical activity going on during this time. However, how do you explain the symptoms of shaking disappearing during sleep or under hypnosis?

META-Medicine® says that we can go through what is called a 'hanging healing'. This is where the client is repeatedly tracking through the healing crisis, as in Parkinson's. They then go through the first part of the regeneration phase, Point 5 (PART B), when they sleep or are in a deep rest. As you can see from this diagram, the stress phase is repeated, they rest and during the healing crisis they shake. In talking to Parkinson's disease patients the shaking gets worse or better on a day to day basis.

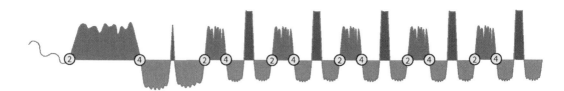

The involuntary shaking of patients who have Parkinson's disease is caused by the healing crisis being continuously repeated during the day. The shaking stops during deep rest and sleep - the regeneration phase.

The stress phase occurs, which can be short, and after a lull the shaking starts again. Sometimes, if the stress phase has been intense, the healing crisis will be more intense and therefore the shaking more violent. The healing crisis repeats itself over and over again. This is because the client has gone over the tracks of the problem, time and time again, maybe for several years. The relay becomes scarred and the person gets stuck in a repeat of the healing crisis.

Epileptic Fits

With repeated healing crisis a person can have regular epileptic fits, as with the diagram below: -

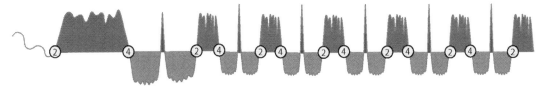

In both Parkinson's disease and with epileptic fits, we can see that there is an association that keeps the issue ongoing; it is being triggered every day or, in some instances, many times a day as I have already mentioned. That association can be the look of a person, the tone of their voice, or a place (such as work). This reminds the body of the original conflict shock at the unconscious level, therefore causing the body to go through an ongoing repetitive healing.

What I have found interesting regarding this phenomenon is that you can predict when a person is going to go through the healing crisis.

The healing crisis is often half way into the regeneration phase, it can vary dependant on water storage in the body. However as a rule of thumb the length of the regeneration phase is the same as the stress phase. So if you know that the stress phase has been active for two weeks, you therefore know that in this example the regeneration phase will also be active for two weeks. The healing crisis will then appear one week into the regeneration phase.

I have found these timings to be incredibly accurate; they allow us to predict when the healing crisis will appear and also what the symptoms will be.

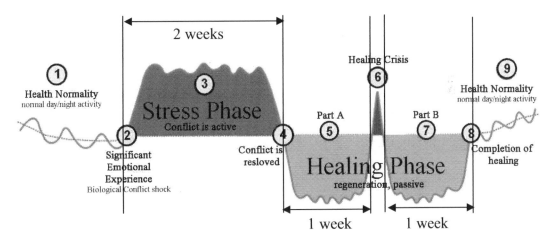

As an example, I worked with a woman who had an ear infection. She had come to see me concerning another problem but the infection was really bothering her and she wanted to know why it was there. She told me that she had had a headache the day before. I enquired as to what time she had got the headache. She replied that it had started at 11.00 a.m. Then I asked her what time it had gone. She told me it had disappeared in the afternoon and that she had not taken any headache pills. She explained that she felt very anxious and out of sorts during that time. She also told me the time when the earache started.

Knowing that the pain happens at point 4, the start of the regeneration phase, conflict resolution, I worked backwards and asked her what had been going on at 12.00 noon on the Sunday. She proceeded to tell me that she had been out clubbing with a friend and her friend had said something that completely shocked her and caught her off guard at 12.00 noon. Her whole face lit up with rage as I asked her what exactly had been said. She could remember the tone of her friend's voice, saying they were no longer 'spring chickens' and that they were too old to be out clubbing anymore. She was single and in her early thirties and, although still a beautiful person in my eyes, she felt she was in competition with younger girls when it came to finding a mate. As her friend had been telling her this, the earache had disappeared. This was something she had not wanted to hear, she knew it deep down but she had been denying it to herself.

I then asked her what had happened a week later (the conflict resolution, Point 4) she told me that she had been out again with her friend, and she had apologised. "What do you remember thinking at 11.00 a.m. the previous day?" She told me that she made a decision that she would stop looking for a man in night clubs and would instead find situations that were more befitting her age to find someone, such as dinner parties, or social engagements. I then worked out exactly how much longer the earache would last and sure enough, she called a few days later and said that ache had healed completely.

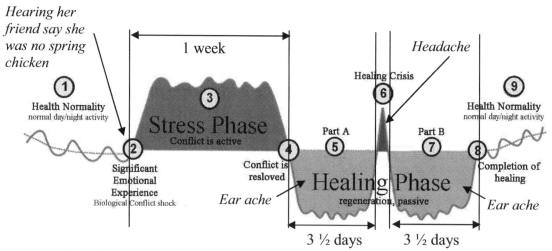

I mentioned in an earlier chapter how I once had a bout of diarrhoea just before delivering a course. From all the information and the times, I worked out what the conflict shock was that had caused the issue to occur.

Knowing why the diarrhoea had occurred was very liberating. I had a meeting with my PR agent which I attended at 4.00 p.m. in the afternoon. I explained to him that I had had a problem and he said, "Oh, was it something you ate?" See the next page for a diagramme of the whole process.

This is where it becomes interesting. The food that we eat and our surroundings have millions of bacteria everywhere. We cannot get away from them even if we bleach our whole environment into oblivion. Products are even sold to us with these so-called healthy bacteria in them. These digest our food, turning it into the energy which we use.

Then the question is - could our bodies use bacteria to clean up after the body has grown extra cells? Could they assist our bodies to rebuild cells after they have been used to deal with the ongoing stress that we have been dealing with? The Herx reaction confirms this is possible.

This is interesting because the body will use the bacteria that it can get from the surrounding environment. So technically it could be something I ate, or more likely the bacteria was already present in my system, bacteria that had been living in symbiosis with my body since I was born. My wife, Kristin, and I had eaten exactly the same food for the past week and she had had no ill effects whatsoever. How microbes work in symbiosis with us is so fascinating that I have added a whole chapter about their involvement in our healing. See chapter 10.

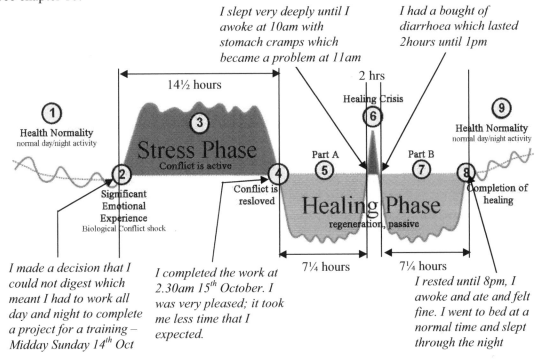

So the answer to his question "Was it something I ate", implying the previous day, was "No probably not". But the real cause of the issue was the indigestible decision I had made, which meant annoyingly that I had to take a whole day, or potentially more out of my life, transcribing some very difficult recordings to complete a project. I had been working on the project for over two weeks and I just wanted it finished. It was dragging on and on. I had expected it to be done well before this time and I was panicking because I needed this material for a five-day training seminar, which I was going to be delivering starting on the Wednesday. The time it was taking was really frustrating me, hence the decision that I did not want to digest - to just work day and night to complete it.

The amazing thing about understanding the symptoms and why they are there, together with knowing how long the cycles are going to take, causes you to relax and just go through the process. In the past I have blamed the person who had cooked a meal for me, believing it to be the food that had been contaminated to be the cause of my issue or because of how the food had been prepared. Now I know that if I get diarrhoea it must have been caused by a stressful indigestible event beforehand, and my body naturally uses bacteria to heal itself. Knowing this I can relax, and let my body do what it needs to do, without resorting to drugs or causing myself further stress by obsessing about the food or the preparation of it. Plus, what I have found is if I let the whole cycle take its course, then it is over quicker and faster than if I obsess and resort to 'over the counter' drugs.

However, just understanding the symptoms and the healing crisis does not mean that this time is not life-threatening in certain instances. Emergency medicine is brilliant at dealing with the effects of the healing crisis.

We can see this in the diagram below. Here we have the two phases. There are times when, during these phases, the issue can become dangerous and the patient needs immediate medical care. In the first phase we can become so stressed that we may have a panic attack or we become violent and dangerous to others. I had a client whose complications stemmed from the fact that she had not slept for over 40 days. Such imbalances in the brain are common, especially with people with mental health disorders. In the second phase the issue can represent itself when we dip too low into the second phase. This could result in a person going into a coma or organs shutting down.

As regards life threatening issues in the healing crisis, we can see in the diagram here where such instances may need immediate medical attention. These may be issues such as a violent fit that does not subside after a few minutes, a stroke where the blood vessels in the brain are damaged by the effects of the healing crisis, causing blood to flow into brain cavities, and damaging other parts of the brain, resulting in brain damage.

There have been instances where the size of the resulting Glial cells (brain repairing cells) that form in the second phase in the brain relays can swell so much with water that this can cause pressure in the brain, resulting in the ventricles, which regulate fluid in the brain, becoming blocked. This causes hydro-encephalitis. The resulting issue can cause extensive brain damage or even death if not seen to immediately. Other serious results of the healing issue may be: A heart attack; extreme diarrhoea (where the person dehydrates due to the loss of so much liquid); and bursting of vessels in the body (this can also affect other organs, having life-threatening consequences, such as a bowel splitting, resulting in poisoning).

There are many things that can go wrong in the healing crisis and emergency medicine is designed to deal with such complications. I am certain you can appreciate how important emergency care is when dealing with such issues.

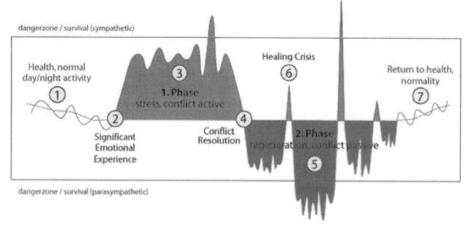

Knowing when to go to a hospital for emergency care and when not to, is a tricky question. I always err on the side of caution, getting advice from a doctor in the first place and then going to Accident and Emergency or Emergency Rescue if required. See the diagram above on when danger zone has been reached and emergency care is required.

It is always important to check the drugs that you are expected to take in the long term after going to Accident and Emergency, because these can stop the completion of the disease cycle (Part B). In fact, many long-term medical interventions may unnecessarily cause further pain and grief.

These drugs actually keep the body under stress, pushing the person back into the first stress phase. The net result is that as soon as you reduce or stop the drug, the person goes back into the regeneration phase, into Part A and then through to the healing crisis again with all the ensuing symptoms that result from the healing crisis.

Take, as an example, anti-epileptic drug treatments. Epilepsy is caused by brain cramping during the healing crisis, often associated with the middle brain which controls our muscles. The Anti-Epileptic Drugs (AEDs) are known not to cure the problem. They are used to prevent seizures from happening but are not used to stop seizures. Some people may not get complete control of their epilepsy from these drugs, others will. These drugs can have side effects. I believe this may be due to the body wanting to complete the cycle naturally. The drugs would artificially keep the person from doing this.

This may sound as if I disagree with drug treatments. That is not the case. Without many drugs, people could die or their lives could become severely hampered. My interest is for you, as the reader, to understand what these drugs are doing in the disease cycle so that you have extra knowledge and can research (via the internet) what each drug does and to give you some idea about their side effects. Sometimes the cocktail of drugs can be more debilitating and more stressful than the original problem. It can even cause death in certain instances.

Death can be caused by the doctors being unaware that there is a disease cycle. Again, I am going to say that you need to get advice from a knowledgeable medical practitioner regarding any changes to drugs you may be taking. Some side effects from reducing or stopping certain drugs can be horrendous. Careful management is required if you choose to go down this path. (Note: Check your insurance policies regarding travelling if you change drug regimes, some companies will not allow you to travel for a few months if you change drugs.) Some medical practitioners are excellent at working with a client to do this, others are not. Remember that you are likely to experience certain symptoms akin to the healing crisis as you go through the second phase.

Reducing the number of drugs a person takes needs to be discussed with a qualified medical practitioner but it does not need to be your present practitioner. Advice concerning reviewing the combination of what you are taking is vital, as doctors can't possibly know how every drug will be affected by another drug. I saw an American who was taking as many as nine different drugs, be reduced to five by a Cuban doctor. (See the movie 'Sicko' by Michael Moore.) As an example regarding Anti-Epileptic Drugs: Not all of them work well for every client, some combinations work better than others. Every woman who has taken 'The Pill' can probably relate to this. I know of women who have suffered for years from the effects of one pill. When they do change to another doctor who reviewed the pill they were taking, the problem disappeared.

Anti-Epileptic drugs cause a person to stay in the stress phase (Point 3). Some of the drugs which are prescribed for heart conditions can also do this. The simple use of small amounts of Aspirin (30mgs) has the effect of continually keeping the person in a minor state of stress. My father-in-law takes this drug. He lives in a continually stressed state which can be really taxing for those people around him, as I have experienced. Most people who work in stressful jobs live like this anyway, so the body can cope with this ongoing stress.

Continually drinking coffee, smoking and working in a fast moving job have the same effect. Our body can take this stress but it does need to repair itself, hence the reason why people often find themselves unwell as soon as they slow down at weekends or on holiday. I know of people who get terrible sneezing fits, have insomnia for a few hours at night as soon as the weekend arrives or they have minor bouts of diarrhoea. All of these are symptoms of the healing crisis. Dr Anton Bader explained to me that the body can survive on forty percent of its optimum functionality. This explains how people can abuse their bodies for years but as soon as they stop, they get really ill and some end up in accident and emergency. As an extreme example - people who retire from high pressure jobs sometimes have a heart attack (the healing crisis of the coronary or pulmonary arteries and veins). The worst is the pulmonary embolism or the silent killer, as there are often very few symptoms that let a person know that they have a problem.

Let me explain what happens in an issue with the heart in more detail. From a META-Medicine® point of view, there are three types of heart attacks. The first is caused by the healing crisis of the myocardium, (the cardiac muscle of the heart) called a myocardial infarction. The reaction is the same as a muscle in the body and is linked to middle brain, the grey matter (cerebral medulla). During the healing crisis the muscle (heart) cramps and sometimes stops. It can be started again using a defibrillator as is sometimes shown in Emergency Rescue or Accident and Emergency programmes. The original stressful cause is the person feeling overwhelmed. Once the heart has been restarted then the person normally returns to full health. The heart muscle is rarely damaged but like any normal muscle that is healing, it will look different and under a biopsy will look diseased, although it is just in a repair state.

The other two issues are related to the coronary or pulmonary arteries and veins. The cause of the heart attack is due to a territorial fear conflict for males or a sexual frustration conflict for females. The arteries or veins in the first stress phase go through a cell reduction and the inner lining of the cell wall becomes thinner. After the resolution of the conflict the arteries/veins then rebuild. Hence the cell wall gets thicker. This is what we call heart disease. This build-up is a plaque called cholesterol. If the length of the first phase continues for many months and is very intense, then the build-up of plaque in the arteries or veins can be so great that it restricts the blood flow to the muscles, which means that the muscle does not get enough blood which is noticed during exercise or intense activity.

Halfway through the second phase, the arteries or veins go through a healing crisis. The plaque that has built up on the inside is shed and it then passes through the blood stream and is processed by the liver.

However, if this plaque build-up has been large, this plaque breaks away forming a blood clot which can block the blood getting to the heart muscles. This results in a heart attack, causing part of those muscles to die. If too much muscle is affected then the heart will stop pumping and the person will die. Trying to restart the heart in this instance is futile since the muscle is already damaged beyond repair.

In nature we see this in deer. A stag that loses his harem to a younger stag in a fight will then go and find another harem. If he is unsuccessful, he is deemed no longer worthy of maintaining a herd, and is therefore useless. The territory is lost, the stag will then go into regeneration and during the healing crisis the heart attack will be fatal.

This happens in people in a similar way. If our territory is invaded and we no longer have a territory to maintain then the ensuing second phase will be fatal, if the length of time has been almost a year. Take, for example, people who retire, having had a high-powered job. They come into a household where the woman runs the house. She is the boss (especially

94

after the menopause, which makes a woman react more territorially). Then the fight is on. If he loses, he will either find another mate or will have a heart attack.

There are other factors too that can cause heart attacks. People who go into stressful jobs, where their territory is continuously invaded and work pressures are intense, are more likely to develop heart disease. The combination of this together with certain foods and habits is also likely to lead to heart disease. Foods that contain highly saturated fats, excessive sugar and refined carbohydrates and habits such as smoking and excessive drinking (which these people tend to do because this keeps the body in the first phase and therefore stressed) can accelerate this process. It is no wonder that these people are more prone to heart disease than others. As they relax and go into the second phase the body deposits plaque on the interior walls of the arteries or veins. If you keep repeating this then the plaque builds up and the heart muscles receive less oxygen, resulting in ongoing issues. The medical solution is a bypass where blood vessels are taken, usually from the leg, to replace the vessels that are full of plaque. It works very well and many people are still alive because of this operation.

However, contrary to belief, the cause of the disease is territorial in men and social in women, not the bad foods, alcoholic drinks, lack of exercise or smoking a person does. Although these stress-related habits do go on to make the whole situation worse, they are not the cause of the heart disease. The cause is the build-up of plaque in the second phase - high cholesterol is a result of a stressful event. This explains why completely healthy people can develop heart disease - people who don't smoke (and never have), who have really good-quality diets, who do not drink and who exercise regularly. It also explains why some people who do the total opposite live to a ripe old age with no heart problems. The real killer is the shock which causes the disease process in the first place and us not dealing with it, or not allowing ourselves the appropriate time and space to fully recuperate. Recognising we are in the stress phase is the key.

However, we often don't know that we are in a stress phase or that there might be the potential for a serious issue to occur. In the stress phase we feel fine - no aches, no pains, no infections and we have the sharpness to deal with problems. Dr Kwesi Anan Odum said to me that as a runner, he would run so much better after an argument with his wife, especially one that dragged on for weeks. This also explains why we need to look after ourselves when it comes to eating healthily and exercising regularly. What is not mentioned is the need to spend time relaxing and taking time out for oneself, as every alternative and complementary practitioner would intuitively tell you. Sports therapists worked this out years ago; the body needs time to heal after intensive exercise. Time off to let your body heal is as important as the time you put into training.

The reason we need to relax, and I mean really to take time out to heal, is simple. If you keep putting your body under continuous strain it will eventually need to heal itself anyway. The other problem that occurs in these instances is that if your body is continuously kept under this amount of ongoing pressure, the chances of reacting to a minor problem in a major way is increased. Just think about how you react to things when you are lacking sleep compared to when you have had enough sleep.

However, the opposite to being caught in the first phase (point 3) stress can occur and we can find ourselves in the ongoing cycle of the second phase with a repetitive healing crisis. Take for example Myalgic Encephalomyelitis - ME or Chronic Fatigue Syndrome (often referred to as 'Yuppy Flu' in the 1980's-1990's). In Britain there was a boom - up and coming people young would work every hour they could in order to earn as much money as possible. We called it 'Thatcher's Britain' after Margaret Thatcher whose slogan was "Put Britain back to work.'

What happened was that many of these people would find themselves getting very unwell, with the stress of work, intense marriages, high mortgages and ongoing changes in social and environment situations - the need to succeed, at all costs was immense. Every Chronic Fatigue client that I have worked with has told me they became unwell after an illness, often a bout of flu. During the healing crisis of the illness, the person goes through another conflict shock. This then gets associated to the whole process and the person tracks continuously through the second half of the disease process. This is what we call a 'hanging healing'.

Let me explain. A client with Chronic Fatigue came to see me. He had had the issue for over four years. Luckily for him he had an insurance policy that paid him reasonably well even though he was not working.

His issue occurred when, after moving from a house where the next door neighbour had been aggressive and violent towards him and his family, he had a bronchial viral infection, resulting in him being laid up in bed with influenza symptoms.

During the healing crisis, when he started to feel a little better, his wife accused him of merely having 'Man Flu', not influenza. This really shocked him. It was unexpected, dramatic, isolating and he had no strategy for dealing with his wife's behaviour. Subsequently her face and voice became associated to the disease process right at the healing crisis point. ('Man Flu' is a term used to describe how a man reacts when they get a common cold. Incidentally, many women tend not to suffer in the same way as men, because many women react with laryngeal issues instead of bronchial issues).

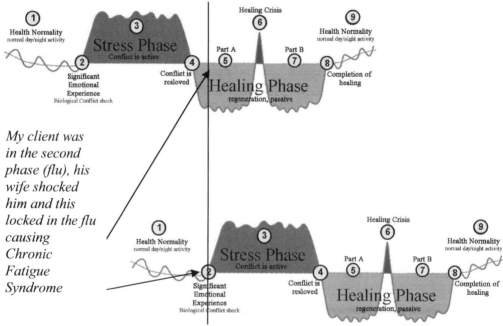

My client was in the second phase (flu), his wife shocked him and this locked in the flu causing Chronic Fatigue Syndrome

This started another disease process to occur. So he was in the stressed phase of the new disease process *and* the regeneration phase of the flu disease process. Let's run the process: Now as he goes into PART B (Point 7) of the flu process he feels tired and has no energy. It is not as bad as PART A but he still needs to recuperate. He is also stressed from the new shock caused by his wife's comments so again, although he is in the process of completing the flu, he has a combination of stress and illness all at the same time. So he is awake but he has no energy. Given time this process would normally complete but when you add the trigger of his wife's face and voice putting him back into the stress phase daily you can see how the whole process keeps going around and around. He told me that he feels stressed when his wife is around, and when she is not there he feels exhausted.

One of the major complaints coming from Chronic Fatigue clients is that they don't sleep very well. My client slept erratically, and dreamt a tremendous amount. He told me he would often wake up feeling more exhausted than he did before he went to bed. Here the healing crisis is at work. During the day he would be going through the second part of the second phase (PART B, Point 7). Then his wife would trigger off the second conflict, by looking at him or saying something to him. The net result was that he would feel stressed. Then she would go to work and he would end up with no energy as he went into PART B again of the second phase - a combination of a deep second phase (Part B) and a minor stress phase of the issue with his wife. Then, when he went to bed, the healing crisis would repeat itself continuously causing restless sleep and would result in him feeling exhausted upon waking up. The whole cycle would repeat itself day and night over and over again - a hanging healing.

I only realised that his wife was a trigger after spending some time with him. He would work with me and feel great, this would last all day until he saw his wife again. He would have loads of energy for hours on end, but as soon as he met up with his wife, the whole cycle would start again. When he was not reminded of his wife and things that he associated with her, the track was not being triggered. Hence, the energy changes.

I met his wife. She was lovely but very, very sceptical of anything that was not traditional medicine. She had no idea that she was triggering off the issue and, unfortunately, she did not agree with my prognosis. My client recognised how the disease process worked, and I worked with him, teaching him to remove the associations. He did some great work in clearing out the problem with his wife. He then went into a full-blown second phase where he had mild pneumonia, only to tell me he was given antibiotics. The antibiotics probably slowed down his recovery but he is now on the mend and doing voluntary work three days a week. He tells me that he is feeling much better, though not totally on form. The pneumonia would probably have been a repeat of the original symptoms, since he said that it had occurred after he resolved everything in his mind that had to do with his wife.

The reason why he has not fully recovered is this: There is one slight problem that occurs with people like my client - he has a secondary motivation for not becoming fully well. Imagine if you hate your job and there is no incentive for you to get back to it, you have a new son with whom you could spend every hour as he grows up and you are being paid more than you were before you became ill. What motivation is there then to become fully well? My client's motivation to get back to work is marginal. He loves spending time with his child, and if he makes a full recovery he will have to go back to a full time job which he hates. His wife loves him being home too, as she has no child care issues and the housework and meals are done by my client.

The body and the unconscious mind are intelligent and the way the mind/body works is designed to allow us to follow the path of least resistance. You know how hard it is to stop a habit - something you enjoy in the moment of indulgence, even though you know it is bad for you in the long term, e.g. smoking, recreational drugs, cream cakes etc. We therefore have to put a lot of energy into changing old established patterns. Most Chronic Fatigue sufferers do eventually come out of their patterns but it takes something pretty major to shake them out of their comfort zone back into reality. Usually it is a change in environmental or social circumstances that removes the triggers from the person, stopping the hanging healing.

There can also be other factors involved that can stop a person from returning to health. These can revolve around the overall energy of the person being inhibited by other erroneous factors, the main ones being toxicity and parasites. In this instance again the body is being held in a hanging healing. Parasites and toxicity can all be eliminated from the body, but it takes energy to do so. If you are in a second phase, all the energy is being directed towards healing the main issue. Parasites need energy to live, so they take it away from the host, causing the whole system to be out of balance.

In this chapter we have discussed the healing crisis in depth. This strange 'spike,' is thought to be a biological test, and the point where water together with cells and bacteria used to heal the stressed tissue from the first phase, are eliminated not only from the organ but also from the affected brain relay. This 'spike' explains the symptoms of many diseases, why there are complications, and why drugs often cannot cure these healing crisis problems. The healing crisis is responsible for so much pain and so much anguish, but the truth is we now know why it is there and, with enough information, we can predict when it is likely to occur. We have now turned a disease, from being static, into a moving process that someone goes through. This is the difference between owning a disease and running a disease process. A person is not their disease! It does not define them. The disease is rather a 'lower level' function, a process that they go through.

With this process and the healing crisis being part of that, we can educate the client and explain why these things are happening. Or we plan when to get the client into hospital so that they are given the necessary emergency care, if we feel the result of the healing crisis could be life threatening. It also explains why people suffer from certain types of reoccurring symptoms, such as migraines or epileptic fits, and why some diseases are left just 'hanging' like Parkinson's, as was the case with John, mentioned earlier. When I asked him "what did your wife say to you in summer 2000 that caught you completely off-guard, something to do with children and not being able to bring them close to you?" John said that she told to him that children were never going to happen; they were never going to have children and to stop even thinking about the possibility that she might change her mind. She was now too old and anyway, she did not want children. You can imagine how upsetting this was for my client, who had devoted his whole life to this woman only to be told that he would never have a child through her. He was devastated by this and he explained that he thought about what she said everyday.

On reflection John's Parkinson's was caused by the ongoing hanging healing. I was never able to help John as he did not really want to do the work to solve the underlying problem.

In the next chapter we will discuss the link between the brain and the organs. We will discover where a stressful event gets stuck in our brains and body, and why specific types of conflict affect us in different organs in differing ways. We are also going to look at what goes on in our brains and how there is an elegant system of relays that switch on and off in line with the two phases.

Chapter 9

Our brain – the biological relay switch and recorder of every disease

In proportion to our body mass, our brain is three times as large as that of our nearest relatives. This huge organ is dangerous and painful to give birth to, expensive to build and, in a resting human, uses about 20 per cent of the body's energy even though it is just 2 per cent of the body's weight. There must be some reason for all this evolutionary expense.
Susan Blakemore (from "Me, Myself, I", New Scientist, March 13, 1999)

"Our organism and diseases are not organized by symptoms, rather by organs and embryonic layers. Based on embryology and ontogenesis we can assign all organs to one of the three embryonic layers (from which our complete body has developed as an embryo). Each organ reacts based on its germ layer connection and the two phases of these organ reactions: cell and tissue plus or minus, over-activity or under-activity, loss of function or increase function."
One of the ten META-Medicine® Models

I have been fascinated by health for many years and have been introduced to many different disciplines in my time, but the thing that really amazed me with META-Medicine® was brain CT reading. Suddenly, here was an area previously limited to a few selected doctors, which allowed a trained individual to get an accurate picture of what was really medically going on inside a person. What is even more exciting is that this information is right under the noses of the medical profession, and they have been so blind that they could not see that the mind and body are connected. What follows, is a story about a brain CT reading, that helped a great friend of mine get her life back.

Birgitte's chronic lack of energy
I met Birgitte in Germany at a META-Medicine® Brain CT scan reading seminar. We hardly spoke but she seemed an interesting person. I then met her again in Norway, at the META-Medicine® Certification training where I was assisting Susanne Billander, another META-Medicine® trainer, in delivering a course.

One night during that course I sat down with Birgitte and a friend of hers, she seemed really tired but she said that she wanted to do an NLP course with me in the UK. Two months later she arrived in Bristol, very excited. On my course we spent a lot of time working through people's problems and they really got a chance to solve issues that had been plaguing them for years. Birgitte was no exception - she had 'a container load of crap' - her words not mine - that she was desperate to resolve.

What was different about Birgitte from the other delegates was that she knew a little about META-Medicine®, and she happened to have her brain CT scan with her.

Birgitte complained that she had 'absolutely no energy'. The only thing that kept her on her feet was strong will power. She told me that she was constantly tired, not sleepy. For example, not only would she fall asleep whilst feeding her young son, she would have to go to sleep after putting him to bed. She had researched and found out that she did not have chronic fatigue syndrome (Epstein Barr) or ME but she knew that something was not right. Birgitte also owns a renowned natural medicine clinic, along with two colleagues, in Bergen, Norway. Not only does she work at this unique clinic, but she has extensive training in complementary medicine and is a qualified Health Practitioner. She told me she had collected therapies in her search to recover from many issues, especially this ongoing tiredness which had been going on for four years.

Birgitte's story started when she was working on a cultural historical farm, where everything was done in the same way as it had been done in the 1940's, before the tractor arrived. She recounted how immensely fit she felt and how much energy she had. During this time she met and fell in love with someone ten years younger than her when she was twenty-seven. She became pregnant with him and, realising this pregnancy was not something she wanted to carry through, she decided to have an abortion. She said, "There was no mental or emotional worry in the decision not to have the child. It was never even a choice. It was okay to let this soul go, it was all done in love. There was no guilt in the decision." She tried all the natural ways she could to induce an abortion but being so fit and healthy, nothing worked. Eventually she went to a hospital to have a surgical abortion.

At the hospital she negotiated with the nurse not to be given the muscle relaxant (which is standard procedure for this type of operation), because she was trained in muscle control. The chief nurse spoke to her for twenty minutes and saw that Birgitte was capable of relaxing her body enough for the operation. She did however, have a local anaesthetic. Everything was fine until the female doctor started the procedure which involved a machine that sounded like a very loud vacuum cleaner and involved a barbaric cutting motion. On recounting the shock that happened at that time, she told me she was thinking "Oh my God! This is brutal! What do I do? I knew I could not do anything because I could not move. I could have said something but I did not. I could not think straight."

All the blood went from her head. She kept thinking 'I cannot move because the doctor has a knife inside me and I will get hurt.' She recounted 'I can't pass out or faint because this was the decision I made, I went all into my head.' After the experience, she just suppressed the whole thing. She got back in shape very quickly, and had been told she would bleed for two weeks but she only bled for three hours. She was fine. She went back to work on the farm, then went for a four week holiday on her own to Thailand. Everything was good, until she came back from the holiday to find that the flat she was living in was getting over crowded with males in what was her 'female territory'. Disliking this, she found another flat where she could be on her own.

As she was moving in she noticed a dull ache in her kidneys. Realising this could be more than a minor problem; she dropped everything and went to see a doctor friend who is also a Health Practitioner. The doctor told her it was a renal pelvis infection. She felt safe as she healed with a very high fever and a horrendous pain, a sharp pain in the kidneys, like a knife that was constantly there. Later on she found out that she was passing kidney stones. She moved in with her mother during these five weeks. She can remember that the two and a half weeks into the healing crisis, the pain disappeared and she thought she was getting well only to seemingly relapse into another two and a half weeks of high fever and pain but where she peed a lot more. (This was a healing crisis).

In the last stages of her healing, her boyfriend came to see her and told her that she could now no longer have the flat she had been moving into and that there was nowhere else for her to live on the farm. This was another shock and she now felt that she had nowhere to go. After being told this, she went into a deep depression that resulted in her staying more or less in bed for a month and a half. The only person she saw during this time was her boyfriend and she became pregnant again. Together they made the decision to keep this baby. Still depressed, she had the child thinking it would solve the depression but instead she felt trapped, more imprisoned and she could not get out of this horrible state.

Eventually she moved in with her boyfriend and, for three and a half years, she battled with the depression and, although she deeply loved her boyfriend, he could no longer deal with her issues and eventually they split up. Unexpectedly the depression lifted at this time but the lack of energy she had been experiencing got worse.

She would sleep at every opportunity; if her son fell asleep in the car she would pull over and sleep too. Amazingly she bought the 'Vital Natur Therapi' Clinic in Bergen during this time. While this was going on, the previous owner tried ever therapy they had to assist her recovery. She had already tried several therapies previously but with little or no change in her symptoms.

Buying the clinic was a wise move from one point of view and a burden from another. Wise because she came across META-Medicine® and through that was able to meet me. However it was a burden because she then felt even more trapped.

She recounted, from when we first talked at the Oslo META-Medicine® training, how I mentioned that my NLP courses were 'all about transformation'. This was the magic sentence that caused her ears to prick up and listen, she recalled. Although during most of this conversation she told me that she had been half asleep.

If you had met Birgitte you would have no idea that she was suffering in this way. On reflection I do remember her sleeping during the trainings. I thought she had been burning the candle at both ends, but she told me later that this behaviour was normal for her - as I said before she had eliminated Chronic Fatigue Syndrome and ME (Epstein Barr). She had flown to Oslo to see special practitioners to try to solve her problem. She had spent a lot of money to get herself back to where she was before all of this started but nothing helped.

During the NLP course we did the normal set of interventions, but they were having no effect on Birgitte's issues. I noticed that she was sleepy and was finding it difficult to pay attention in the class. It was then she told me about her sleep problems and, knowing she had attended the brain CT seminar, I asked her if she had brought her brain CT with her. To her amazement it was still in her bag from that training.

I opened up the CT and started to read it. I started from the base of the brain slices where the brain stem is. Here we find our digestive organs, through the cerebellum where the breast glands and thick leathery skins that protect us are. Up towards the grey matter, the Medulla, which holds our muscles and skeleton together, to the white matter, the cortex, the social/territorial part of our brain, the place that makes us human.

As I travelled up through Birgitte's brain CT, I was reading small ring markings that I knew related to specific organs in the body. I was able to tell her about her old digestive issue whereupon she explained that she had had a problem due to a friend of hers having gone mad and disappearing for weeks.

The most dramatic thing I found that made complete sense to Birgitte was when I asked her if she had a problem with her thyroid. She replied that she didn't. Then I showed her how the area in the front left hand side of the brain in the cortex area had a speckled ring, which meant that this was in the second phase and that it was a hanging healing. I explained that the symptoms of such an issue were a lack of energy and always feeling tired. Some people might call this disease Chronic Fatigue Syndrome or ME (Epstein Barr). She looked at me in total surprise.

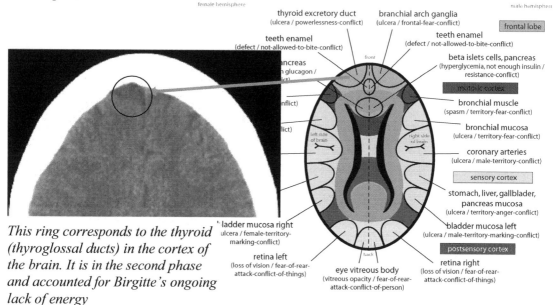

This ring corresponds to the thyroid (thyroglossal ducts) in the cortex of the brain. It is in the second phase and accounted for Birgitte's ongoing lack of energy

She then explained her symptoms to me in depth, whereupon I told her that they seem to fit the symptoms of someone with an underactive thyroid. She was astounded. I went on to explain that we could clear the event that caused the issue to occur in the first place and doing that would mean the thyroid would heal itself, her sleepiness would disappear and her life would return to normal. The stressful event conflict that caused the thyroid to react in this way was a powerless conflict.

To explain what a powerless conflict is - imagine a hairdresser who starts a new job in a new salon. Her livelihood relies on grabbing any new customers that come through the door. Then just suppose that a new, younger, keener hairdresser arrives at the salon a few weeks later. This new girl starts to take all those new customers that the older woman was relying on. This could shock and financially threaten the first woman because she would feel powerless to react. At this time a relay switches on in the brain on the front left hand side of the white matter in the cortex. This relay relates to the thyroid excretory ducts which then become bigger, therefore allowing the two thyroid gland hormones to be released into the system so that they can flow faster into the blood stream. These two hormones thyroxin and triiodothyronine regulate the metabolism in a person (basically how quickly a person burns energy and makes proteins).

The overall effect of this widening of the ducts allows the person to react faster so they can deal with whatever it is that they feel powerless against. In this instance with the extra thyroxin in her system the woman is able to compete at getting new customers who enter the salon. Once the stress resolves itself, e.g. the younger girl leaves, then the ducts need to repair themselves and it is then that the ducts get smaller; allowing less of the thyroid hormones into the blood stream, and less thyroid hormone means less energy.

This was where Birgitte was - stuck in the second phase. She was not depressed anymore but she could not go anywhere. She was continuously triggering off the pattern as a hanging healing, never completing the healing crisis test and forever looping backwards and forwards into the regeneration phase. After reading the CT I asked her to put together a history of her medical issues. That evening she wrote four pages of notes and, from reading what she had written, she worked out what had caused the issue to occur. The next day we used Time Line Therapy® and NLP to resolve the trapped emotion on the point of the abortion where she felt powerless; listening to the machine as the doctor brutally removed the foetus.

The mind body connection and the medical profession

Is there a mind-body connection? Could the medical profession be missing one of the most obvious links there is to disease by focussing only on biochemistry to heal people?

It may or may not be obvious, but when we think, there is no doubt that there is a massive amount of biochemistry going on. Neuro peptides rush through the mind and the body telling us to react in a specific way. This is well understood scientifically and the simple proof of this biochemical reaction and connection is the effect that a positive or negative thought has on a person's body posture, breathing or blood chemistry.

Proof of this is simple; let us use depression as an example. Depression affects a person's blood chemistry in the form of lowering the amount of serotonin in the brain and the body, which in turn affects the breathing and body posture. A depressed person will look at the world, act, walk and talk very differently from when they are not depressed. Their energy also changes when they are depressed - depressed people tend to spend a lot of time doing nothing and nothing seems to interest them.[54]

We can see the effects of lifting this depression by the use of a drug such as Prozac, the first anti-depression drug of its class www.prozac.com. Within three weeks of taking the drug most depressed people find themselves out of this horrendous state.

Even if the drug is designed to do something completely different, such as a beta-blocker (used to reduce high blood pressure) it can have a massive shift in our way of thinking. The wife of a good friend of mine noticed the immediate effect of stopping her beta-blockers - under medical supervision - having taken them for four years. Taking the drugs practically ruined their marriage. She is on another drug (not a beta-blocker) and they are slowly getting back to where they were. Interestingly my friend says that his wife has no recollection as to how bad she was but her life has definitely changed for the better.

Therefore I think it is safe to say that what we think is linked to our bio-chemistry which is in turn linked to our emotions, and vice versa. What I am saying here is neither radical nor new, although I find it strange that the medical profession still do not acknowledge this blatantly obvious mind/body connection.

Energy and the medical profession

Another area that the medical profession conveniently ignore is energy, even though the existence of energy can easily be proven. You may remember from chemistry lessons in school that during a chemical reaction heat is emitted, and that heat is energy. Consider our neural pathways; they use electrical energy to communicate throughout the mind and the body, switching on nerve impulses which in turn cause neurotransmitters to be released into our system which is a chemical reaction, therefore heat is produced.

We cannot see nerve electrical energy but it is the same transference of energy that we use to power an electric light bulb, admittedly with less current flowing through it. So I believe it is safe to say that when we think, we produce heat energy changes, which fire off electrical energy changes along with biochemical reactions, resulting in changes throughout the whole mind and the body. Electrical waves are also responsible for considerable changes in the mind and body which the medical profession has partly ignored although, to a degree, they have been using them for decades.

It is not difficult to prove that electrical waves surround us, our brains and organs, and that we receive and emit electrical waves. Consider the non-invasive use of electro-encephalograph (EEG) that measures brain waves or electrocardiograph (ECG) that measures heart waves, thereby proving that we emit waves through changes in our thinking. We can also stimulate muscles using non-invasive techniques. A machine called 'TENS', which involves placing pads on the skin instead of needles in the body, can be used to show that we can receive electrical waves. This machine is inexpensive and easily obtainable worldwide.

Some interesting experiments carried out by scientists confirm the fact that we produce electrical waves. They invented a skull cap which contained an array of 64 electrodes. Using special computer algorithms, they demonstrated how people could control a cursor on a computer screen using only thought.[55]

I think we can therefore assume that the brain and organs emit and receive electrical information which, in turn, creates a field around them. This information is emitted and received via the nerves, which are embedded in every part of our body and every organ. As soon as an electrical current is passed through a wire, an electrical field is produced - this field is thought to interact with everything around and inside you. Recent research by Professor Peter Fraser has shown that the heart links to the brain and the nervous system, and the work of other people and organisations such as the Heart Math Institute support his findings.[56] The heart seems to contain sixty-five to seventy-five percent neuronal cells. It seems that as the heart beats it is communicating with the blood passing through it, imprinting information which in turn emits an electrical wave and changes the biochemistry in our minds and our bodies.

The fact that we create an electrical field around us is nothing new - police helicopters use specially designed cameras to track down thieves using this principle.

I am mentioning all of this because I want to prove that there is a connection between the mind and body and that thoughts change our energy. Emotions are thoughts and these also change our state - our biochemistry. All of these seemingly separate elements that make us what we are, are not separate, they are totally integrated.

Thinking, emotions and disease

Why this is so important is because the medical profession have separated thinking, and therefore emotions, from disease. If they believed that a thought was connected to the way the body reacted, then they would reconsider the effect a medical diagnosis has on a person, especially one with such implications as a diagnosis of cancer. It is not only the doctors that need to be wary of this, alternative and complementary practitioners do as well. During a diagnosis of any kind, the person is at a heightened state of awareness and this can have a dramatic affect on how a person perceives what they have been told. People are in a trance state and when they are told a horrific or challenging diagnosis, they can and often do go into shock.

Medical doctors and complementary, alternative practitioners all need to look at the wealth of literature that backs up the fact that stress causes disease. They then need to consider which stressful event causes which specific disease.

Looking specifically at modern medicine, we find that research is reductionist in nature. The researchers do not look at the mind and the body, they look at an individual cell and dismantle it, rip it apart in order to find out what is going wrong inside a diseased cell. Then they develop drugs that alter the chemistry in this single cell, therefore repairing or destroying the constitution of the diseased cell. Remember, the researchers work with diseased cells in isolation, omitting the environment and the mental state of a person.

If you disagree with my thinking just consider what effect chemotherapy has on any replicating cell: No consideration is given to side effects since, from a reductionist viewpoint, side effects are an inconvenient by-product. No consideration is given to the person's state of the mind, since the theory is that the chemotherapy drugs only destroy the cancer cells, but as any cancer patient who has had chemotherapy will tell you, the side effects are horrendous. Physical side effects of chemotherapy often cause patients to lose their hair, together with cells that are replicating. The psychological side effects cause loss of self-esteem, mood shifts, irritability, depression, low sex drive and changes in how the patient thinks about him or herself as a person. Even taste and smell changes whilst taking these drugs, not to mention the immense nausea regularly reported to be felt by clients.[57]

Post Traumatic Stress Disorder (PTSD) and diseases

As a person goes through an Unexpected, Dramatic, Isolating conflict shock where they have No strategy (UDIN) to deal with the information, the effect of the emotion that occurs gets trapped in the system as I mentioned in Chapter 8. We can easily prove that emotions get stored in our neurological system. Just think of a happy event from the past, and for most people the emotions reappear. They are in there somewhere and they are often easily accessible. With a UDIN the emotion gets trapped in the system. Research carried out in the United States at Duke University's Centre for Cognitive Neuroscience, Department of Psychological and Brain Sciences, and Brain Imaging and Analysis Centre in 2005 found that people who have experienced a traumatic event get trapped in a cycle of emotion and recall. Post Traumatic Stress Disorder (PTSD) was specifically looked at.

My premise and experience from working with clients is such that the effects of a UDIN have the same reaction as a person who has experienced Post Traumatic Stress Disorder. In essence they are very similar, if not the same. The types of events that affect such people with PTSD are horrendous - accidents, war events or horrific fires. Many of the people who suffer from this type of psychological disorder are soldiers, paramedics and firemen.

By using Functional Magnetic Resonance Imaging (fMRI), which is a relatively new and complex imaging machine that uses magnetism and radio waves to allow us to see inside the body, researchers were able to establish that as a person reassesses the memories of a horrific event, it shows up in the brain. More specifically, in the area for processing emotional memories - the Amygdala and the Hippocampus. These events were trapped and the pictures and emotions were caught in a continuous loop. What was different about this research was the time delay that the researcher used to assess their clients recall. In previous experiments the time difference had only been minutes but in using fMRI the time difference was a year.[58]

Why this is significant for us in META-Medicine® is that people suffering from PTSD are affected mentally and physically by the event that shocked them. They not only have severe psychological changes but are found to suffer from heart-related problems, respiratory system-related problems, digestive problems, reproductive system-related problems, diabetes, arthritis and pain.

What I am postulating is that there seems to be a direct, provable scientific link between a specific stressful event and specific diseases.

Not surprisingly from a META-Medicine® point of view, the medical interpretation of the known causes for these diseases appearing in people with PTSD is not known. They postulate that the stress these people go through affects the body increasing the risk of problems and illness.[59]

Disease and conflicts related to PTSD

In order for you the reader to understand the types of conflicts to which each disease is related, from a META-Medicine® point of view, I have listed them here:

Coronary heart disease (both the coronary veins and arteries);
Male territorial conflict. PTSD will not affect females in the veins or arteries. This conflict affects women as a female sexual frustration conflict.

Respiratory system related problems - bronchial and laryngeal mucosa – Male territorial fear conflicts, or female shocking fear conflict.

Digestive problems (stomach, liver, gallbladder, pancreas mucosa) –A male territory anger conflict or a female identity conflict.

Or

Digestive problems (Relating to the digestive track) - Something that could not be digested – e.g. an event that sits in the gut and cannot be digested.

Diabetes - hyperglycaemia (Beta Islet cells, insulin injecting) – resistance conflict.

Diabetes - hypoglycaemia (Alpha Islet cells, controlled by diet) – fear disgust conflict.

Arthritis – relates to swelling of the cartilage - not valuing oneself conflict.

Pain (presumed muscular) – not valuing oneself conflict.

Reproductive system related problems (probably ovaries and testicles) – profound loss conflict.

All of these issues would relate to the type of issue a person who suffers form PTSD would experience. Here we can start to postulate that there might be evidence that a neurological dysfunction, (known to affect the brain and a person's behaviour), is linked to specific diseases. Therefore a specific stressful event affects the brain in a specific location, which then affects a specific organ for a biological reason.

Brain imaging techniques have also found that there is a direct link between specific areas of the brain and movement associated to Parkinson's disease.

Contributions of functional imaging to understanding Parkinsonian symptoms
Current Opinion in Neurobiology, Volume 14, Issue 6, December 2004, Pages 715-719
Scott T. Grafton www.sciencedirect.com.[60]

Further evidence that the primary and motor cortex of the brain are responsible for basic movement has also been established.

Comparison of neuronal activity in the supplementary motor area and primary motor cortex
Cognitive Brain Research, Volume 3, Issue 2, March 1996, Pages 143-150
Jun Tanji and Hajime Mushiake www.sciencedirect.com.[61]

As well as there being many experiments relating to brain imaging and specific organs in the body, most of the studies relate to movement or diseases that affect neural pathways in the body, such as Parkinson's and MS. There is also research that indicates the locations of specific areas of the brain and their relationship to specific organs of the body.

106

The most well known and easily accepted model of the brain and the related organs comes from Penfield's Institutes Homunculus. This strange example of how a man would look if we mapped the surface area of neurons dedicated to the sensory cells, related to the epidermis of the skin and motor (muscle movement) areas of the body, was first researched by Wilder Penfield in the 1950's. There seems to be no female homunculus model. Wilder Penfield worked with epileptic patients in an attempt to assist them in stopping their fits. He carried out experiments, during open brain surgery, where the clients had localised anaesthetic, meaning they were awake and could speak to the surgeon. Using an electrical probe on certain areas of the cortex of the brain, he could stimulate specific areas of the body. Wilder Penfield established that the brain was organised in a beautiful system going from the toes to the top of the head. He also noticed that the brain was crossed as well, meaning that by stimulating the left hand side of the brain, the right hand side of the body was affected, and vice versa.

From the picture you can see how much room in the sensory cortex is dedicated to the hands and the lips. This Homunculus was obviously put together by an over zealous man. To do a fun experiment of brain probing in the sensory cortex go to www.pbs.org/wgbh/aso/tryit/brain/

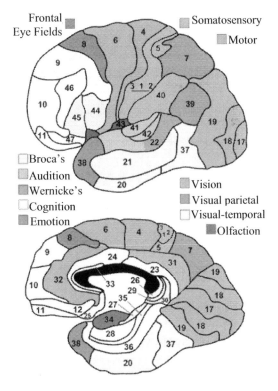

Modern Brain Mapping has defined various areas of the brain and its various related functions. Here you can see the visual areas (19/18/17) at the back of the head the ears(21) on the side and motor (movement) areas (6 on the top).

What I am alluding to in regard to all these brain/body connections is that it appears that the brain is connected to the body in an elegantly organised system. Each part of the body and each organ has a connection to a specific area of the brain. For example, the area responsible for visual processing is at the back of the brain - you do, literally, have eyes in the back of your head. Sound is processed in the side lobes of the brain. The sensory areas responsible for touch can be found on the top of the brain.

This type of brain mapping is relatively old and only covers the cortex of the brain. There is however, an area that is well understood but which has been ignored to some extent when it comes to our design as humans and the link between specific organs and areas of the brain. To understand this we need to look at embryology, an area which is taught for about four days in medical school but from then on is seemingly ignored by the medical profession, unless someone chooses to specialise in pre-mature babies.

Ignoring embryology seems strange. Disregarding the fundamental fact that our organs and brain are organised in a beautiful system which governs how each specific part of the body and brain reacts during and after stress, shows plain ignorance on the part of the medical profession.

To explain this we need to understand the basic fundamentals of embryology: What is happening in the womb from the point of conception to when we have developed into a human being. When we are conceived we start off as one cell that divides into fifty trillion cells that develop to make a grown adult. Within the first thirty days, three specific layers of cells develop. These layers are called the endoderm, mesoderm and ectoderm - inner, middle and outer layers. They are confusingly known as 'germ' layers and, although they have nothing to do with germs and microbes, they do link beautifully to how we react in the second stage of the disease process to fungi, bacteria and viruses. (See chapter 10.)

Each one of these layers makes up specific parts of various organs. Put simply; the endoderm (inner layer) is responsible for our digestive system. This runs from the mouth through to the anus. It includes the meat (parenchyma) of the liver and parenchyma of the pancreas plus the lung alveoli as well. The collecting tubules of the kidneys can also be found in the brain stem and are responsible for regulating the stored water throughout our system. *(NB. The Kidney Collecting Tubules develop from the mesoderm area of the brain and are not endoderm directed organs).*

The mesoderm (middle layer) is the thick leathery skin of the body. It is the dermis area of the skin, and the thick layers of skin that surround and protect our inner organs. The pericardium is a thick layer of skin that surrounds the heart. The peritoneum covers our digestive organs, including the liver and the pleura, which surrounds the lungs. The mammary glands are also directed by the mesoderm – middle layer of the brain.

In the mesoderm we also find the skeleton, striated muscles, the heart muscle, tendons, teeth and cartilage. The smooth muscles of the intestine, stomach and oesophagus are also situated here.

The outer layer, the ectoderm, is responsible for the sensory organs. These connect us with the outside world. The most obvious is the outer layer of the skin known as the epidermis. We also have the mucosas, the slimy areas of our system that are responsible for preventing our organs from drying out, and for giving us vital sensory feedback in order for us to function successfully and survive in our environment. The nasal mucosa is here (smell), the bronchi and laryngeal mucosa, the gall bladder ducts, liver mucosa, stomach mucosa, duodenum mucosa and pancreas mucosa. Interestingly, we find the coronary arteries and veins in the cortex, the alpha and beta islet cells of the pancreas and the thyroid (thyroglossal ducts) and branchial arch ganglia or pharyngeal gland. We also find the seeing part of our eyes, mainly the retina and vitreous fluid and the verbal hearing part of our ears and the upper part of our skin, movement, touch and sensory information of our body.

So, as we develop from the single fertilized cell we divide into the three germ layers. At the same time each germ layer is connected to a specific area of the nervous system and the brain. The endoderm is connected to the brain stem. The mesoderm is connected to the cerebellum – at the back of the brain - and is responsible for the thick skins surrounding our organs - the mesoderm is also connected to the grey matter. The Medulla, which is responsible for support, therefore includes our muscles and skeleton. The ectoderm is connected to the cortex and hence the sensory organs that connect us to the outside world.

Apart from Penfield's homunculus, our understanding of how embryology and the constitution of the brain are linked by a simple map of the organs has been ignored. The thesis that I am about to explain has, as yet, only some scientific verification.

All the experiments to which I have drawn your attention have been done in isolation but the evidence seems to point to the constitution of the body reflecting perfectly in embryology and brain layers. I can only surmise that the medical profession has forgotten that each specific area of the brain is so blatantly linked to the body by the wiring of the nervous system and that these wires also link back from each organ to specific areas of the brain. They also ignore the whole embryological layering of the brain and the link with the body when carrying out modern experiments to determine brain function. In discussions with some of my medical doctors and friends who carry out research, they tell me that embryology is old science and therefore dismissed.

It seems to me that modern medicine and its research has decapitated the head and the brain from the rest of the body, concentrating on specific organs that are completely isolated from any other part of the whole system. Why have some of the brilliant minds in the medical profession not joined the dots and made the assumption I am about to make?

I want to postulate something that will require a simple leap of faith on your part. If a person suffering from Post Traumatic Stress Disorder (PTSD) is more likely to suffer from heart-related problems, respiratory system-related problems, digestive problems, reproductive system-related problems, diabetes, arthritis and pain than someone who has not experienced PTSD, then there is probably a link to the ongoing stressful emotions they experience.

It confounds me that the medical profession postulate that the stress these people go through affects the body, increasing the risk of problems and illness. Yet they do not say that the specific ongoing stressful event that is continuously being triggered in the mind of the sufferer could be directly linked to the specific diseased organ.

Let me explain what I mean. If each separate area of the body and the brain is connected through embryology, then if you were to look at the stress a person is experiencing on a continuous basis with the PTSD and then look at the organ that is affected from an embryological point of view, you would see this obvious link. The ongoing stressful event shows up in the brain in a specific area that corresponds to the organ that is affected, but not the whole organ, just the specific embryonic layer. Take, for example, the lung which is made out of two embryonic layers. The alveoli are connected to the endoderm (inner layer) and therefore the brain stem, and the bronchi mucosa, the ectoderm (outer layer) and therefore the cortex. Two completely different embryonic layers are showing up in two completely different areas of the brain but, from the point of view of the medical profession, it is still the lungs.

The medical profession does not differentiate between these embryonic layers. Even though they are taught and study embryology, they ignore it. I have asked many doctors about this and they all told me what I have explained to you. They ignore this vital connection. Some even told me that the teaching of embryology was a waste of time, that they have never had a use for it. As I mentioned embryology is only used by medical specialists working with premature babies.

Going back to the brain/ body connection, let us explore the basic premise that seems to drive each embryonic level. Looking first at the endoderm (inner layer) which relates to the brain stem, practically all the parts of the organs that are found in this endoderm embryonic layer are to do with digestion. The types of stressful events that affect this layer are to do with an inability to digest something that a person has seen or heard. For example, being told you are a liar when clearly you are not. Diseases that occur here are designed for us to digest these issues more effectively by increasing the surface area of the digestive tract, thereby allowing better absorption of whatever it was that got stuck. This occurs in the first phase.

Looking at the Mesoderm (middle area) which relates to the cerebellum, the stressful events that cause this layer to react are to do with an impending attack against us. An example of the type of stressful events that cause these organs in this layer to react would be an imminent operation on a heart, lung or intestine. Diseases that occur in this layer are designed to protect our inner organs from attack by thickening the leathery skin layer in the stress phase. Another example worth considering is facial acne, indicating an attack against our integrity, e.g. losing face. The skin builds up in the first phase and then is eaten away in the second phase, hence the pimple and puss that is squeezed out from this point.

An issue relating to us not supporting ourselves, or not receiving support from others, would affect out skeletal and muscular system, and would therefore show up in the mesoderm part of the brain – the grey matter called the medulla. An example would be letting people walk all over you - you do not value yourself at a deep level. The cartilage in your lumbar vertebrae became stronger following the resolution of the stressful event in the second phase. Diseases in the mesoderm are designed to strengthen the affected muscles, bones, cartilage and tendons, therefore making you stronger and better able to support yourself. This occurs in the regeneration phase (the second half of the two phases).

If the issue was of a social nature concerning a female or of a territorial nature concerning a male, then the ectoderm (outer layer) - cortex would be affected. As mentioned earlier, an example of a 'social' separation conflict for a woman would be if she was the second wife of a man who dies and is left alone to argue with her husband's children as to whether or not she can live in the matrimonial home. She feels completely ostracised by the children, who have loved her as a mother for the past fourteen years but are now turning against her. She feels a brutal separation conflict. I came across this type of event with a client of mine, and it caused her breast cancer of the milk ducts a 'ductal carcinoma in situ'.

For a 'territorial' issue, imagine a man whose boss, without any consultation, hires someone younger, and incompetent with less experience, to run the department he successfully and profitably built up over the past few years, he could find his whole livelihood threatened. If this carried on for any length of time, i.e. many months, it could cause a heart attack or severe heart issues due to the coronary veins or arteries becoming blocked because of the healing process that occurs in the second phase. A client of mine experienced heart palpitations (a sign of the healing crisis in the heart) following such an experience. Luckily he solved the problem quickly by finding a better paid job with another company within a few months.

The types of diseases we see in the cortex affect the mucosa (the slimy lining of many organs that line specific organs of the body such as the nasal mucosa, stomach mucosa and bronchial mucosa). The ducts of certain organs are also affected, such as the breast milk ducts or the thyroid gland ducts, the beta and islet cells of the pancreas, the motor movements, specific areas of the eyes, the epidermis (outer layer of the skin), nails, hair and the coronary arteries and veins are all in the cortex. In essence, every issue that relates to our 'connection' or lack of it, with the outside world shows up in the ectoderm/cortex. The biological reason for the diseases in the cortex are, basically, for the person to feel less sensitive to the issue that is affecting them, therefore allowing them to deal more effectively with the problem. This always occurs in the stress phase.

What I am postulating here is, if we can speculate that specific embryonic layers of the brain are connected to corresponding embryonic layering of an organ in a structured and organised way, if we were to look at a specific diseased layer of an organ then, in theory, we should find either activity or scarring in the corresponding area of the brain.

One of my students, Robert Waghmare, who is now a META-Medicine® Trainer and Health Coach, had a disease called Nephrotic syndrome. From a traditional medical point of view; this is where the kidneys are damaged, causing large oedemas (excessive water and protein - albumin) in specific areas of the body. In Robert's case it affected his whole body, showing up mainly in his lower abdomen and testicles which would embarrassingly swell up to the size of small rugby balls. It would also cause the rest of his body to swell; his face would blow up and look moon-like.

You can see from these pictures of Sheena how Nephrotic syndrome can affect adults. Notice the massive difference that this issue had on Sheena's face. It looks like fat, but the sufferers of this issue can experience the water collecting overnight. In order to treat the disease, a steroid called Prednisolone is given in large doses. The medical profession say that the moon-face can be caused by steroids. However, according to Robert and through observing sufferers of kidney collecting tubules syndromes, the moon-face occurs before the steroids are taken and not because of them.

The issue causes this excessive swelling due to the water retention and the cause is a UDIN shock of feeling isolated and abandoned. The steroids actually cause more water to collect around the specific areas by putting the whole body into a stress phase. The use of

111

diuretics or 'water pills' can stop any further build up, but like steroids, they are no cure. More information and support for children with Nephrotic syndrome can be found www.nephrotic.co.uk. Where you can see pictures of a young girl called Bethan who suffered from this syndrome.

As regards Robert, being a META-Medicine® health coach he had attended a brain CT seminar and had a brain CT scan. Whilst I was learning how to read brain CTs I discovered a massive array of small white circles in the area that I know corresponded to the kidney collecting tubules.

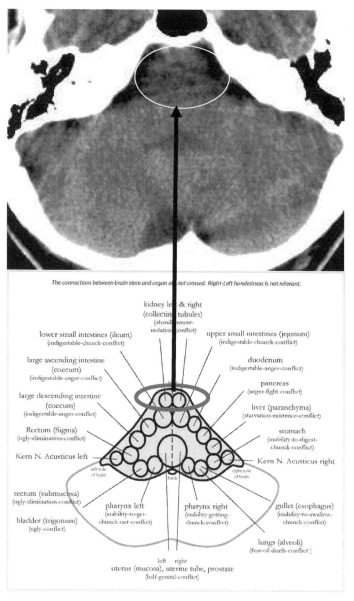

Robert's Brain CT scan from 2005 with numerous white circles in the Kidney collecting tubules area. The white circles are scarring caused by calcium deposits – this means the disease has completed its process

The white circles correspond to scarring, and show up as calcification, which is white in a brain CT. The location of where the scarring occurred had been developed by the doctor mentioned earlier through 10,000 or more observations of CT scans and patient ailments. Unfortunately although this is an amazing discovery, his work has not been verified except by a handful of doctors and at a University in Austria. The reason that this has not been verified is, I believe, because of political pressure and, as I mentioned earlier in the book, this doctor's controversial nature.

Needless to say, in the previous image we can clearly see the number of small rings that have taken form in Robert's Brain CT and that correspond to the brain stem area (the Endoderm - inner layer - of the body).

Speaking to Robert that day and since then, confirmed the reactions that occurred regarding his disease. One day when he was two and a half years old and on holiday in Edinburgh, his parents lost him. This was the Unexpected Dramatic Isolating shock with No strategy that caused the disease. He also remembered how he had strong feelings of a fear of feeling isolated as a child, particularly if friends behaved indifferently or in an unfriendly way towards him. More importantly, he remembers feeling extremely anxious and stressed when his parents went out, fearing that they would not return again. He told me that he used to cry and scream as they left, making it almost impossible for them to have a normal social life. These emotional triggers were the triggers that caused the whole disease process to reoccur, as I discussed in chapter seven.

Robert Waghmare with his partner Joanne Ross, as he looks today, with no signs of Nephrotic syndrome which mysteriously disappeared after he became 18 years of age.

Let us explore this brain/body link by showing other pictures and the mapping that corresponded to brain CTs and diseases in patients.

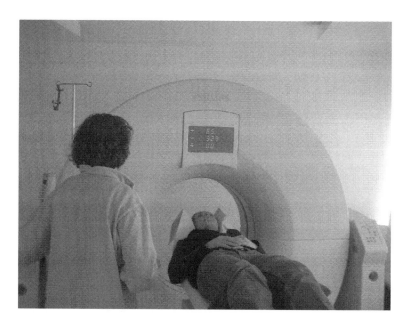

Here we can see Lucille White having a brain CT scan. These amazing machines are complex donut-shaped x-ray machines that create slicing images of different parts of the body. In META-Medicine® we are particularly interested in the brain.

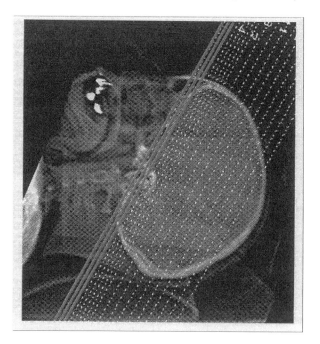

The slicing used in META-Medicine® required for brain CT mapping. Notice the 3mm closeness of the lines in the lower Brain stem and Cerebellum area compared with the 5mm cut of the upper Medulla and Cortex areas of the brain.

Here we can see the slicing and angling that we use for META-Medicine®. Usually we allow a cut of 3mm in the brain stem area and then 5mm as we travel further up the brain. The angle corresponds to the frontal lobes and back of the cerebellum as shown by the thicker lines. I mention this because if you ever require a brain CT image the radiologist will need to know how to set up the imaging. Please also note; NO contrast is required. NB Radiologist do not like being told how to carry out a scan, so be diplomatic.

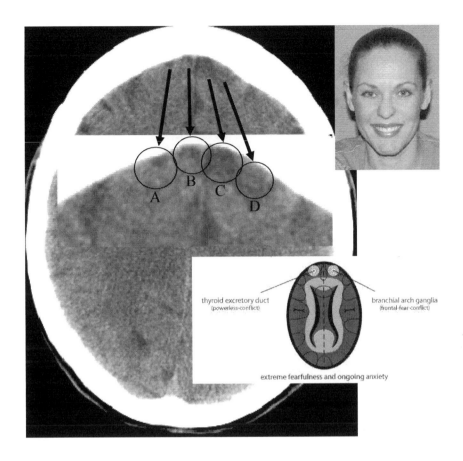

thyroid excretory duct
(powerless-conflict)

branchial arch ganglia
(frontal-fear-conflict)

extreme fearfulness and ongoing anxiety

Figure 1

This client, Lucille White, from the previous page is one of the META-Medicine® health coaches, who I have written about in an earlier chapter. She had experienced ongoing anxiety problems (See Chapter 5). Here (figure 1) we can see the thyroid duct and the branchial arch ganglia, more commonly known as the pharyngeal gland, both active at the same time. This combination of two organs being affected in this way causes a person to experience acute anxiety without the major organ reactions that would be associated if only one ring was present. A similar issue occurs with depression and mania - more about this later in the book.

These rings are in the cortex area of the brain. I have drawn attention to four separate areas. The first two circles A&B show the issue in resolution and therefore in the second stage. They are blurry and dark but there are also many white spots in the centre, meaning this issue is chronic, therefore repeating itself. There are other rings to the right (circle C) which show many small, dark rings (approximately 4). The other lighter ring which is most obvious (circle D), is in the first phase and therefore completely unresolved. However, it is an old issue; this you can see from a small pearling of the outer wall of the ring. This would mean the issue would be continuously there in the background.

115

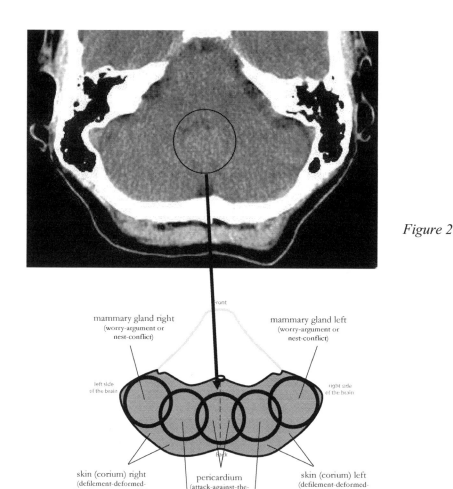

Figure 2

This client came to have a brain CT reading (fig 2) with Dr Anton Bader, and myself. The client had early symptoms of Multiple Sclerosis (MS) and we found symptoms of MS in the reading (the brain CT ring is hard to see so I have not included it here). However, on further inspection of his brain CT, we also found this clear circle corresponding to the heart pericardium. This would have caused a thickening of the thick skin layer around the heart. Fortunately the client did not have any symptoms (it is the first phase). He did however complain that his whole life had recently been turned upside down when his job, which he loved so much, had been threatened by an incompetent manager. Therefore the ring showing as an attack against his heart, the attack being against the job he loved.

A woman, with two young boys, had a bone cancer in her middle thoracic spine area. This CT (fig 3) was taken just days before a healing crisis. She experienced excruciating pain that felt like someone was stabbing her in the back, along with an epileptic fit that lasted three minutes, plus an ongoing migraine headache which slowly disappeared.

Such a disease is caused by a self worth conflict hitting at a very deep personal level (similar to my herniated disc but much deeper) along with Kidney Collecting Tubule syndrome – see page 61. This client had been forced by her co-business partner to do something in her company that she felt was illegal. She resolved the issue and then went through the second phase, with symptoms of pain in the bone followed by the healing crisis. The pain subsided eventually. In normal medical terms this would be considered a brain tumour, but from a META-Medicine® point of view, it is the collection of glial cells (brain reparatory cells that heal the relay) around the brain relay that collect a large amounts of water during the healing phase. As the healing crisis takes place, this water is squeezed out by cramping in the brain, in a similar action to someone trying to squeeze some juice out of an unpeeled orange. The symptoms are severe headaches, migraines and sometimes an epileptic fit. Sometimes the swelling of the brain presses up against the back of the eyeballs and people see flashing lights along with the pain in a separate area of the brain. Sometimes they experience one eyeball being almost squeezed out of their sockets. If left to take its natural course, the amount of water can subside, in which case the eyeball returns to normal. My client did experience her right eyeball being pushed out to some degree, however this subsided very quickly. There is more information about this client in Chapter 14 on Cancer.

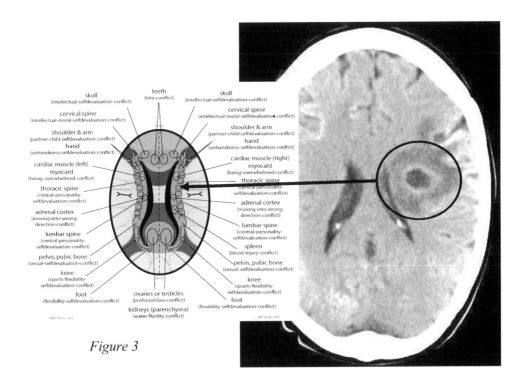

Figure 3

117

In the next brain CT this woman had excessive bleeding and horrendous period pains, and she could not conceive. The doctors were not sure why. After the brain CT we were able to tell her it was her ovaries that needed to be looked at. (Fig.4). We also looked into her past and found that she had had an abortion that she had not come to terms with causing a profound loss conflict, and this coincided with the start of her period problems. After solving the conflicts, she conceived and gave birth to a lovely boy.

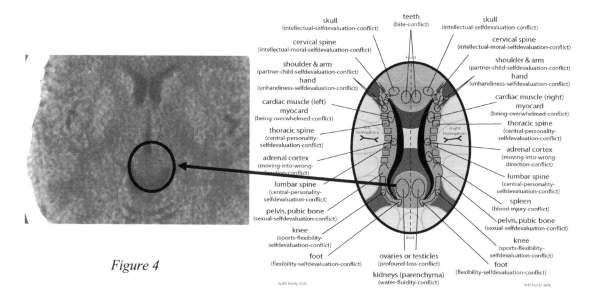

Figure 4

Figure 5 is a client of Dr Anton Bader. Here we have a clear example of the brain stem area where you can see a ring that corresponds to the small intestine area. This client showed symptoms of Irritable Bowel Syndrome (IBS). If you look closely you can see there are clear rings that are broken in places with some white spots inside the rings. This meant that the client is repeating the issue over and over again (see chapter 7). The symptoms the client experienced was constipation and then diarrhoea. However chronic disease, in extreme cases, can cause disease such as Crohn's disease.

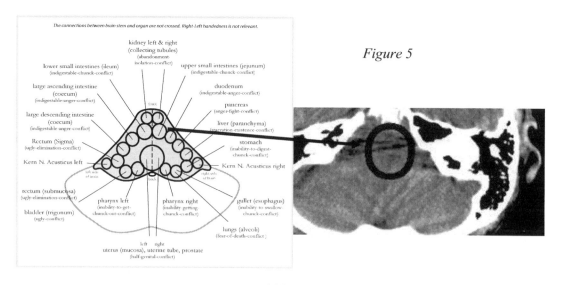

Figure 5

118

Here (fig. 6) is an excellent example of a glandular breast cancer. Twenty-seven percent of breast cancers are glandular cerebellum (middle brain), where seventy-three percent are ductal, which shows up in the cortex of the brain (outer brain). The medical profession does not acknowledge that these two types of cancers have their origins in two separate embryological layers. Here we see that Dr Anton Bader's client has a very clear ring in the location of the breast cancer glands. It is in the first phase and therefore is growing. This type of cancer is caused by a worry or an argument conflict with a son or daughter.

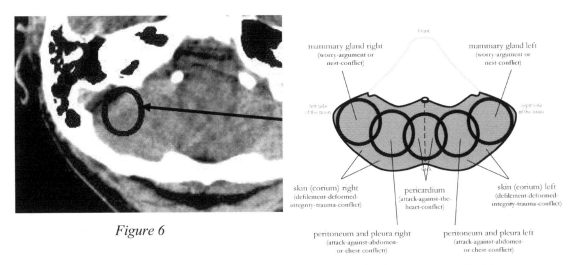

Figure 6

This CT (fig. 7) shows another clear marking for a glandular breast cancer. In this instance it had occurred in the right breast, and was an issue to do with an argument with her own mother over her not being a good mother to her sons. The breast cancer lump was small and was treated with chemotherapy. However the client died of liver cancer caused by the shock of the diagnosis. She had to stop work and since she was the principle bread winner in the family, this caused massive financial issues – hence the liver cancer; which is a starvation existence conflict. She was unconsciously starving herself so the family could eat.

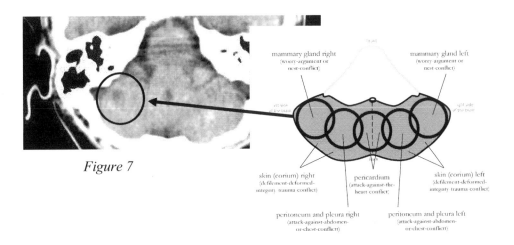

Figure 7

119

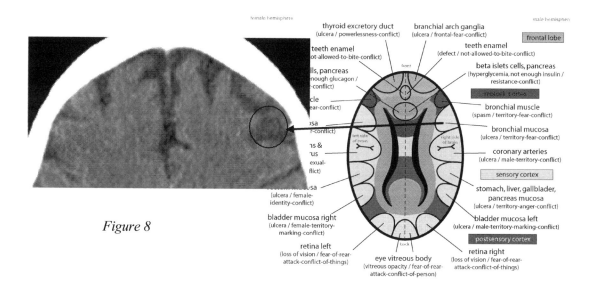

Figure 8

On this brain CT (fig.8) we are looking at the cortex and here we can see a ring corresponding to the Bronchial Mucosa. This is in the first phase and relates to a shocking fear conflict for a woman. This woman showed no symptoms until a month later where she developed a deep cough, a bronchitis which was later diagnosed as pneumonia. She was hospitalised and recovered fully.

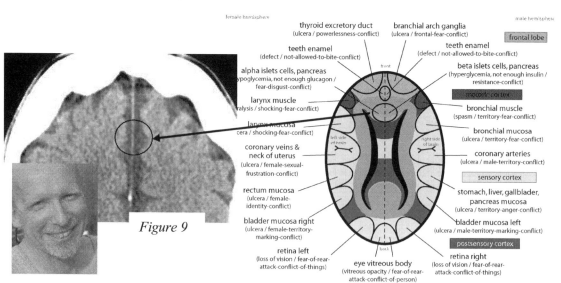

Figure 9

This Brain CT (fig.9) shows Tim Harnden, a friend of mine who was diagnosed with late onset Diabetes. The ring can be seen right in the centre of the upper cortex. The CT also showed us, Dr Bader and I, that the diabetes had not only affected his alpha islet cells but also the beta Islet cells of the pancreas. This meant we needed to address two separate conflicts rather than just one. This posed a problem for Tim who had no recollection of past memories and therefore could not access the original conflicts. I mention about how we have developed ways of accessing old memories using NES on the next page.

120

I hope that I have at least shown you in this chapter a new way in which the body and the brain are connected. I do admit that there needs to be further research in this area to be absolutely certain that we have got this model right. There is an overwhelming amount of evidence proving that there is this amazing link, the implications of which mean that in reading a brain CT you can give an accurate history of a client's illnesses and therefore traumas that they have experienced, plus being able to pinpoint the ongoing issues that a client has been going through.

In my experience of reading brain CT scans I find that it is just as much of an art as it is a science. Interpretation of certain circles can vary from one reader to another. It does have its flaws and, as a diagnostic tool, is not perfect. On the other hand, neither are other modern diagnostic tools. The amount of misdiagnoses has not decreased despite the number of brilliant imaging machines available now to modern medicine. It is experience and knowledge that makes a great brain CT reader.

However, out of this whole understanding of reading brain CTs there has been some amazing cross referencing that has come about, which is very exciting, and I want to briefly mention it here.

Through talking to my friend and colleague Professor Peter Fraser, he revealed some exciting evidence that the rings are indeed trapped energy, and information is starting to appear. Peter, in a conversation in November 2007, mentioned that CT scanners scan the brain at a wavelength corresponding to 10^{14}. This relates to the same energy at which an emotion vibrates. I then went onto share with him that these rings are in fact spheres (although they are not completely spherical). I also told him that these marking spheres or rings do not show up as well in Magnetic Resonance Imaging (MRI) scans, which scan at a different frequency. Peter then made a massive leap in his thinking by saying that what we are seeing is not a sphere or ring but trapped waves of energy with information stored in them.

If we explore that postulation even more, it does make sense. However, Peter has gone one step further in developing special info-ceuticals. Info-ceuticals contain water that has been charged with specific energy, resonating at certain frequencies - similar to the resonation found in homeopathic remedies but far more accurate and potent. On taking a certain number of drops of an info-ceutical, it can have a massive effect on the energetic balance of a client, and on their healing.

Peter and I have developed a new set of META-Medicine® info-ceuticals that work on the energy shifts that occur in the brain itself. Trials using these new info-ceuticals are very impressive. The main info-ceutical used for the brain seems to implode the energy trapped in the sphere outwards, resolving the issue and releasing massive amounts of heat at the same time, whilst putting the client well and truly into the second phase without them tracking back through the conflict. They need to be used with a trained META-Medicine® health coach who has a psychological background, in order to be effective or a specially trained NES practitioner. As an example Bertie, a close friend of Peter, was suffering from an over enlarged prostate 54 mm in diameter compared to the normal 25 mm.

The marker which the medical profession use to determine if there are abnormalities in the prostate, called PSA, was higher than normal, 9.2 compared with an average of 4.0. Peter used the new META-Medicine® inspired brain info-ceuticals combined with other NES drops that he had developed, to bring the size of the prostate down to normal, therefore avoiding any surgery, chemotherapy or radiation.

He also passed a sizable lump of material through his penis, without pain, during the treatment (see photo).

The implications of this treatment have far reaching consequences. The treatment took many months but Bertie told Peter that he would follow this path in preference to the slash, poison or burn treatment offered by his doctor. He also said it probably saved him over £7000, because he could carry on working and he had no side effects. Bertie's prostate is now a very manageable size.

I have come across other interesting encounters through working with a friend of mine Time Harnden (fig. 9) who has late onset diabetes. He had horrendous trouble accessing the original conflict shock that caused the very first pattern of his life of 'not being sweet enough' to occur. Many repeated attempts at trying find the event with me and others failed until he took several drops of the new brain info-ceutical. He subsequently resolved the event and his life changed dramatically. He has reduced his insulin intake from 46 points to 20, overnight. We believe jointly that he will be able to stop injecting insulin.

I believe that we are onto something major that could change how we look and treat disease in the future with the META-Medicine®, psychological resolution of stressful events; and together with work of Professor Peter Fraser through the Nutri Energetic System (NES) we may just be on the verge of creating brand new interventions that work at a totally higher level than modern medical techniques. This is a very exciting time.

For further information on how you can learn how to read Brain CTs, or if you want a brain CT read please do contact us www.meta-medicine.com. For further information on Nutri Energetic System go to www.neshealth.com.

I am now going to refer you to my opening story where Birgitte had suffered for many years with depression and a complete lack of energy. She attended an NLP course with me where I read her brain CT and we found she had a powerless conflict which affected her thyroid excretion, causing a lack of energy. This issue occurred through two shocks, one from an abortion and the other from a losing her home.

After that day on the NLP course, Birgitte's energy changed dramatically. In fact her whole life changed. She told me recently that she has been able to live a normal life, for the first time, with her son Jonas. She told me since then she stays awake until midnight or later and wakes at the same time as her son. On my travels to Bergen, where I have met her, she has been out enjoying evening meals with her friends and me with no problems of sleepiness or tiredness anymore. Needless to say, she told me that what happened that day when I found the thyroid problem through reading the brain CT, gave her back her life.

Birgitte Bakke in 2008
full of life and energy

In the next chapter I want to discuss the highly controversial area of microbes. How fungi, bacteria and viruses are all part of the disease process and are working in symbiosis with our bodies to assist in our healing.

Chapter 10

Bacteria, Virus, Fungi. The Microbes - The evil killers? Or the good healers?

*"In the nineteenth century men lost their fear of god and acquired a fear of microbes
-anonymous"*
*"Microbes are not the primary originator of a disease, rather they are biological,
meaningful helpers and part of a complex disease process.
Viruses, bacteria, micro-bacteria and fungi are organized by germ layer and brain
relay and are active in the regeneration phase."*

One of the ten META-Medicine® Models

The 'cleaning' epidemic – Could this be the reason why we are healthier now?

When I grew up in the 60's there was a 'cleaning' epidemic. Every person in the land started bleaching everything for fear of a deadly virus or bacteria destroying their life. It was a massive fear that was instilled by mass marketing and the media who relentlessly reported the scary consequences of not cleaning everything in your house, especially work surfaces and bathrooms. These were all things that the uneducated public needed to know. Complete sterility was the message.

So what did people do before the introduction of this attitude to microbes? Did the mass population run around suffering from the common cold? Was diarrhoea a regular complaint? Did people suffer horrendously and die terrible deaths from killer bugs and viruses that were targeted as the criminals and villains of our modern understanding of diseases? Are the vaccines and modern medical intervention ALL responsible for our good health? And are we as healthy as we are lead to believe?

My younger sister had continuous colds, and she is still challenged somewhat by nasal and viral chest infections today. She is ten years younger than me and we all grew up in what was called a 'nuclear family' because we lived under the constant threat of an impending atom or hydrogen bomb being sent to destroy our cities and whole country by the 'evil communist USSR'. It sounds farcical now but that is how we grew up - with public information films telling us what to do if a bomb was dropped on our city. The modern nuclear family was clean, efficient and willing to do whatever it could to protect itself. My sister bore the full brunt of this growing up as she did in the modern 'cleaning' epidemic.

Today, cleaning products are pumped into our living rooms by marketing experts who convince us of the perils of the 'nasty, evil germs' that could kill us. Are these bugs the 'so called' killers that we are lead to believe and should they be eliminated at all costs? Are we really under the massive threat the marketing companies and the media say we are? Are we really missing something bigger than what they are telling us?

Certainly cleaning has its benefits but is the whole message correct? Are all microbes dangerous? Are you as confused as me as to what is really going on? I hear of this incredible cleaning product that is endorsed by medical doctors in Canada as their product of choice because it kills ninety-nine point nine percent of all viruses and bacteria (on a humorous note - which of the point one percent of viruses or bacteria do they not kill?) Then we hear about pro-biotic cultures being added to our yogurts. Oh no! Are these bacteria actually being added to our food? There used to be only one type, but now they are selling yogurts with five different types of special bacteria! I was led to believe that all bacteria and bugs are harmful and to put them into our body on purpose just seems wrong. Should we not be adding a branded bleach product to our favourite yogurt as a way of cleaning ninety-nine point nine percent of all the bacteria out of our guts? Have the media and marketing companies gone mad? Or are we mad for believing what they say without really understanding the reason for microbes.

Microbes and healing

Adam Sprackling, a very close friend and an NLP trainer, came to see me. He was complaining of a small sore on his left leg just above his ankle that would not heal. It was caused by an operation to his Achilles tendon, which he had ruptured for the second time in one year. The first time, he told me, was whilst he was playing squash with a friend. The second time happened when he went swimming one night in Brighton during an NLP course I was running with Terry Elston.

He was in a plaster cast for a few weeks followed by a special boot he had to wear after the fourth operation and, although the tendon was repaired, the wound that had been created on the side of his leg during the operation had never properly healed even after antibiotics. He showed it to me several times. We discussed it at length a few months before he came to see me professionally.

I was just really starting to understand the power of META-Medicine® and, as we sat in my office, I started to ask him various questions about the problem. I knew there were two issues. One had to do with the breaking of the tendon and the other had to do with the healing of the skin on the open wound. It transpired that this great man - my friend - upon returning from a yearlong holiday travelling round the world, had decided that life was over. He explained. "I felt after coming home I couldn't relate to my friends and family as I felt they hadn't been through what I had been through."

I was shocked to hear that as he was about to fly back to the UK (his last flight from South Africa), he silently broke down in the airport and said to himself. "My life is over". I looked up 'Achilles tendon' in my META-Medicine® directory and was surprised to read that a person with this type of issue has been through a problem wherein they believe life to be over. This type of shock affects the Achilles tendon, by causing necrosis in the first phase and the rebuilding in the second.

The issue works in this way in the wild. An animal goes through a shock, the tendon becomes weaker and weaker until it eventually snaps, often under pressure; then an animal in this situation cannot run away from any impending danger and becomes fodder for the lions or any other predator. Therefore, in a horrible irony, the biological programme becomes completed. The programme singles out the animals that are not going to bring the rest of the pack down, and an animal thinking in this way would have that effect.

Adam's life certainly seemed like that. He was very depressed. I tried calling him many times after I had heard he had returned home, before he reluctantly spoke to me. Here was a man who had been full of life and energy, and was now miserable, so much so that it was depressing to speak to him. I did think he'd be better off left alone. However, as a friend, I did what I could and invited him to assist on an NLP course I was running in the hope that he would snap out of it and clear this mood, which was so unlike him. That was when the tendon snapped again - swimming one night on Brighton beach. After that incident he disappeared again, and whilst he was sitting at home convalescing, he called me and said that he really needed some help.

In the office that day we dealt with the 'life is over' issue and cleared out the emotions surrounding that decision, and immediately I saw his mood lift. That was great but the real problem that was causing him more concern was the hole in his leg that would not heal as a result of the second surgery. He was concerned because if it did not heal, he was at risk of getting an infection and possibly losing his foot. An infection had crept up his leg after surgery and by using antibiotics. The spreading had stopped though the hole in his leg got bigger and bigger. Recently he had been to see a nurse who had bandaged his leg in order to get a better blood supply to the affected area. She had also swabbed the wound and found MRSA (a bacterium which is resilient to antibiotics, often found in hospitals). I asked Adam how many courses of antibiotics had he taken, to which he replied "several." Then why did this wound not heal completely? Why was MRSA present?

Looking at the wound it was obvious that the upper layer of skin was trying to heal but an area of about 3-4mm was still exposed and you could see pink flesh underneath it. This area is the dermis, the thick leathery skin that protects us from being punctured. The shock that causes this layer to react is one of feeling deformed or attacked. I looked at Adam and asked him if he had felt a deformed feeling towards that part of his body since the operation. He looked up at me, and went red. I looked him straight in the eye and asked 'What's happening inside? Tell me." Sheepishly he recounted how he remembered waking up from the anaesthetic after an operation and looking at this bandaged foot, which was suspended in mid-air, thinking "That is NOT my ankle!" His voice was full of disgust and horror as to what he was saying. We cleared out the shock and the decision using a technique called Time Line Therapy® and left it at that.

A month later he called and excitedly told me that the wound was healing and that new skin was forming around the old hole. Two months later he called again to tell me that it had completely healed over and to thank me. I was overjoyed. This was not the only thing that happened to Adam as a consequence of solving the issue of his life being over.

Microbes play an important part in our healing

I was sitting in a training room in a hotel near Munich on the first META-Medicine® Certification Training. Dr Bader started talking, and what I heard shocked me. I could not quite believe what he was saying. I had heard this particular topic mentioned before by other people but I had dismissed it. This time it was different because it was a doctor telling me this. He was explaining how viruses, bacteria, fungi and microbes play an important part in our healing. I thought Dr Bader was going mad. Running through my brain was my belief system -'viruses and bacteria are killers' - something which everyone knows. Biological warfare would not have any effect if man-made bugs did not kill people in horrible ways. Surely the common cold is caught by breathing in the retro-virus from a carrier. Then what about the killer bugs that eat people? The wife of a friend of mine died in this horrible way. AIDS too – people die from that.

Diarrhoea is a bug you catch from food that has been infected through poor hygiene, isn't it? Fungal infections, like athletes foot, are something you get from the floor of the gym, or because someone else who had the infection has used your gym shoes. What about antibiotics? They kill viruses and bacterial infections that threaten our health, don't they? In America there is collaboration between pharmaceutical companies and TV stations. These companies spend a lot of money promoting their vaccines. One product, called Gardasil is designed to protect women from the Human Papilloma Virus, which has been found to be linked to cervical cancer. Surely eliminating these disgusting microbes is the best thing that has happened to us as a human race? So don't tell me these killer bugs are biological helpers! Are you nuts?

Just so you are aware, here are the side effects of this new HPV vaccine. More young girls have died from its effects than have died from cervical cancer.

"Anaphylactic shock, foaming at mouth, grand mal convulsion, coma and now paralysis are a few of the startling descriptions included in a new federal report describing the complications from Merck & Co.'s Gardasil medication for sexually transmitted human papilloma virus – which has been proposed as mandatory for all schoolgirls. The document was obtained from the U.S. Food and Drug Administration by Judicial Watch Washington group that investigates and prosecutes government corruption, and it has details of ten deaths just since September."[62]

Cleanliness and anti-bacteria products are now everywhere. You can even buy mini-sprays that you can carry with you at all times so that you can spray anything you touch or spray your hands after touching something that could have potentially nasty bacteria or microbes on it. I saw these for the first time in the USA. After the so called 'AIDS epidemic', toilet seats in public toilets would sometimes have special disposable seat covers. What a great idea. I always thought that people were dirty and I wanted nothing to do with that part of their anatomy, so I used them knowing that I was safe from the deadly AIDS virus. As regards the mini anti-bacterial sprays, I wanted some of these as I travel a lot and I like my hands to be clean. But those words of Dr Bader were still playing on my mind.

How could he say such a thing? 'Microbes are biological helpers.' This is rubbish, dangerous and misguided, but he had a point. He said these microbes only work on specific layers of the brain. Old bacteria and fungi work on the brain stem. Newer strains work on the cerebellum. Evolutionary younger bacteria work in symbiosis with the Medulla. And viruses work on the cortex.

Ever the sceptic, I needed to fully understand what was being said. As I started to explore this minefield of a subject, I discovered that many of the things that Dr Bader was saying are true, but how? How do these so-called 'nasty viruses,' bacteria and fungi work? How do they assist us as biological helpers? Could they really be doing something important for us? Could something that meant eliminating them not be the answer? Should we re-think the whole of Louis Pasteur's ground breaking discovery back in the mid-nineteen hundreds, when he came up with our modern 'germ' theory of disease? Should we dismiss Edward Jenner's discovery that having a minor disease such as cowpox could protect a person from something as life threatening as smallpox?

I mention these things because in the META-Medicine® teachings, microbes are there for a positive reason. From a META-Medicine® point of view microbes play an important part in our healing. However, in my research and understanding, not all strains of microbes are going to work well in every person. Some microbes will do the job they are designed to do, which in META-Medicine® terms is to repair the damage that was done after the stress phase, but others seem to have the effect of poisoning, maiming or disabling a person, such as the microbes of botulism, polio and meningitis.

It is strange and challenging to think that we might be living in symbiosis with bacteria. There are 2,000 different strains of salmonella bacteria, which is the most common foodborne illness. They are everywhere, but only ten strains cause illness. They live in the guts of warm-blooded animals and pets, so we come into contact with them on a regular basis. Elimination is impossible. 1,990 of the 2,000 strains are ok - and I believe that animals do not suffer from the other ten strains, so what is going on?

Here are some interesting facts about you as a human. Were you aware that you, as an adult, have ten trillion human cells in your body? And that you also have one hundred trillion other cells that are not human also in your body? Udo Pollmer - food chemist[63]. About eighty-five percent of them are in your gut. There are over five hundred different strains of bacteria inside you. The question, is why? What are they doing there? It is now thought that these bacteria break down our food so we can digest it more effectively. As I mentioned previously, the newest fad the marketing men and women are promoting by branding all over the television in 2008 is pro-biotics.

The gut plays an important part in our lives. Here's an interesting quote from the book called "The Second Brain" by Michael D. Gershon that explains this.

"The gut is different from other organs of the body, in that it contains a complex intrinsic set of nerve cells, called the enteric nervous system, which functions like a second brain. The enteric nervous system is alone among parts of the peripheral nervous system (the nervous system outside of the brain and spinal cord, which are called the central nervous system,) in that the enteric nervous system is able to control the behaviour of an organ independently of commands issued by the brain." [64]

Let's explore what META-Medicine® is saying about microbes. Microbes are biological helpers that assist in the rebuilding of specific layers of our organs once the body has gone into the regeneration phase (Point 4). So they are not active in the system until we resolve an issue.

Each one of the microbes is present in an orderly fashion. The fungi and old types of bacteria, in evolutionary terms, work alongside the brain stem (the brain stem organs are mostly to do with digestion). Such as candida fungi and tuberculosis bacteria decompose any excessive growth that we may have. It comes then as no surprise to find people with Irritable Bowel Syndrome (IBS) often have a large amount of candida in their guts and people with tumours in their bowels start to pass blood as the tumour is eaten away by the old gut bacteria.

Next are the cerebellum bacteria (the protective leathery skin organs). Again, tuberculosis is found here, and so are fungi, for example in 'athlete's foot.' Breast gland tumours also contain the tuberculosis bacteria, and smell particularly unpleasant, if they break through the skin and are exposed to the outside world.

In the cerebral medulla organs (the muscles, bones, tendons, cartilage), the main bacteria is staphylococcus. It rebuilds the bones by filling in the gaps after osteoporosis. It does this by reconstructing the callus by granulating callus forming tissue. Similar bacteria are also present in testicles and ovaries when they are being rebuilt.

Viruses are present in the cortex (the mucous membranes and surface areas of our body). The viruses work by reconstructing the tissue after necrosis and ulceration, and are often accompanied by a fever and/or inflammation.

How do these microbes work? It is thought that the brain tells the body to start producing the microbes as soon as the stress phase has started. This means that these microbes should be visible in the blood system almost immediately. Interestingly, using dark field microscopy they can be seen, but they are not active. It is also thought that the blood cells themselves produce the bacteria; again this phenomenon can be seen under dark field microscopy.

Another noticeable piece of information is that during the stress phase (Point 3) the body is acidic. In the regeneration, second phase (points 5 and 7), the body is alkaline. This fits into the two phases very well, in addition to the fact that there are four hundred cold diseases (stress phase) and four hundred warm diseases (regeneration phase). In the cold diseases there are fungi, bacteria and viruses present, but there is no fever and they appear to be inactive. However, the warm diseases all have active fungi, bacteria or viral infections. This can be somewhat explained by dark field microscopy live blood analysis.

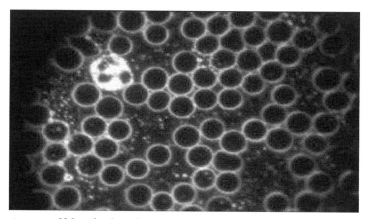

A picture of blood taken from a dark field microscopy blood analysis Red blood cells are seen to be making bacteria in the stress phase. This, I have been told, can literally be seen. The bacteria are then passed into the system and start working in the regeneration phase.

I must mention that dark field microscopy blood analysis is very controversial – it uses a specific type of microscope to analyse live blood. I had this carried out in Australia by Georgie Atkinson. She noticed that my blood was in good order. She did say that there was some activity in the blood that pointed to some bacterial infection which might occur. What was really fascinating was that this infection was not there at all while I was in Australia. It appeared as soon as I got on the plane to fly to the USA from Auckland, New Zealand, after a very relaxing day off. I was very, very stressed while I was in Australia. I had been working every day for over seven days without a break, and the day off in New Zealand was wonderful and de-stressing. On the day of the flight to Los Angeles, I noticed that my foot was very itchy, and when I got on the plane it was quite swollen, as you can see from the pictures on the next page.

When I got to Los Angeles I spoke at length to Johannes Fisslinger President of the IMMA and he said that I needed a medical consultation. I went to an American Emergency Rescue centre and the doctor told me that I had a serious infection of the right foot, which was spreading up my leg. He made a mark on my leg and told me to keep an eye on it. He prescribed antibiotics and said it could be Lyme's disease (a horrible infection that can be caught from a tick. The infection was first noticed in Wisconsin in a place called Lyme.) It is nasty because it can get into your whole system and cause horrendous ongoing symptoms. One of the META-Medicine® Health Coach trainers had had it and he took several months to recuperate. I could not afford six to eight months of recuperation, so I decided to take the course of antibiotics. I wanted to keep my foot as well, and the doctor said infections like this can spread up the whole leg and infect the entire system. He recommended that I take

128

the antibiotics. I challenged him, asking why he thought that, to which he replied that in his professional opinion this was a bacterial infection that, if left untreated, could cause me to lose the use of my foot or leg. He warned me not to mess with this.

I knew why I had contracted the infection. In England, a few days before I had travelled to Australia, I was playing Badminton with Kristin and my family. I remember going to find a stray shuttlecock in the bushes and I know that I was bitten then on the right ankle. It was also a stressful time as I was about to leave for Australia. I was unsure as to whether I could train META-Medicine® in Australia successfully, and if the expensive trip would be worthwhile. I was worried about whether I could put myself forward to achieve this. As it was, the trip was a success and I remember thinking that as soon as I arrived in New Zealand. Hence the stress phase followed by the regeneration phase.

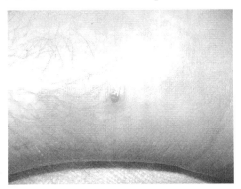

Bite on my right foot; the supposed cause of the infection.

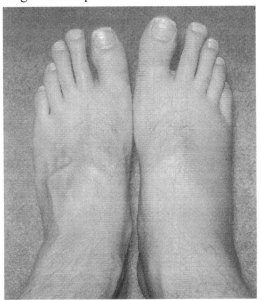

Infection in my right foot, you can see the right foot is swollen – taken on a plane flying from New Zealand, Auckland to Los Angeles, USA.

I also took a separate course of antibiotics but I took a strong course of pro-biotics at the same time, to support my intestines. As soon as the infection disappeared and the swelling went down I stopped the antibiotic course. My intestines did not suffer either.

However in 2010 I had another shock similar to the one that caused my leg to swell up and become infected on my travels back from Australia. This time I did not take medical antibiotics, instead I used homeopathy and B.Propalis painted onto the infected skin area. B.Propalis is a natural antibiotic made from bee pollen. In less than 3 days the swelling and infection completely disappeared. My belief now is the medical antibiotics merely push the issue deeper, therefore not allowing the body to complete its natural healing cycle.

What I want to reiterate here is that it does seem that bacteria are being made in our blood before any infection appears. What I have mentioned repeatedly is that we must rethink our present belief system and work with the microbes and not against them, and we must also understand that some of these microbes can and do cause horrific symptoms that maim and sometimes kill as with Lyme disease. But we should not kill every bacteria in our system. The overuse of antibiotics in the last 30 years has proven this.

129

Bacteria in our system

I mentioned earlier that I would explain how active bacteria get into our system, and why it is important. In META-Medicine® we believe that we live in symbiosis with bacteria and other microbes. Were you aware that eighty-five percent of the trillions of bacteria live in our intestines, that's about 2-4lbs (1-2Kgs) worth of gut flora. If we have an issue that affects our gut, the old style bacteria do the clean up job by eliminating the excess cells that have been created in the stress phase. The viruses and some bacteria that are present in our system rebuild the cells that have been used after the stress phase. (Please refer to Chapters 6 and 9 respectively for the two phases and embryonic layering.)

If the body does not have the fungi, bacteria or virus in the system to do this clean up job then it will use the microbes that are available in the local environment to complete this healing. Some of these microbes are very aggressive in their nature. As an example, I was recently in Egypt at the Red Sea, learning to dive. I was with a group of friends and we all went out to the same restaurants and, half-way through the week, we all came down with the same stomach bug at the same time. We had all eaten in the same restaurants. A few days before this we had been to a restaurant where we were ripped off, not badly but it left us all feeling as if there was something we could not digest. A day later we all came down with the same bug.

My colleagues took a small course of antibiotics. I took one set of them as an experiment and my wife took none. We all recovered at the same time. My wife suffered marginally more pain than I did but we all got better at the same time. My conclusion was that our bodies used the bacteria from the surroundings to complete the regeneration phase. Taking the antibiotics helped to a degree to alleviate the symptoms but the whole problem would and did, disappear if it had been left alone. The problem is, as white Caucasians we are not accustomed to this type of 'Egyptian' bacteria and if something stressful upsets us, as in being ripped off, then our bodies will use the local bacteria that is available. In this case it was a very unpleasant strain of bacteria that caused excessive diarrhoea, instead of what would normally happen where we might have had an unnoticeable loose bowel movement.

We believe that the same occurs in other microbes such as fungi, parasites and viruses. However, the reason why we get these strains is, as I mentioned before, if we do not have the necessary microbes in our system then the body will go out and find the microbes in our local environment. It will build up a reserve of the bacteria in the blood in the stress phase, and then during the regeneration phase the microbes become active doing their work.

If the microbes are not there then the body encapsulates the issue in the brain stem and cerebellum issues. It literally puts a fine tissue around the excessive growth. In muscle or cortex related issues it does not rebuild the used tissue that has necrotised, therefore leaving the body scarred and weaker, as in Osteoporosis or ongoing muscle weakness.

As an example of encapsulation I remember listening to a story of an eighty-year old lady in Australia. After having a terrible argument with her husband, she developed a breast gland tumour in her left breast (she was left-wired, so it affected her on the partner side). She had the tumour removed but the surgeon commented that it was unusual because it looked like a silver bullet. The whole tumour had encapsulated itself. Normally, if she had had tuberculosis in her system, then she would have had an infection and the tumour would have been eaten away by the bacteria. She would have felt a swelling in her breast during this time.

I also worked with a person in St Lucia, who called me and was very worried. As a gift for doing some work for a newly wed couple who were doctors, he was given a full body CT screen. During this time they found a large tumour in his left lung. I questioned him at length and he had had no recent fear of death issues. However, when he was eighteen he did fear for his life, he explained that his mother was an alcoholic and had tried to kill him.

Since he was living in paradise (his words when referring to St Lucia), very happily married, no issues whatsoever, lots of money, a wonderful life, I explained that this was likely to be the shock and that what he must do is have as many chest CTs until he was reassured that the tumour was not getting bigger or had not moved. The doctors told him that he must have it removed. To this day, some 3 years later, he has had two extra lung CTs carried out and the tumour has remained exactly the same size, in the same place, and is doing nothing.

He was asked to have a biopsy and I said he should avoid this because this would puncture the thin membrane of the tumour and this may start the cells multiplying again. This would then mean he would have to have surgery. He has no symptoms whatsoever and has had no symptoms since we spoke. When I spoke to him recently he told me that he is thankful that he has not had surgery or a biopsy. He did the extra CT scan and he told me that he feels as fit as a fiddle. I explained that surgery would have been very invasive and may actually have caused the issue to grow or cause other complications to occur. The doctors wanted to remove a large part of his lung. I also recommended that he check the tumour regularly, using CT, perhaps once a year or less until he was one hundred percent reassured that it was benign, doing nothing. I also explained that he must watch out for any changes in symptoms in his lungs, just to be on the safe side. He has followed through with these recommendations and his doctor friends are also happy with his lack of symptoms, and have stopped asking him to get a biopsy and/or surgery.

He did ask me what would happen if he did get the tuberculosis bacteria into his system. I explained that because the growth had completed its process, then the tuberculosis bacteria would not remove the tumour. He felt reassured by this.

Each person has at least 10,000 times more bacteria inside them than there are people on earth. Each adult human has 1,500 different microbes, of which only about 100 are potentially dangerous. In 1980, The International Committee on Systematic Bacteriology agreed to reduce the accepted number of named species of bacteria from more than 30,000 to about 2,500 species. Yet, without these organisms, life would cease to exist.

Bacteria can be more deadly than snake venom or strychnine, but the majority are actually beneficial. Many are used in the production of antibiotics, as well as enzymes for detergents, for leaching out metals from low grade ores, in the making of foods, and for the conversion of milk sugar (lactose) into lactic acid. Vinegar is produced through bacterial action. Bacteria are even used in the manufacture of cocoa and coffee.

Microbes and the brain layers

Each brain layer has an evolutionary component to it going from the brain stem, cerebellum, cerebral medulla, and cortex. As our brains and embryonic layers have evolved, so has the symbiosis with each layer. I have listed each brain area and added the common microbes that do their repair work in the second phase. You will see there is an overlap between the layers. Therefore in the brain stem and cerebellum some overlap occurs, likewise between the cerebellum and the medulla and the medulla and cortex.

Most bacteria work happily in symbiosis with our bodies. However, some bacteria produce waste products that cause toxins in the system as with some strains of Listeria. Plus if bacteria are starved of oxygen, then they produce toxins that are harmful in the regeneration phase.

Brain Stem

The oldest microbes are directed by the brain stem. Considered to be the "destruction crew" they decompose issues that are formed in the stress phase e.g. colon, lung, kidney or liver. This reparation process takes place only in the regeneration-phase (second phase) and is usually accompanied by fever and a night sweat. If no mycobacterium is available during this healing, then the tumour is encapsulated in scar tissue and stays without further cell augmentation (in cancer this is diagnosed as a benign tumour). Mycobacterium starts multiplying from the point of the conflict shock to the resolution at the same rate of the excessive cell growth. During Part A of the resolution phase (Point 5), the bacteria decompose the excessive cell growth and this waste comes out through the sweat glands or other excretory areas. Symptoms are warm sweat (that leaves a stain on your clothes), and a bad smell from your pores and breath. There could also be bleeding or abscess' forming - as the bacteria eats away at the conflict mass. From Dr Guinée Les Maladies Mémoires de l'Evolution (Diseases, Memories of Evolution - the book is not yet available in English).

Common example of fungi and bacteria that are used in the brain stem directed organs:

Mycobacterium – Fungus – Tuberculosis.

Avium-intracellulare – affects the Pulmonary veins and Lungs.

Mycobacterium scrofulaceum – affects the Cervix.

Histoplasmosis – is a Fungi.

Cryptococcus – causes yeast (Fungi) infections.

Sarcoidosis – is similar to tuberculosis.

Syphilis Spirochaetes bacterium – causes sexual infections.

Candida – is present mostly in the gut.

Tuberculosis – is present mostly in the gut.

Listeria monocytogenes –thought to cause meningitis in new borns.

Cerebellum

Cerebellum directed bacteria are considered the "clean-up worker" as they help decompose issues like acne or tumours, melanoma or breast gland tumours and assist in clearing the remnants. These bacteria play a major role in helping to restore tissue by forming abscesses and filling them with scar tissue.

Common example of fungi and bacteria that are used in the cerebellum directed organs:

Athlete's foot is usually caused by the anthropophile fungi. The most common species are Microsporum, Epidermophyton and Trichophyton. These account for ninety percent of all skin fungal infections, commonly referred to as ringworm.

Tuberculosis – often found in Peritoneum, pericardial and pleura issues.

Listeria monocytogenes –thought to cause meningitis especially in new borns, Septicaemia, and encephalitis.

Endotoxins which include Bacillus, Listeria, Staphylococcus, Streptococcus, Entrerococcus and Clostridium.

Diseases that have bacilli-shaped bacterium include the following: tuberculosis (TB), whooping cough, tetanus, typhoid fever, diphtheria, salmonellosis, shigellosis, legionnaires' disease, and botulism.

Cerebral Medulla

Cerebral Medulla directed bacteria (like staphylococcus) take part in the process of filling the gaps in bones caused by meltdown of callus cells and play a major role in reconstructing the bone with granulating callus forming tissue. Bacteria will also present in the rebuilding of cell loss (necrosis) of ovarian and testicular tissue.

Common example of bacteria that are used in the medulla directed organs:

Staphylococcus aureus - the most common.

Also methicillin-resistant Staphylococcus Aureus or MRSA.

Staphylococcal sepsis – affects the blood.

Tetanus causes lockjaw.

Diseases caused by cocci include the following: pneumonia, tonsillitis, bacterial heart disease, meningitis, septicaemia (blood poisoning), and various skin diseases.

Note: Cocci are round (spherical) cells. They may be true spheres (e.g. staphylococci), helmet-shaped (e.g. pneumococci), or kidney-shaped (e.g. Neisseriae). Cocci may occur alone, in pairs, or in groups. If found in pairs they are called diplococci, threes are a triad, etc. Other group types include: Tetracoccus (groups of four), Streptococcus (chains), Sarcina (cubes of eight), and Staphylococcus (irregular clusters).

Cortex

From an evolutionary point of view viruses are the youngest microbes. Found in organs of the ectoderm such as skin-epidermis, bronchi, the nose or intra-hepatic bile ducts or the cervix and directed by the cerebral cortex. Viruses are part of the "reconstruction" of the regeneration phase; they help replenish the tissue lost during the proceeding ulceration process. Viruses start dividing and multiplying only after the conflict resolution. The regeneration phase involving viruses can be intense and is often accompanied by fever or inflammation.

Common example of viruses that are used in the cortex directed organs:

Human Papillomavirus (HPV) often found in the cervix and penis head

Pneumonia – lungs.

Hepatitis – liver and gall bladder.

Herpes – Sexual organs, lips and skin.

Flu – Bronchi and larynx.

Epstein Barr - Chronic fatigue.

Helicobacter pylori stomach and epithelia cells.

Viruses are present in diseases such as cervical cancer, multiple sclerosis, chronic fatigue, the common cold, Gastric flu, cold sores, smallpox, measles.

I describe other common viruses and microbes in the following chapter about vaccinations plus treatment in the form of antibiotics, including MRSA. In the rest of this chapter I want to explore two other highly controversial subjects, epidemics and AIDS.

Epidemics: Why do they occur?

Often in the teachings of META-Medicine® during this section this question comes up. Why are so many people affected at once with the same infection? In this situation, the collective consciousness is affected and when, as a whole, this group resolves the issue, then they all get the disease. Here is a good example: Before, during and after the First World War and the Second World War there was a massive increase in tuberculosis (TB) that affected the lungs. It was so bad that there were hospitals wards completely dedicated to the treatment of TB. TB was once the leading cause of death in the United States.[65]

What is noticeable is that the increase in the amount of people suffering from TB occurred slowly from the First to Second World War, and by then there were many hospitals all dedicated to its treatment. These hospitals have now all but closed worldwide. Could this have been down to immunisation, or has it occurred because of a shifting in mass consciousness?

TB has been in our systems for a long time. Traces have even been found in Egyptian mummies. It has been known to be a terminal illness for centuries, but since the mid-1800's sanatoriums were used to treat TB. Hermann Brehmer built the first sanatorium in Germany in Gorbersdorf, where treatment consisted of good nutrition and continuous exposure to fresh air. Patients were found to recover from what was thought, at the time, to be a terminal disease.

The strange thing about TB is that the bacteria (mycobacterium tuberculosis) which causes it is known to be in the system of many people. Just because a person may have the bacteria, it doesn't necessarily mean that they feel sick and from a META-Medicine®'s point of view it is only when the bacteria becomes active that is it called the disease 'TB'.

Tuberculosis (TB) in META-Medicine® is the second phase of symptoms from the active bacteria that rebuilds the lung alveoli. The relay for these cells is present in the brain stem. The conflict shock is fear of death. Obviously with two world wars and the ongoing threat of death back then, we would see this type of threat as very real. Many soldiers were diagnosed with tuberculosis in these wars, and often whole barracks in prisoner of war camps were dedicated to the treatment of this disease. The tuberculosis was probably due to the fact that the stress they had been going through and the fear of death, abated when they were captured and then they went into the second phase. During the late 1940's and early 1950's hospitals popped up everywhere to treat the public epidemic of TB. However, today there is no longer any need for hospitals dedicated to the treatment of TB and most of them have closed or are being used as nursing homes. I can hear you say that the closure of these hospitals was caused by the use of vaccinations, notably the BCG (Bacille Calmette and Guérin) vaccination named after the two scientists who discovered it in France in the late 1920's. It is the only vaccine still used against TB. However, this is not the whole story, so before I elaborate on the use of this vaccination in our society I want to mention that TB is very difficult to get out of the system once it is there. It is not a rare bacterium either - one third of the population of the world have it.[66]

In order to eliminate TB from a person, an intensive drug regime of six to nine months has to be administered. It is well known that many people with latent TB hardly ever develop the disease nowadays. (Source: Centre for Disease control and prevention). After the massive increase in TB after the World Wars, the use of chemotherapy was considered, but then the widespread vaccination of whole countries, using the BCG vaccine, came along. However, vaccination and its subsequent extensive use being heralded as the reason for the demise of TB is far from the real story.

From a META-Medicine® point of view, TB is caused by the shock of possible invasion or a threat against a person's life, (fear of death). If this is ongoing, then the person is under of lot of repetitive stress. The disease works like this: During the stress phase there is an extra increase in alveoli (these are the tiny air sacks in the lungs that allow oxygen into our blood and carbon dioxide out). This allows the person to be able to get more oxygen into the system. A person with more oxygen is better equipped to be able to get oxygen to the muscles and therefore fight more effectively, hence overcoming the fear of death.

During this build up of extra cells we also see an increase in the mycobacterium tuberculosis which is lying dormant in the blood. Once the threat of the fear of death has gone, the excessive lung cells that originally had built up are no longer required and therefore not needed by the body. The brain/body tells the bacteria to eat away at the now unnecessary alveoli cells. The symptoms associated with this removal are deep wheezing due to restricted air flow, fever, lack of energy and, most importantly, coughing up blood and sputum from the depths of the lungs.

This coughing up of blood is actually the excessive alveoli having been digested by the mycobacterium tuberculosis being expelled. The easiest way to get these unnecessary cells out of the system is to cough them up. The body uses the most obvious and easiest way to eliminate the unwanted cells. The problem is that it is very scary and when people see blood in their phlegm they think they are dying (mass media explaining the symptomlogy and death rate also causes the cycle of fear of death to repeat itself.)

The Second World War was a great example of this. Once the threat had disappeared, the influx of people suffering from TB increased. Once the fear of death had dissipated along with the subsequent introduction of a vaccine and a cure, the belief systems in people changed and the disease also dissipated.

However vaccination is not the reason for the decline in deaths because the decline in the number of deaths from TB was happening before the introduction of mass immunisation. According to the Commonwealth Year Book No.40, the official figures on TB deaths are: 1921 - 3,687,000. 1931 - 3,167,000. 1941 - 2,734,000. 1951 - 1,538,000. 1961 -   447,000.

Mass immunisation using BCG only started after the Second World War in 1945-1948. However, the decline was already happening before then.

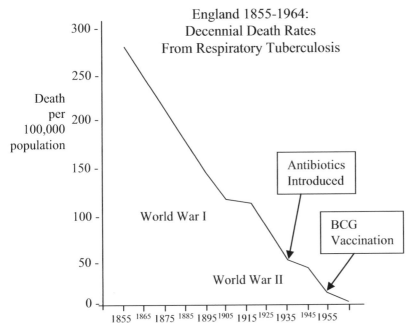

England 1855-1964: Decennial Death Rates From Respiratory Tuberculosis

An interesting graph showing the decline of TB related deaths and the introduction of Anti-biotic and mass immunisation. Clearly we can see the reduction occurring well before these medical interventions.

67

Changes in diet and cleanliness by understanding how the active bacteria got into the system (more on why this is important later) really changed the death rate. This, together with knowing META-Medicine®, the cause being a fear of death conflict, shows that reduction is not due to mass vaccination.

To prove this point, there has been recent increase in TB cases in the United States. This has been attributed to people coming from infected areas and breathing the airborne bacteria over others. But this does not make sense, since people have been travelling into the USA from infected areas during the last fifty years or more. From a META-Medicine® point of view however, the reason is probably due to the aftermath of 9/11. People in the US live in a continuous state of fear. A third of the world's population is infected anyway, so the increase is probably not from these people, but from the fear created by the actions of Al-Qaida, fuelled by a power-hungry US military machine and the media.

I observe the American media, who are masters of prolonging a drama to sell more advertising, and the United States government, who fuel the need for an enemy, probably to maintain the excessive funding of their oversized military machine. They seem to do what they can to make the problem worse. I live in Canada, near Toronto, for six months of the year and the difference in political attitudes between these two neighbours is quite incredible. People don't carry guns in Canada, and therefore their attitude to the threat of an attack is very different. Their military machine is minute in comparison. Al-Qaida did not attack Canada. Canada did not send troops to the Second Gulf War. The Prime Minister of Canada at the time, Jean Chretien, told George W. Bush that Canada would not send troops to the Gulf War. He did not think that the evidence was sufficient to justify invading the country. He wanted to follow through with the UN Security Council's recommendations. He proved to be right.

Statistics from both countries regarding TB show that there was a difference after the 9/11 attacks in the United States. Both countries have consistently seen a reduction in TB. Canada continued to decline after 9/11 but there was a blip in the US, as mentioned here:

"In the United States, the latest national surveillance data show a significant, but slowing, decline in the case rate of TB. In 2004, a total of 14,511 TB cases were reported in the U.S. The overall TB case rate – 4.9 per 100,000 persons – was the lowest rate ever recorded since reporting began in 1953. However, the decline in the case rate from 2003 to 2004 was one of the smallest in more than a decade (3.3 percent compared with an average of 6.8 percent per year). And despite the nationwide downward trend, TB continues to exact a severe toll on many U.S. communities. Seven states now bear more than half the total burden of TB disease in the U.S. California, Florida, Georgia, Illinois, New Jersey, New York, and Texas account for 59.9% of the national case total. The toll continues to be greatest among minority and foreign-born individuals, who consistently have higher rates of TB disease." Centre for Disease Control – Tuberculosis in the United States 2004.[68]

This would fit with META-Medicine®, that is, the decline stopping in the years 2003-2004, would have been after the height of the stress during 2002 following the 9/11 attacks in 2001 and the invasion of Iraq in 2002-2003 - remember that tuberculosis is the second, regeneration phase of the fear of death conflict. America was looking at total eradication of tuberculosis before these events.

What is also interesting is that Canada had no increase in tuberculosis during this time. A report on tuberculosis in Canada up to 2006 shows no change in the decline in the years 2001-2006 in all provinces.[69]

On a smaller scale, regarding epidemics, I remember working with the staff of a school for severely learning-challenged teenaged children in England. I know the Principal very well, he is a personal friend of mine. I spoke to him one day in 2005 and he told me that he had been through hell regarding his work. He had been suspended after being accused of stealing funds from the school. He was found to be completely innocent after three to four months of intense investigation into his personal and business affairs. Naturally he was very, angry during this time and so were all his students with whom he got on very well. The senior staff members, who had instigated the investigation, did not have his charisma, and having alienated the Principal, they also alienated the children.

When my friend was exonerated, he went back to the school, and carried on with his job. The students were very happy about his return, expressing their gratitude in many wonderful ways as Autistic and Asberger children can do.

What was very interesting was that two weeks later the whole school went down with a stomach bug. It affected mostly the students and many of the staff. The whole issue was over in two to three days. There was a mass cleanup in the kitchen area which was blamed for the outbreak.

In META-Medicine® this was the healing crisis of some information that could not be digested. What is surprising from my point of view is that all the students went down with the issue, in addition to those staff members who had shown an affinity towards the Principal. The people that had instigated the whole problem and the people that supported them did not get the stomach bug. He told me that they were the ones who had to work day and night to get the school back to normality. There is natural justice so my friend told me.

I have also seen pockets of people in trainings get the common cold as a whole group bar a few individuals. The question is, 'why do the majority get the issue whilst a small minority is okay?' Surely this virus should attack everyone, but it does not. The only explanation seems to be in a mass belief system that affects a group with similar belief systems, similar to what happens when large groups of people get together for a sports game or a concert - there is a field that affects everyone en masse. I am sure you have experienced this type of field if you have ever been involved with a group of people and, unwittingly, you find yourself dragged into something that you would never normally do - dancing, or taking on a challenge at work as a group. It is not unusual and a recognised phenomenon called morphogenic fields - see Rupert Sheldrake. Lynne McTaggart also wrote a whole book on this subject called 'The Field'. It is therefore not difficult to see how a whole country, a large group or even a small cluster of people (such as a family) could become infected with a microbe simultaneously. The key is to understand that the illness is the regeneration phase of the problem. There would have been a common shock at the start that would have affected the whole group and this then feeds into the group psyche bringing everyone into resolution simultaneously.

AIDS – Acquired Immune Deficiency disorder

AIDS is a regular disease + HIV virus. Without the HIV associated it would just be a regular disease. HIV is not always associated with AIDS; people with AIDS do not always have HIV and people with HIV do not always have AIDS.

Interestingly there are too many different symptoms of AIDS to classify it as a disease. But how was it discovered, here are some interesting facts about AIDS. Luc Montagnier, a French virologist, first isolated HIV in 1983 It was named lymphadenopathy-associated virus, or LAV. When Montagnier first published the discovery, he said LAV or HIV's role in causing AIDS "remains to be determined." He also said he never saw the virus. A year later, a team led by Robert Gallo of the United States confirmed the discovery of the virus and that it caused AIDS, whereupon they renamed it Human T-Lymphotropic Virus type III (HTLV-III). Both men were later credited with the discovery of HIV and AIDS.[70]

Root-Bernstein, a professor of physiology at Michigan State University, suggests that HIV, while involved in the development of AIDS, may be no more important than "co-factors". He states that "HIV is neither necessary nor sufficient to cause AIDS. Both the camp that says HIV is a pussycat and the people who claim AIDS is all HIV are wrong." He

137

has distanced himself from AIDS denialists who argue that HIV is harmless, saying, "The denialists make claims that are clearly inconsistent with existing studies. When I check the existing studies, I don't agree with the interpretation of the data, or, worse, I can't find the studies at all".

This then brings to our attention the whole issue regarding AIDS from a META-Medicine® perspective. When asked about AIDS, Dr Bader explains that the AIDS virus has never been found but on reading through Montagnier's literature, he does say that he did isolate the virus but because it was very fragile he could not photograph it at the time. This is important for science, since other scientists have said that without a picture and other clarification, the virus cannot be verified. However, he now says there are pictures of the virus and that he has seen them.[71]

It still brings us to the point that a receptor T-cell (an antibody that attaches itself to the virus) is the way a person is diagnosed with having the HIV virus. Dr Bader did say that there is a virus in our system that is normal and which only becomes active during territorial sexual encounters. These are caused when a male or a female steps away from their respective life partners and has an affair.

To explain this on the end of the penis (in uncircumcised men) and under the hood that protects the clitoris, the body produces a natural lubricant called smegma[72] which for each one of us has a unique smell. During female-male sexual intercourse, the smegma is rubbed onto the pubic hair of the opposite partner. This smell is designed to ward off other females and males to say, 'this person belongs to me.'

If that person, male or female, has an affair and their main life partner smells smegma on them from someone else, then this can cause a sexual territorial conflict. Apparently a person can detect even the slightest smell of another person's smegma on their partner. If the conflict is resolved, the end of the penis and under the hood of the clitoris becomes inflamed and in the resolution phase of this conflict, this is what the scientist found to be the positive antibody test for HIV. This is HIV, according to what Dr Bader is saying. Also this is a brain stem directed organ and therefore a bacterium, not a virus is produced in the system. The symptoms are similar to a bad cough - enlarged glands, weight loss and some diarrhoea. It does not kill.

When they experience this conflict a person will become diagnosed with AIDS, and an HIV test will be positive. When another conflict, for example, hits the bone, they will get bone symptoms. Hence the diagnosis of a bone issue plus having a HIV positive test means the person has AIDS.

With AIDS there are no specific AIDS symptoms, unlike in the case of measles or pneumonia. AIDS is a set of different symptoms that vary from person to person. When someone shows symptoms of cancer, rheumatism, tuberculosis or pneumonia they get a diagnosis of that specific disease. If they have one of these diseases and they test positive for the antibody, which means HIV is present, then they have AIDS.

From a META-Medicine® perspective, no-one has ever died from HIV. There are many people who have tested HIV positive and are not ill, they do not even display even a single symptom. Trillions of dollars that have been spent on trying to find a cure/vaccine for aids but they still do not have one. Clinical trials are being carried out for a vaccine but none have been proven to work yet. One of the side effects of this vaccine is that the client tests positive to HIV. I guess it is a waiting game to see if the vaccine works, and therefore how many people go on to develop AIDS. As I discussed later in chapter 11 on vaccines, I have my doubts as to whether this will work or will simply be a way of the pharmaceuticals to make money.[73]

The only way to establish if a person has HIV is to test for antibodies. However, people have been known to test positive for HIV after having been vaccinated with the Salk Polio vaccine. There has been some research into the Salk vaccine, for Polio may be linked to AIDS.[74]

Dr Stephan Lanka, a virologist who was one of the first people to separate a virus in the lab and who is also a very controversial figure, has mentioned that the AIDS virus has never been found, though in my research Montagnier has said otherwise. Dr Lanka was one of the first people to isolate a virus in sea algae. He isolated, photographed and biochemically marked it. This is what you do to prove the existence of something biological in science. When he went on to research into the AIDS virus, he could not find any evidence whatsoever in any scientific literature to prove that the AIDS virus exists.

Nor could he find proof of a virus for measles, mumps or rubella. He also says that there are no viruses freely moving around in the body. Many of the pictures that you see of viruses are either bacteria or stains in an electron microscope, or some proteins that are in a specific pattern. It is similar to trying to prove that a black hole exists; it cannot be done. The surroundings give some indication that black holes exist but no one has proven it, as yet.

If Lanka is right, then the medical profession and the pharmaceutical industry will be proven to have made a massive mistake. He does have a good argument and he has written to many universities, asking for evidence that viruses exist in humans. To date not one university has been able to prove this fact.

Here is a small extract taken from an interview with Dr Stefan Lanka.

"While most people in the U.S. and Western Europe go right on believing that the so-called Human Immunodeficiency Virus [HIV] is the sole cause of AIDS, debate rages even within the alternative AIDS community over whether HIV exists at all. Though Peter Duesberg, Ph.D. -- virtually the only alternative AIDS theorist with any significant public reputation -- continues to insist that HIV exists but is harmless, other alternative AIDS researchers and activists are coming to the conclusion that the virus doesn't exist. The main proponents of this view are Australian researcher Eleni Papadopulos-Eleopulos and her colleagues, who argue that HIV has never been isolated according to the Pasteur Institute criteria of 1973, and therefore it's probably what's called an "endogenous retrovirus" -- a creation of the body's own genetic material that looks and functions partly like a virus, but is not an infection because it comes from the body's own cells.

Stefan Lanka, Ph.D. takes the challenge to HIV's existence even further. A German researcher, Dr. Lanka is usually referred to as a virologist. But that hardly begins to describe his wide-ranging fields of study. Based on experiences in marine biology, biochemistry, evolutionary biology and virology, he's worked out a whole new view of HIV and AIDS. He believes that all so-called retroviruses are actually the body's own creations; that hepatitis is an autoimmune disorder (a disease in which the body is attacked by components of its own immune system) rather than a viral disease; that AIDS has nothing to do with immune suppression; and that it should really be called Acquired Energy Deficiency Syndrome -- AEDS -- because its true cause is a breakdown in the delivery of oxygen to the blood and/or body tissues."[75]

What about the expensive drugs designed to stop HIV? AZT, the drug supposedly used to 'cure' AIDS was only tested on a small handful of people before it was licensed. It was later discounted as preventative medicine in the Concorde tests after it had been handed out to thousands who were HIV positive but still healthy.[76] Now HIV positive people take a combination therapy, which contains AZT.

My belief is that HIV is probably of the body's own making. The body is healing itself from the conflict caused by a person having sex with another person who is not their main partner. That person can smell the smegma of the other person on them after they have had sex. This causes a stress conflict that, once solved, will cause the common symptoms associated with AIDS.

Gay men are more promiscuous than heterosexual couples, and having many sexual encounters is normal for a gay man in the gay community. However, the territorial issues produced by smegma are 'mother nature's way of keeping partnerships together and creating monogamy. Plus gay sexual practices can cause the immune system to be under threat. The doctor, Paul Gallo, who discovered the HIV and AIDS, did so in gay men who were having very intense and invasive gay sex with multiple partners. This often involved digesting other people's faeces, along with taking lots of recreational drugs. Their systems would have been severely compromised over time by these practices. The respiratory symptoms could lead to pneumonia and muscle wastage followed by diarrhoea all common symptoms of AIDS[77].

Another pointer to this fact is that the epidemic that should have occurred in the heterosexual population has not materialised.[78] Every heterosexual male or female would have to have at least five extra, unprotected sexual encounters a year to reach the same incidence of AIDS as in the gay community. Heterosexuals and even lesbian women just don't have this number of sexual encounters, hence, the reduced incidence of HIV in these groups.

There is also a belief that once a person has been told that they have HIV, it can become a self-fulfilling prophecy. You may argue with this point, but what we know of conflict shocks and metastasis in cancer clients, suggests the same thing that is happening when a person is diagnosed with AIDS.

In Africa the increase in AIDS could be put down to malnutrition, a man having multiple partners (male and female), and mass vaccination.

In conclusion, do microbes cause disease or is it more complex than we are led to believe? I am fully aware that some bacteria can cause serious issues to occur. However what we have been sold by the media and the medical profession needs to be re-thought. We do need to re-think our approach to microbes, as can be found in the treatment of bladder cancer, where immunisation using the BCG vaccine has been found to be more successful than chemotherapy.[79]

So the cleaning epidemic has had an effect on all of us. I believe that this has probably been the reason why we are so much healthier than before the introduction of cleanliness but the belief that these microbes are the reason for disease is misconstrued. It is not as simple as we have been lead to believe. We need microbes in our system to survive.

This leads me onto the next chapter where I will discuss antibiotics and immunisation and here we shall see what the belief that microbes are evil killers has created in the way of trying in vain to eradicate certain viruses, bacteria and fungi from us all.

Can we believe what we are being sold by our doctors, the pharmaceutical companies, the media and governments for our long term benefit, or is there sometime more disturbing going on?

Chapter 11

Antibiotics and Vaccination

"The trouble with being a hypochondriac these days is that antibiotics have cured all the good diseases."
Caskie Stinnett (American writer)

Antibiotics

What effects do antibiotics have on our systems? What do these do to our bodies?

My wife recently gave birth to our wonderful son. It was a challenging time. We live in Canada now and being from the UK, I was not familiar with the health care system or the attitudes of nurses and doctors here. Overall the experience was very good. However, I do want to mention something that happened that seemed completely out of our control.

It is common procedure in Canada to test for the Group B streptococcal bacteria in a woman's birth canal prior to giving birth. Because Kristin, my wife, was not tested for this, the doctors wanted to give her antibiotics as soon as we entered the delivery room. We questioned this, asking why, and after a very intense meeting with one of the nurses, where emotional blackmail was used, we were told we could be putting our baby at risk. The doctors did not give her the antibiotics after all. However I was not happy with the pressure we were put under, so I started to research into what happened.

I found out that that this bacterium can affect the baby and may cause a blood infection of one or more of the following: Sepsis, pneumonia and meningitis. I have since found out that about a third of the population has this bacterium and live happily with no effects whatsoever. The bacterium Streptococcal resides in the gut and vaginal canal of many healthy women. The chance of it affecting the baby is only zero point five percent.[80] What is even more frightening is that the use of intravenous antibiotics during pregnancy does not seem to stop babies getting blood infections. In fact there seems to be some proof that suggests that the use of antibiotics actually depresses the immunity of the baby in later life, causing even more complications. The overuse of antibiotics has caused the development of many strains of antibiotic-resistant bacteria. And just so you know, the most common type of infection from streptococcal bacteria is 'strep throat' and the people most affected are five to fifteen year olds.

My wife's waters had broken early, and unfortunately this carried with it many complications, including a greater than normal risk of the baby becoming infected with this particular bacterium.

As I mentioned, we did not have the antibiotics. We were certain that all was well with the baby, so we planned on having a natural, vaginal birth. Unfortunately there were no signs of the baby coming out so, after a lot of deliberation, we had a semi-elected Caesarean section. The birth went well; we had used hypnosis for much of the labour, and the positive suggestions through hypnosis during the Caesarean section meant that Kristin made an incredibly fast recovery from the surgery. She came home after two days and was carrying baby Oliver. Many women take a lot longer to recover from undergoing Caesarean sections, so we are told, and cannot hold their babies or carry anything for up to a month. The use of positive suggestion through hypnosis seemed to make a difference.

However, I found out that Kristin was given intravenous antibiotics after the surgery, without being asked. So was it right? Was it wrong? After all, she did have major surgery. About six percent of women develop complications from a Caesarean section. This apparently is very high, and as a lay person I cannot question these facts. What I can question however, using META-Medicine® when we look at this type of intervention, is the dilemma of how and when antibiotics are prescribed.

Antibiotics – how are they used?

The issue with antibiotics is not whether they are good or bad. It is how they are used and their over-use that I have to query. I want to answer this question from a META-Medicine® perspective. Lynn McTaggart, in her excellent book 'What Doctors Don't Tell You' mentions a very emotional story about how her mother was saved through antibiotics. In 1942 her mother could have died through a massive infection that was caused by the unwise removal of a tooth by her dentist. She had a streptococcus infection in her neck from the minor surgery, which Lynn says would probably have killed her. She was administered the 'Last Rites' but luckily she was given an experimental drug called Penicillin. The infection disappeared within two days and Lynn's mother survived to tell the tale to her then unborn daughter.

Antibiotics have defined modern medicine and I do believe they have played an important part in saving many peoples lives. However, many bacteria have become resistant to antibiotics, the most well-known of these are the so-called super bugs, MRSA and Clostridium Difficile. All medical doctors have recently been told not to administer antibiotics as freely as they did in the past, due to this worrying drug resistance.

The question is, why? Why is this happening? It is obvious that bacteria can mutate but why would they do that? In META-Medicine® I have mentioned that bacteria are there for a reason (Chapter 10). When you look at the two phases in the regeneration phase, microbes are there to rebuild or remove the effects that have occurred during the stress phase. Therefore we say they are doing something positive. However, the body uses the bacteria that are available in the environment to do its work. It will use whatever it thinks will do the best clean-up job. This means that during the stress phase, extra bacteria are being created in the blood, as I discussed earlier when I mentioned dark field microscopy. If these bacteria are eliminated through the use of antibiotics, and the body is under stress, then the body will find whatever bacteria it can in the environment to complete the disease process.

If practically all bacteria in a person's system have been eliminated by antibiotics, and the only bacteria that is available is MRSA or Clostridium Difficile because they are resistant, then the body will use those to do the work. Both bacteria are probably very poor at completing this work in comparison to the millions of other bacteria that we have in our system, which are living in beautiful symbiosis with our bodies, until they get killed off by the over use of the antibiotics.

We could then postulate that giving large amounts of antibiotics over an extended period of time actually weakens our whole system, making the person's body more likely to use the superbugs as a way of resolving the second phase.

The most vulnerable people likely to get superbugs are the old, young and very ill. They have found that the spread of these superbugs can be reduced by good hygiene. In fact, very good hygiene can eliminate the spread of many unpleasant bacteria. This is an argument that I will come back to later when we look at vaccines. Each year, at least 100,000 people who go into hospital get an infection there. MRSA is one example of this.

What is MRSA and why don't antibiotics work against it?

Staphylococcus is a family of common bacteria. Many people naturally carry it in their throats, and it can cause a mild infection in a healthy patient. MRSA stands for methicillin-resistant Staphylococcus aureus, but is shorthand for any strain of Staphylococcus bacteria which is resistant to one or more conventional antibiotics.[81]

Another interesting issue with antibiotics is their use by the medical profession to combat viral infections. Viruses are effectively the rebuilders of our system after the stress phase that caused necrosis in the organs. During the second phase, (the regeneration phase) the viruses are active. Antibiotics work by killing off the bacteria in our system. ANTIBIOTICS DO NOT WORK AGAINST VIRUSES! They never have and never will work. So why do doctors prescribe them to clear up viral infections?

Apart from placebo which I mentioned earlier, an answer is that the patient wants a pill or a course of pills to stop their symptoms. Sometimes the course works, sometimes not. We can only postulate as to why they sometimes work. More often than not it's because the person heals through the belief that the drugs are having an effect - the placebo effect. This often happens and is how many drugs are tested. Most placebos do an excellent job of healing people, sometimes even better than the drug itself. Another assumption is that the bacteria carry the viruses in them and killing the bacteria through antibiotics stops the viruses from spreading.

Dr Stefan Lanka, who I mentioned earlier, reported that viruses in the body are not able to exist independently. They must have a host cell in order to do their job. They are viruses but they cannot be separated from proteins that often collect in living cells.

Dr Stefan Lanka also says that the brain creates viruses as a symbiotic instruction to complete healing. He is controversial because he says things such as: 'There is NO AIDS virus'. No one has ever proven its existence. They have only established that there is an antigen. No one has ever separated an HIV virus in a lab anywhere in the world. So does HIV exist? Can you develop a test for a virus that you have never been able to isolate? His argument is no.[82]

Back to antibiotics: Are they good or bad? The answer, when we consider META-Medicine® is, 'good if used correctly and if used sparingly.' They do work in small quantities for bacterial infections that are life-threatening or that could severely disable a person. In using antibiotics for dealing with common, annoying infections such as a persistent cold or an aggravating ear infection, (both of which are viral infections), we need to look deeper into the stressful causes to find better solutions than giving out antibiotics as the be all and end all to solving every ailment.

So how should we be dealing with bacterial infections? If the body's symbiotic relationship with bacteria and viruses is upset by the use of antibiotics, and since eighty-five percent of all of these bacteria resides in our gut, then after taking a course of antibiotics we need to replace the missing bacteria by taking pro-biotics. This is what my wife did after we found out that she had been given antibiotics following her Caesarean section. I believe that the antibiotics were useful; hospitals are not clean places and there would be many different strains of bacteria about in a confined place. If she had got an unpleasant strain of bacteria from the surgery, it could have infected her womb as it healed and caused many complications.

As regards the original antibiotics that the nurse forcefully tried to persuade my wife to take, I believe we did the right thing. Streptococcus is not dangerous, it is in the throats of many people, and it lives happily in symbiosis with us as humans. Different strains have become immune to antibiotics due to mutations. So killing off your own good strain of bacteria could easily cause you to get a mutated strain in hospital. Since, in this instance, the chance of the bacteria in my wife's birth canal affecting the baby was ten thousand to one, we made the right choice.

Generally, if we have been under a lot of stress and we have had surgery or a deep infection which required us to have antibiotics, then we need to be more careful to avoid unhygienic places which are full of dangerous bacteria, ironically places such as hospitals or doctors' surgeries. We need to cook food carefully until we have rebuilt the reserve of our own symbiotic bacteria which can be deployed if we have a stressful event. We also need to be careful about putting ourselves under extreme stress again. After we have had a proper medical diagnosis, a good rest is possibly the best tonic. I am not saying anything controversial here since this is often what doctors prescribe when a person arrives with a persistent cold or ongoing earache. As long as the issue is not life threatening, bed rest is often the best solution, and was a genuine prescription before our lives became so busy.

Vaccinations

This brings me to vaccinations. Two months after the birth of our beautiful little boy, my wife announced that we had an appointment in two days time to have him vaccinated. She asked me what I thought. I said that I did not know and I needed to do some research. Both of us had been vaccinated as school children and both have had chicken pox, mumps, and measles; we came out unscathed and are both in good health.

However, knowing that META-Medicine® says that fungi, bacteria and viruses are all there for a reason and that the only thing that causes a person to get a disease is a stressful event, together with the fact that the strains of any of these microbes alter daily, I felt that I needed to study this in more detail. But I had no time to do this so we went to the doctor and asked her. She persuaded us that we were doing the right thing for our child. The arguments were very convincing. She told us about a local Dutch community who refused to have the whopping cough vaccine; one of the unvaccinated children died because they contracted whooping cough. She also mentioned a case where a child had developed autism after having the combination vaccine against measles, mumps and rubella, was probably because the child had signs of this issue before the vaccination.

At two months we had Oliver vaccinated against various diseases (HIB, Pc, DTaP, Rotavirus, and Polio - each one of these vaccines/diseases will be explained later). We were told to come back two months later for the same vaccinations to be given again. He was full of fever for that day but he quickly recovered. What went through my mind was: Was this really necessary? Did he really need to have these vaccines? What was he really being vaccinated for? Why did we need to go back two months later? Surely that was it? He had been given the vaccine so why did he need more? This chapter will answer those questions.

I was not convinced by what had happened that day in the doctor's surgery. There seemed to be an air of vigilantism, as if we were killing the bad guys and helping the good.

We were also both scared; it is our beautiful baby boy, our only child. We want to protect him as parents. Because of the circumstances, emotions were running high that day.

144

When I set out to write about vaccines I did so with a completely open mind. I wanted to find the facts and the details so that I could approach our excellent medical doctor with information that would prove the validity, or otherwise, of the vaccines that were being given to our young son. To my horror I found very little evidence from bona fide sources to back up the mass vaccination of all children at such young ages. This appals me. I am truly shocked. What follows is my research along with the META-Medicine® perspective.

What do doctors know about vaccination?

I know and respect the medical profession. Especially doctors. I know they have little time to do research into many subjects, and they only have time to look at their medical association's journals, and listen to naturally biased pharmaceutical representatives. Doctors are people too. They work extremely hard, and they do terrific jobs, but they cannot possibly follow or know everything that is going on in the world. Vaccines have been the main stay of a doctor's arsenal against infection and disease since they were introduced. They would never and could never question them.

Governments promote vaccinations with a vengeance. In many states in the USA you have to have your children vaccinated before they can attend school. It is the same in Canada, except you can object to your child having the vaccines and they can still attend school. In the UK and Europe it may go the same way as the some of the states in the USA.

Ever the sceptic, I looked further into this minefield of a subject. As I delved into the world of vaccinations I was shocked to find so little evidence to back up their use. I became fascinated with the subject and wanted to find out more. On our next visit to the doctor I had a different opinion as to having Oliver vaccinated.

There is so much written, for and against vaccinations that I do not want to go into depth in this book. What I do want to outline is some basic information that can be used in a META-Medicine® context and also as material for an educated debate.

I have used Lynne McTaggart's book, 'What Doctors Don't Tell You' and 'The Vaccine Book' by Robert Sears M.D. F.A.A.P. as my major references. Both seem to give a good, well researched idea as to the 'why we should vaccinate' and 'why we should not'. For a full in-depth review of vaccines I do recommend you buy both books. Lynne McTaggart's book is still available and was updated in 2005, and you can also download it on www.wddty.com. Dr Sears book is also available via Amazon or in bookstores worldwide. His website is www.thevaccinebook.com.

With the knowledge of META-Medicine® that the microbes are only active in the second regeneration phase, and that they are there as repairers of our system, we can look at why we get specific diseases in the first place and also what these diseases are repairing.

From this we can deduce preventative measures and perhaps look at the whole picture and make a good, well informed decision as to what works and what does not. I am going to take each disease and look at the vaccine, add the META-Medicine® element along with some facts for you to consider. I will not say whether you should or should not get your child vaccinated. I will merely point out the facts and if you, like my wife, and me have a young child that needs to be vaccinated, I urge you to buy the books and make up your own mind.

Right up front, I want to say that doctors are taught a lot about disease but they are not taught a lot about vaccines. What they are told in the United States is that the Federal Drug Administration (FDA) and the pharmaceutical industry do a lot of research into vaccines to make sure they are safe and effective. Doctors don't review the research themselves. They trust and take it for granted that the proper research is carried out.[83]

Here is a list of all the Vaccines given to a child in America in 1983 compared with 2007. Note the massive increase in vaccinations over the past 25 years. My wife said she had been vaccinated and it did her no harm. The difference here is she and I only had 10 vaccine shots for 7 diseases, my son would have 35 vaccine shots for 16 diseases. The question is, is this necessary? You be the judge as I go through each of the 2009 vaccines.

CDC recommended Vaccine schedule 1983 (7 seperate vaccines)

2 months	Diphtheria Tetanus Pertusis DTP
2 months	Oral poliomyelitis vaccine OPV
4 months	Diphtheria Tetanus Pertusis DTP
4 months	Oral poliomyelitis vaccine OPV
6 months	Diphtheria Tetanus Pertusis DTP
15 months	Measles Mumps Rubella MMR
18 months	Diphtheria Tetanus Pertusis DTP
18 months	Oral poliomyelitis vaccine OPV
4 years	Diphtheria Tetanus Pertusis DTP
4 years	Oral poliomyelitis vaccine OPV

CDC recommended Vaccine Schedule 2009 (16 seperate vaccines for boys, 17 for girls)

Birth	Hep B
1 month	Hep B
2 months	HIB, Pc, DTaP, Rotavirus, Polio
4 months	HIB, Pc, DTaP, Rotavirus, Polio
6 months	HIB, Pc, DTaP, Rotavirus, Hep B, Flu
1 year	MMR, Pc, Varicella (Chickenpox), Hep A
15 months	HIB, Pc, Hep B
18 months	DTaP, Polio, Hep A, Flu
2 years	Flu, Pc (if high risk)
3 years	Flu, Hep A Series (if high risk)
4 years	Flu
5 years	DTap, Polio, MMR Series, Flu (yearly), Varicella Series (Chickenpox)
12 years	Tdap, Meningococcal, Hep A Series, Hep B Series, HPV (3 doses girls only)
13-18years	Tdap, Meningococcal, HPV Series (girls only)

*CDC – Centre for Disease Control in the USA. The UK often follows the CDC recommendations as do Europe but changes do occur with each country, please visit your relevant health websites for more information.

Haemophilus Influenza Type B – HIB Vaccine

Here is my summary of what Dr Sears says about HIB. HIB is a bacterial infection that causes mostly nasal, ear and throat infections. It can also cause meningitis (inflammation of the lining of the brain) blood infections and pneumonia. It is transmitted in the same way as the common cold. Most cases of HIB go undiagnosed. Diagnosis requires a blood test or a spinal tap. The infection does not give a person life long immunity. It affects mostly young children and the elderly. It is different from the Meningococcal bacterium which can affect anyone at any age.

HIB is not common now; before the vaccine came into use in the mid 1980's there were 20,000 cases a year in the United States, where as now there are only 25 each year.

The biggest issue is meningitis, since it has a five percent fatality rate and a twenty-five percent probability of some residual brain damage occurring. The other problem is that it is difficult to diagnose, so even if a child has it, it can take up to two days to identify the HIB in a blood sample.

It is treatable by intravenous antibiotics over several days in hospital.

There are several vaccines given over many months until the age of two. The vaccine is made from the bacteria. The sugars that form the outer coat are filtered out and these sugars are then bonded with other agents which come from the tried and tested, diphtheria/tetanus vaccines, and that is what the vaccine is produced from. There is some aluminium used in the PedVaxHIB brand. Research has not proven that the aluminium in vaccines is harmful. Some studies indicate that if too many vaccines containing aluminium are given at once, a toxic effect can occur.

Side effects of the vaccine affect five percent of the babies. Of these side effects, the most serious includes Guillain-Barre syndrome, which causes severe muscle weakness and paralysis. In vaccine trials more babies caught HIB than those who did not get the vaccine. The pharmaceutical industry said that they were infected by another HIB bacterium, and because it was already in their systems before they were vaccinated, the vaccines had not had the chance to build up immunity. This has changed over time since there is less HIB bacteria in the population.

Looking at the HIB vaccine, it appears that the incidence of the disease is now widely unreported, largely because surveillance procedures have declined.[84] It also seems that the incidence of adult HIB meningitis has increased and the average age for contracting the disease is now twenty-five.

From a META-Medicine® perspective the HIB bacterium is affecting the meninges, which are the protective membranes of the brain and spinal chord. These are probably connected to the cerebellum, meaning the cells grow in the first phase, and then the HIB bacterium eats away at the excessive tissue in the second phase. Hence, the infection and the resulting symptomology of swelling of the brain. Coupled with a kidney collecting tubule, excessive water collecting around parts of the brain and spinal chord, this would cause excessive pressure on the outer cells of the brain. Here we have the motor sensor areas (as per Penfield) and other sensory areas, including the eyes (hence seeing stars and getting a headache plus blurred vision). This would also explain the Guillain-Barre symptoms that occur with HIB meningitis.

The conflicts are an attack or fear of attack aimed at the head, or fear of having a psychiatric or neurological disease – therefore the attack is focussed against your centre of command (your intellect, brain) which is probably why it affects college students as they can feel threatened by a possible attack against their intelligence. Also fear of protecting your head in some situations - see below for infants.

The most likely cause of the brain and spinal chord being affected in this way is if the baby has been hit on the head, or around the spinal chord. The resulting attack would have to be unexpected and follow the UDIN criteria mentioned earlier, in chapter 4. The reason the meninges increase the number of cells is to protect the delicate brain and spinal chord areas from attack, literally creating extra layers of leathery skin to stop any further impending attack. My postulation is that this type of shock could occur in a kindergarten setting, by one child repeatedly hitting another child over the head or on the back in the spinal area. Children can be very cruel to each other.

It does make sense then that if the child does not attend child-care and has been breast fed (probably has the anti-bodies in the blood stream from the mother's milk) then the likely chance of getting this disease in the US or the UK is now rare. Also, as a parent it is worth noting that the vaccine has one of the safest side effect profiles of all the vaccines.

Pneumococcal – Pc vaccine (Prevnar in the US)

Here is my summary of what Dr Sears says about the Pc. Pneumococcus (Pc) is a bacterium; its proper name is streptococcus pneumoniae. It causes a wide range of illnesses from the symptoms of a mild cold, severe pneumonia, blood stream infections and meningitis. It is transmitted in the same way as the common cold. It is dangerous when it affects infants, toddlers and the elderly. Most people experience symptoms similar to a common cold. It is diagnosed by a blood test or spinal tap. It is the most common cause of infant meningitis. It has never been a reported disease, so it is not known how widespread it is. However, it is a common bacterial cause of respiratory infections (although cold and flu viruses are more common).

Pc is common and there are reported incidents in hospitals. On the whole, unfortunately, there are few statistics available. There also seems to be an antibiotic resistance to Pc occurring as well.

The vaccine was introduced in 2001 and the Center for Disease Control (The CDC) in the United States estimate that there were 60,000 cases of severe pneumococcal diseases occurring each year before vaccination began. About 17,000 were children under five years of age. These figures have decreased since the vaccination was introduced.

How they can tell this I do not know because, as I said earlier, there are few statistics available. The vaccine is made in a similar way to the HIB vaccine. It also contains aluminium, which could be toxic if given in large quantities.

Recently the number of reported cases of Pc shows that the strains of bacteria used in the vaccine account for only four percent of people who are infected. The PC vaccine has either worked or the more likely reason is that the bacterium has mutated. This is not a new phenomenon because it happens with the Flu virus and the common cold.

Lynne McTaggart does not have an opinion about the Pc vaccine in her book but her website talks about a trial carried out in Sweden in 1998, where they conclude that the vaccine had an opposite effect; they concluded that you were more likely to get the disease if you were vaccinated.[85] The trial was carried out in middle-aged people and elderly, not babies, to whom the vaccine is usually given. Interestingly at ages two, four, six and fifteen months of age for the US and, since September 2006 two, six and thirteen months for the UK. I have no idea why there is a difference as to the timing.

In META-Medicine®, it appears that the tissue which is probably affected is from the brain stem. Since it affects the pharyngeal gland, the middle ear and the lungs (most probably the bronchi and alveoli, although I cannot be certain of this), the meningitis causes swelling of the brain stem, interrupting the flow of brain fluid and causing damage to the brain structures. The most likely reason for the swelling is the Kidney Collecting Tubule syndrome during the second phase, with the healing crisis being the point of which to be very careful. I discussed this syndrome, page 61 and the healing crisis in chapter 8.

There are two conflicts that relate to this issue. The first is not being able to develop your gifts as a person, literally being suppressed in some way, held back. Another conflict is hearing words that you are forced to take on and you cannot shut them down in yourself (this affects the throat). You are told something about yourself but inside you know it is not true. E.g. a child is told he/she is a liar, and told to tell everyone when they clearly know it is not true.

The reason that one child can be affected by Meningitis in a different area/way than another child is because of the different issues that the child has experienced. Occurrence in the brain stem would mean that the person or child has heard or swallowed something that they cannot digest. The different strains occur because the body uses the bacteria that it finds locally in the environment to complete the regeneration phase. Since this bacterium is in all of us and it mutates rapidly then vaccinating to eradicate it will probably be impossible. I want to reiterate that it is well known that we all carry this bacterium in our system and it lives happily in symbiosis with all of us, and has done for millions of years. Just like the tuberculosis bacterium, which again affects the brain stem organs; eradication is impossible. Cleanliness and interrupting the spread of the bacteria by not taking an infected child to a nursery is probably the best form of defence.

The Prevnar vaccine and its substitutes around the world will never be able to keep up with bacterial mutations. In April 2008 in the UK a new strain of the pneumococcal appeared, the same has been reported in the US. It appears that as soon as the vaccine stops one set of the bacteria, a newer and sometimes more aggressive bacteria develops. This fits in with the META-Medicine® theory that the body uses the bacteria in the local environment to solve the issues caused by the stress stage. The filling of a gap seems to be what is happening. We get rid of a group of one type of bacteria and it is replaced with something far worse, which we cannot treat with antibiotics as in the case of MRSA.

This fact alone would make anyone question the long-term validity of this vaccine. The vaccine has only been in use in the UK since 2006, and the reported incidence of data to establish its effectiveness is also unavailable in the UK, as in the US. The UK and the US vaccine authorities often seem to work closely with each other. Is this vaccine pharmaceutically and/or politically driven? Or is it of a real benefit to society at large? There are no concrete facts to prove this and doctors rarely question these facts. The reported side effects of the vaccine are mild in comparison to other vaccines, such as the MMR.

Diphtheria, Tetanus and Pertusis (Whooping cough) – DTaP vaccine

Diphtheria. Here is my summary of what Dr Sears says about Diphtheria, it is a very severe throat infection which is caused by a bacterium called Corynebacterium diptheriae. It releases a toxin that irritates the lining of the throat and upper lungs causing harsh coughing and breathing problems. About ten percent of cases are fatal. Sometimes the swelling is so intense that it can close off the airway completely. It is also treatable with antitoxins. Diphtheria is not common now but was in the early 20th century.

Lynne McTaggart explains and I have summaries that diphtheria vaccine wears off its immunity as we get into adulthood, and in the new Russia the vaccine has proven not to curb epidemics. Eighty-six percent of people a year have diphtheria after being given booster shots. Even the vaccine review, which was sponsored by the US, concluded that this vaccine was not as an effective immunising agent as had been anticipated.

A recent topical example: Dr Ossi Mansoor, a principal doctor regarding vaccination policy, stated on Radio Pacific, "The figures we have show that there were 800 deaths every year in the 1920's" (from diphtheria). Yet the New Zealand Government's statistics show the average yearly number was below 100, also that the average death rate per 10,000 mean of population fell from 6.08 to 0.20 before the use of the diphtheria vaccine (Southland Times 30-Sep-1998). This statement, coming from a doctor, created a good deal of 'fear' in people, around what was an extremely mild case of diphtheria in an unvaccinated child.

META-Medicine® says that Diphtheria affects the cortex and the infection affects the throat and the lungs in the second regeneration phase. The cause of the conflict is a shocking fear of dying because you are incapable of calling for help. This affects the larynx or bronchial muscles. The closing of the throat which stops the person from breathing is likely be the healing crisis, as the swelling seems so severe.

149

Tetanus. Here is my summary of what Dr Sears says: Tetanus is caused by a bacterium that thrives in soil and on dirty, rusty metal and contaminated needles. Once in the system the bacteria secretes a toxin that gets into the nervous system causing paralysis, starting with the jaw first, hence it's commonly referred to as lock jaw. It is not common because nowadays people with infected wounds have them cleaned with water and disinfectants. Internationally it is far more prevalent in young children, probably due to unsterilized instruments being used during birth. It is fatal in fifteen percent of cases. It is not really treatable if the toxins have got into the system; it has to run its course. A person will, however, need life support and intensive care for a few weeks.

If a person does get a deep wound and there is a chance of tetanus being present, then an injection of the tetanus immune globulin (TIG) can immediately deactivate any tetanus bacteria.

The incidence of people dying from tetanus was decreasing well before the introduction of the vaccine. Tetanus is very rare in developed countries and the chances of dying from it small.[86]

META-Medicine® would say that the tetanus infection would be the body's way of cleaning a wound. The issue occurs in the tetanus bacterium releasing such paralysing toxins that it cripples a person. There may be a biological reason for this. Perhaps, from nature's view point, the wound may be so deep that it renders the animal useless to the rest of the herd, therefore the animal becomes paralysed, causing it to be left behind whereupon it dies without holding back or endangering the remaining healthy members of the herd therefore survival of the fittest. This issue affects the Cortex area of the brain, hence the paralysis.

Other conflicts that I have noted from my readings from META-Medicine® are conflicts of dirty blood or stained blood, or blocked nerves, due to an internal conflict of feeling separated from oneself. This causes a person to have to go further than they are capable of going. They are being asked to go beyond what they think they are capable of doing as a person. The nervous system feels it is being attacked by the suggestions. What happens is that the nerves become blocked so they do not carry out the order that will force them to go beyond their capabilities. The spasms caused by the muscular contractions are to get them out of the entrapment that has been imposed upon them.

Pertusis or whooping cough. Here is my summary of what Dr Sears says that Whooping cough is caused by secretion of a toxin from a bacterium called Bordetella Pertusis that infects the upper lung and throat. Symptoms are similar to the common cold in the first week and then the cough gets worse with fits of prolonged coughing which can last thirty seconds or even up to two minutes. The cough is so bad that the person can barely breathe, and when it is finally possible the sound is like 'gasping for air' or a 'whoop', hence the name. You catch it like the common cold and infection creates lifelong immunity, although the medical community recommends a person should continue with vaccination after they have had the disease. It is common and it seems to be cyclical, repeating itself every three to five years. The last outbreak was 2004-5 in the US, and the next will probably be 2008-10. Data for the UK or other parts of Europe was not available at the time of writing this book.

Strangely, the effects of the whooping cough vaccine seem to wear off and many teens become infected. However the cough can often be confused with bronchitis and therefore people go longer without treatment consequently spreading the disease. It has a fatality rate of one percent during the first six months of life. Most fatalities occur in babies younger than two months who are too young to have the vaccine. Death from whooping cough in children after six months is unheard of. Vaccination is carried out supposedly in order to decrease the disease in our population.

Lynne McTaggart says and I have summarised; that whooping cough is not serious beyond six months of age. Most young children get it from their vaccinated siblings, plus half the cases occur within vaccinated children. A study carried out by a Dr Stewart on 6.000 babies concluded that the vaccine did not protect infants. During the reported epidemics in the US and the UK, most of the cases did not have whooping cough and of the ones that did, had been vaccinated. It has also been noted that there has been a decline in the number of whooping cough outbreaks.

Dr Michael Ordent wrote a letter in the Journal of the American Medical Association (JAMA) (1994) where figures show the rate of asthma occurring in Pertusis immunised children was five times higher compared to non-immunised children. Here are some other interesting quotes regarding whooping cough.

"Up to ninety percent of the total decline in the death rate of children between 1860-1965 because of whooping cough, scarlet fever, diphtheria, and measles occurred before the introduction of immunisations and antibiotics." - Dr. Archie Kalokerinos, M.D.

"Dutch scientists are struggling to identify the exact cause of an epidemic of whooping cough that has swept throughout the country despite vaccination rates as high as ninety-six percent. Similar problems are also being reported from Norway and Denmark." –

"Whooping cough infections are common in an immunised population." -Journal of the American Medical Association, 1998.

META-Medicine® says that Pertusis or whooping cough is a cortex infection that affects the bronchial and laryngeal muscles of the lungs and throat. Being muscle-based it affects the musculature of the breathing mechanisms in the lungs and throat area. A repeated healing crisis would account for the horrific cough as the body eliminates the waste products produced by the rebuild of the muscles in the second phase. The toxins produced by the bacterium would also cause ongoing irritation as the body would want to remove these through the easiest possible means, via the mouth. The severe whooping, where the child cannot breathe is most probably the healing crisis.

What causes this is a fascinating conflict that comes from being separated from ones parents as a child. Essentially it is a shocking fear conflict that comes from a child being left alone, mostly at night, by the parents (likely the mother). They feel threatened and anxious and that death is waiting for them; they literally fear not waking up and not hearing the sounds of the morning. It can also relate to not being the preferred child of the parents. Or a child might feel it has been left to die having been separated from its parents, most likely the mother, either due to another sibling or being unceremoniously dumped at a day care centre, where they feel that the parent will not come back for them hence they fear death.

In conclusion this vaccine seems to be very problematic in that there seems to be little evidence for the continued vaccination for diphtheria or tetanus in highly developed countries. If you are travelling to foreign regions where there is diphtheria then it might be worth having the vaccination, but it appears not to work. Tetanus, however, does pose a threat but only for those who work in places such as the construction industry, or with gardening/farming where there is a possibility of getting a deep cut or a large wound. As regards the Pertusis vaccine, as I have said, it is cyclical, occurring every three to five years regardless of continued mass vaccination. Taking into consideration that there are very few or no reported deaths due to these diseases occurring in young children from between the ages of a few months and a few years, it seems strange that the recommended immunisation for a young child is at the age of two, four, six, eighteen months and five years. I believe the

151

continued reason for the mass immunisation is to maintain what is called 'the herd immunity'. However clearly from what I have researched, this idea does not work.

Hepatitis B – Hep B vaccine

Here is my summary of what Dr Sears says about Hepatitis B, it is a virus which affects the liver, causing liver damage and failure. It can be fatal. There is a hepatitis A, B, C, D, E, G, (no F; it is a theoretical virus, it only exists in the laboratory probably in a computer programme). There are only vaccines for Hep A and B. Hepatitis B is a sexually transmitted disease, but can also be caught through sharing intravenous needles or through tattoo needles. Dr Sears mentions that anyone who is participating in any of these dangerous activities could catch hepatitis B. There are other ways of catching Hep B. Through blood transfusion, which is rare, or theoretically through saliva, which is virtually unheard of, and also through blood. The virus can survive outside the body for up to a week, perhaps on a razor blade. It can also be passed to a child during birth from an infected mother, although this is extremely rare.

Records show that over 6000 cases of Hep B are 'reported' in adults per year; 1300 amongst teens and college students. About 70 cases are reported in children over five to fourteen, 30 in children between one and five and 30 in children below that age. It seems rare but the total is probably nearer 200,000 in the US per year, many cases go unreported. (I will explain this when I talk about META-Medicine®.) A study was also carried out by a group of doctors, several US medical centres and two pharmaceutical companies in which they somehow reached the conclusion that Hepatitis B was common in children and therefore all newborns should be vaccinated against it, instead of just vaccinating those whose mothers tested positive for Hepatitis B. It seems strange that the estimates concluded that 30,000 newborns had Hepatitis B, almost a thousand times greater than the reported amount. Dr Sears has the actual case studies listed in his excellent book.[87] He goes into a lot more detail and mentions that there have been only 130 reported cases in children from newborn to the age of fourteen each year - a far cry from the estimated 30,000.[88]

Hepatitis B is very serious with death occurring mainly in adults. There is no cure for Hepatitis B and it usually passes without being noticed in most adults. The only treatment is a form of therapy similar to chemotherapy. One third of people are cured by this treatment, even children. A very good friend of mine is presently having this treatment but it is for Hepatitis C.

There are many unpleasant side effects from the vaccine. Ten to fifteen percent suffer flu like symptoms while other side effects can be as severe as seizures and MS. The vaccine is sometimes given at birth without consulting the parents. The normal procedure for vaccination against Hep B is at birth, one month, and six months of age.

Lynne McTaggart does not mention anything about this vaccine in her book, but there are plenty of articles on her website www.wddty.com which are worth looking through, including a piece about the French government stopping the vaccination of school children against Hepatitis B, following research that suggested there was a link between MS and the vaccine.[89]

When we consider Hepatitis B through META-Medicine® all the strains of the virus are the rebuilders of the liver after the stress phase, so they are not the cause of liver disease but the repairers. The Hepatitis virus is very unpleasant, but it has already been mentioned that most people do not even experience the effects of the regeneration phase, which are similar to flu-like symptoms which affect the gall bladder ducts and liver mucous membranes.

The principle conflict is one of hatred, resentment or a grudge, likened to an injection of some sort. Being pushed onto something they do not want to do. Interestingly drug addicts who get Hep B start injecting the drug often by force due to peer pressure. It could be seen the same for sexual intercourse - being forced to have sex with someone you do not want to have sex with. Again, this could be perceived as an injection of some sort.

From my point of view, the facts as to whether this vaccine is good or not, really has to be considered. Since mass immunisation the incidents of Hepatitis B has decreased significantly. According to figures from the Public health authority in Canada, the group that is mostly affected are the twenty to thirty-nine year olds.[90] This could be due to the extensive use of condoms from the AIDS scare which, after all, is a sexually transmitted disease. The number of incidents amongst zero to nine year olds has not been affected, but there is also a significant decrease in people over forty. These people were not vaccinated, and are less likely to be sexually promiscuous. There is an interesting flash presentation on Hepatitis B with some remarkable facts on www.thinktwice.com/hepB_sho.htm. One slide mentions that in 1993, eighty-seven percent of interviewed paediatricians and practitioners said they thought the vaccines were NOT needed by newborns.

I find the vaccination of children against Hepatitis B to be very strange. The evidence for administering the vaccines is odd and has never been challenged. Inoculating newborns with a vaccine has not changed the incidence rate in the last fifteen years, and has to be questioned. It is really unnecessary at that age, since in reality, the forecasted death rate is not what has happened. The World Health Organisation (WHO) is introducing this vaccine worldwide, probably based on the US and Canadian figures, in the hope, as they righteously say, of eradicating Hepatitis B from the world.[91] The UK, Ireland and the Nordic countries do not vaccinate against Hepatitis B, considering it to be a very low risk.

From what I know of META-Medicine® and the reason why the body uses this virus in the first place as a repairer of the liver, it will be replaced by a different strain, the A, C–G when the 'B' strain gets wiped out. The WHO may be doing one of the largest human experiments in the world to establish something that may or may not work. Time will tell. However, it will probably be just as difficult to establish the true facts in ten years, as it is now. The fact that many of the major developed countries are choosing not to use mass immunisation says a lot about this vaccine.

Rotavirus – Rotavirus vaccine

Here is my summary of what Dr Sears says: Rotavirus is an intestinal virus that causes vomiting and diarrhoea. It is transmitted by the stools or saliva of an infected person, and is resistant to common disinfectants and antibacterial cleaners. It often gets spread in day-care centres. It is different from other types of gastric flu in that it last longer, usually a couple of weeks instead of a few days. It is common - about two million people become infected each year, mostly infants and children. In the US it usually starts on the west coast in November and balloons out across America and reaches the east coast by March. It then dwindles, and the cycle is repeated every year. Most kids will have had a bout of it by the age of two or three. It is most dangerous during the first year of life and after the age of two, cases are less likely to cause an issue.

Rotavirus can be a problem, because it causes such ongoing bouts of diarrhoea and vomiting that dehydration is not uncommon. Each year in the US about 50,000 children become hospitalised because of it. Rotavirus is the cause of death, through dehydration in about twenty to seventy children each year in the US. . Half a million children die each year worldwide because of the illness, mostly in developing countries.

The vaccine is given orally to infants at the age of two, four and six months. Of the side effects, the most worrying one being intussusception. This is where part of the intestine telescopes itself and the intestine becomes blocked. It requires surgery in many cases. Rotavirus also causes the same issue.

Lynne McTaggart does not mention Rotavirus but in the www.wddty.com website there are some interesting articles. One of them points out the fact that a new vaccine, which was allowed on the market in 1998 caused intussusception. The present vaccine seems to have fewer side effects, however the introduction of pro-biotics into the diet of young children dramatically eases the effects of rotavirus. Pro-biotics are naturally found in breast milk.

In META-Medicine®, the rotavirus would be there to rebuild damaged tissue in the second phase of a territorial anger conflict or a female identity anger conflict, both found in the cortex. Both of these conflicts are likely to occur in a kindergarten or day-care setting. As I have mentioned before, the body uses the microbes in the environment that are most easily accessible to solve the problem. This is gastric flu and not typical diarrhoea, which normally affects the lower intestinal track as part of the brain stem. This is cortex-related and therefore affects more of the duodenum, liver, gallbladder and liver mucous membranes, hence the vomiting and the continuous diarrhoea symptoms. My speculation is that the intussusception is most probably due to the excessive release of bile during the healing crisis.

Rotavirus is nasty. As Dr Sears points out in his book, it is not a question of *if* your child will get it, but *when*. Vaccination is an option; it contains the live virus in quantities that do not cause an attack. However there is still live rotavirus in the stools seven days after the vaccine has been given.

The likelihood of children at a very young age coming up against a social or territorial issue is minor; therefore being exposed to the virus would cause little or no issue. However, if a child that has to be in day-care has these issues and then is exposed to the virus orally, the body will use rotavirus to complete the healing. Dr Sears suggests, at the end of his chapter, that there is a possibility that rotavirus will, with time, die out. I am not convinced it will mutate. Instead the body will use it to heal itself, and by giving vaccines containing active rotavirus to children it will still be active within our environment. Time will tell. The best course of action is to make sure your baby is well-nourished, is happy in a non-threatening environment, has regular courses of pro-biotics, and to be prepared for when, not if, they get gastroenteritis, which is rotavirus.

Rudolph Steiner, the German philosopher and anthroposophist, suggests that viruses may be the way the body updates our biological system, and that we need these updates to survive more effectively in our environment. He also advocates that experiencing diseases as a child is not only normal but also conducive to our good health. It actually stimulates and builds a normal, healthy immune system that protects us through life. META-Medicine® would not dispute this way of thinking, as viruses are not the cause of disease, they merely do the clean-up job. Why the body chooses life-threatening microbes to do this, I do not know, other than survival of the fittest as I mentioned in the section on Tetanus.

Polio – Polio vaccine

Here is my summary of what Dr Sears says: Polio is a disease that is caught like the common cold. Most people show no symptoms. Some people have a minor sore throat and fever. It is not fatal, but in one of every two hundred and fifty cases the person develops muscle weakness and paralysis. Polio can only be caught once. It is not common - there have been no cases of polio since 1985 in the USA. There are a couple of thousand cases that occur each year in Asia and Africa. The disease has to run its course - it cannot be treated.

154

The person affected has to be put into an iron lung machine which enables them to breathe until the paralysis wears off. Older people may remember this happening frequently to polio victims. The vaccine is injected at the ages of two, four, eighteen months and five years. The side effects are minimal.

Lynne McTaggart says and I have summarised; that of the polio vaccine, after its introduction, the number of cases of polio doubled and almost tripled in some states during the late 50's and early 60's. The health authorities printed opposite findings. They also changed the name to 'viral or aseptic meningitis', or 'cocksackie virus' - an easy means of proving that a disease has been eradicated due to vaccines[92]. She also points out that polio is cyclical in nature, coming around every twenty years. The vaccines took the credit for eliminating it, not nature. Salk and Sabin were cited with causing the eradication of polio. However, recent studies in immunised populations where there are sudden breakouts do not seem to back up that the vaccines caused the eradication. Which started out with the live Salk injection under the skin, and was later replaced with the Sabin oral injection. More out-breaks occur in immunised people than in non-immunised people. The virus mutates; proven by the discovery of various strains which have been found to exist. People who had been vaccinated were tested for the anti-bodies and found not to have the immunity that would be necessary to stop an attack.

In META-Medicine® this virus affects the cortex region of the body in the motor-related areas. This would mean it would be related to an 'inability to flee' conflict or a 'hold on' conflict. In the first stress phase the body stops communication to the muscles, stopping the person in their tracks. They cannot move. It is as if the defence mechanism is 'playing dead'. In the United States, there were major recessions during 1907-8, 1929-39 and in the 1950's. People would have been severely stuck, unable to move or even breathe. Maybe there is a link. I have seen people who have been paralysed by their jobs, due to the lack of money or financial situation, causing them to have severe muscle weakness and paralysis of certain muscle groups. Usually there is a link to malnutrition as well.

I came across these interesting quotes: - "Official data shows that large scale vaccination has failed to obtain any significant improvement of the diseases against which they were supposed to provide protection" --Dr Sabin, developer of Polio vaccine.

Jonas Salk, inventor of the IPV, testified before a Senate subcommittee that 'nearly all polio outbreaks since 1961 were caused by the oral polio vaccine.'

"That the polio virus is the sole cause of polio is accepted by most people as gospel, and that the Salk and Sabin vaccines eradicated polio in the western world is etched into our collective consciousness as the major medical miracle of our time. But the history of polio and its vaccines is shrouded in a murky mist of politico/scientific manipulation, altered statistics, redefinition and reclassification of the disease, increased cases of vaccine induced paralytic polio, and monkey viruses transmitted by contaminated vaccines to millions of people worldwide." – Edda West[93]

Measles, Mumps, and Rubella – MMR vaccine

Measles. Here is my summary of what Dr Sears says: Measles is a virus that travels through the body, causing fever, a rash, a runny nose, and a cough. It is transmitted through the common cold, and infection usually gives life-long immunity. It is not very common any more; there are 50-100 reported cases in the US yearly. The number may be higher, but it is either rarely reported, or goes unnoticed. It is not serious; most children get it, and it is over within a week. It is not treatable and it must run its course. However one in 1000 cases is fatal.

155

Lynne McTaggart says and I have summarised; that the measles vaccine has been promoted by saying that the likelihood of encephalitis (water on the brain) was very high and that the fatality rate was also high. However, in the UK, before the vaccine was introduced, six died out of the 42,000 children that were infected. Most deaths now occur in adults. Measles can kill, and the death rate is higher in underdeveloped countries, where children are malnourished. She also mentions that the measles vaccination does not protect people. In a recent outbreak half of the sufferers had been vaccinated. Norman Begg (a highly respected Consultant Epidemiologist) said that deaths from measles were directly related to poor vaccine coverage. However, in Italy, after mass vaccination was carried out, the death rate from measles increased three-fold. It seems that through vaccination, the childhood disease which affected ninety percent of all children under five years of age, has passed to young teenagers and adults. In adults it is a nasty disease to catch, and the effects are far more serious. In her book, Lynne has much more to say about the response that the Centre for Disease Control in the US has to measles.

Some other quotes: -

"Among school age children, (measles) outbreaks have occurred in schools with vaccination levels of greater than ninety-eight percent. These outbreaks have occurred in all parts of the country, including areas that had not reported measles for years." (Morbidity and Mortality Weekly Report, 29/12/1989).

Atypical measles (measles contracted from the vaccine) has been known about for almost as long as the measles vaccine has been around, and it is ONLY found in those who have been vaccinated. It is typified by a milder rash than the one found in wild measles, which is probably where the ugly rumour originated that vaccinated people get a milder case of measles than the unvaccinated. Though the rash may be milder, the symptoms can be much worse and the chances of lung involvement are higher than with wild measles (twenty percent +) and liver involvement (three percent +). The earliest medical journal study I have about this is "Altered Reactivity to Measles Virus" Atypical Measles in Children Previously Immunised with Inactivated Measles Virus Vaccines. Fulginiti, V.A. et al; JAMA 18/12/67, Vol. 202, No. 12.

Dr Viera Scheibner is an active controversial lecturer on vaccines and vaccination has said that the chances of dying from wild measles are point zero three percent, while the chances of dying from atypical measles are between twelve to fifteen percent. It was thought at one time that it was only the early-inactivated vaccine that could cause atypical measles, but it is now known that any measles vaccine can. It seems that the vaccine corrupts the immune process, which may explain the reason why those who are vaccinated can get measles again and again without developing any natural immunity and may not be able to pass immunity onto their unborn child through the placenta.

Measles vaccination produces immune suppression that contributes to an increased susceptibility to other infections. (Clinical Immunology and Immunopathology, May 1996; 79(2): 163-170.)

META-Medicine® would say that measles is a conflict of 'I am fed up to the back teeth with something.' It may also be a conflict of 'being unable to smell'. 'I am sick of that' or 'Unable to express things'. This affects the oral cavities and the sinuses. During the regeneration phase you get the measles with a rash.

The virus also affects different areas of the body dependant on the conflict problem. Skin - separation. Mouth - I cant get the morsel of information or food I want, or I want to spit out something I have taken in, verbally or literally. Nose - I can't smell the situation around me. Larynx - notion of surprise. Bronchia - shock to do with territory.

156

Measles is also about a child becoming more autonomous. From a biological standpoint, children become more of a master of their surroundings if their senses are better developed. They are not relying on the parents' senses anymore. Ironically this is one of the most important diseases to help with development of a child's personality.

Mumps. Here is my summary of what Dr Sears says: Mumps is a virus similar to measles; it affects the saliva glands, causing swelling, a fever, and a rash. Once you get it you are immune for life. It is not common; there are only 250 reported cases in the US per year. There are outbreaks and most of those infected had been vaccinated. It is not serious for youngsters, but in adults it can cause swelling of the testicles, arthritis, kidney problems, heart problems, and nervous dysfunctions. It is not treatable so it must run its course.

Lynne McTaggart mentions and I have summarised; that vaccination does not mean that you are protected from mumps. Over ninety-eight percent of outbreaks occur in highly vaccinated populations. The vaccine was developed because of the severe side affects following mumps that rarely occur.

Since the widespread use of the mumps vaccine, the incidence of the disease has shifted to adolescents and adults, who are much more susceptible to the complications of testicular and ovarian infection, which can lead to sterility. During the period between 1967 and 1971 the annual average cases of mumps in persons greater than or equal to fifteen years of age was eight point three percent. In 1987 this same age group accounted for thirty-eight point three percent of cases, which is more than an eightfold increase.[94]

META-Medicine® says that Mumps is caused by being unable, being not allowed to or not wanting to eat. A child is not allowed to eat what they like to eat. In the stress phase there is ulceration of the Parotid gland ducts, the largest of the salivary glands, which often goes unnoticed apart form a dragging pain, then in the resolution phase you get the Mumps. It is a cortex related issue.

Rubella. Here is my summary of what Dr Sears says: Rubella is caused by a virus that causes a fever and a rash all over the body, commonly known as German Measles. It can also cause aching joints and swelling of the glands behind the ears and in the neck. In children it is so mild that it often goes unnoticed. It is caught like the common cold, and once you have it you are immune for life. It is not common any more, nor is it serious, but it is not treatable and it has to run its course. If a woman catches Rubella during the first 3 months of pregnancy, the foetus can be severely affected. This is why we immunise. However, only ten babies in the last twenty years have been born with congenital rubella syndrome.

Lynne McTaggart says and I have summarised; that rubella vaccine (the R in MMR) mutates and that the present strain used probably only protects ten percent of the time. Most women who give birth to congenital rubella syndrome babies have been immunised. She also mentions that five percent of children and twenty percent of grown women get symptoms of arthritis after the vaccination.

META-Medicine® says that Rubella is a separation conflict, since it affects the whole outer skin and causes conjunctivitis which is a visual separation conflict. This is most probably due to parents leaving their children with someone else, e.g. kindergarten. The disease is mild; purposely infecting the whole population with the virus seems strange to protect women in their first trimester. It would be better to test women for the virus as soon as they get pregnant.

The conflict for rubella is the same as for measles with an extra element of someone hitting another person so hard that it is not justified.

157

When we look at the Measles Mumps Rubella (MMR) vaccine as a whole, there have been many links made with its introduction and Autism. A British researcher, Dr Wakefield, published an article in the Lancet in 1998, saying that the measles vaccine, not natural measles, triggered inflammatory diseases in the intestines of autistic children, he never said the MMR caused autism. However this link has been categorically dismissed by study after study. New research shows that there is no link between MMR and Autism.[95]

META-Medicine® would say that the reason for the link is all the MMR viruses affect the Squamous mucosa of the stomach and duodenum and the laryngeal mucosa. This would fit with the conflicts noticed that relate to autism, which is caused by two separate stressful events occurring at the same time. There is also the element of poisoning caused by the vaccine which causes the body to go straight into the regeneration phase as it attempts to heal itself from the poison. Two shocks such as these occurring at the same time can cause a child to stop maturing. See the latter part of chapter 13 for more details.

Dr Sears mentions in his book, that the horrendous side effects of the MMR vaccine outweigh the effects of the symptoms from the diseases by far. After reading the whole chapter of Dr Sears book on the MMR vaccine, my wife came to the conclusion that it made no sense to subject our son to the possibility of these side effects, the consequences of which were far worse than those of him catching the actual diseases. Even Dr Sears mentions that he has little foundation in convincing parents they should give their child this vaccine if they object. Moves are being made towards giving the vaccines separately. My advice is - look at the facts and the side effects carefully, all of which are listed in Dr Sear's book.

Another quote says "Measles, mumps, rubella, hepatitis B, and the whole panoply of childhood diseases are a far less serious threat than having a large fraction (say ten percent) of a generation afflicted with learning disabilities and/or uncontrollable aggressive behaviour because of an impassioned crusade for universal vaccination.......Public policy regarding vaccines is fundamentally flawed. It is permeated by conflicts of interest. It is based on poor scientific methodology (including studies that are too small, too short, and too limited in populations represented), which is, moreover, insulated from independent criticism. The evidence is far too poor to warrant overriding the independent judgements of patients, parents, and attending physicians, even if this were ethically or legally acceptable." (Association Of American Physicians & Surgeons).

Chickenpox – Varicella vaccine

Here is my summary of what Dr Sears says: Chickenpox is a virus that causes fever and spots all over the body. It is transmitted in the same way as the common cold. Once a person has become infected the virus is in the nervous system and it can flare up later on in life causing shingles. It is not common. Since vaccination, the number of reported cases has reduced dramatically from 3.5 million to 50,000 reported cases in the US. It is not serious anymore either; it used to kill 55 people a year in the US, now there are only 2 deaths a year attributed to chickenpox. It is treatable; the vaccine is given when the child is one year old.

Lynne McTaggart does not talk about this vaccine in her book. The website mentions that the vaccine is not available in the UK, and that those at risk have lowered immunity; the side effects of the vaccine outweigh the effects of the disease by far.[96]

The website also mentions; the effects of the vaccine seem only to last six years. "Another concern is the effect of injecting into one-year-old babies and children a live virus which has a tendency to lie latent in the nervous system and reactivate many years later. A majority of patients who have had chickenpox as children may go on to develop herpes zoster, commonly known as shingles, later in life. This condition causes painful and highly sensitive blisters on the skin along the nerves infected by the virus, often on only one side of the body. The severe pain may last from two to five weeks and in older patients, this jabbing pain can go on for several months."

META-Medicine® says that this is a conflict concerning separation from the flock, separation from the mother due to a change in circumstances as with eczema. It can also be related to smothering by a mother, being over protected therefore the child wants to be separated. This can also be triggered by a change in the attitude of the mother causing a forced separation. It is in the second phase, the regeneration phase of the disease. It comes from the upper cortex area of the brain. There seems little to be gained by having this vaccine if you have a healthy child. It is not offered routinely in the UK as it is feared that there will be a greater number of shingles in adults if this vaccine is given to all children.[97]

My belief is that mass vaccination is driven by business. Each chickenpox vaccination costs $40, and in the article already mentioned from www.wddty.com they talk about this at length. Many doctors do not believe that the vaccine helps, and consider that such a mild disease is all part of growing up as a child. Immunising against it is unnecessary.[98]

Hepatitis A – Hep A vaccine
Here is my summary of what Dr Sears says: Hepatitis A is a virus that attacks the liver, causing temporary liver inflammation. Most children who get the virus do not have any symptoms at all. Adults who get the virus do have the severe reactions of intestinal flu that can last a few weeks, often jaundice (a yellowing of the eyes and skin, due to liver damage) - this is when the issue is diagnosed. It virtually never occurs in children. It is transmitted through infected stools and can be spread by carers not washing their hands, and also in restaurants and other venues where an infected person does not properly wash their hands. Entire beaches can also be infected with Hepatitis A. Most of the third world, which has poor sanitation, has been infected with Hepatitis A and have lifelong immunity.

Hepatitis A is common, with 10,000 cases reported per year in the US. It is serious if caught by adults who have liver disease, but most people recover a few weeks later after a bad bout of intestinal flu. Vaccination has not been administered to all children but in those states in the US which have high percentage rates, it is being given to infants aged eighteen months in an effort to eliminate it from the population.

Lynne McTaggart's book does not mention Hepatitis A and there is little information on her website.

META-Medicine® says the same as for Hepatitis B - it is a rebuilder of the liver in the regeneration phase. It is cortex-related and therefore is a female identity anger conflict or a male territorial anger decision conflict. Most likely the virus is in all our systems anyway. It is only when we have a liver issue to resolve, that the body will produce the virus, and then the antibodies will show up. Eradication is probably futile since the virus will mutate as we have already seen with the Hepatitis B-G (no F).

The conflict is linked to not having the basic foods in order to survive and bearing a grudge against those who caused the problem. An example might be a person who cannot feed their family because the boss is not doing a proper job due to negligence so there is no money to pay the employee. They hold a grudge against this person but they cannot do anything about it because there are no other jobs available.

Interestingly enough, the vaccine is not given in the childhood vaccination programme in the UK nor can I see it being administered in the same way in Europe. It is recommended as a vaccine for those who travel to undeveloped parts of the world with poor sanitation where the Hepatitis A virus is rife. Good personal hygiene is the best way to stop the spread and also to inhibit you and your family from getting the virus. The vaccine is heavily advertised on American TV.

Influenza – Flu vaccine

Here is my summary of what Dr Sears says: 'Flu' or influenza is a virus which mutates yearly. It is transmitted in the same way as the common cold. It causes fever, headache, body-ache, sore throat, vomiting, diarrhoea, runny nose, etc. It is common and every year is supposed to be the worst flu season ever, but, as Dr Sears pointed out, ever since he has been practicing each year is about the same as the previous. It is not serious for the majority of the population, and it passes without consequence. However, the elderly are most likely to suffer and hospitalisation due to complications does happen in this age group.

It is said in most literature concerning flu that 36,000 people die from flu and pneumonia every year in the US. However, the real number of deaths from flu is very low; about 20, according to the American Lung Association who carried out a study in 2004.[99]

It is treatable with Antiviral medication. However this will only lessen the symptoms and most people just let it run its course.

Lynne McTaggart says and I have summarised; on her website that new evidence released by the Center for Disease Control (CDC) in America suggests that attempts to protect our elderly against flu is a little like catching smoke in a sieve.[100]

In META-Medicine®, the flu is as a result of a territorial fear conflict or a female shocking fear conflict that affects the bronchi mucus membranes or the larynx mucus membranes in the cortex. A combination of both conflicts causes asthma attacks during the healing crisis which makes sense, as there is some evidence to suggest that this vaccine makes asthma worse.[101]

Flu is caused by various related conflicts. A dispute conflict - you are ordered to do something that you disagree with. Also separation conflict - not being able to breathe or not being able to move. Feeling powerless in a physical or verbal way. As an example in winter all the children cannot go outside, they are forced to stay inside and feel they cannot move. A higher order of power affects the children so their freedom is affected.

"Nine die in flu tragedy as epidemic hits nursing home. Nine pensioners died within days of each other after a suspected flu epidemic swept the nursing home where they lived. An investigation has been launched after it emerged all the victims suffered severe chest infections despite having the flu vaccinations." (Daily Express UK 1/1/1999.)

My thoughts are that to immunise a child against flu is probably futile, unless they are around vulnerable elderly people, since the side effects of the flu vaccine are akin to getting the flu and, with most people, it passes after a few days. Every year there is a mass 'exodus' to be vaccinated in the US, Canada, and the UK. What I personally know about mass hypnosis and group belief systems is that if you tell people it is the flu season, they can create the disease in themselves. Many people who have had the flu vaccine, catch the flu. The excuse of the drug companies is that they did not predict the right strains of flu virus. This apparently happened in 2007. "The 2007-08 flu vaccine was only 44 percent effective," the Center for Disease Control and Prevention (CDC) has admitted in a study published in Morbidity and Mortality Weekly Report, making the flu season the worst since 2003-04. It's flu season here in the Canada as I am writing this; we watch American TV as well as TV from Canada and the way the flu jab is marketed is very scary. It is enough for most people who are not even aware of what the advertisers are doing, to become quite frightened. It is thought provoking to imagine what would happen to the number of cases of flu if the media did not market the 'flu' jab.

Meningococcal – Meningococcal vaccine

Here is my summary of what Dr Sears says: Meningococcus bacterium causes an infection in the blood which runs throughout the body to various organs, and sometimes into the brain causing meningitis. It is transmitted in a way similar to the common cold, and has a rapid onset into the system. It causes fever and aches, but the unique thing about this bacterium is the fine pinpoint rash which does not disappear when you depress the skin. This rash develops into larger purple blotches later on. The vaccine is given at age twelve, but moves are being made to develop the vaccine so that it can be given to infants.

Meningitis is common; about 3000 cases a year in the US, mostly affecting babies of six months to two year old toddlers. It is extremely serious for the young age group; ten percent of children die. Amongst older children, the death rate is higher, nearer to twenty percent. Most people who get it end up in intensive care. Fifteen percent of those who survive will have some form of permanent disability such as hearing loss, nerve damage or loss of a limb. It is treatable with antibiotics, given intravenously for a week.

Lynne McTaggart says and I have summarised; that the death rate from this disease is small in comparison to other diseases and accidents occurring in the home, and that to inoculate a whole population seems a knee-jerk reaction. The disease affects children under the age of five and fifteen to twenty year olds.

"A case-control study has shown that forty-one percent of meningitis occurred in children who had been vaccinated against the disease. The vaccine's protective efficacy was minus fifty-eight percent. This means that children are much more likely to get the disease if they are vaccinated." JAMA 1988[102]

META-Medicine® says that the most probable issue is one of being hit over the head - and the disease is in the regeneration phase. There could also be a link to intellect as well. Look at the meningitis section regarding the HIB vaccine. There may be some connection with being away from home for the first time since it mostly affects young students and shows up as a rash.

Human Papillomavirus – HPV vaccine

Here is my summary of what Dr Sears says: HPV causes genital warts. It is transmitted through unprotected sex. It is also said to be the cause of cervical cancer. Most women who have the virus are not aware of it until they get a cervical smear. Men can carry the virus on their penis, often without any genital warts. Most women who are sexually active carry this virus. HPV is the most common sexually transmitted disease. Approximately 20 million women get infected each year. Certain strains are serious, some cause genital warts which come and go, and others can be disfiguring. Some cause cervical cancer; 10,000 of the cases are found by smear tests but still it kills 3,500 women a year in the USA. It is treatable by removal of the top of the cervix through a procedure called LEEP (Loop Electrosurgical Excision Procedure), or through chemotherapy if the disease has progressed too far. Warts can be removed through freezing.

On Lynne McTaggart's website it says "The HPV vaccine – which is being given to girls aged between eleven and twelve to prevent cervical cancer in later life – may be a killer. So far three young girls have died after being vaccinated, and there have been 1,637 adverse reactions reported in under a year. The vaccine, Gardasil, has courted controversy since it was approved for use in 2006. Some states in the USA have decided to make the vaccine compulsory, which has caused an outcry among parents who see the vaccine as a license for sexual relationships outside of marriage."

161

The vaccine contains 4 HPV viruses but there are over a 100 HPV viruses. 10-30 if them can cause cervical cancer. The HPV virus is very common as I mentioned earlier. Even the Center for Disease control admits that in ninety percent of cases your body's immune system will clear up the HPV infection naturally within two years.

Gardasil is advertised relentlessly on US television. Many girls have been subjected to this new vaccine and until all the side-effects and its long term use have been ascertained, to advertise it like a new cereal is, in my opinion, irresponsible. As with all viruses this vaccine is unlikely to stop or prevent cervical cancer – which is the main killer, since the virus will undoubtedly mutate. The virus does not cause the cancer, a UDIN shock does.

META-Medicine® says this is a female sexual frustration conflict that affects the coronary heart veins and the cervix at the same time and it occurs in the cortex. The HPV virus rebuilds the cervix in the second phase. The warts are also part of the same system, therefore the cortex. They are likely to be separation conflicts from a sexual partner.

Conclusion about vaccination

Throughout this chapter I have been explaining to my wife that the information I have found just does not stack up. It seems that the whole mass vaccination of society is driven by the pharmaceutical industry and politicians. It has a lot to do with power, money and the need of the lay person to believe they are being protected. There is nothing wrong with this approach. I am in business and I know I have to tell people about what I do otherwise they won't train with me. I have to make a living and I do so with a conscience.

I am certain that there are many doctors who have this consciousness too, who are not fooled by very well-trained pharmaceutical salespeople. However, how many doctors and how many politicians take the two months it has taken me to research into this area, adding the META-Medicine® elements, to educate themselves? Very few and I don't blame them either. A lot of my research also came from the web, I dislike websites that say such things as 'vaccines are useless' without any foundation and without stating the reasons as to 'why' - of which there are plenty. I just think we have been carried along by a mass belief that 'vaccines are the answer to eradicate all disease' instead of looking at the real, simple facts of disease control such as good hygiene, good housing, better sanitation and general cleanliness. And I would add to that - the removal of the threat of war.

Microbes are there for a reason and to eliminate them will be impossible, I am sure of that. To vaccinate is also not an answer. Does it save lives? We will see. As mass vaccination covers the rest of the globe and with some of the poorer developing countries not being able to afford the high cost of vaccination; as better sanitation, housing and as peace arrives in these countries, we may see a massive reduction in diseases without vaccination. Time will tell whether this will happen, along with carefully considered, independent research.

Some other useful websites about vaccination

www.nvic.org - National Vaccine Information Centre
www.vaccines.net - A website about many health issues
www.whale.to - Interesting Website on all things to do with health

In the next chapter I want to look at vitality and how drugs, food and energy determine our ability to complete the disease process. How acidity and alkalinity play a significant part in this process and knowing this information explains so much about the complex subject of nutrition.

Chapter 12

Vitality, food and drugs.

A Short History of Medicine
2000 B.C. - "Here, eat this root."
1000 B.C. - "That root is heathen, say this prayer."
1850 A.D. - "That prayer is superstition, drink this potion."
1940 A.D. - "That potion is snake oil, swallow this pill."
1985 A.D. - "That pill is ineffective, take this antibiotic."
2000 A.D. - "That antibiotic is artificial. Here, eat this root."
~Author Unknown

"Our self healing qualities can be influenced by eliminating factors aiding disease and supporting factors aiding healing. A strong immune system, high life force and vitality are essential aspects of this healing process. Especially during the conflict phase and the regeneration phase additional energy and nutrients are needed. The biological, meaningful disease process can be supported by therapeutic measures at all levels of our organism."
One of the ten META-Medicine® Models

Go on a Vegan diet – you must be joking!

I was in Germany at a META-Medicine® Certification training and I was having my CT scan reading in front of the class by Dr Anton Bader, when Qualified Health Practitioner Christa Uricher, (one of the founders of the International META-Medicine® Association) after my reading carried out a therapy session using EFT*. I immediately became hot and very lethargic - to feel so completely relaxed in such a short space of time was very unusual for me. I became calm, quite euphoric and very tired. I recognised these symptoms as the regeneration phase. I had just gone through complete resolution of the conflict. Christa focussed on my personality and my worthiness or lack of it at the time, focussing on Terry who was in the audience, who had triggered the whole issue in the first place. (I do want to say that Christa is so talented at this work; she specialises in working with cancer clients, and Terry, as I have mentioned before, was merely a trigger - he did not cause my unworthiness - I did.)

EFT is a therapeutic intervention that is similar to Acupuncture but without needles. You tap on the main acupuncture points whilst making specific suggestions. It also incorporates changes in beliefs in order to resolve simple and complex problems.

It was during this time that Christa said that I needed to change my diet. She told me that I must become vegan. I looked at her surprised because I had been following a diet based on Dr. Atkins work. The Atkins diet involves cutting out carbohydrates and eating a lot more protein in the form of meat and cheeses plus plenty of vegetables and fresh salads - it can be a very acidic diet. I told her she must be crazy but she insisted it would be the best thing for me. However, she softened the vegan part saying that I could eat some protein in the form of white meat or fish twice a week although she told me my healing would be quicker if I followed a vegan diet.

I got up from the therapy session feeling very, very different. I found it difficult to concentrate on the rest of the lesson that day. During the following break I called Kristin, my wife, and explained what had happened and I explained that I wanted to change my diet into a vegan one. After a year and a quarter of suffering I made a decision that I would do whatever it took to solve the problem and if that meant no meat at all, so be it. I knew it was not forever so it was easy to persuade Kristin of my intentions. More importantly and to my surprise she was ecstatic because she disliked the amount of meat we had been eating - her metabolism did not do well on the Atkins diet. She also laughed because she had just come back from the shops having bought a large amount of meat products. I told her to freeze them. I said it was not forever and we could give it away anyway.

During the rest of the course I ate, as close as I could, as a vegan and noticed that I slept really well. I was tired but at the same time I was euphoric.

When I arrived home I carried on with this diet, eating organic bean casseroles, salads, organic vegetable medleys, some fruits and nuts. The effects were quite profound. I was still in the second phase and I did not track back into the first phase at all. I had very little energy but I felt fantastic - I had a continuous grin on my face. I also noticed that work was useless. I am self-employed but I had no energy for work whatsoever. I just needed to rest, and rest I did. I remember sitting in front of my computer in my office trying to answer emails. I found this very difficult and trying to do any business was also very challenging. I would sit in my office and fall asleep in front of my computer, so eventually I gave up attempting to work and just rested during the day. However I found myself dozing during the night and not getting the deep profound sleep that I was experiencing during the day. Luckily through my teachings I knew that this was normal.

Vitality and the two phases

The two phases have an effect on our bodies at a deep level and understanding the effect of our diets on our system can help assist us in our healing. In the first phase our body and muscles needs instant energy, hence why we crave carbohydrates, sugars and proteins/dairy, high quick energy burst foods. Our body needs to be naturally acidic in order to achieve this. In the second phase, our body needs foods that heal and build our cells so that they regenerate effectively - fruit, vegetables and pulses - so our body naturally becomes alkaline. During the healing phase we need to squeeze out the water from our system. Many pharmaceutical drugs have the same effect as stressful events on our body. Chemotherapy and radiation, push the person right back into a very stressful phase and shocks the system, killing many microbes and other newly multiplying cells required for regeneration. This renders the person very susceptible to foreign microbes that are present in the environment, so the body becomes confused. Some drugs such as steroids keep people in the stress phase continuously.

Vitality is important for a person if they are going to survive the resolution stage. This is why many people die. They don't survive this phase because their bodies have used up all

164

their energy reserves. Also, damage from the chemotherapy and radiation literally pushes people back into the stress phase, destroys their immune system, the microbes that work in symbiosis with the whole body, and depletes their energy by stripping away the very life force that allows a person to heal. The mitochondria often called the cellular power plants of the body are damaged for life by radiotherapy. There is more about the effects of cancer treatments in Chapter 14.

A tremendous amount can be done through a change in nutrition to assist with our vitality. However the doctor that developed much of the foundations we use in META-Medicine® is quoted as saying that nutrition plays no part in our healing. In META-Medicine® we categorically disagree with him. If you are not a convert to how important nutrition is for your body then watch a brilliant movie called 'Super Size Me' by Morgan Surlock.[103] Just Google Super Size Me, Morgan Surlock.

Morgan eats nothing but McDonalds for a month and his health suffers horrendously.

Many people throughout the world have known that through nutrition alone you can heal people. Food plays a significant part in our wellbeing and overall health. In the previous chapter I mention that good nutrition and hygiene are one of the main contributors to the decrease in disease, not vaccinations.

However - why? Why does nutrition play such a significant role and what is happening inside a person that causes them to heal when they change their diet?

To explain this we need to go back to the two phases again. When I first heard this I was amazed. I remember Christa Uricher explaining something so simple yet so enlightening regarding nutrition it amazed me why no one had made this connection before.

In the first phase the body is under stress and the cells are working so they produce waste which is acidic.

In the second phase the body is regenerating so the cells are repairing so they are in an alkaline state.

The simple truth is when a person is in the stress phase (phase one, point 3) the body is acidic. The cells are working and they need energy. The muscles are in a state of fight and flight. The body needs to react quickly to any impending danger. The blood is pumped full of adrenaline, the blood is thin, there is high blood pressure and the body, if you were to measure its PH, would be found to be acidic. During this time we need energy foods, stimulating drinks, supplements/remedies or drugs that keep the body in a state of alertness. (Foods such as red meats, many dairy products, foods with high sugar and salt levels, processed foods, drinks such as alcohol, coffee, tea or high energy drinks, supplements such as caffeine tablets, drugs such as cortisone, smoking and chemotherapy (which massively increases the acidity of the body – more in Chapter 14). Activities such as doing a sport, watching certain sports, intensive travel, fighting, arguing, worry; all contribute to raising the acidity of the body.

In the second phase the body is healing, the cells need to repair themselves and the environment that best suits this repair is one of alkalinity. The blood thickens, the pressure decreases and the PH is alkaline. Foods such as organic vegetables, beans, grains and nuts and drinks such as camomile tea and fruit teas, supplements like magnesium and selenium all help this healing process.

It does not end there. Certain therapies assist the body to become more alkaline as well. Massage, meditation, energetic healing, yoga and emotional clearing techniques.

165

Insomnia

In the regeneration phase all the typical symptoms of slow heart rate, feeling tired and weight gain will happen but something else that is vital that I did not explain earlier happens as well. Whilst you are recovering you will feel very tired and sleepy during the day, often taking naps that are so deep you can literally forget who or where you are. These naps are essential for your healing because you will find that you cannot sleep that well at night, often finding yourself very tired but awake whilst everyone else is asleep. This is completely normal. It is a programme that runs in all animals. Being unwell, you are likely to be slower should a predator attack the herd but because you are only lightly resting at night, you will have a head start in getting away. During the day because the herd is wide awake, you are protected and can be awoken if an attack occurs.

If you know you are in the second phase and you find yourself very tired during the day, sleep if you can. Know you will not sleep that well during the night and feel relaxed about it. If you find yourself having to soldier on because of work, see if you can take a day or two off. It is false to think that you are very efficient as a worker if you are deep in the second phase. I have seen people turn up for work almost dead to the world with a cold because they thought it was their duty to work; they are inefficient and the cold lasts a lot longer than if they stayed at home for a day. Our modern work system allows us to take such time off, so take advantage of it, if you can.

However, also look out for the stress signs as well as these will indicate if you have something underlying that is unresolved. In my personal experience I have found that when I am stressed following a shock of some sort, my diet changes, e.g. in a challenging work situation, I find that I eat dark chocolate - I want to change how I feel with sweet things such as pastries and breads. I will drink wine (I very rarely drink alcohol) or sometimes even normal coffee (I only drink decaffeinated coffee and one a day, if that). I find I will over-eat, stuffing myself with comfort foods such as breads made from wheat even though I know that wheat bloats my stomach and is disastrous for my metabolism. If I am at a family gathering or at a restaurant with friends, I will eat the puddings or ice cream I am offered. I hate ice cream and I don't eat sweets as a rule but when I am stressed, if it is put in front of me, I seem to have no will power and I end up eating foods I rarely eat and don't much like.

As an example, I recently, rather ly, worked myself to the bone. I flew to Norway and delivered fifteen straight days of training without a break. I had planned to have three days off in-between but such is the nature of my work that people were clamouring to see me morning, noon and night. Before I arrived I had been very stressed. We had a young baby - he was three months old at the time - I was leaving a very stressed wife, and I had been working every day without a break to prepare for the trainings.

All in all it was a really difficult time and I arrived in Bergen airport, Norway, in a wheelchair having popped a vein in my lower left leg. I worked on solving the trauma that caused this and it took only two weeks to fully heal. Although I had planned three days off in Norway as I mentioned, I never got them and I arrived in Brighton in the UK having to deliver another seven days of training. I was stressed to say the least. The last day before I left Norway I rested a little, and then the following day I started the META-Medicine® Part B training with no voice. I had gone into resolution during my small time off.

I completed the seven days training and the following day I met my wife and child off the plane in London, Heathrow. I was exhausted and had no energy left. This time I really needed to rest but I could not with baby Oliver waking up in the middle of the night, and a completely jet lagged, stressed out wife. We were staying in London with my fantastic older brother and his lovely wife and beautiful three-year-old daughter who live a very fast and furious life-style, full of energy but really challenging.

I drank a lot of wine. I ate anything that was put in front of me. I ate chocolate bars and gorged on sweet things whenever I could. We had planned to meet and stay overnight with many friends during this trip and we did stay with one friend for one night after leaving London. However, finding myself with sciatica (nerve pain in the buttocks that travels down the leg), my wife with no voice and Oliver with a deep cough, when we landed at my parents' house, we did not budge. Five days after we arrived I found my diet starting to return to normal. I refused alcohol, and I ate what I wanted to eat, not what was put in front of me. I drank green teas and I eventually lost the sciatica. My wife's voice returned and Oliver's cough disappeared.

So you can see our diets reflect what we are going through in our lives as well. Naturally the body is attracted to the foods that it requires in order to do the job it is meant to do.

During the stress phase we will eat acid inducing foods, and in the regeneration phase we will be attracted to alkaline foods. However, when we look at our lifestyles we can quickly establish that many people are eating foods through habit which keeps them in a stress phase. Therefore they never give themselves time to regenerate and heal. This ongoing barrage of stress has an accumulative effect and ends up lowering our vitality, which in turn makes us more susceptible to a conflict shock.

In the UK in the past few years there have been many programmes dedicated to showing the disastrous effect of these first phase, stressful diets. One such programme delivered by Dr Gillian McLeish called 'You are what you eat' takes an overweight person who, through bad nutrition, has made themselves obese. At the start of the programme she gets the person to log what they eat and drink in a week and then she displays their whole week's diet to them on a large dining table. It is frightening to see how much stress-inducing foods these people are eating. These people have many psychological issues, obvious problems with their digestive systems and of course, they look dreadful. They also suffer extensively from many diseases such as skin disorders or Type II diabetes.

In the following weeks during these programmes, Gillian McKeith shows these people how to eat. Most, if not all, of the foods are alkaline-based. What is amazing is that so many of the issues that these people present disappear completely by the time they finish the programme.

As regards alkalising your body, I spoke to Georgie Atkinson; the lady with breast cancer from whose story I mentioned in chapter 6. She is a qualified nutritionist she sent me her chart of 'Alkalising Your Body.' She actually uses these methods herself and does not just preach them. She also mentioned to me recently that mental work is also needed to maintain some of the dietary changes that are necessary for the body to remain alkaline. I am really grateful for her input.

Alkalising Your Body to Return to Good Health by Georgie Atkinson
Basic Information
- The optimal pH for blood is 7.365. This must be kept within very narrow limits for the human body to function.
- If the foods you eat and the drinks you drink are too acidic, the body will neutralise them with powerful buffering compounds in your blood. Any further acid excess will be excreted by the kidneys via your urine. Your urinary pH will therefore vary according to what you have eaten in the past, together with the last meal.

- Once your blood buffering systems and kidneys are overloaded with too much acid, the excessive acidity will accumulate in the tissue and cells, allowing disease processes to get a hold. (Only if there is a conflict shock – Ed.)
- Your saliva which is produced by the salivary glands in your mouth will reflect your blood pH much more closely than your urine, as it is part of the body rather than a waste product.
- To correct such a situation and help return the body to health it is recommended that you eat mostly (80%) alkaline forming foods and only a few (20%) acid forming foods each day.
- Depending on your past eating patterns, it may take a few months of eating a balanced diet, before your tissue and cell acidity is brought back into a healthy range.
- During this time it is expected that you would begin to lose any excess fat stores as well.
- While you are making the transition to an alkaline way of eating, measure your salivary pH regularly, say 4 times a day, first thing in the morning and then between meals.
- If you cannot maintain it at a pH of 7 or above, use an alkalising product that has sodium, potassium, magnesium and calcium bicarbonates.
- To get started quickly and if necessary dissolve 1 tsp of sodium bicarbonate (Bicarb of Soda) in a glass of water and drink 1 hour after eating.
- To test your salivary pH, use pHStix, by ph ION Nutrition ™, available from any good health food store, nutritionist, naturopath or chiropractor. Experience says they are better than litmus paper as the colour matching is much more accurate.

Foods to Eat

Alkalising Foods – potential alkalising effect of 25 grams

Food	only +	mg of calcium	grams of protein
Summer black radish	+ 39.4	7.5	2.5
Soy lecithin, pure	+ 38.0		
Wheat grass	+ 33.8		6.25
Cucumber, fresh	+ 31.5	6.25	2.5
Soy bean sprouts	+ 29.5	12.0	1.5
Alfalfa grass	+ 29.3		6.25
Barley grass	+ 28.7		
Sprouted radish seeds	+ 28.4		2.5
Kamut grass	+ 27.6		
Soy nuts	+ 26.5		8.5
Dandelion, greens	+ 22.7	46.75	6.75
Cayenne pepper	+ 18.8		
Red radish	+ 17.6	7.5	2.5
Avocado, Hass	+ 15.6	2.5	5.5
Endive, fresh	+ 14.5		
Cabbage lettuce, fresh	+ 14.1	10.5	
Tomato, fresh	+ 13.6	3.25	4.5
Celery	+ 13.3	9.75	
Garlic	+ 13.2	7.25	5.0

Spinach	+ 13.1	23.25	12.25
Soybeans, cooked	+12.8	16.75	2.75
Lima beans	+ 12.0		
Navy beans	+ 12.0		6.5
White beans	+ 12.0	7.5	
Sorrel	+ 11.5		
Fresh red beetroot	+ 11.3		
French beans	+ 11.2		
Lemon	+ 9.9		3.25
Carrot	+ 9.5		
Coconut water	+ 9.0		
Chives	+ 8.3	17.25	
Lime	+ 8.2		2.25
Banana, un ripe	+ 4.8		
Marine lipides	+ 4.7		
Evening primrose oil	+ 4.1		
Almonds	+ 3.6	58.5	4.75
Flaxseed oil	+ 3.5		
Linseeds	+ 3.5		
Cherry, sour	+ 3.5		
White cabbage	+ 3.3	10.5	
Borage oil	+ 3.2		
Tofu	+ 3.2		10.75
Swede	+ 3.1		
White radish	+ 3.1		
Cauliflower	+ 3.1	6.25	
Onion	+ 3.0	12.75	3.75
Soy flour	+ 2.5		
Caraway seeds	+ 2.3		
Lettuce	+ 2.2	5.0 – 17.0	3.0 – 10.5
Green cabbage	+ 2.0		
Comfrey	+1.5		
Artichokes	+ 1.5	12.75	7.25
Fennel seeds	+ 1.3		
Asparagus	+ 1.1	5.75	6.25
Cumin seeds	+ 1.1		
Olive oil	+ 1.0		
Lentils	+ 0.6	19.75	7.5
Peas, ripe	+ 0.5	6.5	1.5
Coconut meat, fresh	+ 0.5		
Sesame seed	+ 0.5	290.0	

This above table has been assembled from the book "The pH Miracle" by Robert and Shelly Young. ISBN 0 – 7525 – 3406 – 4.

Cooking/Eating Suggestions

- ✓ If you are going to cook foods with oil, use coconut oil.
- ✓ Following are some simple dishes and snacks to get you started. They are not divided into breakfast, lunch and dinner, as the idea of traditional foods for certain times of the day is an artificial constraint that will only hinder your forward progress. For your own sake, eat whatever you like, when you like as long as it is from the list of alkaline foods above.
- ✓ Eat 5 – 6 small meals a day.

> Fresh home made green vegetable juice.
> Essene (a very old grain) bread with avocado and tomato slices
> Vegetable lasagne
> Buckwheat crackers with cucumber and tahini
> Buckwheat crackers with fresh pesto
> Pureed silken tofu and berries
> Buckwheat pasta with salsa sauce
> Stuffed zucchini
> Sautéed vegetables with homemade tomato sauce and navy beans
> Avocado dip with vegetable sticks
> Tuscany soup with soybeans
> Miso (a Japanese sauce) soup
> Tossed green salad
> Millet porridge
> Lentil curry – dhal
> Vegetable stir-fry with tofu
> Soaked almonds

Eating Out

- ✓ Drink mineral water with a slice of lemon when out.
- ✓ Chose a salad meal with fish.
- ✓ Leave the bread roll.
- ✓ Take your own salad dressing with you if you need one.

Green Juice

Using a low speed, crush and press juicer such as the Vitalmax Juicer from Oscar, combine any of the following leaf, stalk or flower vegetables. Experiment to find out which combination you prefer.

- Wheat grass
- Cucumber
- Dandelion greens
- Cabbage, all colours red, green, white
- Tomato
- Celery
- Garlic, onion, chives
- Spinach
- Sorrel
- Beetroot
- Carrot
- Cauliflower
- Lettuce

Special Juices

Some vegetables have specific compounds in them that have very specific effects on the body.

- If your blood needs building add parsley. Parsley has good levels of iron.
- If you have hormonal problems add broccoli. Broccoli has indol-3-carbinol.

Nut and Seeds

- Nuts and seeds are excellent sources of good oils and protein. Feel free to eat all of them except peanuts.
- Almonds are good if soaked in a jar of filtered water overnight. Only ¾ fill the jar with almonds as they absorb the water and swell. Drain them in the morning and keep in the fridge. They will keep for 3 days. They have a great new texture.

Resources

Some good books on the subject are:-

- Alkalise or Die
- The pH miracle
- The Acid-Alkaline Diet

- The following sites on the Internet are very helpful. Please note that there are considerable differences in the alkaline food lists from the different organisations. Be conservative to begin with.
  - www.essence-of-life.com
  - www.acidalkalinediet.com
  - www.phmiracleliving.com
  - www.energiseforlife.com/AlkalineLifestylePay/alkaline_diet_course.php

Georgie's experience using the Alkalising diet.

Georgie recently wrote to me explaining her background - how she is a qualified practicing nutritionist who trained in Deakin University in Australia and did a naturopath nutrition qualification as well. She wrote that she has always been fascinated by nutrition ever since a biology teacher put a digestion chart up on the blackboard. Here follows an extraction from her letter explaining how even to a nutritionist, food is not the only acid-giving factor in changing vitality - you need to change your thinking as well.

"To my utter astonishment on the first day of my second spontaneous remission, after doing the 70 x 7 *(a technique used for getting to the bottom of a deep seated issues which I am not aware of – Ed Richard)* I burst into tears, cussing and swearing at myself like I have never done before. The self-loathing and hatred took me by surprise. I let it all pour out of me. I allowed my body and mind to get right into it, sobbing and uttering profanities at myself for a very long time. Put simply, I was disgusted at myself over almost everything I had ever done in my life. I have talked to my inner critic during voice dialogue sessions in the past, but with this there was a subtle difference. It was straight out rage and fury at myself. Since expressing all this pent up anger I have stayed on a very strict alkalising diet ever since."

Georgie has had breast cancer. After surgery she developed some small dermis tumours where the incisions were made when the breast was removed. In META-Medicine® the body is defending itself from the attack of the surgery by growing the extra skin. She also developed lymphomas in and around the breast area and a self-worth conflict from removal of the breast (not being/feeling womanly enough due to the removal of the part that makes her look female.) When I spoke to her she had done a lot of the mental work, including clearing self-hatred. She started using her real name again, Sarah, which was perfect to hear because that made a massive difference to her eating and following through with an alkaline diet.

Georgie has stayed in contact and recently she needed to really address the dermis scars that were still growing from the cut caused by the operation. Having had some success with her nutrition plan she travelled to a retreat in the USA near San Diego to study further see www.phmiracleliving.com and did a two week programme. There she learnt a tremendous amount about pH balancing and returned home excited and started administering a more comprehensive alkalising programme herself. She explained that you need to use bicarbonate IV and intravenously inject several grams a day of this solution. This she said has made the biggest impact on her pH levels. Another part of the alkalising is to have a lymphatic massage and a sauna each day.

What has been so dramatic is that the dermis tumours have completely disappeared. However, recently she called me at 3.30 a.m. her time in Australia. She was in excruciating pain due to the lymph glands swelling in the second phase. It was so bad she told me, that the pain-killers were having no effect and the next step would be morphine. I knew this was a Kidney Collecting Tubule Syndrome and I worked with her. It all transpired that the pain started before Christmas and was due to her splitting up from her partner. I assisted her in resolving the abandonment/isolation issue and the pain went from a ten (being unbearable) to a one in thirty minutes. She went back to bed and slept.

The moral of this is that nutrition alone will not heal everything. Psychological work as well as other integrative methods of healing is necessary to become well. This I will explain in a later chapter.

Vitality can also be addressed by environmental and social changes. I was in Brighton having a meal with a group of friends. The venue was a curry house and the music and general environment was basic. I then suggested we go to Hotel du Vin, and enjoy a drink in their luxury lounge. The change in all our moods was easy to notice, we all commented on how our spirits lifted as we sat down in large comfortable settees and drank gorgeous hot chocolate, some of us drinking glasses of delicious dessert wines.

Our environment plays a significant part in our healing. Retreats, walking in tranquil places, getting away from the hustle and bustle of the inner cities, away from noise and traffic all add to our inner energy reserves being charged.

The people we mix with, the programmes we watch on television, our friends, all add to giving us a boost. The ancient Hawaiians, a culture I find very interesting because it remained untouched by western civilisation until two hundred years ago. They have a saying about life-force energy: 'If something gives you energy do more of it, if something takes energy away from you, stop doing it'.

The same philosophy can be applied to what we watch - if the news depresses you, stop watching it. If a television programme has a negative effect on you, switch it off. If a friend seems to drain you every time you see them, stop seeing them. If people in your workplace or your boss are causing problems, look inside as to how you are causing the issues in them and find ways of changing the situation. (NLP can help with this)

Book a regular appointment with yourself to resolve inner issues in yourself and get organised. It is good advice we rarely use but it pays dividends in our well-being, knowing that all the minor things such as bills are paid, conversations that need to be had are planned, chores are organised and emotions we need to resolve are solved.

I recently had a major set of deep buried issues arise in myself that were causing me a horrendous amount of stress. I was eating badly (mostly sugar related products) and I had some horrible conversations with a very good friend who was triggering off past issues in me. I booked myself in for an appointment with myself and did the emotional work to clear the problems. I also stopped speaking to my friend. I took time out as well for myself and went to the gym, without feeling guilty that I was leaving my wife alone with our son. It was time well spent because the problems were resolved and now I am talking to my friend again and everything is clear. I stopped the excessive sugar eating and although I have some aches and pains from the original issues which had healed, I feel one hundred percent better.

I have in the past let these things go and soldiered on as I mentioned before, but I knew if I let these issues fester I would only find them arising at a later date and probably the resulting pains would have been much deeper and worse than they were.

What drugs and supplements can keep us in the stress or regeneration phase

Here is a list of drugs and supplements that keep us in the stress phase. Point 3.

Cortisone, adrenalin, digitalis, antihistamines, anti-allergens, antibiotics, cytostatic drugs (damaging to cells) such as chemotherapy, radiation, caffeine, tea, coke (drink and herb), guarana and many other stimulating, sympathetic methods, recreational drugs, many prescribed medications and therapies.

It is worth mentioning cortisone or steroids, as many people take these as prescribed medications, e.g. Prednisone is a common drug used in the treatment of many diseases. What this is literally doing is putting the body back into the first phase. The symptoms disappear and the pain and swelling goes. The problem occurs through continued use of such drugs because the body never heals the issue. Eventually when the drugs are stopped many other symptoms appear. Steroids can and do help in therapy, but what we have found is that these drugs are overused. What we recommend is to reduce the amount (along with medical supervision) and carefully allow the body to go through the second phase.

Another use of stress-inducing drugs is if a person is experiencing epileptic fits that keep repeating themselves, cortisone can be administered by a medical doctor in order to get people over the hump of the healing crisis. The reason why this is so effective is because the body wants to squeeze the excessive water out from in and around the tumour. In epileptic fits the issue is in the brain, where a relay is squeezing out the excessive fluid so it can complete its healing. If a doctor will not give cortisone during this time, then you can give a couple of shots of espresso coffee. I have done this with clients and I use this theory to great effect when I have a headache. After drinking the coffee you experience excessive urination. You will find that you will be urinating more fluid than you have drunk during the day.

Listed below are some supplements and therapies that assist with the second phase:

Magnesium, selenium, valerian, massage, meditation, yoga, energetic healing, and many other relaxing, second phase therapies, medications and methods.

How to stay healthy and live longer

Vitality is therefore very important in all our lives. If you want to be healthy and live a long life then changing your diet is not the only answer, however it is very, very important.

In META-Medicine® you also need to change your whole lifestyle and you need to continuously work at it. You need to deal with any underlying emotional issues as and when they arise (EFT is one simple solution to this - I like it because you can self-administer the treatment, www.emofree.com or my friend Karl Dawson's site www.e-f-t.com). You need to review what you watch on television or read, take regular exercise, do something you love - it could be as simple as walking or playing golf regularly - its not just about going the gym.

Choose your tranquil place where you can close the door and switch off the world. Talking with good, positive friends is also empowering, having fun time-out with them can also energise your body and mind. Doing a spiritual practice of some sort such as connecting with who you are as a person and your place on this earth, all have benefits that can and do energize us. Relaxing and meditating can also make such a world of difference that some people swear by it. Look into Holosync - www.centerpointe.com/holosync/ as a fast way of getting to deep levels of meditation known only to Tibetan monks. Treat your body to massages and look after yourself. De-stress regularly; I personally notice I get so much more done the less stressed I am. Taking time out pays ten-fold in the long run.

Conclusion of eating a Vegan diet and the affect it had on my back

After I had worked with Christa, I came back to the UK and I stated to eat like a vegan. I kept this up for over two months and during this time many things changed and I found that every day my back was getting better and better. The pain started to disappear until I felt no pain whatsoever. I also took drastic action socially and in my environment and noticed that my personality changed. I was working with a person who had me contracted to a large multinational telecommunications corporation. I had let her put me down and I even found myself saying: "I let her walk all over me." I called her and told her I did not want to work with her again. This cost me a fortune in lost fees but then again, being able to walk with no pain was the price I was willing to pay because after two months I was walking and running again with no pain.

In the next chapter I want to explore psychological diseases and how they are caused. This is one of the most exciting developments to come out of META-Medicine®. Imagine knowing how and why a person gets depressed and then knowing the process that can trigger the depression. Using a modern emotional clearing technique such as Time Line Therapy™ or EFT, you can get rid of a deep-seated life long issue forever. Look at www.stressintohappiness.com for more information and trainings about these teachings delivered by myself.

Chapter 13

with Rob van Overbruggen Ph.D.

Basic psychological symptoms finally explained

Depression, mania and sexuality

As I say; I don't want to kill myself, I just wouldn't mind dying. - Stephen Fry
Popular gay British comedian and actor talking about his manic depression

NOTE: This chapter discusses sexuality in detail. Some of the points raised are challenging. If you find this subject difficult please go onto the next chapter.

The story of Kari and her clinical depression

Kari Reed came to see me in Sea Isle, USA. She was a demonstration subject and also one of the assistants, helping with the filming of 'How to Tap using META-Medicine®'. This would be made into a DVD set, designed to teach EFT' Practitioners where to tap on a client following a META-Medicine® diagnosis.

EFT is a therapeutic intervention that is similar to acupuncture but without needles. You tap on the main acupuncture points whilst making specific suggestions. It also incorporates changes in beliefs in order to resolve simple and complex problems.

When I met Kari she was morose, she did not speak much and she looked really unhappy at having to be there. What's more, she was on the verge of going into another deep depression, as I discovered during the consultation. In order for you to fully understand what she was going through, I have included her notes which she sent me before we met.

There is a lot of information here and the reason I have included it all, is because there are many people in the world who suffer from depression, and who have no solution other than having to resort to anti-depressants, which can have horrendous side effects. The traditional psychological community doesn't seem to have an answer either. Kari experienced both the prescribed drug issues and the limited techniques available for healing depression available to her via her therapist. Also, as we have found in META-Medicine® such psychological issues affect sexual preference.

She writes well and the story is really interesting. I have changed a few names to protect certain individuals for obvious reasons. As you read her story and then the rest of this chapter, you will see what happened to her regarding her depression and sexuality. After reading this chapter if you read through it again, I am sure you will discover the patterns of depression and mania that she went through and how her sexual preference was influenced.

"Five years ago, when I was just about 20 yrs old, I was diagnosed with Clinical Depression recurrent (meaning that the depression itself tends to manifest in 'episodes' that can last anywhere from a couple of days to a couple of months or longer). Even worse, I was told by my original therapist, and all of those that would follow that this would never go away, no matter what I did, what medications I took, or how many counselling sessions I sat through. Simply put, it is something that I am apparently destined to deal with for the rest of my life and that can be triggered at any time, no matter how well things seem to be going for whatever length of time.

Just before my diagnosis, I was a sophomore (second year student) in college – I attended an art school in Philadelphia – and things were going really, really well. I felt happy, I was maintaining a 4.0 in school and enjoying my classes; I was involved in volunteer programs and had an active social life, etc. etc. My childhood was not ideal – things like divorce, feeling very responsible for my siblings when my parents were unable to act like parents, drug and alcohol addictions in the home, being sent off to live with grandparents rather unexpectedly, and my parents somewhat complicated relationships and marriages after the divorce are just some of the things.

Around that time, I met a woman who remembered my parents divorcing and the events that surrounded it. She was 12 years older than me. While I did not know it at the time, my parents had been involved in affairs with another couple that attended their church. To further complicate things, my family was a very 'visible' family in the church.

We immediately became friends, and, out of curiosity or concern, I suppose, she began asking me questions about what had happened, what I knew, and how I felt about it all. I had never been concerned about telling people what I thought; I knew that she was a therapist with a master's degree in clinical counselling, so I had no problems talking to her. There was one specific time that I remember fairly vividly – we had run a youth retreat one weekend in the fall of my junior year of college and were returning the van we had rented. Sally (name changed – Ed; the therapist woman) and I were in the van alone. She starting asking me questions about my dad, him leaving, our current relationship, etc. etc. – and I had a small but considerable 'breakdown' that was highly emotional and a very new experience for me. She called my parents when we got to the van place and told them that since we were so far away, I was such a mess, and it was so late that she was going to have me stay at her house (which was closer) that night to talk about what had happened. Since my parents knew her from the church and knew that she was "a real therapist" they consented.

From that point on, I remember things spiralled steadily downward. She, with the consent of my parents (who had pushed since mid to late adolescence for me and my siblings to 'deal' with the emotional things that were caused by their past activities) took me on as one of her 'clients' – though I'm not sure if my parents paid her or not. The sessions were informal and very laid back, and we spent most of our time together as friends. Eventually she and I became interested in each other as 'more than friends' so to speak, and in the middle of all of this we embarked on a romantic relationship that was very involved, complicated, and secretive – she was still a counsellor for the church we attended and it would have been detrimental to her career and position at the church if anyone knew that she was involved with another girl, let alone one of her clients. As the relationship progressed, I moved into her house with her and her two female roommates (who were also ex-girlfriends, as I would later find out) in the name of "helping me" and "my therapy" – or that was what was told to my parents and others who asked.

Sally had, from early on in my therapy, said that I exhibited signs of depression and "a little borderline personality disorder" – but I had never felt highly depressed. A few weeks after moving into her house, I had my first major "break" – I became severely depressed, to the point that I couldn't even get out of bed. I cried A LOT and had never experienced anything quite like that before. She maintained being my therapist, my girlfriend, and my friend in public – and suggested that I see my family doctor for anti-depressants. My parents were again supportive if it meant I would be 'normal' again, and my family doctor put me on a new anti-depressant at the time – Lexipro, to which I had a severe reaction – I found myself unable to sleep for days upon end, hyper, and had a significant loss of cognitive understanding. I was sent back to the family doctor where they prescribed something different. This pattern continued until I had been on several medications. Finally a drug called Effexor XR seemed to work.

I continued to live with my girlfriend/therapist and her roommates for about a year and a half – she continued to administer sessions and I continued to take medications to cope, however, my life was in no kind of coping order. I nearly failed out of school for missed classes and inability to participate, I contemplated suicide on many occasions, I had no contact with my old friends or my family, and I would spend most of my time in bed – alone during the day and with my therapist/girlfriend at night.

Three events happened that changed these things – First, my girlfriend/therapist woke me up one morning around 4 a.m. and told me she could no longer be with me or see me and that I needed to leave. I had nowhere to go and felt completely and utterly blindsided, but got some things and left. I would later return to get the rest of my stuff. I moved back in with my parents and continued to both take meds (with some relapses in how consistent I was) and battle my depression, many days not getting out of bed at all.

The second thing that happened was; it was discovered that I was having terrible side effects to the Effexor that I was on – my blood pressure was through the roof and I was having blackouts and dizzy spells. The third thing that happened was Sally went to my parents (my step-father, who I consider to be my father, was also the pastor of the church we had been and were attending) and told them about our relationship – without me. I came home that night and walked into a big mess. The conversation was long and difficult, but it was decided that I would no longer see her as my therapist. (There were many other, more public consequences to that conversation that I will leave out here, for the sake of time and space).

From that point on I saw another therapist and a psychologist to regulate my meds (one of the best in the area). I was put onto Wellbutrin, another anti-depressant that seemed to work very well. I eventually got things in my life back in order (for the most part) and started back in school. However, I was told by both of these people (as well had I been by Sally) that I had clinical depression and it was never going to go away – no matter what. They all maintained that I would have to struggle with it for the rest of my life.

My relationship with Sally continued to be tumultuous, and I eventually moved to Pennsylvania (from New Jersey, another state entirely) so as not to have to deal with her and the pressures of the church to 'confess' and do things I decided I did not believe in. I have since stopped going to traditional therapy (with the blessings of my therapist) and am no longer on medication of any kind (also with the blessings of both my therapist and

177

psychologist) – while this sounds great, I still struggle on a day-to-day basis with depression – both with episodes that last anywhere from a couple of days to more severe ones that last weeks, and with the constant fear that I will fall back into the kind of state that I was in when it was at its worst. I think the fear is the worst part, because it is constant. Recently, I have been struggling greatly with the worst 'episode' that I have had in a long time. I do not want to go back on medication, but feel I may be running out of options. I now use EFT fairly regularly, and it has taken the edge off of some of my fear (though not much) and has been able to 'pull me out of' several smaller episodes. It, so far, is making this one slightly more bearable, but I would like to be free from it altogether, though part of me may believe that I will have to struggle with this forever."

I carried out a META-Medicine® diagnosis with Kari on camera. I explained to her how her depression worked (something I am going to make clear in this chapter), at the same time Lynda Wood, the EFT practitioner who was going to do the therapy work, was listening and taking notes. I told Lynda what events and patterns she needed to work on. Lynda's sessions lasted only a few hours, and in that time the changes in Kari were astonishing. I will tell you about this later.

The question is: How did I know where to look? How was I able to give Lynda a simple road map to follow? She is one of the most skilled EFT therapy practitioners in the world, and would have assisted Kari over many sessions but with no guarantee of solving her problem, so how, that in two hours, she could assist someone diagnosed as clinically depressed and borderline suicidal, in changing her life forever? This was something that university trained counsellors, medical doctors, clinical psychologists, and therapists were unable to do, even with the best will in the world and with the array of different anti-depressant drugs available to them. How did I know where to tap?

The question I was asking myself was why does a young twenty-year old girl who is highly religious and sexually heterosexual, end up having a same-sex relationship and being clinically depressed?

In order to answer these questions and many others about psychological issues we first need to study the cortex area of the brain and hormonal differences between men and women.

Gender and masculine and feminine energy

Men and women are obviously different. We all know from an early age that we carry different genitals, but why do we act differently? Why do little boys like engineering and structural things from a young age? And likewise, little girls are more interested in social interactions, babies and dressing up. This is all to do with masculine and feminine energy, and that energy determines how we behave in the world, as you will discover in this chapter.

Our gender is assigned in the womb, six weeks after conception; the genes determine if we are to be a man or a woman. However, at six weeks you cannot tell if the foetus will be a boy or girl as the gonads (the sex organs) look the same. Only at sixteen weeks will the changes be noticeable. Before the hormones start to develop, the foetus is female. When the genes want to make a male body, then the body starts to produce more testosterone. This testosterone develops the primary and secondary male sex organs. Without this testosterone the body would stay female. Testosterone is what makes a man.[104]

However, as we grow up these differences are obvious to see. Most people grow up to act like a woman or a man, but I am sure you are aware that some women are very masculine, and some men are very feminine. Why do these people act and behave as they do?

The difference in feminine men and masculine women is caused by gender energy. This energy determines how we interpret a conflict as a man or a woman.

Therefore a masculine woman will react in a masculine way to a conflict. A feminine man will react in a feminine way to a conflict.

As we discuss this difference, whenever we talk about a biological WOMAN we are referring to a person who has a vagina, a womb and breasts. A biological MAN has a penis, testicles and prostate. When we refer to 'feminine energy' this is soft and caring, whilst masculine energy is hard, protective and assertive.

The four types

1. Man
2. Woman
3. Feminine energy
4. Masculine energy

In ancient times, when we all lived in caves, there were distinctive roles for the women and men. Women were responsible for 'internal' group coherence; holding the tribe together, bringing up the children and producing the food. The men were responsible for hunting and protection from 'external' threats.

Hormones

There are also effects from hormones; women ovulate and get pregnant through oestrogen, and testosterone gives men their strength, deeper voice and facial hair. Women who inject testosterone grow excessive hair and become more muscular; in effect the woman becomes more masculine, so she has more masculine energy. We see this in women who take testosterone (anabolic steroids) e.g. in bodybuilding. Likewise a man who takes oestrogen will start to grow breasts, his facial hair growth will subside, and he will become more feminine, so he has more feminine energy. We can notice this in transgender males who purposely take oestrogen.

What makes a woman feminine are the female hormones - estrogens and progestagens.

What makes a man masculine are the male hormones - androgens, of which testosterone is the most widely known.

In order for us to understand the major difference between feminine energy and a masculine energy, it is worth looking at the stereotypes.

Stereotypical feminine energy

Stereotypical femininity focuses on nurture, friendship, socializing, empathy, and emotional expression. Because women need to interact with their surroundings and maintain a lot of social issues at the same time, their brains are wired to handle this. The woman's brain is wired in such a way that both hemispheres work more often together than a man's brain.

Women tend to be better in:

- Emotional expression (oral and written)
- Multitasking
- Communication
- Ask for help when they need to

179

Stereotypical masculine energy

Women take care of the group coherence and structure, whilst men take care of food and the protection of the group from external threats. These functions have developed themselves in the brain too. The brain of a man is wired for these primary functions.

During hunting, men need to communicate fast and efficiently. It makes no sense to sit down and communicate extensively when you are trying to catch a deer. Communication is geared towards a specific task that needs to be completed. Interfering signals from the surroundings which are irrelevant to the task are disregarded.

Men tend to be better in:

- Factual expression
- Focussed working
- Physical action
- Solving things on their own

How shocks affect masculine and feminine energy

Hormones change how we react socially and territorially in our environment; they change our energy - more feminine or more masculine. In META-Medicine® these energy changes affect how we react to shock. Do we experience the shock as masculine or feminine? e.g. A person with feminine energy reacts to social conflicts, where as one with masculine energy to territorial conflicts. The energy determines which side of the brain a conflict lands.

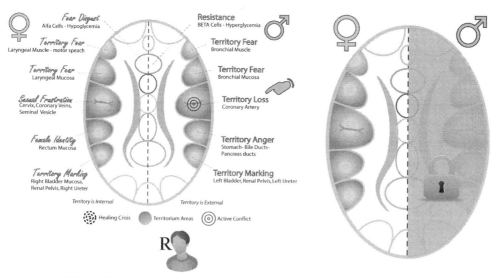

If a right-wired man has a conflict it lands on the right masculine hemisphere, this then closes. The left feminine energy hemisphere is still open so he reacts with a feminine energy.

An example of a masculine conflict over a loss of territory may be a man who gets fired from his job, something which is unexpectedly shocking for him. If this man is RIGHT-WIRED then the conflict will land on the right hemisphere. This right hemisphere then closes. The only way then for this man to react is on the left hemisphere; he will therefore become more feminine.

180

The right hemisphere is the <u>masculine</u> energy side; the conflicts are territorial (external). If there are multiple conflicts and the right hemisphere conflicts are more intense, the person will feel DEPRESSED.

An example of a woman experiencing a feminine sexual frustration conflict could be for example; a man cheats on her and this is unexpectedly shocking for her - If this woman is RIGHT-WIRED the conflict lands on the 'left' hemisphere. This left hemisphere then closes. So the only way for this woman to react is on the right hemisphere; she will therefore become more masculine.

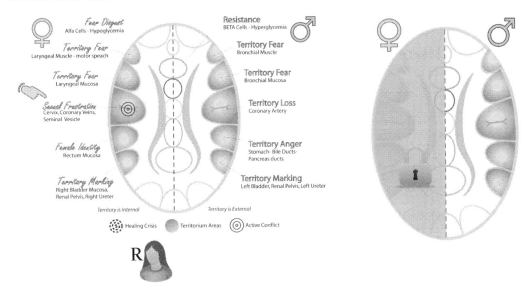

If a right-wired woman has a conflict it lands on the left feminine hemisphere, this then closes. The right masculine energy hemisphere is still open so she reacts with a masculine energy.

The left hemisphere is the feminine energy side; the conflicts are social (internal). If there are multiple conflicts and the left hemisphere conflicts are more intense the person will feel MANIC.

Multiple conflicts in the cortex

If two conflicts occur, one after the other, in the brain stem, cerebellum and cerebral medulla, it causes the same relay to be activated; it adds to the intensity of the issue, along with a greater organ reaction.

In the cortex this is different.

If a conflict lands on one side of the brain, it closes that hemisphere. However, the opposite side is still open. Any new conflicts then land on that hemisphere.

If a conflict lands on the feminine hemisphere, it closes it off, leaving the masculine hemisphere open. The person then reacts to conflicts in a masculine way.

If a conflict lands on the masculine hemisphere, it closes it off leaving the feminine hemisphere open. The person then reacts to conflicts in a feminine way.

If you have a conflict that you cannot solve in a masculine way, you are given time out and start to react in a feminine way; therefore you become a non-threat to the person causing the conflict. The opposite is also true; if you have a conflict you cannot solve in a feminine way, you are given time out and react in a masculine way.

If a man gets into a fight for his territory, he can either win or lose. If he loses he can either fight again, or give up the fight and that leaves him more feminine or submissive. If he is submissive, he is no longer a threat to the original opponent, which is a biological way of protecting himself and his family.

How all this happens is determined by whether you are a man or a woman, right or left-wired, feminine or masculine energy, or hormonally suppressed. As conflicts hit relays, they can cause either depression or mania, and cause a person to react in a more feminine or more masculine way, and either an organ reaction to occur, or not.

Different combinations of conflicts cause psychological symptoms, such as bulimia, anorexia, manic depression and other issues, which are explained later in this chapter. These, until now, had no process or structure to them. People knew that they came from imbalances of the brain. For the first time, we can explain with META-Medicine®, how and why this happens. People knew that in the case of bulimia there was a stomach issue, and in depression there was often a sexual problem, but there was no model to explain the relationship.

Now let us go into more detail about each type. In these explanations we refer to:
- 'Territorial conflicts,' which are in the external world. This can be a company, a job, a house, or a partner (man or women) who leaves a relationship.
- 'Social identity conflicts' which refers to the internal world. This can be a perceived position in a social group, nurturing, protecting the children, and communication.

In the following paragraphs we describe in more detail what happens to each one of the types of person, a right-wired man/woman or a left-wired woman/man. It is not as straight forward as the other brain layers, but really worth studying.

Right-wired man

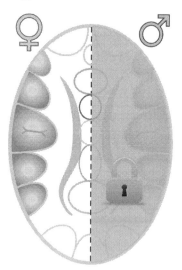

After a right-wired man experiences a single territorial conflict, his RIGHT cortex (the masculine hemisphere) closes. He will have a stress phase organ reaction.

The left feminine hemisphere is still open and he starts to react with feminine energy. (This is the only way he can react.) He will be less worried about making a career, more interested in expressing emotions and taking care of children. He will be more submissive and will avoid conflicts.

He will associate with and be attracted to masculine women or feminine men. He is now in a feminine energy; any new conflicts will be experienced in this way and so his conflicts will be more social and internal; they will land on the left feminine hemisphere.

Example:

A man, before he lost his job, was aggressive, career orientated, enjoyed competitive sports, and was attracted to feminine women. After the conflict he is in a more feminine energy and enjoys the company of masculine women and/or feminine men, along with home-making and focussing more on communication and being more emotionally involved in conversations.

If this RIGHT-WIRED feminine energy man experiences a new conflict, this conflict will land on the left hemisphere. Now both hemispheres contain an active conflict. He is in constellation. The original organ reaction stops and he will experience psychological symptoms of mania or depression depending on the intensity of each conflict.

If the feminine conflict is very intense then the man will become MANIC. If the masculine conflict intensity is more intense the man will become DEPRESSED.

Triggering the tracks (refer to chapter 7)

Imagine that the right hemisphere issue is connected to work and the left hemisphere issue to home life (e.g. a wife). In work this person will feel depressed followed by feeling manic when at home with their partner. E.g. depressive-manic.

Right-wired woman

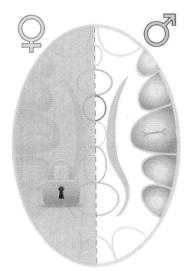

After a right-wired woman experiences a single social identity conflict, her LEFT cortex (the feminine hemisphere) closes. She will have a stress phase organ reaction.

The right masculine hemisphere is still open and she starts to react with masculine energy. (This is the only way she can react.) She will be less worried about expressing her emotions and taking care of children but more focussed about making a career. She will be more aggressive and will take on conflicts.

She will associate with and be attracted to feminine men or masculine women. She is now in a masculine energy - any new conflicts will be experienced in this way and so her conflicts will be more territorial and external; they will land on the right masculine hemisphere.

Example:

A woman, before her partner cheated on her, was attracted to masculine men. She was submissive, family orientated, enjoying social interaction and gossip.

After the conflict she is in a more masculine energy and enjoys the company of feminine men or masculine women, along with making a career and focussing less on communication, and being less emotionally involved in conversations.

If this RIGHT-WIRED masculine energy woman experiences a new conflict, then both hemispheres contain an active conflict. She is now in constellation. The original organ reaction stops and she will experience psychological symptoms of mania or depression depending on the intensity of each conflict.

If the masculine conflict is very intense then the woman will become DEPRESSED. If the feminine conflict intensity is more intense the woman will become MANIC.

Triggering the tracks (refer to Chapter 7)

Imagine that the left hemisphere issue is connected to work and the right hemisphere issue to home life (a husband). In work this person will feel manic followed by feeling depressed when at home with their partner. E.g. manic-depressive.

However in left-wired women and men different reactions and symptoms occur.

Left-wired Man

For left-wired people the brain relay hits on the opposite hemisphere than right-wired individuals.

An example of a masculine conflict over a loss of territory may be a man who gets fired from his job; something which is unexpectedly shocking for him.

If this man is LEFT-WIRED then the conflict will land on the 'left' hemisphere. This left hemisphere then closes. Now he can only react on the right hemisphere (the masculine energy side), so he reacts like a masculine man, an overly masculine man, a macho man.

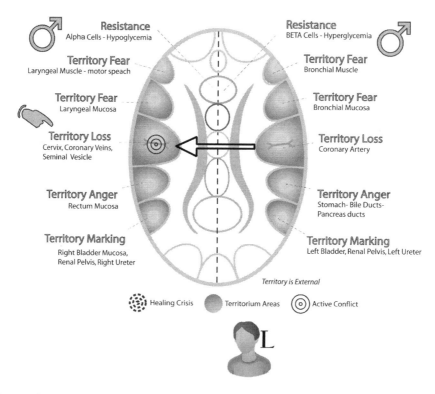

Left-wired man the first conflict lands on the left hemisphere. He still experiences it as a masculine conflict. Unlike in right-wired people, this first conflict will cause a change in behaviour - he will feel manic.

Left-wired woman

If a woman experiences a female sexual frustration conflict - for example a man cheats on her and it is unexpectedly shocking for her. If this woman is LEFT-WIRED, the conflict lands on the 'right' hemisphere. This right hemisphere then closes. Now she can only react in a feminine way, so she reacts like a feminine woman, an overly feminine woman.

Left-wired woman.

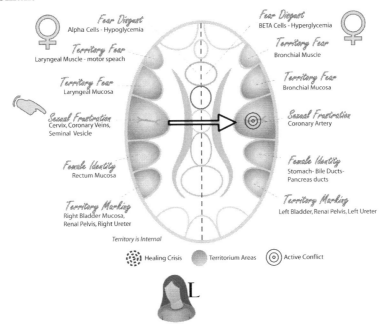

In a left-wired woman the first conflict lands on the right hemisphere, she still experiences it as a feminine energy conflict. Unlike in right-wired people, this first conflict will cause a change in behaviour - she will feel depressed.

Two conflicts in a left-wired man

After a left-wired man experiences a single territorial loss conflict, his LEFT hemisphere closes. Although this is the left (feminine) side, he still reacts territorially as a man. He will have a stress phase organ reaction and he will feel <u>MANIC</u>.

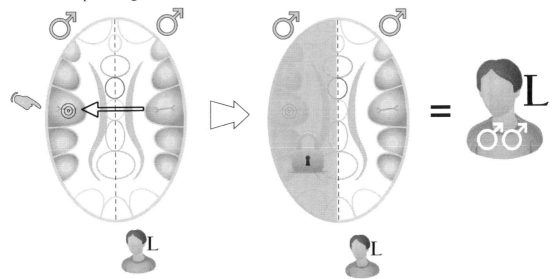

A diagramme of how a left-wired man reacts with a shock. After two shocks he will become a macho man.

185

How a left-wired man's behaviour changes following two or more conflicts

The right masculine side is still open and he starts to react like a <u>macho</u> man. He will attack any alpha male (see Alpha Males and Females) in his group because he feels that an alpha male is a mating threat to him; he now has a second chance to solve the original territorial conflict.

The competing alpha male fights back, and when this happens there are three possibilities:

Either:

He wins and he takes over the alpha male position and takes that position in the group.

Or:

He fights again with the alpha male because he wants to resolve the first conflict. He fights manically, with his full strength; until he is exhausted or severely beaten, or the more likely outcome is that he gives up and lives with the situation (survival of both males in the pack is the key). There are now two conflicts; the first conflict shock brain-relay on the left hemisphere, and the second on the right hemisphere.

If he wins the second fight then he is master of the territory again, and he solves the first conflict – if he waits more than nine months to do this, he will die of a heart attack during the healing crisis, usually 6-8 weeks after conflict resolution.

If he gives up and decides not to fight, the first conflict becomes downgraded. It is still under stress (active) but not serious. The coronary veins are affected – the organ reaction will be a light angina pectoris, but he can live with it.

He will become a macho man, not attracted to women. He will lose his sex drive to mate with women, but he will still be able to have sex. He is no longer a threat to the alpha male. He will become submissive and possibly become homosexual, gay (see homosexuality in wild animals). He will not be able to become an alpha male or be able to claim a leadership position.

Example:

I talked with one of my good friends, who is left-wired and gay. He told me that he grew up with three older brothers. He would fight with them until he was totally exhausted. He said he knew he was gay from age seven. This happened when he gave up physically fighting his brothers.

Or:

He gets an opposing conflict, (a constellation, both conflicts are opposite each other,) e.g. coronary veins - left side and coronary arteries - right side, the organ reaction stops at the moment of the constellation. He will become a 'court jester', a 'clown'. He therefore poses no threat to the alpha male, so no women are attracted to him and therefore none want to mate with him. This has a special biological significance; if the alpha male dies or leaves, he becomes the next alpha male. This causes a complete resolution of both sides, and since there was no organ reaction there will be no heart attack. Nature literally creates a biological 'spare' for the group.

Two conflicts in a left-wired woman

After a left-wired woman experiences a single social identity conflict, her RIGHT hemisphere closes. Although this is the right (masculine) side, she still reacts socially as a woman. She will have a stress phase organ reaction and she will feel DEPRESSED.

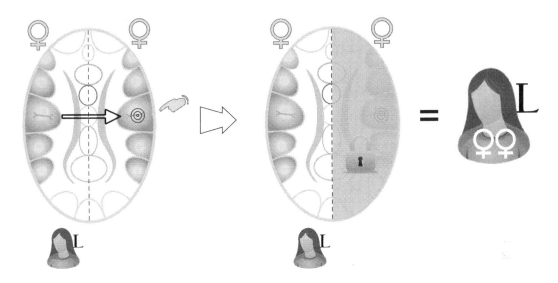

A diagramme of how a left-wired woman reacts with a shock. After two shocks she will become a super female woman.

How a left-wired woman's behaviour changes following two or more conflicts

The left feminine side is still open and she starts to react like a super female woman. She will challenge any alpha female by trying to attract the alpha male sexually in her group (see Alpha Males and Females) because she feels that an alpha female is a mating threat to her. She now has a second chance to solve the original social conflict.

The competing alpha female challenges her, by showing her who is the boss; she does this by establishing the alpha male as hers sexually, or by socially pushing out the LEFT-WIRED feminine energy woman. When this happens there are three possibilities:

Either:

She wins and she takes over the alpha female position, and takes that position in the group.

Or:

She challenges the alpha female again because she wants to resolve the first conflict. She will challenge with all her social abilities and sexual prowess, until she is ostracised or is socially inferior or as is the more likely outcome, she gives up and lives with the situation. There are now two conflicts. The first social conflict brain relay on the right hemisphere and the second on the left hemisphere.

If she wins the second conflict then she is master of the social group again and she solves the first conflict – if she waits more than nine months to do this she will die of a heart attack during the healing crisis, usually 6-8 weeks after conflict resolution.

If she gives up and decides not to fight, the first conflict becomes downgraded. It is still under stress (active) but not serious. The coronary arteries are affected – the organ reaction will be a light angina pectoris, but she can live with it.

She will become a super feminine energy woman, not attracted to males. She will lose her drive to mate with males but she will still be able to have sex. She is no longer a threat to the alpha female. She will become aggressive and possibly become lesbian (see homosexuality in wild animals). She will not be able to become an alpha female or be able to claim a leadership position.

Or:

She gets an opposing conflict, (a constellation, both conflicts are opposite each other, e.g. coronary arteries - right side and coronary veins - left side, the organ reaction stops at the moment of the constellation. She will become a 'joker', a 'clown'. She therefore poses no threat to the alpha female, so no males are attracted to her and therefore none would want to mate with her. This has a special biological significance; if the alpha female dies or leaves, she becomes the next alpha female. This causes a complete resolution of both sides and since there was no organ reaction there will be no heart attack. Nature literally creates a biological 'spare' for the group.

What else can close down the feminine hemisphere side or affect the feminine energy?

Drugs; such as alcohol, morphine and heroin.

> It is interesting to observe young women in the UK who have developed a culture of drinking heavily. The alcohol shuts down the feminine energy side and turns the woman into a masculine woman or a super feminine woman, dependant on how they are wired. If she becomes more masculine she can turn into a 'ladette'; a female lad (a lad is a young sixteen to twenty-one year old boy). These ladettes can be very threatening to young males, as often they are the ones out-drinking the lads and demanding sex from them. Alcohol in large quantities releases testosterone into the blood. Hence the reason why many males fight when drunk, and so do ladettes when drunk.

The contraceptive pill

> The pill reduces the amount of female hormones in the body, thus making the woman react with masculine energy.

Chemotherapy

Cytostatic - (toxic to cells) drugs used in the treatment of cancer.

Radiotherapy

> Both chemo and radiation destroy the ability of the ovaries to produce oestrogen, the feminine sex hormone. Consequently oestrogen is significantly reduced but the sex hormones produced in the adrenal glands are still active. In effect, there are more of the opposite hormones so the person becomes more energetically masculine.

Hormone replacement therapy (HRT)

Menopause - Around age fifty to sixty

During pregnancy

During lactation

> Whilst a woman is lactating she will want to protect her offspring so she will act with masculine energy. Usually one ovary is enough for a woman to remain female. If a woman stops ovulating for whatever reason, this will block the feminine energy side.

Being in Hormonal Standoff

> A woman can often be in a situation where there is a more dominant (alpha female) woman that she naturally has to be submissive towards. In this instance she can be in hormonal standoff and the masculine hemisphere is closed

Brain operation in the cortex

Healing of an ovarian cyst - More production of oestrogen, so more feminine energy.

Removal of ovaries - one ovary is enough to maintain feminine energy.

Less oestrogen; if both are removed then the women has more masculine energy.

What else can close the male hemisphere or affect the masculine energy?

Chemotherapy

Radiotherapy

Both chemo and radiation destroy the ability of the testicles to produce testosterone, the masculine sex hormone. Consequently these are significantly reduced but the sex hormones produced in the adrenal glands are still active. In effect there are more of the opposite hormones so the person becomes more energetically feminine.

Hormone replacement

Such as female hormones taken during prostate cancer. More feminine energy.

Healing of a testicular cyst - More testosterone, more masculine energy.

Old age - Around age seventy - less testosterone, more feminine energy.

Castration

Less testosterone, more feminine energy. One testicle is enough to maintain masculine energy.

Being in Hormonal Standoff

A man can often be in a situation where there is a more dominant alpha male who he has to be submissive towards. In this instance he can be in hormonal standoff and the masculine side is closed. NOTE: No organ reaction occurs on this hemisphere in this instance.

Brain operation in the cortex

Hormonal Standoff in children and teenagers

A young boy or girl, before puberty, will be balanced in their hormones. They will still act like a girl or boy and the reactions will still be the same as already mentioned. However, once puberty starts and a girl starts to ovulate and a boy to produce sperm, then they will go into hormonal standoff in and around the alpha male or female. This is usually the parent but it can also be another sibling. This continues until the child reaches biological maturity, which stops them from being hormonally suppressed.

Hormonal standoff in adults

This can occur in adults at work, or other situations such as playing sports or in a group. The leader, who could be a boss (the designated alpha male or female) can immediately put a person into hormonal standoff. This can force the changes I have written about; the person can become submissive or macho or super female around these alpha males or females.

Intensity of conflicts on both hemispheres

When one hemisphere of the brain is closed and a conflict occurs on the opposite hemisphere, if the person then experiences another third or even fourth conflict on the same side, these will add to the overall intensity. Therefore a person, who has three active and intense conflicts on one side of the brain compared with two low-intensity conflicts on the opposite side, will really feel the intensity of the three issues and therefore as an example have severe depression (right side) or severe mania (left side).

189

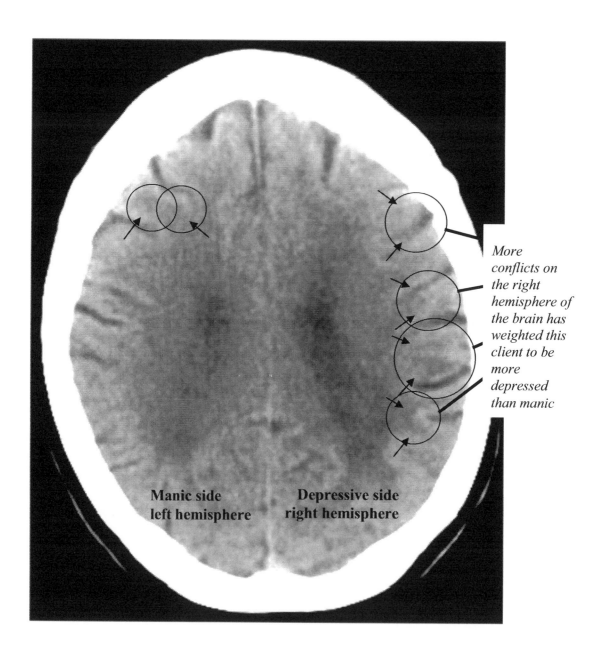

More
conflicts on
the right
hemisphere of
the brain has
weighted this
client to be
more
depressed
than manic

**Manic side
left hemisphere**

**Depressive side
right hemisphere**

Here is an example of a lady called Sally who was medically diagnosed as Bi-polar, the brain CT shows that she is weighted towards the depressive side. I carried out a META-Medicine® consultation and discovered that she had several conflicts. I was able to trigger off the conflicts and make her feel depressed and manic within minutes of each other. Her main issue was triggered by her husband leaving her and not returning because he had died of a heart attack. The issue repeated itself seasonally, every winter around mid-January she would switch from the depression into mania. You can view this consultation on www.meta-medicine.com.

Sexual conflicts

Sexual conflicts are so significant and they can affect us in so many different ways throughout our lives. Many psychological symptoms are caused by sexual conflicts in both men and women. This can cause people to become lesbian or gay, or have strange sexual situations, such as requiring bondage in order to reach orgasm, or becoming sexually addicted. My experience of working with many psychological issues with women and men indicates that so many of them stem from abuse that turned into a conflict shock when they were little. This is the reason why I want to mention these problems.

The conflict content of these sexual issues can vary. The way a person has an orgasm can determine how a man or woman will try to resolve the underlying conflict. e.g. If a women only can orgasm through clitoral stimulation, then the sexual content gives a practitioner some idea of what to look for in order to solve the psychological conflict. We will write extensively about these orgasms in our next book.

*Look out for conflicts that affect the penis, the vagina, the anus, the breast and oral sex plus violence and bondage. These are often pointers to the original conflict shock. You will be surprised as to how many people have experienced these sexual conflicts. Many of these conflicts are caused by parents, uncles, aunts, grandparents or next door neighbours of both sexes, therefore male to female, male to male and female to female. These issues are often passed down family-lines as well.

Nymphomania in a right-wired woman

If a right-wired woman experiences a sexual frustration conflict where the conflict is of a specific sexual nature*, (this could be as simple as being seen naked), this will affect her coronary veins and cervix. E.g. she catches her husband in bed with another woman. The organ reaction will be a loss of her period, or her menstrual cycle will become very irregular if the conflict is constantly being retriggered. This will close down the left hemisphere of her cortex. She then reacts like a masculine energy woman.

If she has another conflict (this time on the right hemisphere) related to a masculine territorial conflict where the conflict is also of a specific sexual nature*, then she will become sexually addicted - a nymphomaniac. Then all the organ reactions from previous conflicts stop and her period returns. This reaction (nymphomania) is a biological way of trying to solve the conflict. She cannot handle both conflicts individually, so a new behaviour is needed. She is trying to resolve the underlying conflict by having as much sex as she can. These women are often lesbian. They might sleep with men but without passion, mostly because they cannot avoid it. She will often not be bothered about who she has sex with, women or men. She will not be able to build deep meaningful relationships with men or women, and she will not want to either.

There is nymphomania and nympho-depression, depending on which side is most accentuated: Mania - then she cannot experience a vaginal orgasm; depression - she cannot or finds it very hard to have a clitoral orgasm.

Nymphomania in left-wired woman

If a left-wired woman experiences a sexual frustration conflict where the content is of a specific sexual nature*, this will affect her coronary arteries. This closes down the right hemisphere of the cortex; she will not loose her period. She will react like a super feminine woman and will dress in a very sexy way trying to attract another feminine man or masculine woman. Because she is now operating from the left feminine side of the brain, she can experience another female sexual frustration conflict where the content is of a specific sexual nature*. If this happens she may lose her period or it may become irregular and she will become a nymphomaniac – and/or she may become bisexual or lesbian.

Example:

I worked with a right-wired woman who, at the age of five was giving oral sex to an older man. She told me he found this exciting but, at age five, it could just as easily have been brushing his hair or cutting his nails. She really did not know what she was doing. After a while the man pushed her away and said "You're fucking useless." This caused many conflicts; one in the thoracic vertebrae, one as a massive boil (wart) between her legs, and a hearing conflict. Plus a sexual conflict pattern was probably started at this point.

The question is, how would a five-year old girl know how to please a man? Many women are unaware of how to please a man, even as they get older. The experience gave her a self-worth conflict which made her feel that she was not liked. As she matured she developed a nympho-depressive conflict and became addicted to sex. In my experience, this was in order to solve the original conflict which ran like an unconscious loop in her head. See CT scan on the next page. She was a masculine woman, the feminine side was closed and she would have sex with women or men, mostly people she knew and cared about. The sex, ironically, was pleasurable, but rarely heartfelt in the way that most women without this conflict would experience intimacy. She did tell me she would want to please other people, a throw back to trying to solve the original conflict of 'like me'. She did not lose her periods and they were not irregular, since this is an opposing combination of conflicts. It was clearing out this original (age five) conflict and other conflicts to do with her heart that stopped the nympho-depressive. She still enjoys sex, especially around her period (which is normal) but whereas in the past she had to go out and search for sex and embrace it with a man or women, she tells me the urge is no longer there. The need to chase has gone. This is the key to nympho-depressive or nympho-mania is the chase.

In solving the conflict she stopped being addicted to sex. She was in a lesbian relationship for a while but is now single. She told me this was the first time she had had a relationship with a woman, and that it was not just about sexual pleasure, it was a heart-felt relationship.

When we look at this from a META-Medicine® perspective, she was born a balanced woman and she had a female sexual frustration conflict followed by a territorial loss conflict that caused the nympho-depressive behaviour. She is right-wired. My thinking is that this lesbian relationship was a test to see if she could connect with another person on a heart level, something that had been stopped by the sexual frustration conflicts. She has one child and she told me that eventually she would like to find a male partner and maybe have another baby. As we look at what 'mother nature' is doing here, we see that it is possible for same sex relationships to exist for pleasurable reasons, at a heart-felt level. We see in 'mother nature' that due to the combination of shocks, there is not the complication of other children being born which could cause alpha male and alpha female issues to occur in her group, and the obvious problems of raising extra children.

Women naturally bond together to bring up children and sexual pleasuring from the same sex is normal in the wild, probably after a conflict occurring with the animal. (See sexuality in animals in the wild in this chapter). It would therefore be normal in modern society if religion or other beliefs had not conditioned us to believe otherwise. Discrimination of same sex relationships still plays a significant part in our society even today.[105]

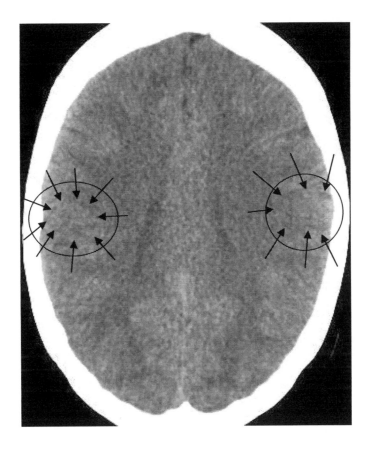

Coronary veins

Coronary arteries

My client's CT scan shows active (in the stress phase) coronary arteries and veins conflict, along with the sexual frustration conflicts this caused nympho-depressive and bisexuality. The rings are there but difficult to see. The conflicts are not excessive so the rings are not prominent.

Casanova (male form of nympho-depressive or nympho-mania) in a right-wired man

If a right-wired man experiences a territorial fear conflict, where the conflict is of a specific sexual nature*, this will affect his coronary arteries. e.g. He catches his wife in bed with his best friend. This will close down the right hemisphere of his cortex. He then reacts like a feminine man. He will not be able to build deep meaningful relationships with men or women, and neither will he want to. He does not have many friends and is a typical egoist.

If he then has a sexual frustration conflict where the conflict is also of a specific sexual nature*, this will affect his coronary veins and his spermatozoa vessels, and he will become sexually addicted - a male nymphomaniac, a Casanova. This is a new biological program to resolve the underlying conflict by having as much sex as he can. He is not bothered about who he has sex with, and it is more likely to be with women than men, but he is likely to experience sex with a man if no woman is available.

There are two types of Casanova; Casanova-manic, who will find enjoyment having a penile orgasm and Casanova-depressive who will have trouble getting a penile orgasm and find it a lot easier to have anal orgasm.

Casanova (male form of nympho-depressive or nympho-mania) in a left-wired man

If a left-wired male experiences a territorial loss/fear conflict where the content is of a specific sexual nature*, this will affect his coronary veins and his spermatozoa vessels. This closes down the left hemisphere of the cortex. He then reacts like a 'macho' man, and will think he is God's gift to women in order to attract another female, because he is now operating from the right masculine energy side of the brain. If he experiences another territorial loss/fear conflict, where the content is of a specific sexual nature*, he will become sexually addicted; a male nympho-depressive, Casanova-depressive, but this time it is likely to be with men. Bisexual or homosexual, if connected to the depressive right-hand side.

Example:

I heard about a gay man who could not sleep unless he had sex. He would be on the internet daily and go out and have sex with a different guy everyday.

Examples of famous Casanovas:

Actor Errol Flynn, famous for his lead role in the 1938 'The Adventures of Robin Hood,' had a reputation as an original Hollywood hell-raiser with his off-screen exploits, often overshadowing his prolific film career.

Screen legend Marlon Brando, famous for his roles in 'On the Waterfront' and 'The Godfather,' had at least 11 children with three wives and various other women.

The real Casanova, who, in his memoirs, boasted of relationships with more than a hundred women, was the son of actor parents. He rubbed shoulders with luminaries such as Russia's Catherine the Great and French philosopher Voltaire.

Case Study

Here is a case study for you to read so that you may understand how 'normal' people can be affected by conflicts of this nature. This example has been adapted and extended from a real-life experience of a client. As you read it, notice how each one of the shocks the people go through changes their personality and how it affects their sexual behaviour. The therapy session which I (Richard) carried out with the client, is written in the way it happened.

A client, Mark, came to see me. He is right-wired. He was engaged to be married to a beautiful woman, Fiona (right-wired), and had been in this loving relationship for five years but was now having serious problems. He was in a mess because he had a sexual addiction problem. His fiancée Fiona had recently experienced a major conflict with her best friend Beth, who was to be her maid-of-honour. Beth had accused her of having sex with her boyfriend, Peter. Fiona denied this but said that she had kissed Peter, but that it had gone no further than that. This was a shock for Fiona and consequently closed down her left feminine energy hemisphere, making her act with a masculine energy.

Mark said his fiancée, Fiona, started acting very aggressively towards him. It was as if he was living with another male in the house, similar to PMT (Pre Menstrual Tension) but instead of lasting a day or two, it carried on and on without any respite. She lost interest in him sexually. Her period stopped too. This carried on for six months, but eventually the conflict was solved when her best friend Beth, split up from her partner, Peter, who had caused all the trouble in the first place. She had found out he had been unfaithful with several other people whilst seeing Beth. Fiona, his fiancée, then stopped being so masculine and her periods returned. However during these six months of Fiona acting very strangely, Mark gave up fighting for Fiona's affections; he felt that he was no longer the man in the house. He was in hormonal standoff because Fiona was acting with a masculine energy. Therefore his right hemisphere was closed whenever he was around her, even though no conflict had occurred.

When Mark was out of the house, at work or with his friends, he felt normal, masculine, a man, but as soon as he went home he felt 'like a pussy' - his words - i.e. feminine energy. Mark was in hormonal standoff when around his fiancé Fiona because her left hemisphere was closed due to the social conflict with Beth, her best friend.

It was during those six months, when Mark was out with his friends one night drinking, that he met a very 'sexy' younger girl (left-wired woman) called Susan, to whom he was immediately attracted. This girl was all over him and he liked this; he said it made him feel masculine again. Both of them got very drunk that night and he went back to her house and they had sex. He told me that the sex had been amazing.

He went home and thought nothing of it. His fiancée Fiona at that time was still acting in a very masculine energy way and there was no sex because she wanted a feminine energy 'softer' man. He felt a little guilty about the affair but he also felt better inside because he felt the masculine energy again. He still loved his partner and was still happy to marry her even though they were going through a rough patch.

The affair carried on with sexy Susan for three months. However, Susan became pregnant and had an abortion. The abortion closed her right hemisphere, leaving the left feminine hemisphere open, so she was now acting with a doubly feminine energy.

Mark felt like a man because of the pregnancy, he had never got a woman pregnant, but also felt deflated by the abortion; it was, after all, his child. Although he knew rationally he did not want it, he felt that the abortion was somehow wrong. He assisted Susan through the situation but one day, very shortly after the abortion, Susan said that she did not want to sleep with him again. He was totally shocked. A territorial fear conflict – hitting his coronary arteries on the right hemisphere, he had not expected this.

Mark told me he felt very feminine after that shock, as if he wanted to nurture Susan. The right hemisphere was now closed because of the 'not sleeping together' shock and the left feminine hemisphere now open. She was his territory and now she did not need him anymore. He said it felt similar to the feeling when he was around his fiancée Fiona. He felt feminine but this time the feeling was there all the time, at home, at work, with his friends. Rationally he knew that the abortion had been for the better, but deep down he was really scared of losing Susan. He maintained contact with her, she had changed and she was totally uninterested in him sexually.

A few weeks later he saw Susan kissing and fondling another woman and he was <u>really</u> shocked by this. This was a feminine sexual frustration conflict for him that hit on the left hemisphere. Susan told him that she was going out with this girl; men were not worth the effort and this woman was what she wanted. Susan's girlfriend seemed quite masculine in her nature.

At exactly that point Mark said he changed. He became obsessed with sex. Casanova manic, coronary arteries and veins active in both hemispheres; the coronary veins with the most intensity, hence feeling manic. He had sex with anyone he could, he would 'chase' after women, always scheming of ways he could get them into bed; he was regularly successful. He also went to prostitutes, something he had never done before in his life. He would not build any relationship with any of the women he went to bed with. Sometimes he said he even considered sex with men, but this never happened.

Mark started having sex with his fiancée Fiona again but not in the normal way. She seemed to enjoy being the dominant partner. Her left hemisphere was closed so she was still acting like a masculine woman. He experimented with her, wanting to please her as if he was a woman (the right hemisphere was being triggered hence he felt a feminine energy) and she was attracted to his softy masculinity. He downloaded lesbian porn and would watch it intensely, wishing he was a woman so he could replace Susan's girlfriend, in an effort to unconsciously solve the underlying sexual frustration conflict. He experimented with anal orgasms, with his fiancée and prostitutes.

Mark told me he was really angry with Susan and frustrated sexually, but he also kept in contact with her although he knew nothing would ever happen between them again. This was driven by him unconsciously wanting to hold onto his territory and wanting to solve the sexual frustration simultaneously. He was confused because it felt as if he had fallen 'in love' with the Susan. This seemed strange because the relationship was all about sex and never about building a long- term bond. This had been a mutual agreement between the two of them from the start. She had told him that she loved the sex and she enjoyed his company but he was not what she wanted in a man. He felt exactly the same way towards her. So this 'love thing' really confused him. This was because he was acting as a feminine man; he wanted to nurture her, to help. It was not a masculine trait, hence the confusion.

The sex between Mark and his fiancée Fiona changed when she solved her conflict with Beth, her best friend. Fiona started acting with a feminine energy again and disliked Mark sexually, but this time the reason was because she did not like his Casanova-style behaviour. She told him that, in bed, he was not the man she had originally met; there was little or no intimacy. He was distant in all areas of their lives, uncaring at home and an animal in bed. However, she still loved him.

Mark had been to see many therapists but none of them had been able to help him. He also tried going to Sexaholics Anonymous, similar to Alcoholic Anonymous, but this did not help either. He said he found sharing the problem was useful but some of the peoples' issues stemmed from childhood and some were really damaged through abuse. His difficulties only started a few months ago and he was not abused as a child. He felt the meetings did not solve anything; in fact they made it worse, since he was still addicted to sex.

I worked on the two major conflicts, starting with the most recent shock; the shock of Susan rejecting him for a woman, followed by resolving the shock of Mark being scared of losing her, i.e. his territory. The whole session took two hours. As we were clearing the two events he felt a tingling sensation down his left hand side of his body followed by the right side. Plus his breathing changed dramatically during this time. He also said that his heart twinged momentarily as things cleared, a sign of the issues resolving themselves. Since he had a Casanova conflict, I knew that doing the therapy posed no threat to his heart, and that a heart attack would not occur as long as I cleared both conflicts in the same session.

That night Mark went back to his fiancée Fiona and made 'normal' love to her. They both started enjoying each other's company again - they were back to normal. He told me two months later that immediately after I worked with him, all the need to chase went. He feels a 'normal' man and he has lost contact with Susan the 'sexy' woman. The wedding was wonderful, he is very happy to be married and he says it was a miracle that the session took so little time to establish the conflicts and do the therapy. Mark also told me that he would have called off the marriage if the problem had not stopped. He felt that he could not take that problem into his relationship on a life long basis. In essence the session saved his marriage.

Sexuality - Lesbian, gay or bisexual

Ever since puberty I have been amazed as to why some people are attracted to and in 'same sex' relationships. I remember liking girls from an early age and that was considered normal. Even though I was and have been taken aback as to why same sex relationships occur, I have been fascinated as to what makes someone gay or lesbian. In an effort to fully understand, I started to research the subject in order that we can all understand it and remove any fear that often becomes associated with ones own sexuality.

Obviously after we have experienced many conflict shocks where one hemisphere closes, thus changing our reactions from feminine to masculine, this throws up the whole question of homosexuality, of being lesbian or gay.

Many people find this whole area difficult to talk about. Many men dislike gay men (even closet gay men) with such ferocity that they can become violent towards them. Any suggestion that a man is showing homosexual tendencies makes many straight men act macho. Now we know why. It doesn't seem that lesbian women find it so challenging. Lesbian women are not as obvious as gay men, because women can be openly affectionate to each other in public, whereas for men, this is taboo. Women can dress up and they can dress in a masculine way, but when a man dresses up in a feminine way it can be very obvious that they are acting in a feminine energy way. Then again, some lesbian women can look so masculine it is obvious that they are acting in a masculine energy way as well. Men can dress with a feminine energy without being noticed. Men who stand for a long time in front of the mirror finding the right tie are behaving in a feminine manner. Masculine energy equates to practicality, feminine energy equates to beauty.

Religion has firm opinions on same sex relationships for both men and women. They are seen as disgusting and wrong in the eyes of God. Is it no wonder that on the whole, in western society, such subjects are not discussed and in some parts of the world gay men can become completely ostracised and sometimes killed. This still goes on today in some African countries, (which is causing the whole AIDS issue in Africa to become worse because the church is responsible for practically all AIDS education programmes).[106] In many African states 'same sex' relationships are punishable by death.[107] It is also strange to believe that it was not long ago that homosexual acts were illegal in the UK and USA. The laws were changed in the 1960's.

It is interesting to observe wild animals. We can see what happens when we take away the many taboos that surround same sex encounters; animals have no such interference from media or religion to consider, just survival and pleasure. I mention this because, as a heterosexual male brought up in a right wing society and with a Church of England background, my experience of homosexuality was probably very similar to many men. It was not until I came across a man who wanted to take me to bed at age eighteen that I really had to think about this subject, and I certainly did think. Only since META-Medicine® have I really understood why people can become attracted to the same sex.

Sexuality in animals in the wild

What is fascinating is that in the animal kingdom, where the males are mounting males, and females are pleasuring females, homosexual behaviour has been observed among fifteen hundred species and five hundred of those are well documented.[108]

In the dwarf chimpanzee (a group of apes very closely linked to humans) homosexuality is all part of the group's lives. With lions, the males will often mate with each other to ensure loyalty. Female apes will not only share rearing of the young and food to maintain the continuity of the group but the will also have sex with each other just for pleasure. In swans who are renowned for pairing for life, four to five percent of the couples are homosexual. Single females will lay their eggs in these couples' nests and it has been observed that these homosexual couples often make better parents than heterosexual ones. Female baboons have even been observed taking wooden sticks and using them as sexual toys (dildos).

197

It amazes me that scientists have focussed mainly on survival in animals. It is as if we as humans think we are the only ones designed to have pleasure. If an animal is in a hormonal position in the pack because of one of the sides of the hemispheres is closed, they will still want sexual pleasure and this is what has been observed. Therefore sexuality is about maintaining the balance of leadership in the pack and the sexual acts are about pleasure. Sex can feel really good. Same sex pleasure also does not produce offspring. So in nature there is now a valid reason for same sex relationships.

In fact there is not a single species that has not been observed exhibiting homosexual behaviour, but researchers have ignored these acts, their own religious backgrounds and taboos getting in the way of good science. Petter Boeckman of the Norwegian Natural History Museum.

It seems that same sex relationships are all part of the pecking order. There are alpha males and alpha females; likewise there are beta males and beta females. An alpha male or female is the natural leader in a pack.

In wolves, alpha males and females are usually the main breeders in a pack. Their offspring leave the pack after two years, to establish their own packs. During that time the alpha females and males will hold their tails up and urinate by cocking their legs (yes the alpha females do this as well.) The beta females and males keep their tails between their legs and urinate by squatting. These animals are under hormonal standoff or have had conflicts with the alphas, therefore their masculine or feminine hemispheres are closed and they do this to maintain the survival of the pack. I am sure that same sex relationships occur in these groups as well although there is no mention of this from my source.[109]

Another interesting point about homosexuality comes from Joan Roughgarden, a professor of biology at Stanford University. She has documented and explored animal homosexual behaviour in her book "Evolution's Rainbow" (2005), and she says that "biology has neglected evidence that mating isn't only about multiplying. Sometimes, as in the case of all those gay sheep, dolphins and primates, animals have sex just for fun or to cement their social bonds." According to Roughgarden, homosexuality is "an essential part of biology and (it) can no longer be dismissed."[110]

Here's my deduction from a META-Medicine® perspective. When we look at how the sides of the brains close, it would be natural for a man and a man or a woman and a woman to engage in pleasurable bonding in some way; women on the whole get on better with women than they do with men. Men likewise. To have sex before contraception was a risky business that caused offspring that the pack could ill afford to keep. So these biological changes are animalistic and normal. The stigma of same sex relationships is brought about by religion and social beliefs, not by what we are naturally drawn to do as humans.

I believe the same of mating, and having more than one partner. Are we destined to be with the same person for the rest of our lives? Who said so? Most likely it is religion again. When the Bible, the Koran and other religious books were written many thousand of years ago, the belief systems adopted then were positive and useful.

Take as an example circumcision, which is even carried out today in modern America and Canada by religious denominations and even agnostics. A non-circumcised penis is believed to be unhygienic but modern science and the whole uncircumcised animal kingdom says otherwise.

Beliefs and social constraints can play a significant part in whether a man has a same sex relationship or whether a woman does as well. Lesbians are far more accepted in society than are gay men. This is perhaps because of the way men see a woman-woman relationship or how women see other women. A straight woman can look at another woman and see beauty in her and her body, where as a straight man does not look at another man in the same way; - he does not see beauty. There is also the question of penile penetration or lack of it in woman-woman relationships compared with the thought of anal sex in gay relationships. How much of this is down to religion or common sense, since a sexual encounter between a woman and a man, before contraception, could easily produce an unwanted child.

Woman-woman relationships and man-man relationships were and are considered normal in some societies. It was normal for a man in Roman times to have many male partners. In some Islamic countries, men are openly affectionate to other men. When I was in Egypt my friend Dr Khaled Al-Damallawy met me at the airport with a flower. I saw other men give men flowers. Women are 'off bounds.' Many women will cover themselves up from head to toe. For many women this is because they want to, and not because they are being forced to by men. They do it out of respect for their religion. I am not sure what happens with woman-woman sexual relationships in some of these countries. I do know that female castration is carried out in many Islamic countries which in my opinion, is barbaric and strange. Men are very predatory by nature; women on the other hand are the opposite. This is displayed in the number of sexual encounters a gay man will have in comparison to a heterosexual or lesbian person.

Gay men on average will have many more sexual partners in their lifetime[111] compared with heterosexual and lesbian women who will have nine. Globally the number of sexual partners is nine. [112]

With bisexuals the emphasis switches constantly. When the right side is emphasized they are depressed and feminine. They are attracted to masculinity (men or masculine female). When the left side is emphasized they are manic and masculine and are attracted to femininity (women or female men).

Cortex Constellations

There are many combinations of possible conflicts. We call them constellations, because a specific combination of conflicts creates a new super-supposing biological meaning, which is often characterised as a psychological disorder. I do not want to go into detail about each one of these. I will mention a few of them, and their make-up. I plan to write another book about these issues with Rob van Overbruggen Ph.D.

Dual hearing conflicts – I cannot believe what I am hearing

I mentioned earlier in the book how I worked with an Australian guy, called Sam, who is a musician and was the lead singer of his band. He came to see me for coaching as his life was really in a mess and he was manic too. After three long sessions I was getting nowhere; he kept saying "I don't trust anyone and I don't trust myself." I threw down my writing pad and said, "OK let's look at this using META-Medicine® because the NLP techniques I am using are not working." I asked him if he had had any medical complaints recently, to which he said he had, and explained that he had a re-occurring ear infection in both ears. He was taking antibiotics but they were having no effect.

Immediately I told him, "That's a combination of active hearing conflicts in the left and right temporal lobe, which causes you to not believe what you are hearing from anyone, including yourself." I asked him when had it all started, and what had happened. He explained that a female friend of his, who was living in the same house as he was went mad and became clinically depressed. She shouted at him one day and it shocked him. Another incident involving a friend, one of the band members, again shocked him. He had experienced tinnitus in both ears before they became infected. We cleared both issues in that session and the infections cleared up after a few days. He also changed dramatically. He left the house he was living in, moved in with his girlfriend and life became much happier and more positive. See Chapter 5 and the story of Sam.

It is also worth mentioning that schizophrenia is often diagnosed as the person hearing voices, this includes hearing the voice of God, and channelling information from the dead. This happens with the combination of conflicts. The issues must be very deep seated and there must be two separate conflicts for this to happen.

Anxiety

Lucille is one of the META-Medicine® Health coaches, and I noticed her combination of conflicts when I was looking through her brain CT. There are two conflicts that cause anxiety; one lands on the thyroid gland relay and the other on the pharyngeal gland relay of the cortex. I have already written about Lucille's conflict. (Chapter 5) These conflicts are either a powerlessness conflict or a fear of being attacked from the front. What follows is a short explanation by Lucille of how she got the shocks that cause the Anxiety to occur.

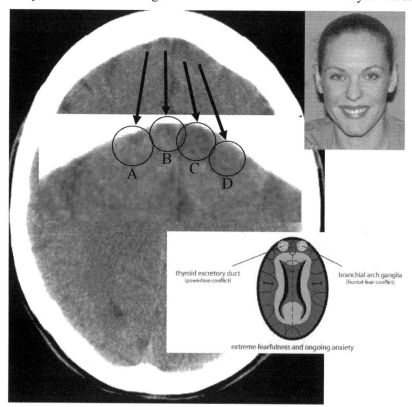

Lucille's CT showing the combination of the two conflicts that cause anxiety.

"My anxiety started when I was only seven months, still in my mother's womb, my father beat my mother by thumping her in her pregnant belly. This shock affected my infant years; right through my teenage years, and most of my adult years. I cleared the emotion with Richard on a META-Medicine® Certification Training course, this started me on a journey and I have subsequently cleared all the other associations to the anxiety. I can now be who I really am, not that little scared and anxious girl, but a powerful woman ready to embrace the world, which is what I am doing, enjoying the magic that is now my life."

Down syndrome

This is caused by a hearing conflict with a sound that resembles a predator. What happens is that a child, or any young animal, that cannot run away from an impending attack will play dead. This is a protection system. You can see it in the wild, a mouse being chased by a cat plays dead until the cat shows no interest and walks away, whereupon the mouse escapes. Rabbits chased by dogs do the same thing. The roar of an animal or something that resembles an animal roar such as a wood-saw can create the same issue. If the noise is repeated many times, the baby in the womb comes out playing dead. In a famous example of this, a doctor read the CT scan of a young Down's syndrome girl and diagnosed multiple ear conflicts, and because of a current constellation in the hearing areas there was also a maturity stop (see next page). The parents moved from the noisy city, to a farmhouse and put noise cancelling headphones on the girl. Over time her senses came back and she started to react to things. It took nine months of being away from the noise, and then the girl started developing normally again.

Dr Bader showed a picture of this girl at age five. She looked completely normal apart from her eyes, which had astigmatism. People have asked me, "What about the extra chromosome?" DNA is built up of a code that switches issues on and off and the DNA responds to the environment and emotional shocks.[113] Changing the environment (in this instance) removes the need and any noise as a trigger to 'play dead' and the extra DNA will switch off.

Asthma

Asthma is caused by an active conflict on one side of the cortex and, either a laryngeal muscles conflict and/or a bronchial muscles – Territorial fear or social identity conflict, which has been resolved, but is now going through the healing crisis (point 6). The conflicts for this issue are: A territorial fear conflict, or a female identity fear conflict. If someone is having regular occurrences of asthma where the issue is repeating itself, over and over again, then I would suggest you look at bullying or someone invading a person's inner or outer territory. The use of inhalers that contain steroids puts the lungs back under stress, therefore causing symptoms to disappear and the problem to repeat itself as the lungs then go through their whole cycle again and again. Most people grow out of being asthmatic because they leave the school environment, where the bullies resided.

Laryngeal Muscles in healing crisis

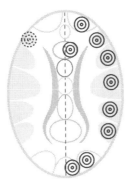

Another active conflict on the right hemisphere

Laryngeal Asthma – Defined by a healing crisis on the left hemisphere, laryngeal muscles and one active conflict on the right hemisphere. You can tell this type of asthma by the extended and stronger inhale. During the healing crisis the larynx muscles cramp on the breath out.

Bronchia Asthma

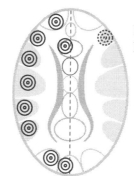

Another active conflict on the left hemisphere

Bronchial Muscles in healing crisis

Bronchial Asthma – Defined by a healing crisis on the right hemisphere, in the bronchial muscles, and one active conflict on the left hemisphere. You can tell the type of asthma by the extended and stronger exhale. During the healing crisis the bronchial muscles cramp on the breath in.

Status Asthmaticus, which is a disease that does not respond to steroids and causes horrendous breathing problems in clients, is a combination of the larynx and bronchial muscles going into a healing crisis simultaneously. The conflicts are the same as I mentioned above.

Maturity stopping

When there are two active (under stress) relays in the cortex, the person stops maturing on a physical and emotional level. As an example, if a person enters into this type of combination at the age of fourteen, they will stop maturing. Physically and emotionally they are age fourteen for as long as this combination of active relays last. Intellectually they continue to grow; they can look very young in the face, but have a university degree and still play with model trains (something that usually only a child would want to do).

The meaning behind the maturity stopping is so that the other members of the tribe don't see this person as some sort of threat. They are still viewed as a child who needs protection. This can happen in many combinations, not just territorial ones. As an example in motoric conflicts that affect paralysis and movement of our muscles or sensory conflicts that affects the skin. We can usually tell when the conflict occurred because maturity stopped at that point.

An example that some of you may have come across could be a university professor who lectures on particle physics during the day, only to come home and play with toy trains and kites. The playing with toy trains and kites are children's games, which indicates the issues occurring at an early age, maybe eight to ten years of age.

Autism

Autism is caused by an active conflict in the laryngeal mucosa in the left hemisphere, with an active conflict in the stomach mucosa or gall bladder, or liver mucosa area. These are all conflicts that occupy the same relay, and only one has to happen in order for the relay to become active. There is also an issue when two conflicts occur that stops maturity. The conflict is ongoing and probably caused by the use of vaccines; although there is evidence that the MMR vaccine does not cause autism. However, if we look at the shocks that

202

surround this, there is a feminine fear/fight conflict (the larynx – not being able to speak up) plus a territorial anger conflict. The MMR vaccine is given at age five just as a child is entering a school (many children are advised to have this vaccination at this time). It would not be unusual for a child to experience these two conflicts one after the other. Even going to the doctors and having the vaccine could cause one of the conflicts to occur.

Autism constellation

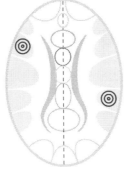

Laryngeal Mucosa

Stomach, gallbladder, pancreas, duodenum mucosa

Demonstration of Bipolar - Manic Depression

On a DVD set called META-Medicine® and EFT, (which is available for purchase from www.howtotap.com) I worked with a woman who had been diagnosed as bipolar. This is the same constellation as the Nymphomania and Casanova syndrome and she was definitely a very hot-blooded sexual female. In it I found the conflict shocks and I triggered them off, one after the other. I demonstrated weighting of the brain using NLP techniques to reduce and increase the depression and the mania, all within ten minutes of each other. With my good friend Karl Dawson, an EFT Master and inventor of an incredible therapeutic technique called Matrix Reimprinting see www.matrixreimprinting.com. In the DVD we removed the underlying patterns that caused this problem to occur. It was sexual abuse from a close relative at a very young age. The last I heard from Kathy was that the bipolar had completely disappeared. She told Karl that she liked to ride, but every time she went to the stables, she would cry her eyes out. She also recounted that if she fell off the horse she would not get back on for weeks. The next time when she went to the stables, after the treatment, she did not cry at all. She also fell off her horse, only to jump straight back on. She said that this was amazing, and proved to her that the bipolar had completely disappeared. After eight months she has reported that she has joined an amateur dramatics society, something that was inconsiderable before. She says she has up and down days. She asked is that 'Normal' the answer was yes. Most people have up and down days. Her husband is also a very different person, being far more involved in the marriage than before.

Frigid

Frigidity can be caused by several different issues. Frigidity, or recently called Hypoactive Sexual Desire Disorder (HSDD), is a lack, or absence, of sexual fantasies and desire for sexual activity. Clinically, there is a difference between a general lack of desire and the lack of desire for the current partner. However, in reality it is much harder to differentiate.

From a practical point we could say that frigidity is when one or the other partner loses interest in having sex.

For example, a woman is attracted to a man. As a feminine woman she was attracted to the masculinity of the man. They spend some time together and they fall in love. Eventually they marry and live happily ever after. In this fairy-tale there is not a single conflict for the man or the woman. The man is still masculine and the woman is still feminine.

Scenario 1

If the woman has a "not being able or allowed to mate" conflict, it will affect her vagina mucosa. During the conflict active stress phase there is a widening of vagina by necrosis of the vaginal mucosa. During the regeneration phase there is a swelling, bleeding and pain in the vagina. Imagine that the woman leaves this man, finds another man but maintains contact with her ex-partner. Whenever she is on the phone with her ex-partner she is re-triggered in the original conflict, and the necrosis starts again. Then when she has sex with her current partner the conflict is resolved and a little later she gets the swelling, bleeding and pain. This discomfort is connected to having sex with her current partner. She therefore does not feel like having sex.

Scenario 2

A women's partner loses his job through cutbacks. The man (right-wired) experienced this as a loss of territory. The right hemisphere becomes closed so he can only react with his left hemisphere, and becomes more feminine.

Problem 1:

The woman was attracted to this 'masculine' man, but he is no longer masculine. The woman might lose her attraction. Diagnosis: frigid (at least for this partner).

Problem 2

The man, because of his right hemisphere being blocked with a territory loss conflict, now has trouble getting a penile orgasm just for intercourse (ejaculation). (The activated brain relay on the right is responsible for ejaculation.)

As a feminine man, having trouble with a penile orgasm, might become more focussed on anal orgasms, because the left hemisphere is still open, acting with a feminine energy.

Problem 3:

The man might become homosexual

Scenario 3

The man and woman are without any conflicts. One day when the woman walks through the park she encounters a flasher and is shocked by it. She experiences a sexual conflict, and as a right-wired woman her left hemisphere closes and she will react in a more masculine way.

Problem 1:

She now is attracted to feminine men. Her husband is a masculine man. She loses her sexual attraction to him.

Problem 2:

The conflict on her left also closes down her ability to get a vaginal orgasm. She is still able to get a clitoral orgasm, but usually that is not what men are good at. She is no longer satisfied with the sex between the two of them.

These are just some scenarios where someone can become frigid. As an example; think of the muscles of the vagina when they do not open anymore/or enough, as in Vaginismus. Think of a depression where one of the partners has no interest in sex anymore. We will be writing more about this subject in our next book.

Anorexia

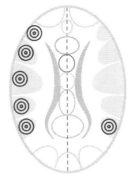

Another active conflict on
the left hemisphere

Stomach, gallbladder,
pancreas, duodenum
Mucosa

In Anorexia there is an active conflict in the left hemisphere, usually something to do with a female identity conflict followed by a territorial anger conflict in the stomach mucus membranes. As a common example, a right-wired female has an issue with her identity as a woman. This closes down the left hemisphere, and she then has a masculine territorial anger conflict that affects her stomach mucosa. She stops eating because of the ulcer in her stomach (from the stress phase) but is constantly reminded of her identity each time she looks at herself in the mirror. Therefore the problem swings from side to side.

Bulimia

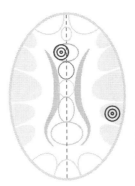

Islet cells of the Pancreas

Stomach, gallbladder,
pancreas, duodenum
mucosa

In the case of Bulimia there are two conflicts; one in the stomach mucus membranes in the form of an ulcer (first phase) and the other in the Islet cells. The right hand conflict of the stomach mucosas is an identity or territorial issue, and the Islet cells, a fear/disgust or resistance conflict. How Bulimia works is fascinating. The Islet cells of the pancreas are responsible for glycogen (sugar/energy) or insulin throughout the blood. As the body goes through the two phases the energy fluctuates due to glycogen and insulin changes and at times they have low blood sugar levels. At this time the person feels 'hungry' and needs to binge on sugar, carbohydrates and quick 'sweet fixes' to make them feel better because of the low blood sugar. There is often an underlying theme of a person feeling they are lacking sweetness in their life. If we combine this with the second shock of the stomach ulcers in the right hemisphere then the person will feel constantly nauseous as they eat, due to the ulcers, so they vomit because the stomach cannot take in all the excessive sweet food at the same time. The person then vomits the food back up because they feel the stomach ulcers and this reminds them about their identity conflict. They yo-yo between low blood sugar and the identity conflict, triggering the issue, over and over again.

To summarise; they binge eat due to feeling under-sugared, low blood sugar, and need to vomit due to the identity stomach ulcer in the right hemisphere.

Example

A boy was forced to eat brussel sprouts, and he hated the taste. This little boy was disgusted by this, and showed it. He was forced to eat this by his grandfather, with whom he was staying at the time. Being forced to eat brussel sprouts, he experiences a territory anger conflict which affects the stomach mucosa. The right-hand hemisphere then closed.

A couple of weeks later he stayed at his grandparents again and they fed him brussel sprouts again. Now he is even more disgusted and he refuses to eat them. However the sprouts are forced into his mouth. He experiences a fear-disgust conflict.

Now the boy goes into a bulimic constellation.

Whenever he sees brussel sprouts, the first territory anger conflict is triggered and he has to vomit. The same event triggers a fear-disgust conflict which makes him want sugar, so he wants sugar all the time.

As we conclude this chapter what we have explained means that we now have a road map for how to work with psychological issues. This work is profound, so much so that we believe that a whole book dedicated to this amazing subject has to be written - so Rob and I are in the process of doing this. As a final word, after working with Kari, her life changed. She wrote to me a month after the diagnosis and therapy and this is what she said: -

The conclusion of Kari and her clinical depression

"I just want you to know that I feel like a COMPLETELY different person. I know that I've worked on some pretty big stuff with EFT before, but I don't know if I've EVER experienced a change quite this huge. While I was working with Richard and Linda I had said that depression felt very much like drowning - like being trapped underwater with no feasible way out - and this is the first time in a long, long time that I haven't felt that to some extent - before, even when I wasn't completely 'depressed' it was still always there - it sort of lingered in the back of my head so that I always felt some of it and it could completely overtake me in a matter of hours. I never thought this could go away - EVER. Now, the only thing that's left is this sort of vague recollection of how it felt and me waiting for it to suddenly come back - but there's nothing. It's amazing. Not only have I not felt this good in the last few months, but I'm not sure I've felt this good in years - if ever!

On my way back home from the shore, (this was where the DVD were shot - Ed) I made a point to stop and see my mom - just to gage how I felt and how I acted around her. It was definitely interesting, and, honestly, I felt no way depressing at all -- I mean, she's always making some comment about something and she can be very passive aggressive - and none of that necessarily changed, but I didn't feel the need to react in anyway at all. It was crazy. And - maybe for the first time ever- when I left, I just left - I didn't take anything with me, nothing she said, no worry about what she might be thinking or doing or complaining to Bill (Kari's step father - Ed) about - nothing. Even better- when I got home, the first thing Nate (Kari's fiancé - Ed) said to me was - "Holy shit, you look different." I hadn't TOLD him ANYTHING that had happened.

I'm sitting here tearing up because I don't remember the last time I've been this happy and felt this free and I am so grateful to everyone that was involved, I am beyond thrilled about EFT and META-Medicine® and my amazing new life!"

In the next chapter I want to look at the highly controversial subject of cancer, how META-Medicine® can assist in the process of healing.

Chapter 14

Cancer – The ultimate disease process

"The moment my doctor told me, I went silent. My mum and dad were with me. Then we all fell to pieces." Kylie Minogue (singer) - On being diagnosed with breast cancer

"I feel more inspired than ever, and think that I will finally achieve what I have long been wishing for: a balance of work and privacy" - a harmony. Kylie Minogue (singer) - On getting through her battle against cancer

Kim and her Meningioma - Part 1

When Kim came to see me she was in such a state, very stressed indeed. She told me she had had brain cancer, and although it had been operated on, she had been told that it was likely to return. She could feel it growing again. She told me that she did not want to die. She had no idea that she had a tumour until one day she had a driving accident in which she hit her head. The normal procedure following a car accident involving a head injury is to have a brain CT. This, she did. It was then that the medics noticed that she had a large growth in her brain called a Meningioma. It was so large that it was causing a lot of pressure on the rest of her brain. She explained that she had been experiencing many headaches before the accident, and she had been drinking more wine than usual to escape from the pain.

She sat in my office and explained how the brain tumour had been operated on and how the doctors were not able to remove all of it. They explained that there was also a forty percent chance of it coming back. She told me that she could feel activity on the right-hand side of the head, in the location where the tumour had been removed.

We got to work: I knew that the tumour was because of an increase in skin due to the meninges increasing in size to protect the brain from being hit. The meninges are the special skin that protects the brain from the skull. A growth of this sort will be in the first phase, similar to the cerebellum directed organs such as the pleura and the peritoneum.

Knowing that the type of conflict that causes this increased growth in the body is due to it protecting the inner organs from being attacked, I asked Kim if anyone had tried to hit her on the head recently.

She went red and started shaking: "I have always been scared of being hit over the head by men." She told me. "All my previous boyfriends and husbands have attacked me on the head, some with knives and some have hit me violently. There have been men who did not hit me but even so I have always feared being hit over the head since I was a little girl. My Dad hit me over the head regularly."

We worked and cleared out all the fear associated with the problem. A couple of hours later once we finished, she looked relaxed and happy. She commented that she felt tired, that it was getting late and she needed to drive home. She also said that the activity that had been going on in her head had changed. It was strange because it felt warm, really warm and she made me touch both sides of her head. There was a remarkable difference in temperature between the two sides. She left and I lost contact with her. A few months later I received a phone call from the friend who had referred Kim to me. She told me that she had just received a letter from the medical centre saying that Kim's recent CT scan showed no activity and they asked her to come back in six months' time.

That was the last I heard from her for three years.

Healing is not as easy as it seems

When I got into META-Medicine® I wanted to find the answer as to why my mother had died of cancer. It was a horrible death, long and painful, with secondary cancers, surgeries and the removal of one part of her that made her a woman - her breast.

I have worked with many cancer patients since then, and in META-Medicine®, I was looking for a way to be able to heal cancer. Little did I know that healing is not as easy as it seems. Once the body goes to the extremes that it does to produce certain tumours, it makes sense that the beautiful balance, that our bodies normally maintain, has been massively upset. In many of the cases I have dealt with, the clients have made the decision that they do not want to carry on with this life.

I have a postulation: The word 'cancer' is linked to 'not getting well', and if we cure this disease once and for all then where will people turn? We do have the free will to check out of this planet if we wish. Some people just switch off - depression is a great example of that. Others create debilitating diseases that paralyse or cripple them, such as MS.

I have written about my good friend Birgitte earlier in this book - she was the one who had the sleep issue, where she had no energy and would sleep in front of her child as she fed him. Recently, Birgitte lost the ability to use her muscles - a paralysis. She said she felt as if she was carrying the weight of another person around. She had energy but she had no power in the muscles throughout most of her body; she could not type, talk or walk very easily. It was linked to her identity, doing something that she fundamentally does not want to do.

She is an intelligent person who fully understands what is happening to her. However, let us look at the circumstances, because there is a lot to be learnt from this. I know that Birgitte does not have cancer, but the circumstances of how she has created the disease have parallels. She will and is solving it, like she has the many other medically unsolvable problems in her life. She is already much better since my writing this. The interesting thing is that although she has access to some of the best minds in the world in the emotional clearing business and the META-Medicine® medical field at her disposal, she is working through the situation herself. She has the tools to do that.

There is a lesson here for every therapy practitioner: She has stubbornly told me that she did not want me to assist her. This surprised me at first. It is in my nature to want to help people heal, and I wanted to help Birgitte with healing this massive problem. After all, we had solved the seemingly impossible before.

We recently had a few conversations that were very challenging for me. She is one of my best friends so her not wanting my help really surprised me. However, as in all interactions with people we love and care about there are two sides. This one for me was very difficult; she told me to let go of 'the need' to help her heal.

After long deliberations about this, and having to deal with my own anger and frustration, I cleared out 'the need' to help her heal. As I did that I learnt something fundamental, something I had mentally understood but this time I truly integrated it into myself.

208

Healing does not come from the doctors, from a change in diet or better nutrition. It does not come from a pharmaceutical pill or specialist energetic drop of liquid, or from a therapy practitioner. Healing must come from within the client – their spirit, their will.

Birgitte has been on the biggest journey of her life and she is doing a fantastic job of healing. Her will and spirit have made this happen and I have seen an amazing shift in Birgitte's personality as a result.

In META-Medicine® we have the ability to explain why a cancer is there, what caused it to occur, where the person is within the disease cycle, and what is happening to them on a mind, body, spirit, social and environmental level. As caring people we all want to help. If you have been diagnosed with cancer and are reading this, you probably know this all too well. You also will want to get well, to live. It is possible, but healing has to come from within you.

I recently worked with a young girl in her late twenties, who had cancer of the liver. She and her mother had tried everything to stop her cancer. When I met her she was yellow through jaundice and had severe body wastage. I spent two long days with her and I put together hypnosis CDs, so we could get her to focus on wellness. I was in this for the long term and was willing to do whatever it took to assist her. She had very little energy, but we did some great work together and I knew that what I had recorded, especially for her, would assist her even when I was in Canada and could not be there for her. Overall, I was pleased with the work we achieved together.

Then, just as I was about to leave after two days working solidly with her, she announced to her mother and myself that she wanted to die. She was fed up. She was lucid - she knew what she was saying. I spoke to her and nonchalantly told her that if she wanted to die, it was okay, but I also told her that she still had life in her and that she could survive this. I remember her face turning away from me as if to say, "You have not truly heard me." She said it again. "I want to die, I don't want to do this anymore, I hate my life." The truth is that truly was the problem - she hated her life in many ways. Her father had died of cancer recently, she had a job she hated, a boss who was a bully, she had no life partner and she was being cared for by her wonderful, loving Mum. A Mum whose life she had seen had not turned out as either would have wanted.

I arrived in Canada from the UK exhausted. It took me several days to recover from the long trip. During that time this girl passed away, gracefully, happy in her soul and without pain, so her mother told me. I was sad, I was looking forward to helping her, but I guess she helped herself and that was a wonderful thing.

This taught me a big lesson and one I want to share on these pages. My friend Christa Uricher, is a specialist in cancer and META-Medicine® www.meta-medicine.com (you can order and/or download the 12 CD pack and manual from here). She said "people are born into this life and people pass on, and they die. It is normal. Our job is to assist them through their journeys, whatever that may be." And 'assist' is the key word here.

Cancer is the ultimate disease process. In diagnosing a client, when the cancer has been there for some time, I often find that they have made a deep spiritual decision to give up on the problem that they are facing. Frequently the client will say that they would rather die than go through this whole problem again. The body then hears this, and acts upon it.

Christa knows this, and has a wonderful exercise for cancer patients. She gets the clients to write down a hundred reasons why they want to live. This is a really challenging exercise for a cancer patient. If you ask yourself the same question I think you will find a big spark of light inside you, meaning you want to live. For many cancer patients, in my experience, that light is very, very dim or non-existent.

Doing this exercise with my clients taught me a lot about life and the purpose for living. Again, Christa taught me so much, and the story of one client, where Christa assisted me, says it all. A woman, who was in her thirties, called me from Copenhagen asking for help. She had a loving husband and two young boys. Her main cancers were breast cancer and bone cancer. She also had a brain tumour.

I consulted with her over the telephone for a month or two and helped her while she had ozone therapy (a form of therapy that baths all the cells in the body in oxygen, see the last chapter for details) in a foreign country. She returned to Denmark and seemed to recuperate reasonably well. However, during that time she suddenly started to get worse, and near Christmas her husband called me saying that she was in excruciating pain. I told him, as I always do, to see the doctor, but he told me that all they wanted to do was to give her morphine. I know that the long term effect of morphine is not good. As a painkiller it is the gold standard, but long-term use means that the person stops caring about anything; life becomes irrelevant, friends, family and anything of importance become pointless. After a while, or so I have been told by people who have taken it, morphine ceases to alleviate the pain but the person just does not care about the pain - it is a horrible way to die. You just don't care about anything, so that even dying becomes irrelevant. Morphine also shuts down the digestive system and the client ends up starving to death because they cannot eat.

The family begged me to travel to Denmark and help. I jumped on a plane and flew to Copenhagen. As soon as I arrived at the family's apartment, I saw she had a massive oedema in her right arm (caused by the lymph rebuilding in the second phase) and a kidney collecting tubule syndrome - an abandonment isolation conflict (see page 61). When I saw her she was screaming the whole apartment block down with such a deathly bellow, it was no wonder the family called me. She had also had many epileptic fits and even the morphine, which her desperate husband had decided to give her, was having no effect.

Within twelve hours, working throughout the night, I was able to completely get rid of the pain, and the swelling in her arm disappeared. We had some wonderful conversations after that. She went from a dream state to lucidity, and back into consciousness over and over again. She also did not sleep at all and she would have hallucinations of people coming to visit her. She would have happy conversations with these people. This is normal in the terminally ill. A bit freaky for the family and others, but I knew it was normal. She had not slept for over a month; it was as if she was squeezing every last inch of life out of herself. I want to thank Anne Sweet for explaining this to me. Anne is a META-Medicine® Health Coach who practices in London. She was also one of the first Hospice nurses in the UK.

It was during these amazing times, whilst we were able to just sit and be, that I asked her the question: "Tell me, why do you want to live?" She said, "I don't want to die because I have two lovely boys, I don't want them to have to be brought up without their mother."

This brought tears to my eyes as I thought back to my own mother's death. However, when I spoke to Christa she queried me as to whether I had asked my client the 'hundred reasons why you want to live' question. I said yes and told Christa about her reply. Christa, to my surprise, said that that was not enough. "To live because of someone else in not good enough, even if it is for your children. You have to want to live for yourself." I went back to my client and asked her again: "Tell me a hundred reasons why you want to live?" She asked me, "Is wanting to bring up your children not enough?" and I replied, "yes, it is", knowing that this was not going to be an exercise that she would do. Inside I knew my answer should really have been "No" - but who is going to fight with a dying person? In hindsight and with my experience now, I would have fought her, coming from a place of love not anger.

210

I left Copenhagen happy that this beautiful woman and mother of two lovely boys was at least pain free. She remained pain free without any medication for a few weeks, whereupon I received a phone call telling me that she had been rushed to hospital. She was in a coma. She had had another epileptic fit but this time she did not come out of it. The medical profession said that they would give her radiation treatment on the brain tumour. I knew that if she had any chance of survival at all, radiation was not an option. I explained to the family what radiation does to the body and carefully said "You must make the right decision for her." The husband, who had to make the decision, was in turmoil. He spoke at length with the doctors.

They elected not to do radiation, and a few days later she passed away peacefully; she did not come out of the coma. The doctors said that her brain tumour was too large, and that even with radiation she would maybe have lasted a few days more. I was very sad at this news. I spoke to Christa and she told me, "All of us die. It is natural, we do our best as healers and that is all we can do. We are not God; we cannot make someone live. As therapists, we merely give our best for people to get the most they can from life. That is our gift."

Metastasis – Cancers that spread or a second or third conflict shock?

In cancer we need to look deep inside, to distinguish whether it is a life-threatening illness or a long-term reoccurring problem. There is a difference. If the issue is being triggered off over and over again, the tumour can seem benign; it may be big but it is growing very slowly, like Kim's. These types of cancers are often not life threatening until they get too large and press against other organs. The other types are aggressive as with my client in Copenhagen. They grow and grow and take over entire organs, causing other organs to work harder whereupon these organs eventually give up.

We also need to look at the medical diagnosis. This often is a shock and in META-Medicine® we are certain that this is the cause of the majority of secondary tumours - metastasis. So even if the person has a benign tumour, the shock from the diagnosis can cause a secondary cancer, which is often what kills them.

Looking at metastasis, it is very interesting to discover that cancer and secondary cancers (metastasis) are rare in primitive peoples. Diet and regular exercise may be a major factor but even so, the occurrence of cancer is rare. What seems even stranger is the lack of metastasis. My postulation is that with modern medical approaches to diagnosis, the secondary or tertiary diagnosis causes another conflict shock, which then causes subsequent secondary cancers.

Medical anthropologists have found little cancer in their studies of technologically primitive people, and paleopathologists believe that the prevalence of malignancy was low in the past, even when differences in population age structure are taken into account.[114]

Let us look at breast cancer as an example of how diagnostic shock could cause metastasis in modern day life. A woman who finds herself diagnosed with breast cancer, will often go onto develop lymph cancer, liver cancer, lung cancer, bone cancer and often cancer of the dermis layer of the skin where the incision to remove the breast has taken place.

From a META-Medicine® perspective the reason is quite clear. Firstly on finding a possible lump in the breast, most women immediately run to the doctor to get a diagnosis. The underlying assumption is she will have to have her breast removed. Even if she does not, the general belief is that is what is going to happen. If the diagnosis is cancer, this can shock the woman and causes a self-worth conflict; she no longer feels she can be a woman if her breast is removed. This affects the surrounding lymph glands, which are in the first phase, these go into necrosis (cell minus, less cells) this goes on unnoticed.

211

A woman's breast defines a woman. If you are male reading this, consider having a large chunk of your penis removed and I think you can understand how removal of a breast affects a woman. I mention this because I know of male doctors who have questioned the emotional connection between removal of a breast in a woman and this self-worth conflict, believing the women is over-reacting - 'the breast is just a gland, after all'.

There is also another assumption, made by doctors that the cancer will spread. So once the breast is removed then she will be recommended to have chemotherapy and radiation, to catch any travelling cancerous cells and possible micro-metastasis.

The likely next cancer is of the liver - most liver cancers are secondary. In META-Medicine® the reason for this is that liver cancer is a 'starvation existence' conflict. The woman cannot provide for the family, or believes that she should starve in order to feed the rest of the family. The liver becomes a super nutritional absorbing organ in the stress phase as it grows to absorb more nutrients.

Cancer of the lungs comes from a fear of dying. The alveoli and the bronchi react to support the person in the possibility of dying; more oxygen getting into the blood means she has more fight in her to solve the problem.

The bone cancers are self-worth conflicts - the diagnosis affects the person at a deep personal level. The second phase of this will strengthen the bones so that they can better survive the conflict the next time. Osteoporosis is the first phase - a bone cancer with leukaemia in the second phase. The skin is a dermis reaction where the body does not want to be cut; basically it does not want the operation to occur, fear of being operated on again, being cut open. The skin gets thicker in the stress phase.

Combine all these fears, then add chemotherapy and radiation, which puts the body under immense stress and seriously compromises the whole biological system, and you have a perfect environment for metastasis/secondary cancers to occur.

All these conflicts can be seen under brain CT scans. Reading the CT scan of a woman who has had a diagnosis of a breast cancer, shows these separate issues in the different embryological layers. In a recent preliminary study we carried out within META-Medicine® we took the brain CTs from thirty women with confirmed breast cancer, and we found the breast cancer stress ring clearly showing in twenty-nine of them. The one that did not show the ring baffled Dr Bader, who did the readings. However, he went on to explain all the other cancers and health issues this woman had, to Professor Raef from the University of Alexandria in Egypt. He knew all the patients personally and he carried out all the brain CTs; the professor, apparently, was stunned.

So we can observe that metastasis is probably due to other stresses, some caused by the fact that we worry others by generalised belief systems. I know of a mentally disabled girl who has had pancreatic cancer for four years and she has no secondary cancers. She is still alive, she has had no chemotherapy or radiation, she was given six months to live after the diagnosis, and chemotherapy was considered pointless. Talking with her cousin, who I know, she told me that she just does not understand the implications of the cancer. She simply has no fear and therefore has not produced a secondary cancer.

I also want to add that it seems that not all secondary cancers are caused by a client's fear. I recently came across some observed postulations that eighty-five percent of all cancers are caused by secondary shocks, as we have discussed. Five percent are caused by cells that have broken away due to a cyst that has exploded (because of a Kidney Collecting Tubule syndrome, page 61) these do travel through the system and grow in separate areas. E.g. you can find breast tumour cells in the lungs, but they are rare. The last ten percent are because the person is worrying that they will get a cancer so the body creates the cancer as a way of solving the conflict.

So diagnostic shock is very important to consider when working with clients, or as a patient you must look at your beliefs and the shocks that occurred when you were in the doctor's office. Fear is probably the major killer in cancer, causing secondary cancers. Ironically the original cancer is often not the cause of death. The metastasis cancers, which are frequently more aggressive, cause the person to pass on.

Chemotherapy

I have mentioned chemotherapy and radiotherapy many times in this book. These interventions are hailed in modern medicine as the solutions to people surviving cancer. In reading the enlightening book by my friend Lothar Hirneise called 'Chemotherapy Heals Cancer and The world is flat,' - the title says it all. He mentions that chemotherapy has not provided all the answers that we are led to believe it has. I read that chemotherapy increases survival rates by certain percentages, and every day new, experimental chemotherapies have better survival rates. Just type 'survival rate chemotherapy' into Google and you will see what I mean. Lothar mentions that many of the percentage increases really amount to days rather than months or years. He also asks, 'at what cost?' When you look at the side effects of the new chemotherapies, is all the extra suffering really worth those few extra days?

Let us look at what chemotherapy is. It is the use of medicines to stop or slow the growth of cancer cells. These cytotoxic (toxic to cells) drugs work by interfering with the ability of rapidly growing cells (like cancer cells) to divide or reproduce themselves. Because most of an adult's normal cells are not actively growing, they are not affected by chemotherapy. All that are affected are bone marrow (where blood cells are produced), the hair, nails, mouth stomach and the lining of the gastrointestinal tract, plus the gonads (sexual organs - causing temporary or permanent sterility) and the lymphatic system. Effects of chemotherapy on these and other tissues give rise to the horrendous 'side effects' during treatment. It is strange that these are called side effects, since these are the <u>main</u> effects of chemotherapy, NOT 'side effects'.

It is also worth mentioning that seventy-five percent of cancers are epithelia cancers which come from shocks generated in the cortex. The subsequent secondary cancers are more fundamental life or death issues such as lung alveoli (fear of death), or liver parenchyma (fear of starvation) cancers, which are directed from relays in the older brain stem. These lung and liver cancers are rare as primary cancers. This is further evidence that shocks caused by a medical diagnosis that makes a person fear for their life and/or fear that they cannot feed their family, are responsible for secondary tumours.

Chemotherapy puts the body under stress, forcing a person back into the first phase. Epithelia cancers (cortex driven) grow in the regeneration phase and therefore when chemotherapy is given the tumours shrink, since there is no tumour in the stress phase. Lung and liver brain stem cancers grow in the stress phase therefore chemotherapy causes these tumours to grow even more. This fits in with the findings of what happens in oncology and further evidence for thinking twice about using chemotherapy as a way to treat tumours.

Modern Cancer Therapies

However, to really understand modern cancer treatment we need to look at the types of therapies used and their apparent success rates, plus how these are related to META-Medicine®. There are four main types of medical interventions for cancer: Chemotherapy, radiotherapy, surgery and hormone therapy. (There is also interferon and interferon 2 but these are rarely used). The first three main interventions have not changed since the 1950's. Only the recent introduction of hormone therapy and interferon which accounts for less than four percent of all cancer therapy interventions.

Since the 1950's, there have been massive advances in engineering, computing and science as a whole. We sent people to the moon in the 1960's, and my laptop was merely science fiction in the 1950's. Medical technology and diagnostic systems equally have increased at a rate that is astounding. We can look inside people and see their beating organs through modern imaging machines. Through an fMRI (see page 70) scan, we can actually observe changes in brain activity as we think. So much has happened to advance our understanding of our bodies and the function of cells, genes, and our general understanding of how the brain works. The advances made in thinking and science is mind blowing, and all of this has happened with business and government money. Trillions and trillions of dollars, pounds, yen, Euros etc. have been spent on these incredible breakthroughs.

The War on Cancer
Then I ask the question: 'What about cancer?' What about the wars against cancer and the trillions and trillions of pounds, dollars and Euros spent on this war – what amazing advances have there been? None. And I will explain why.

A good friend of mine recently sent me a Christmas card that was supporting a very well known cancer research charity in the UK. As much as I like the idea of supporting charities, I questioned where all the money has gone if chemotherapy, radiotherapy and surgery (with a small percentage of other therapies) are all we have to offer in the war against cancer? Where have all the vast sums of research money gone, if nothing has changed? I looked on this charity's website and there are many studies into the use and development of chemotherapy interventions, along with other interventions such as Photo Dynamic Therapy (PDT). - This is where a special chemical agent is injected into the tumour and then, when a specific frequency of light (usually a laser) is shone onto the area, the chemical in the agent is activated to destroy the tumour - just another localised chemotherapy, in my opinion. (Georgie Atkinson was involved in failed trials of advanced PDT - see Chapter 6.)

I know you may think that the death rates for cancer have decreased dramatically in the last few decades due to this research and the war against cancer, but unfortunately this is not the case. The truth is, the death rate has increased.

America has spent 2 trillion dollars since Ronald Regan declared 'war on cancer' in 1975. However, you have no better chance of being cured today than you did in 1975. In fact one in four people would be diagnosed with cancer before they died in the 1960's, one in three in the 1980's, now it is one in two in America. That amounts to 1,500,000 deaths a year due to cancer.

People against cancer www.peopleagainstcancer.net have some wonderful quotes about the war against cancer and also chemotherapy. I have listed a few that I think you need to be aware of.

"Virtually every significant effort to investigate and validate alternative and innovative methods of cancer prevention and treatment has been buried by the National Cancer Institutes and the American Cancer Society. The fixation on chemotherapy and radiation therapy has doomed all efforts to cure this deadly disease." – Frank Wiewel, former Chairman, Pharmacological and Biological Treatments Committee, Office of Alternative Medicine, National Institutes of Health, and Founder, People Against Cancer.[115]

Dr Watson, a member of the National Cancer Advisory Board, said that the National Cancer Plan was having no impact and more than doubling of funds had merely doubled the pre-existing programs. "As for those claims of steady progress," Dr. Watson charges that, "the American public is being sold a nasty bill of goods. While they are being told about cancer cures, the cure rates [since the 1950s] average only about one percent."

In response to claims by the National Cancer Institute (NCI) of the excellent effectiveness of chemotherapy treatments, Dr. Dean Burk, serving as head of the Cytochemistry Division of the NCI, addressed a letter to his boss Dr. Rauscher, which stated, "I submit that a program of FDA-approved [chemotherapy] compounds that yield only five-to-ten percent 'effectiveness' can scarcely be described as 'excellent,' the more so since it represents the total production of a 30-year effort on the part of all of us in the cancer-therapy field. Even that five-to-ten percent effectiveness," he adds, "is suspect, possibly being more than offset (in the majority of patients who do not benefit from chemotherapy) by shorter survival and lower quality of remaining life occasioned by the (widely acknowledged) great toxicity of nearly all approved chemotherapies, most of which, are capable of causing cancer in their own right."

Researchers at Oxford University in England published a paper, which concludes that the best treatment for inoperable lung cancer is *no* treatment. In the study, patients were divided into three groups, those receiving no treatment, those receiving continuous single-agent chemotherapy and those receiving an intermittent combination of chemotherapies. The conclusion: no treatment "proved a significantly better policy for patients' survival and for quality of remaining life."

Scientific American featured a recent cover story entitled: "The War on Cancer -- It's Being Lost." In it, eminent epidemiologist John C. Bailar III, MD, PhD, Chairman of the Department of Epidemiology and Biostatistics at McGill University cited the relentless increase in cancer deaths in the face of growing use of toxic chemotherapy. He concluded that scientists must look in new directions if they are ever to make progress against this unremitting killer.

In a comprehensive review in 2005, entitled The War on Cancer: An Anatomy of Failure - A Blueprint for the Future, Dr Guy Faguet wrote, "Despite the most assiduous and lengthy efforts by the largest number of researchers ever assembled to conquer a disease, most advanced cancers respond only marginally to cytotoxic chemotherapy drugs."

In an exhaustive review of cancer therapy entitled Chemotherapy Heals Cancer and the World is Flat, author Lothar Hirneise states, "Sooner or later the use of chemotherapy will go down in history as medical malpractice, and it is certainly a medical error today to use it as the sole means of treating breast cancer, colorectal cancer, prostate cancer, pancreatic cancer or lung cancer".

"Scientist McGill Cancer Center in USA sent a questionnaire to 118 oncologists and asked them which of the 6 usual therapies they would use on themselves. 79 responded, 64 said that they would never undergo therapy with Cisplatin – quite a normal chemotherapy with annual sales of 100 million Euros. Much worse was the response of 58 of the 79 doctors who said they would never undergo chemotherapy because in the first place it is ineffective and secondly it is much too toxic". From 'Chemotherapy heals cancer and the world is flat' - Lothar Hirneise (Page 187).

The truth is that we are losing the "war on cancer." The cancer establishment has promoted one "magic bullet" after another - first radiation, then chemotherapy, then interferon, then interleukin-2. Where are they now? Each one of these turned out to be little more than a public relations ploy to sell dangerous, toxic, ineffective therapies that were extraordinarily profitable. - Lothar Hirneise.

Speaking at the Sixth National Cancer Conference in 1968, Dr. Phillip Rubin, director of the Division of Radiation Therapy at Washington University School of Medicine said: "The clinical evidence and statistical data in numerous reviews are cited to illustrate that no increase in survival has been achieved by the addition of irradiation." Sharing the same platform, Dr. Vera Peters of Princess Margaret Hospital in Toronto added: "In carcinoma of the breast the mortality rate still parallels the incidence rate, thus proving that there has been no true improvement in the successful treatment of the disease over the past 30 years, even though there has been technical improvement in both surgery and radiotherapy during this time."

In the journal Radiology, researchers concluded in the treatment of lung cancer, "…the actual prolongation of life was discouragingly small. Of the patients given radiation, only four percent more were alive at the end of one year, and their median survival time was only 30 days longer than that of those who received an inert compound (lactose)."

This statement says it all regarding the war against cancer "The war on cancer is a bunch of shit." – James Watson, discoverer of DNA, Nobel Laureate.

Screening for cancers in women

The use of screening for cancers in women such as Pap smears (cervical smears) and mammograms (breast cancer screening) have not had good results either. In PAP smears the death rate from cervical cancers is just as high for those that are tested as those that are not tested. Within two years fifty percent of all abnormal smears regress to normal status. How many unnecessary operations have been carried out because of an abnormal smear?[116]

My wife had an irregular smear. We solved the underlying conflict and she regressed to normal in the next test a few months later. In the meantime she was asked to go in for a LEEP (Loop Electrosurgical Excision Procedure), a brutal operation that is carried out as an outpatient, which removes the top of the cervix and causes excessive bleeding for some time afterwards. She did not have the operation. I am certain we would not have our beautiful son if such an invasion on her body had been carried out. Though to be fair, there is no proof to say such an operation affects the ability to conceive. In Canada, Pap smears are carried out every year, in the UK it is every 5 years. Why? I do not have an answer, but it does seem strange.

However, in my opinion it is important to have a cervical smear test to find out if there is an abnormality, so that if you do find a problem you can do the necessary therapeutic work to resolve the conflict and immediately clear out any fear associated to a negative result. This is an integrative medical approach and in line with META-Medicine® thinking.

What about Mammary Gland screening? In an article in the British Medical Journal by Susan Ott, it was reported by Swedish researchers that mammograms led to an incorrect diagnosis in over 350 women. In 1994, the Canadian government screened 50,000 women. In the group that received the mammogram, thirty-three percent more women died than in the comparison group (this has also been confirmed by studies in Sweden and the USA). More tumours were detected but then the death rate shows this was not necessarily a positive thing (in the detection of cancer - Ed) especially when you consider the next paragraph.[117] Screening does not seem to assist according to a recent report in the Archives of Internal Medicine[118], which I found from Lynne McTaggart's website (www.wddty.com) which said that in a test group of women in Norway who had not had regular mammogram screening,

216

their cancers had disappeared. The incidence of breast cancers in those that were screened rose by twenty-two percent.[119]

J.P. van Netten from the Royal Jubilee hospital in London also proved that the incidence of earlier ductal breast cancer increased by two hundred percent caused by the excessive pressure the x-ray plates that are used in mammograms.[120]

How chemotherapy was developed

I think it is worth knowing how chemotherapy was developed and how it works so that as a practitioner, and as a patient, you know what you are dealing with. Most chemotherapy drugs were developed from Nitrogen Mustard gas, yes - mustard gas, a chemical warfare agent used in First and Second World Wars. It was noticed in an accident that happened in Bari (an Italian port) that the merchant seamen and soldiers who were exposed to this gas were found to have very low counts of white blood cells. Later two pharmacists Louis S. Goodman and Alfred Gilman were recruited by the United Sates Department of Defence to investigate the potential for therapeutic applications of chemical warfare agents based on these findings.[121]

People who had died from mustard gas had shown severe reduction in their lymphatic system and bone marrow. These two pharmacists reasoned that these agents could be used to treat lymphomas. Along with Gustav Linskog, a thoracic surgeon, they injected the nerve agent into mice who had induced lymphomas. They then did the same with a patient with non-Hodgkin's lymphoma. They observed a dramatic reduction in the mice and in the patient's tumour masses. Although this effect only lasted a few weeks, this was the first step in treating cancer with pharmacological drugs.[122] From this Alkylate chemotherapies were born. (See the next few pages for more information on different types of chemotherapies).

Later, after World War II, Sidney Faber, a pathologist at Harvard Medical School, carried out a study into folic acid, and found that this stimulated the proliferation of acute lymphoblastic leukaemia in children. Drugs were then designed that interrupted the enzyme involved in folic acid production in our bodies. These were injected into children who had this disease, and remissions occurred, although brief. The principle was clear. From this Antimetabolites chemotherapies were born.

Chemotherapies work by interrupting cell division. Cells divide in four phases: prophase, metaphase, anaphase and telophase. Different chemotherapies affect different parts of this cell division. This is very important to know because if you want to understand how chemotherapies work you need to know that the desired result of these toxic chemicals is the death of a cell. NOT a transformation of the cell. Plus they are not smart; chemotherapy agents cannot single out cancer cells, they disrupt the cell division in all dividing cells. Because cancer cells divide rapidly, they are naturally more sensitive to such toxins and are therefore destroyed in increased numbers. However, if a tumour cell is dividing slowly or at the same rate as other non-cancerous cells, then the tumour will not decrease in size.

The body is also incredible in that many times when a patient is given these toxins, the system identifies the toxin and naturally eliminates it. Therefore the chemotherapy is found not to work. This happens in many cancer patients. The medical profession noticed this and then started to administer a 'cocktail' of chemotherapy drugs, each one attacking the cell division at a different phase. Let me explain how this works.

You may have experienced this type of effect with alcohol, if you have ever drunk too much of the same alcohol over a significant period of time. You can feel the effects of the beer, wine or spirits, and then if you keep drinking the same product, (and it must be the same product), you can drink yourself sober. It is very weird and something I have noticed in others and myself from the ten years that I spent in the wine trade. However, as soon as you mix a different type of alcohol with what you have been drinking, e.g. you could drink the same type of white wine, two to three bottles, over many hours and then have a gin and tonic, you would find yourself extremely drunk and often very ill. We had a saying in the trade that was 'Never mix the grape with the grain' - this was excellent advice.

With a single variety of chemotherapy the body recognises the type of toxin and eliminates it through the urine. The 'cocktail' chemotherapies, however, push the body over the edge and the body cannot eliminate the toxins. It literally gives up.

However, cocktail chemotherapy interventions do not seem to have any better results than administering a single type of chemotherapy. The side effects are much greater. You may ask why are they still used, the answer is simple; these combination therapies are very expensive. The winner, it seems, time and time again, is the pharmaceutical industry. These cocktails produce greater side effects, and amazingly, even then, the body can fend off the effects of these toxins changing the permeability of cells to protect themselves.[123] It is also known that the larger the tumour cell mass, the greater the resistance to chemotherapy drugs and cocktail infusions. Also, many people often forget that tumour cells become more malignant and therefore aggressive after chemotherapy, which fits into META-Medicine®, epithelia cells multiply in the second phase; and there are even studies that conclude that the potential for the dreaded metastasis are increased.[124] The reason, as I mentioned earlier, is most secondary tumours are directed from the brain stem; these tumours grow in the stress phase. Chemotherapy puts the body into the stress phase.

I think that it is also relevant to understand the types of chemotherapies that are administered and a bit about their origin. I will briefly go into each preparation, but Lothar Hirneise's book 'Chemotherapy heals cancer and the world is flat', covers them in a lot more detail. Plus I mention the names of many of the well known preparations. I do this because I have often been told by patients which chemotherapies they have taken and I need to know what effect they have had on my client's body. Knowing the background to each chemical is very useful, so here is a small sample of each major strain.

Alkylates

These change DNA coding, so it therefore cannot be read. Cells divide as if they have been exposed to strong radioactive agents. Yperite belongs to this group; it is mustard gas, the same preparation that was used in the First and second World Wars and killed thousands of soldiers, as I mentioned earlier. Today Yperite is 'nitrogen yperite'. It destroys bone marrow and other tissue structures - it seems to affect mainly Cerebral Medulla based organs such as lymph, the testicles and the ovaries and certain other soft tissues. Therefore, and this is only a postulation, the muscles, tendons and kidney parenchyma veins and arteries, plus the heart muscle, would all be weakened by these preparations. This seems to be the case in my readings.

Additional compounds are Chlorambucil (Leukeram) and melphalan (Alkeran). Other groups are oxazaphosphorines, like cyclophosphamide (Endoxan). Ifosfamide (holoxan) trofosfamide (Ixoten). Relatives of Yperite are used for brain tumours. These include nimustine (ACNU), fotemustine (Muphoran), carmustine (BCNU), bendamustine (Ribomustin) and Lomustine (CCNU). There are also platinum combinations like Cisplatin (Platinex) or Carboplatin (Carboplat). These have horrendous side effects.

Antimetabolites

These work again by affecting the DNA, causing the strand to break by introducing a certain combination into the cell. The cell cannot divide because of a lack of folic acid. Normal practice is to give the person large doses of medication, such as 5FU and then, shortly afterwards, folic acid, e.g. Leucovorin (also known as calcium folinate). This combination of 5FU and Leucovorin is mainly used in intestinal cancer therapy, however, as Lothar explains in his book, although it has become a gold standard therapy, it was never approved because it has been found to cause fatalities. During treatment 2.3 % died with the combination therapy compared to 0.5% when only 5FU was used.

There is also controversy over giving Gemzar, another popular antimetabolite used in pancreatic cancers (pancreatic cancer survival rates are horrendous using chemotherapies, compared to nutritional therapies such as the Budwig diet. According to Lothar however, no research has yet been carried out). The pharmaceutical literature says that patients using Gemzar live longer. Here are the figures: 5FU lived 4.7 months compared to 5.7 months on Gemzar. Differences such as this happen so many times in testing because they do not compare the results with people who did nothing, or those that did complementary or alternative therapies.

Lothar also goes onto explain how many people are persuaded that they should attempt a new chemotherapy, based on a few facts that do not include doing nothing, or doing alternative approaches such as nutritional changes. Max Gerson used intense detoxification and introduced important nutrients through a low-fat low-salt diet. It is not an easy diet to follow. Mainly it involves re-addressing the balance between potassium and sodium in the body. This is done by drinking fresh fruit juices and having several coffee enemas a day. Coffee enemas are the procedure of inserting coffee into the anus as a way of flushing out toxins from the bowel and liver. (NB. This is not possible to do if you have just been through chemotherapy.)

Intercalants

These chemotherapies came originally from the First World War; they are extracted from bacteria. The most important intercalants are anthracyclines, basically antibiotics - extracted from streptomycin. They are used with leukaemia and lymphomas. They can cause permanent damage to the heart muscle. The most common are adriamycin, doxorubin, epirubicin (farmorubicin).

Taxanes

These chemotherapies come from the bark of the yew tree and were only approved in the 1990's. Paclitaxel (Taxol) and Docetaxel (Taxotere) are the most well known. They are very popular in breast cancer treatments; they are also very expensive, which is wonderful for the drug companies. They have shown an increase in life expectancy by an extension of one month. Lothar says that this could just be statistical deviation. 87% of all patients said they had additional complaints with its use. These are also used with non-small cell lung cancer.

Conclusion of Lothar on Chemotherapy

Lothar also goes onto explain that with the exception of testicular cancer and certain leukaemia's which account for only 0.6% of all cancers, chemotherapy can and does stop a tumour from growing but it never heals cancer. How many people die from the chemotherapy itself and not from the cancer? Admittedly there were successes in the treatment of bone marrow disorders using chemotherapies, but to then approve the use worldwide of these preparations for all cancers is quite simply beyond comprehension. Lothar Hirneise's brilliant book title says it all, 'Chemotherapy heals cancer and the world is flat' and he mentions Dr Abel, an employee of the German Cancer Research Centre and author of a book called 'Chemotherpie fortgeschritter Karzinome' (Chemotherapy of advanced carcinomas). He examines most of the chemotherapy studies in detail and in the process he has determined that there are virtually no studies to prove that chemotherapies contribute to patients with epithelial cancers living longer. Epithelial cancers are cancers of the cortex, therefore the skins or mucous membranes inside and outside the body. They make up 85% percent of all cancers, and are referred to as 'carcinomas'. The only conclusion I can come up with for this is that money plays the major part in this whole charade.

Radiotherapy

Why radiate? There is so much literature that says radiotherapy is not the answer. Radiation can completely kill healthy cells and tumours too. In oncology terms, if the tumour has gone that means the cancer has gone. But this is only half the story.

Irradiation therapy costs a fortune; the machines and therapies are very, very expensive. Radiotherapy can be easily executed. Patients also believe that 'tumour gone' equals 'cancer gone,' plus that the micro-metastasis' are also going to be killed by the radiotherapy. Radiotherapy cannot be seen or heard, and it does not hurt. Frequently the side effects of the therapy do not kick in until months later, and if things go wrong the response is often 'The cancer was stronger'. All these things have caused radiotherapy to have a position in oncology that is unexplainable based on statistical data.

Another interesting fact comes from Dr Zabel, who as early as the 1960's describes that a tumour only bears the brunt of 0.5%-4.0% of the total radiation administered. The remaining tissue absorbs the rest, killing the surrounding immune cells that are there to fight disease. The body is then robbed of its vital defence functions in the exact place where they should be. Radiation also kills, for good, the vital mitochondria, which are the energy makers of our body, found in our cells, and are absolutely necessary for health and therefore anybody fighting cancer. Killing them is literally killing the life force inside a person.

Do not be lead into false security by literature that says radiation has developed since the 1960's. It is still the same. In fact the amount of radiation, which is measured in Gy* accumulates over time. Often the literature says the dosages are smaller and more focussed than before, but the truth is that the same damage is done. The normal dose of 30 rounds at 1.8 Gy* is often given over several days, in a sandwich format, before and after surgery. This amount will destroy healthy cells, influence and in many cases is the initiator for new tumours.

*The amount of radiation used in radiation therapy is measured in gray (Gy), and varies depending on the type and stage of cancer being treated. The typical dose for a solid epithelial tumour ranges from 60 to 80 Gy, while lymphoma tumours are treated with 20 to 40 Gy.

My experience has been that new cancers appear after radiotherapy. I have lost many a patient after they have elected to have radiotherapy. The doctors said that the tumour had shrunk or disappeared and a few months later the client would be suffering horrendously with new tumours and then subsequently die. What is more frightening is that patients who had radiotherapy then got cancers in the exact place they were irradiated.

Chemotherapy heals cancer and the world is flat by Lothar Hirneise

I also want to mention that Lothar Hirneise's book is extremely comprehensive; it covers more than just chemotherapy and radiotherapy. It goes into a lot of detail explaining the traditional 'Gold standard' treatments for many of the common cancers. It extensively covers alternative and complementary approaches. He has developed his own programme from his studies called the 3E programme, which is written out in detail in the book. I highly recommend his book to anyone who has cancer, or is working in this challenging field. As a patient, if you are considering chemotherapy as a treatment option then you <u>must</u> read his book. As he says on the back of his book, "In the future there will be two groups of cancer patients; those who have read this book – and those who are uninformed."

META-Medicine's® approach to chemotherapy and radiotherapy

When we apply the META-Medicine® models of the two phases, repeating the disease process (see Chapter 7) by reactivating the conflict shock and the purpose behind the growth in the first place, we can understand why chemotherapy works and why it does not. Plus what happens when we use radiotherapy.

For the two phases, for brain stem (intestines, lungs, liver) and cerebellum (pleura, breast glands, dermis skin) driven issues, there is cell growth in the first phase. Then in the second phase, this tumour is either encapsulated or eaten away by bacteria or fungi in the system. (See chapter 10.)

Chemotherapy in brain stem directed organs cause tumours to grow even faster, as I mentioned earlier. Once chemotherapy is stopped, if the issue is retriggered or the stress is ongoing, the tumour will carry on getting bigger. If the cancer is encapsulated then the chemotherapy will have no effect whatsoever. Unless a biopsy has been performed, then the cells inside the encapsulated tumour start to multiply, and the tumour gets bigger again.

Also, in both phases if there are bacteria or fungi available then they are killed by chemotherapies and radiotherapy because they divide like normal cells. Therefore the tumour does not get eaten away. If the brain stem tumour is in the regeneration phase it has stopped growing, therefore chemotherapy has no effect. The tumour is unaffected. This answers why so many people do not respond to chemotherapy.

There is even proof that chemotherapies put such a stress on the body that the person is pushed back into the stress phase, and may cause metastasis (secondary cancers) to occur. Wenzel-Seifert and Lentzen and others noted this, years ago.[125] In META-Medicine® it seems that the toxins stop the cell growth so the tumour appears to be getting smaller but only slowly. In my readings and experience, I have found that all of these reactions appear to be normal in cancer patients who have chemotherapy.

The Cerebral Medulla (bone, muscles, tendons, testicles and ovaries) and cortex (outer skin, mucous membranes, breast ducts) directed organs: In the first phase there is cell 'depletion', cell necrosis (or death) and then in the second phase there is cell 'multiplication' as the damaged area of the body is rebuilt by more advanced bacteria and viruses (Chapter 10). The growth happens in the second phase and therefore the person is already going through the healing. If correctly supported, and if the person does not repeat the issue over and over again (Chapter 7) then the tumour will shrink on its own – in practice this is more difficult than it seems.

In this instance the cell growth is in the second regeneration phase, so the chances of chemotherapy being successful is a little higher, since the body is already healing and therefore reduction in the tumour cells will be normal. This we saw in the first initial studies of chemotherapy in the 1950's. These showed that the production of white blood cells was seriously diminished through the use of chemotherapy. From a META-Medicine® the point of view; after Osteoporosis or breaking a bone, during the rebuild stage a person will develop excessive white blood cells. In fact, if a lab technician looks at the blood of a person who has broken their bones, they will see excessive amounts of white blood cells. People have been diagnosed with leukaemia following a fracture of a bone. Most doctors are aware of this and dismiss leukaemia.

In brain stem and cerebellum tumours – (commonly referred to as 'Adenocarcinoma') if the person is in the first phase the tumours stop growing when chemotherapies are administered but as soon as the chemotherapy stops they start growing again. If the person is in the second phase because all the bacteria that are designed to eat away at the tumour are killed, or the chemotherapy stops them multiplying, the tumour does not shrink. In this instance more rounds of chemotherapy are usually given.

People do die from cancers in this second phase, which can grow to quite large sizes. Armed with the knowledge of the two phases, I believe it may change how people view the use of chemotherapy. From a META-Medicine® perspective what the person needs is to resolve the issue mentally, get plenty of bed rest, remove all stresses and stressors, have surgery if the tumour invades specific parts of the body or is getting too large and restricting vital organs. It is important to support the vitality of the body (see chapter 9), get onto a strict alkalising regime and use what ever is required to assist the body to heal. (See chapter 10). Other non-invasive therapies such as Reiki can also assist.

A very worried mother called me because her young son had been diagnosed with osteosarcoma of the right knee. His father had left his mother a few months before. His issue showed up in the right leg (the 'father' leg). He wanted to be a footballer and everyday he would play football in the park. One day he fell over onto his knee, which is when the problems began. This falling over caused the thin layer of skin that covers the bones known as Periosteum to split, and the bone issue (which was in the second phase) underneath the Periosteum started to grow out of control. A lump appeared and his mother took him to hospital to have it looked at. She was told it was osteosarcoma, a particularly unpleasant cancer, where the survival rate is twenty-five percent without treatment, and forty percent with chemotherapy and amputation of the affected joint. The boy had chemotherapy and the tumour shrank. Then it grew back again.

When the mother called us she was desperate, because her son was booked in to have his leg amputated. She never went ahead with this. Instead she flew abroad and made her son rest the leg for two months. In that time it completely healed; doctors in the foreign country could not find any trace of the osteosarcoma. He is playing football again.

All that had to happen was for him to stop using the leg and rest it so that the healing could complete. I wonder how many cancers could benefit from such a simple treatment. I am not advocating that all cancers should be treated this way but I am saying that the use of chemotherapy and radical surgery, which would have maimed this boy's life forever and probably have killed him, needs to be reviewed. Chemotherapy and surgery, at the drop of a hat, is not the only answer.

What doctors really know about cancer and the mutation theory
I was horrified to read that doctors learn very little at medical college about cancer, it usually accounts for two to three days. Yes, you read me correctly. They also believe that cancer is a mutation. However, regarding META-Medicine®, this is definitely not the case. The medical profession has no clear theory on how cancer is caused. In META-Medicine® we do. We do not believe that cancers are caused by viruses or microbes, as in META-

Medicine® these are the rebuilders or the cleaners following the stress phase. There are substances that can and do poison the body and then the body produces cancer from these. An excessive exposure to radiation causes cancer, this includes the radiation used in the treatment of cancer. Chemotherapies can cause cancers as well. In META-Medicine® we believe that the majority of cancers are caused by stressful events.

The way doctors see it (and are taught), is that as our genes are affected by a myriad of chemicals and radiation over time, which affect the DNA in our bodies, causing cancer; a cancer is therefore a 'mutation'. You need to know this if you are working with cancer patients or you have been diagnosed with cancer. This is what your doctor learns and is also the way the pharmaceutical industry approaches and tackles the problem of cancer. From the doctor's point of view, destruction of the tumour and any metastasis means the cancer has gone. The mutation has been eliminated.

This whole approach is flawed because the theory falls flat on its head. When, for example, you take the nucleus of a cancerous cell which has mutated DNA and put it into a healthy cell, theoretically the healthy cell would become cancerous. Or if you take a healthy nucleus and transfer it to a cancerous cell, the unhealthy cell would theoretically become healthy again, but in both instances this is not the case. What happens is not what the mutation theory suggests. If you replace the nucleus of an egg of a leopard frog with a cancerous nucleus, then you should get frogs with cancer. This does not happen - the frogs are born completely healthy. This was demonstrated by McKinney and B. Mintz. Karl Illmensee published it later in 1975[126]. There are plenty of other experiments that contradict the mutation theory. Bruce Lipton has a whole chapter based on this in his book 'Biology of Belief.' He says, "It's the environment, stupid, that causes change in a cell." Lothar also goes on to explain why the mutation theory is incorrect, and has a whole chapter in his book dedicated to this subject.

Metastasis cancerous cells travelling through the blood

One interesting thing is the metastasis theory which traditional doctors believe. Cancerous cells break off from the main tumour and attach themselves to other organs. Then why is it that when these cells are inspected under the microscope, they consist of many different cell types - as descendants they should be made up from the main cells of the primary tumour. Also, cancerous cells have not been found travelling through the blood to get to other parts of the body. Most metastases occur in the lungs, liver and the brain. Why they don't appear in the pancreas, spleen or a little finger has never been explained. However META-Medicine® explains secondary cancers fully. Allopathic medicine has categorically got it wrong. Your doctor is working on a premise that is outdated and that has very little or no science to support the mutation theory, and therefore the therapies that they administer must be rethought.

Cancer tumours are made of trillions of cells - a tumour of 1 cubic centimetre is made up of 1,073,741,824 cells. Usually a tumour can only be detected when they are 6-8cm in size. A cubic millimetre consists of more than a million cells.[127]

It is now understood that we all have cancerous cells in our body all of the time. In META-Medicine®, every time you have a UDIN (Unexpected, Dramatic, Isolating, No strategy) shock you either produce more cells in the first stress phase or in the second phase, depending on the embryological layering, as discussed before. The difference in cancer is that if the shock is very deep, the obsession continues, sometimes for years. Hence a cancer can take some time to grow. I have known cancers taking as long as three years before the tumour was noticed and diagnosed.

We can then deduce that primary cancers often take some time to grow. Metastatic cancers are different. They are often emergency programmes, such as liver and lung cancers, which are a response to a starvation existence programme, or a fear of death programme, respectively, as I mentioned previously. Doctors often prescribe chemotherapy and radiotherapy immediately upon diagnosis, saying micro-metastases (possible unseen small cancers) will be destroyed by this therapy before they grow too large because they believe, incorrectly, that there are micro-metastases from the primary cancer.

Brain cancer

According to META-Medicine®, brain cancers are caused by the resolution and regeneration phase of a cancer in the body. The relay in the second phase has to heal. There is a proliferation of glial cells (these are brain reparatory cells which are not cancerous). However, the medical profession see them as a cancer and use radiotherapy, chemotherapy and surgery to remove them. This is a mistake. I have heard and seen in my clients how these so-called 'brain cancers' can and do shrink if they are left alone. However, emotional clearing therapy and other changes in a client must take place for this to occur.

Problems really start when the person has a kidney collecting tubule response at the same time. This causes excessive fluid to be retained and therefore stops the fluid in the ventricles in the brain from equalising. Therefore pressure builds up in the brain causing horrendous headaches, bulging eyes and, in some cases, death. Blood vessels can also be affected, which may result in a stroke that can cause paralysis of complete muscle groups, or death.

Brain issues such as these are very serious. The removal of the so-called tumour through surgery and the use of radiotherapy (which shrinks the tumour) and chemotherapy only make the problem worse. Time and time again I have seen clients die, not because of the tumour but because of the therapy given. In order to release the pressure on the brain, the solution is to solve the abandonment isolation conflict first (the cause of the Kidney Collecting Tubule syndrome) and then tackle what caused the underlying issue in the first place.

META-Medicine® knows the location of the primary tumour from where the brain relay is situated. I did a META-Medicine® diagnosis with a client whose primary cancer was pancreatic, although he had been diagnosed with inoperable brain cancer. I was able to deduce this from an MRI. I told him to see his doctor and to check up on his pancreas and small intestine. The shock that caused these issues was an indigestible anger conflict with a boss he just did not get on with. I heard from the family after the diagnosis that there was a problem in the pancreas but they wanted to follow traditional methods to solve the brain tumour. I explained that the inoperable brain tumour was linked and that it was in the second phase. I also explained both sides of therapy; a traditional and alternative approach, and that he could assist his recovery with dietary changes and mental changes, to resolve the underlying stressful issues. The family still decided to follow traditional therapy. Unfortunately he passed away a few months after the chemotherapy and radiotherapy.

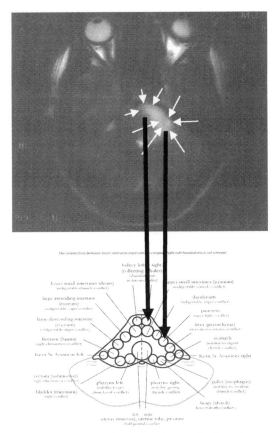

My client's inoperable brain tumour (MRI) in his pancreas and small intestine. This was in the resolution stage and also he was suffering from Kidney Collecting Tubule syndrome, hence the swelling. The original issue was an indigestible anger conflict related to his boss.

In META-Medicine® the theory is that the brain tumour can disappear, though I have not seen it myself yet (unfortunately all my clients have had chemotherapy and/or radiotherapy.) I have spoken to several people who have experienced the disappearance of a brain tumour and I did work with a client who lived for many months without pain relief or other medication. However, she was bed-ridden because when she moved her head, she had a lot of pain caused by excessive pressure. Several times we worked on the abandonment - Kidney Collecting Tubule syndrome issue and she improved dramatically, sometimes overnight. During these times she found herself being able to live a normal life, even if it was only for a few days or a week.

However, the triggers that caused the abandonment kept reoccurring, and she would relapse into the state as before. It was a double bind. As soon as she became freer, her sons and daughters would not need her and so go about their own lives again. Then the problem would reappear and the family would rally around her again. We had many discussions about this and she tried to solve it, but her nature was to have the most precious people in her life there for her. We call this a 'secondary motivation' or 'secondary gain'. This can be so huge that it overrides the healing (as I discussed at the start of the chapter).

The family (who were lovely), needed a break from giving their mother twenty-four hour care; they had looked after her for over a year and they were offered a respite by their oncologist who said she could stay in hospital for two weeks, on the condition that she have radiotherapy. The tumour shrank but she lived only another two months after the hospital stay. In my opinion what killed her was the radiotherapy, not the so-called tumour. Killing the glial cells which were doing the healing meant damaging the very mechanisms that were making her well.

225

What do you do if you have been diagnosed with cancer?

What I am about to explain goes completely against the ideas of normal medical practice, so you follow these guidelines completely at your own risk. I explain this procedure because people ask me what they should do - follow their doctor's opinion or that of META-Medicine®. I am completely happy with whatever you decide to do. As I have said, time and time again, doctors do a fantastic job, although many are not well informed with modern scientific proof and their teachings are out of date. Also, the pharmaceutical industry is incredibly powerful in persuading and maintaining the status quo regarding the use of chemotherapy, radiotherapy and surgery. It is your choice.

However, cancer is not a death sentence. It never has been and a person must do the mental and dietary changes and if necessary, undergo surgery, to recover. It is important to get a proper medical diagnosis. The type of therapy offered by the medical profession for cancer is chemotherapy or radiotherapy. According to all of META-Medicine® research, these therapies are outdated, apart from in extreme circumstances. It should also be emphasised that carrying on with the same lifestyle as if nothing had changed could mean that one could face an early death sentence. If you have already had chemotherapy or radiation, I implore you to rebuild your immune system immediately. Start with detoxification and work through the programme listed below.

The following are what we in the META-Medicine® association, have found to work. These are what we teach and - I openly admit – they are controversial. I hope these points will assist you in making the right decisions, whether you are a therapy practitioner wanting to know what to do, or a patient who has been diagnosed with cancer.

Diagnosis

First things first: If you find a lump or suspect a growth - relax - it has probably been there for many years, so panicking will do no good. In fact, in the opinion of META-Medicine®, 'fear' is probably the number one killer. Relax and work on the fear using one of the recommended emotional clearing techniques listed below, or any other you may be comfortable with.

If you are going for tests and you suspect a cancer diagnosis, take a good friend with you to record everything told to you during the consultation. Brief them to be supportive but to try not to get into the overall emotion of the situation, as you will need this vital information. After the meeting, log in detail all the shocks you experienced.

Buy and then refer to Lothar Hirneise's book, 'Chemotherapy Heals Cancer and the World is Flat'. You can find a link to it on my website www.meta-medicine.com.

An absolute must: Change your diet radically. There is a wealth of literature that supports the fact that diet can literally save one's life. One diet I know of is called the 'Budwig diet'.: Search the Amazon website for the 'Oil-protein Diet' or the 'Budwig Diet'. There are many diets for cancer out on the web. Please research thoroughly the validity of the diet before attempting to work with it. Lothar Hirneise's book covers some of the best-researched diets for cancer care and Georgie's 'Alkaline diet' is also excellent, and fits the META-Medicine® model, (see Chapter 12).

Have loved-ones and friends read the important chapters, especially about doctors and what they know? If you cannot get hold of Lothar Hirneise's book, get them to read chapter 14 of this book. If these people still want you to have chemotherapy or radiation, get them out of your life, or get them to do the research for themselves. Time and time again we have found that the influential people, the main carers - well-meaning family members and/or friends - persuade clients to do therapies that end up killing them. This is of vital importance and I cannot stress this point enough.

Inform your doctor or consultant of your personal choice – research into chemotherapy or radiotherapy – there is little evidence to support their ability to heal. If you do have chemotherapy, there are options you can discuss with your doctor such as localised or hypothermia interventions which are less invasive. These treatments can be found in Germany. Be prepared for the barrage of emotionally-charged use of clever language to persuade you otherwise. Remember - doctors are unaware of the latest research, and they believe that "'tumour gone equals cancer gone'. The medical profession is generally twenty to thirty years behind scientific studies. Do not allow your judgement to be influenced by a doctor showing you data from a drug company. Do your own research - the internet is a magnificent resource. Scientists tend to be neutral, but I will say that many are being paid by pharmaceutical companies to carry out research because they pay very well, so how neutral are they you will have to decide for yourself.

Hormone therapies do seem to buy people time, but they are not a cure. They do have their side effects, and if you are aware of what they do, they can help. They tend not to do that much damage, but they will change your personality. I do not know of the side effects of interferon or its usage and the long term effects. Ask your doctor to research www.naturalstandards.com, a massive database designed for doctors to get integrative medical interventions that have been tested using traditional research methods.

Do not be baffled by the use of 'Response rates and survival times' from your doctor. Your doctor will often use arguments to make you see their reason for doing a course of chemotherapy. For example Breast Cancer Studies by Henderson and Canello, by Schwartsmann and Pinedo, or by Plosker and Faulds, which prove chemotherapies such as Doxorubicin or Epirubicin in high doses have achieved response rates of seventy percent. However, they often omit to tell you these did <u>not</u> achieve a twenty-five percent remission (disappearance of the tumour). Nor do they explain the most important thing and that is that a seventy percent response rate and a twenty-five percent remission has no effect on your survival time. In other words; 'survival time' is what you need to know.

Do not buy into survival times that say you have 'x' amounts of months to live, based on statistics that say '1 in 5 people survive this type of cancer'. These are statistics based on chemotherapy and radiation treatments against doing nothing.

Buy Christa Uricher's CD set about META-Medicine® and Cancer from my website www.meta-medicine.com. Learn about all the other forms of therapies you will need to assist your body back to health.

Contact a Licensed META-Medicine® Health Coach www.metamedicine.com or www.meta-medicine.com who is experienced in working with cancer clients. Have a stress-based diagnosis. Be prepared to change social and environmental situations. Your META-Medicine® Health Coach will explain in detail what you will need to do. This can be very challenging. You will be asked to complete a history of your personal conflict shocks.

Solve the underlying conflicts using NLP, Hypnotherapy, Time Line Therapy™, Emotrance, and EFT (to name but a few approaches to this). Your META-Medicine® Health Coach will know some of the top people in each field with regard to these therapies.

Solve any diagnostic shocks that you may have received before, during or after the medical diagnosis, or any other realisations you may have that do not support you.

Learn EFT, it is an excellent tool for removing emotional conflicts in the moment, and, unlike other therapies such as NLP, you can self-administer it. Go to www.howtotap.com

where you can buy DVDs on EFT, and my good friends Karin Gustafson or Karl Dawson www.matrixreimprinting.com.

Do your research into chemotherapy, radiotherapy. This is little or no evidence to suggest that these therapies work or affect your survival time. (They may if you do nothing at all.) However they will destroy your immune system, which you need to heal yourself. There is evidence to suggest that lymphomas, leukaemia and testicular cancers have a good response to chemotherapy. I suggest with reticence that if you do decide to do chemotherapy for these diseases then find a place in the world that will administer chemotherapy alongside hyperthermia. This involves heating up the body and administering a tenth of the amount of chemotherapy. This seems to have the same effect as chemotherapy carried out at normal body temperature. Obviously the effect of the chemo on the body is significantly reduced. I have heard of patients who had this treatment, saying that the side effects were minimal and that the tumours reduced in size. However sometimes their tumours returned, so only testicular cancer, leukaemia and lymphomas come under this bracket.

Avoid biopsies at all costs if you can. These can aggravate tumours, splitting the thin layer of skin that often forms around them. When this happens, the once tightly-grouped tumour cells can and do leak out in and around the surrounding areas, causing more growth and often more damage to other organs in the vicinity. A CT scan, or MRI, or ultrasound can usually tell a doctor what the tumour is, but they are expensive and a biopsy is cheaper. However, sometimes a biopsy is necessary after other imaging techniques have been exhausted, and then a doctor will need to find out exactly what the cancer is. It will be your judgement call as to what you do in these instances.

Do have surgery if the tumour is operable and easily removed, with the exception of brain tumours, unless the issue is life-threatening. A brain shunt to remove the excessive pressure is recommended to overcome the Kidney Collecting Tubule Syndrome. I have recently developed a way of solving this syndrome. For more information go to www.meta-medicine.com.

Contact a NES practitioner and start using the NES info-ceuticals, These are a combination of homeopathic remedies incorporating acupuncture energies, that readdress the energetic balance in your body. Along with Professor Peter Fraser, we have jointly developed special brain info-ceuticals that work in accordance with META-Medicine®, plus other emotional unblockers that can assist you in releasing deep emotional trauma in your system.

Either get an NES pro-vision scan carried out www.neshealth.com or get a brain CT (which will cost you a lot more) if you can. We can assist you with both scans, please email us at ct@meta-medicine.com. CT scans are extremely expensive in the UK - we can arrange a CT to be carried out in Germany at a fifth of the cost. I have no idea of costs outside of Europe or how easy it is to get a CT carried out.

Many countries have special stipulations for having a brain CT done, and you will need to abide by their laws and costs. For example, I know you can get a brain CT carried out in Norway through a friendly doctor for the equivalent of £20. However, in the UK it is almost impossible and it will cost you around £600. If you do require a brain CT, there are specific stipulations that the clinic will need to follow in order for us to be able to read it. Brain CTs for cancer patients are read by one of our small group of medical doctors who are trained in this discipline. We prefer to use less invasive techniques such as the NES Pro-vision but, as yet, many of these techniques have yet to have side by side analysis with a brain CT carried out. Please look at our website for more information. www.meta-medicine.com.

Look at and work out bona-fide therapies that will work for you. I mentioned earlier a website that has a massive database with a wealth of background information on all natural based integrative medical interventions, including foods, dietary information and alternative and complementary therapies. It has up to date figures and studies taken from research papers around the world. It is designed for doctors and medical staff as a resource for understanding integrative medicine. I have looked around the comprehensive database and it is excellent. However, it is expensive, costing $350 a year (at the time of writing). It is really designed for academics. I am in the process of persuading them to allow access to the site for a week, for a respective donation. www.naturalstandards.com.

Please contact us at www.meta-medicine.com for more information on new therapeutic interventions that we have found to have a great effect on certain cancers. E.g. Electro Cancer Therapy ECT for prostate and epidermis skin cancers such as basal cell carcinoma and Ozone Therapy for diabetes and brain tumours.

Remember that I mentioned at the start of this chapter how cancer can be a death wish for some people? The answer to this is to change your whole life into one where you want to live. Secondary motivation; where the motivation has more of an emotional charge than the primary motivation which is to get well. E.g. the person would die, in order to get back at a parent. Secondary motivation is also very challenging to solve but must be done.

Remember to embrace life, enjoy it to the full, taking holidays, having regular sex, eat amazing foods that support your whole immune system, and give up stressful work and people. You will end up feeling more alive than you ever thought you could; this is the state you want to be in, in order to heal.

Remember, this is also a spiritual journey. Be prepared to learn at a very, very deep level, and do expect to change your whole life for the better. I have never met a cancer patient who did not say that the journey was the most incredible one of their lives.

Kim and her Meningioma - Part 2

Jane, Kim's friend, called me one day out of the blue and said "I think you should call Kim." I was scared, not knowing if it was good news or bad. I called, and a very excited Kim answered the phone. She told me she was well but she would like to see me again. I agreed and we met up one evening at her home. I was still apprehensive, but what she told me was amazing. She introduced me to her son, who was just turning eighteen. Although this was not significant at the time, little did I know that meeting him was to end a major chapter in my life.

After Kim and I worked three years ago, she could remember how tired and sleepy she felt and as soon as she opened the door to her house she went straight to bed. She had stayed there for two weeks with a fever. She had no energy and felt exhausted. She had some headaches but they were not extremely bad, not like before. Slowly she got back to health and felt much better. This was obviously the second phase, the regeneration phase. A few months later she had the brain CT that showed there was no sign of any growth. After that she moved to Spain, (she had always wanted to live in Spain), then three years later, she decided to move back to the UK. In that time she set up an amazing equestrian photography business and she is really happy.

Then a serious tone came over her as she told me that she had been to the hospital again for her regular brain CT check up and that was why she wanted to see me. I was worried because my immediate thought was that the Meningioma had come back. She gave me a letter and I carefully opened it. It was from Plymouth Hospital and, as I read it, I realised it was not something to be scared about, quite the opposite. It said that because there was no sign of any new growth whatsoever and since this had been the case in all the previous CT scans, the consultant recommended that she did not have to return for another check up in another three years. Kim then looked at me and smiled a big happy smile. I was overjoyed, so was she, a big tear rolled down my cheek and we hugged each other.

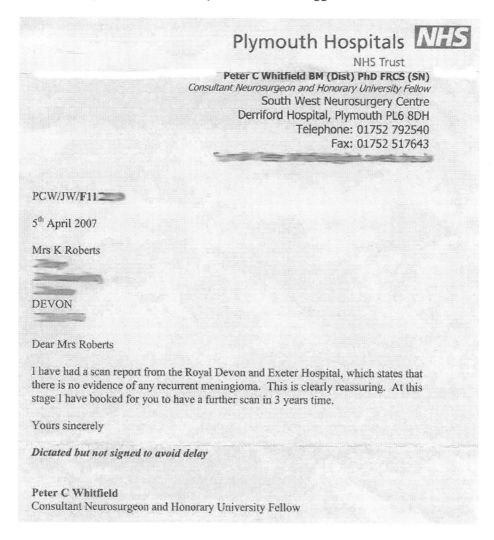

PCW/JW/F11

5th April 2007

Mrs K Roberts

DEVON

Dear Mrs Roberts

I have had a scan report from the Royal Devon and Exeter Hospital, which states that there is no evidence of any recurrent meningioma. This is clearly reassuring. At this stage I have booked for you to have a further scan in 3 years time.

Yours sincerely

Dictated but not signed to avoid delay

Peter C Whitfield
Consultant Neurosurgeon and Honorary University Fellow

That night, as I drove home something amazing happened to me. But you will have to wait till Chapter 15 to find out what it was.

In Chapter 15 I will conclude the book and give you insights into the future of medicine, as I see it. There are massive changes afoot in the medical world and we are on the brink of a massive shift in how we treat all diseases.

Chapter 15

Conclusion and the future of medicine

"The doctor of the future will give no medicine but will interest his patients in the care of the human frame, in diet and in the cause and prevention of disease."
~ Thomas Edison, famous American inventor

It has been two years since the idea for this book came about. I had been discussing with Johannes Fisslinger the possibility of translating his book META-Medizin® from German to English. He said "Write your own instead." Little did I know back then that it would take me two years to complete. In that time there have been many discoveries, and the most important has been turning this amazing wealth of information into something that a person can understand and believe in, enabling them to find out what it is that is <u>really</u> curing the illness, and then how to fix it.

"Why am I sick?" I believe that this has finally been answered. We have a structure and a process for disease. It is no longer just something people suddenly acquire out of the blue, that hits them whilst walking down the street. Most people intuitively know that something happened to them to cause their illness but what? Louis Pasteur's 'Germ theory', is the basis for how modern medicine treats many diseases. However, the theory that, Germs cause disease so you need to take antibiotics and vaccines, add some steroids now and again in order to get well, needs to be rethought.

The Medical profession was born from this way of thinking and everyone bought into it, because it worked for their diseases, and then the assumption was made that every disease would respond in the same way. You 'pop' a pill and you get well. What an amazing philosophy! The pharmaceutical industry embraced this one hundred percent and has grown into one of the biggest businesses in the world today. Diseases are there to be eradicated and we have a drug somewhere that someone will buy. In fact it worked so well they and the medical profession were able to persuade governments and the media to believe whatever they were told.

However, as we are finding, pill popping does not solve every ailment. Cancerous growths, psychological disorders, skin issues, irritable bowels, strange syndromes such as Parkinson's disease or MS are supposed to have been 'cured' by now, using the magic bullet of 'dropping' a pill. All diseases should have been eradicated, that was what we were all told and we believed it. But it has not worked. Instead we have a massive business that has grown so large, so complicated and so stuck in its own red tape that it has lost its way. Instead of evolving and asking fundamental questions and using science in the way that engineering has, it has carried on thinking in the same old way, refining the same protocols and doing the same thing, hoping that no one notices that what they are doing is <u>not</u> working.

231

If you challenge the medical profession or the pharmaceutical industry with this, you get nowhere; it is a closed shop. It is very similar to the Communists who fervently believed that 'all are equal'. For a time it worked, but communism did not evolve as people realised there was more to life than the secret police and being told how to think and behave. Eventually 'the people' tore communism down, the old belief systems did not evolve with 'the people'. If the medical profession and the pharmaceutical companies do not heed this message they will find themselves in the same position, which, in my opinion, would be disastrous, because to change medicine we need the infrastructure not the outdated beliefs.

I do want to mention 'emergency medicine', which is something very different. It does save many lives, and many drugs such as antibiotics can be crucial in those instances. There are many things that the medical profession do brilliantly such as reconstructive surgery, the healing of bones, and the delivering of children. Medical doctors know a lot, but it is time for their information to be updated worldwide.

We need to think creatively and differently in order to educate the medical profession as well as the general public, and to change beliefs from 'disease is a mistake (of the body)', 'germs cause disease', into 'most diseases are caused by conflict shocks'. The body has a wonderful order to it for how and why it creates a disease. The mind and body are connected to each other, and the environment and our spirit play a massive part in how and when we react to a disease. Fundamentally, disease is not a thing that is in our way, like a tree blocking the road which we would cut, burn or remove in order to go forward.

Disease is a process, like a journey from A to B and the road and the tree are all part of it. Therefore we need a different approach to solve the problem of disease. We need to step up, take an overview of the journey and see the entire picture. That way we can establish alternative routes, a way to balance or complement our journey by working alongside nature before the tree (being the problem) becomes to large, perhaps by using traditional techniques to trim the branches in order to manage the problem.

What I am leading to is an 'integrative' approach to dealing with disease. META-Medicine® finally allows us to take an overview of the process of a disease. It gives us a road-map to follow. Alternative, complementary, energetic and traditional therapies all have their place in assisting a person on their journey. No single therapy is right; no single intervention will solve a disease. There are times when modern medicine works brilliantly (emergency medicine is a great example of this). Emotional clearing techniques such as EFT and Time Line Therapy®, complementary medicine such as homeopathy and the brilliant NES system, alternative methods such as Reiki and nutritional changes, all add to the overall picture of how we can now assist a person to get to the end of their journey.

All these practitioners of all these disciplines will say that their method is the only way, but when we look at a disease from a META perspective (Meta means overview) then we can see how an integrative approach of alternative, complementary, energetic and traditional therapies is really the answer.

Now that we have the reasons 'why' we need to integrate medicine, and META-Medicine® finally has answered the fundamental questions of disease, we can get on with educating the practitioners as to the benefits of different alternative, complementary and traditional approaches to solving a disease.

The real question is - do the practitioners want to be educated? Or are they afraid that their beliefs of many, many years will reveal that their thinking needs to be dramatically changed? Sometimes we all need to be shown what is obvious and not be fooled into accepting something for fear of our position in society. It is the Emperor's New Clothes syndrome. Re-education will come about but it will take time. It is well known in scientific circles that in order to change anything in the scientific and the medical world, first the professors need to pass away, and then the students of the professors.

This is happening - we hold a conference every year called the 'Integrative Medicine Conference' in Germany. We have speakers from all over the world who come and share their knowledge and different approaches to healing. Some of these are doctors, such as Dr Schuppert (who has an excellent cancer clinic in Cologne), some are writers who have researched certain subjects (such as Lothar Hirneise 'Chemotherapy heals cancer and the world is flat'). We record the lectures, which can be downloaded for a small fee from www.meta-medicine.com.

I mentioned in chapter 14 the website called www.naturalstandard.com, so I won't go into further detail. In the USA the integrative approach is changing medicine. Things are happening. President Obama has a completely different approach to health care from his predecessors.

Education on META-Medicine® has also started; this book, a film called The Living Matrix www.thelivingmatrix.tv, and integration with other disciplines such as EFT www.metamedicineandeft.com. I am certain that as META-Medicine® grows, many more disciplines will be added. Look at my website www.meta-medicine.com for more products.

As far as education is concerned, I have developed a certification training programme that means anyone in the world can learn META-Medicine® over the internet to become trained and licensed as a META-Medicine® Health Coach, see www.meta-medicine.com for more details. We also have an array of trainers who deliver live programmes worldwide. As regards the medical profession, education programmes are being organised. Dr Bader has programmes running that are designed specifically for doctors.

What of the future of other disciplines?
Nutri- Energetics System - NES

The brilliant NES system (www.neshealth.com) integrates homeopathy and acupuncture in bottle form, called 'info-ceuticals' (remedies which have imprinted information in them) to assist a person to heal. Designed by Professor Peter Fraser and Harry Massey, this system uses a quantum measuring device to examine our human body field. It can determine imbalances in our field and then using the info-ceuticals it assists the body, via the heart, to re-imprint the field with updated information so that we get well. What Peter and Harry have done is astonishing. The results that people are getting from the NES system are amazing and it is further proof that healing is not caused by changing biochemistry alone. The remedies have no active ingredients in them, yet our biochemistry changes when they are used.

Their excellent book called 'Decoding the Human Body Field' will enlighten any practitioner, including sceptical medical doctors, that there is so much more going on inside and outside our bodies. The explanations they give as to why NES works has plenty of science behind it. NES are doing what the medical profession and pharmaceutical industry should have done years ago. Keep your doors open to new scientific ideas such as quantum physics, and experiment; think outside the box and you will discover the way the body uses the environment as a reflection.

I know Harry's vision is to have an inexpensive medical system that anyone can afford. The NES Pro-vision and info-ceuticals are exactly that. It needs a practitioner trained in the system to use it, the client then purchases the specific remedies and takes these as drops in water. The client is checked weekly and their symptoms are assessed alongside a medical practitioner. It works. I know of people who have solved their Chronic Fatigue Syndrome, have survived cancer without having chemotherapy or radiation. Harry tells me that NES is not designed for cancer treatment. Nevertheless, in my opinion it works.

Myself, Peter Fraser and Harry Massey in Spain during the development of the new Brain info-ceuticals that unblock emotions directly related to META-Medicine®.

Peter and I have also developed info-ceuticals that work alongside the two phases; assisting people to heal by following the process that a disease takes. We have also developed emotional un-blockers that assist the brain to open up the underlying emotional causes of conflict shocks. I have been successfully using verbal emotional clearing techniques since 1992, and in that time I have worked with thousands of people. When I use the emotional un-blockers and some of the other brain info-ceuticals, the speed and depth of the clearing is incredible. Our mission is for practitioners trained in emotional clearing techniques to be able to get the same results as I do, without having to have the years of practice that I have. I now know this is achievable with META-Medicine®, NLP, Time Line Therapy®, EFT and the use of the NES emotional un-blockers. If these techniques are of interest to you then go to www.meta-medicine.com for more information.

Harry has also developed a machine that you can use at home called the 'NES Mi-Health'. It measures your human body field and then, by using electrodes attached to the machine, you can administer a therapy session that alters your human body field, thereby changing the underlying problem.

The NES Mi-Health, see next page, combines three proven powerful technologies that have come out of decades of research; NES Matching software, NES Information Imprinting, and Russian Adaptive Electro Stimulation.

In essence you can put it anywhere on your body, connect to your computer and see on the screen an animated picture of your body showing highlights of potential problem areas for treatment.

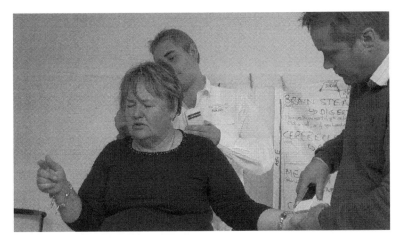

Richard Flook and Cyril Burke (of the Zap House) treating Wendy Maclarn with the NES Mi-Health, the first true 'Star Trek' type scanning and informational treatment device that both fits in your pocket for everyday use, yet docks to a computer for full scanning ability.

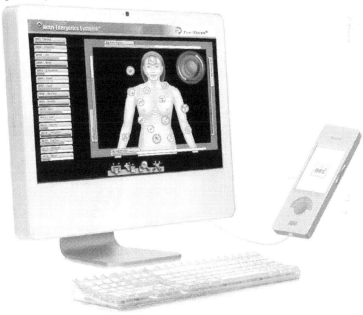

Having done a Human Body-field scan, you can then either directly treat that area via Informational Electro Stimulation, Infra-Red, or further refine your area of treatment with the inbuilt specific treatment area locator and use the NES Mi-Health's auto-treatment mode to assess when the treatment has taken effect.

While the NES Mi-Health is the first to combine these technologies, no claims can yet be made. Existing research and results behind the technologies is quite staggering both from NES and from the Russian Space program. Their research can be seen at www.neshealth.com/research and www.scenar.info. This device has the power to revolutionise the way healthcare is done.

NES have also produced NEStrition, (NES and Nutrition) where NES information is combined with the best essential vitamins and minerals. The outcome is supplements whose effects are two to four times greater at entering the body's system, and assisting with healing than just taking the supplements themselves. www.neshealth.com.

NES Health is truly revolutionary and is being used the world over by qualified practitioners including many medical doctors. Recently, when I was travelling in Australia I met up with Rose Hayman and Bruce Bourke and I saw what I think is the future of modern energetic medicine for everyday people. What Bruce and Rose have done is combined all of this incredible technology and created a place where everyday people can get treatment. They call it The Zap House. A great name and with their friendly, open and accessible approach I believe we will see Zap Houses in every corner of the world.

Rose Hayman of the Zap House with Richard Flook in Australia; this is truly the way energetic medicine is going to go in the future. www.thezaphouse.com.au

Clearing emotional conflicts EFT, NLP and Matrix Re-imprinting

When it comes to Emotional Clearing Techniques these are imperative in dealing with disease; if you don't clear out the conflict shock and the underlying emotion that caused it in the past, then you risk the conflict reappearing over and over again. There are plenty of techniques out there in the world. My personal favourites are: NLP (Neuro Linguistic Programming) (which is the study of human excellence) coupled with Time Line Therapy® (the system developed by Tad James to clear deep-seated emotional conflicts and unwanted beliefs about yourself). Most people believe that changing takes a long time and many hours of therapy. Psychologists and counsellors believe this. This is not the case; a deep-seated traumatic emotion can be cleared by a trained specialist using Time Line Therapy®, in minutes. An emotion a person has held all their life can totally and utterly disappear in the time it takes to make a cup of tea. I train people in these skills and how to use them with META-Medicine®.

There are other techniques that use the similar principles, EFT (Emotional Freedom Technique) invented by Gary Craig, referred to as acupuncture without needles. It uses tapping on the end of the meridian lines along with reframing (an NLP technique) to release energy, emotions and beliefs that are stuck in people. My friend Karl Dawson has gone one stage further; using EFT he has created a technique called Matrix Re-imprinting www.matrixreimprinting.com which I mentioned in Chapters 13 and 14. If you want to see more about how all these techniques are done go to www.howtotap.com. You can order DVDs that will teach you EFT, Karl's DVDs on Matrix re-imprinting and EFT & META-Medicine® with myself and Karl. We also have developed a training DVD set that teach a person who is trained in EFT to take a META-Medicine® consultation and use that as a road map to solve a client's underlying issues. This was recorded in America with an EFT Master David Rourke and a brilliant EFT practitioner Linda Wood, who has developed the use of a cuddly bear that you tap on, which is great for releasing emotions in young children. (www.howtotap.com.)

I love EFT because you can self-tap when you are experiencing a negative emotion; you don't need a practitioner to do it for you and you can tap in the moment, you may look a little stupid, but it's a small price to pay for the outcome. I personally got rid of the eczema on my left hand using EFT. NOTE: you will still need to resolve the major underlying UDIN conflict shock, and that often requires a session with a qualified practitioner in EFT, NLP, Time Line Therapy® or hypnotherapy. Following that any tracks/triggers or associations can be solved by EFT self-tapping.

There are other emotional clearing techniques, and all of them do similar things to NLP and EFT. Some are derived from EFT, such as TAT and Emotrance. There is also hypnosis, which is a brilliant tool for assisting clients to heal. I use hypnosis with many of my clients and teach it too.

The Spirit and the Human Design System

What about the Spirit? In this book I talk about the spirit and I have found that many clients find themselves in situations where their hearts and minds are disconnected from who they really are. A excellent system that explains our personality and our unconscious design is the Human Design System. It is a synthesis of astrology, the Kabbalah, I Ching and genetics amongst other things. It not only tells you about your personality in great detail, it also enables us to look at the fundamental motives and urges that run your life – aspects that you may not even be aware of, and provides you with the necessary information to de-condition from false beliefs by giving you a specific strategy and inner authority that you can work with.

I heard about Human Design in 2005 and I thought it was good but it was not something back then I was interested in learning. As I looked further into META-Medicine® and the spiritual side of disease I realised there was a big chunk missing from the diagnosis. On the recommendation of two friends and students of mine, Lucille White and Birgitte Bakke, reluctantly, I had a Human Design reading. It took two hours and Richard Beaumont, who heads up Human Design in the UK. We spoke at length about my energy, my spirit and who I was in the world. What he told me about myself was nothing new, I have worked with many psychometric tests in my time and I am really very aware of my personality and who I am.

When I came off the phone I thought that the reading was okay. Then I realised that Richard Beaumont had spoken for two hours continuously about me, he explained things about my personality and behaviour that I knew were one hundred percent true all based solely on my birth date, time and place of birth. The thought stopped me in my tracks. The accuracy was outstanding and on reflection the reading confirmed to me that I am doing the right job for me, it also has made me rethink some of the approaches to my life that I had taken on from other people. Something Human Design people call the NOT self.

My two friends Birgitte and Lucille also experienced the same things. Lucille has blossomed, as a woman, since the reading. Birgitte realised what she was doing in her life was not right for her. She has dramatically changed as a person truly acting as she should, as she stopped doing the NOT self. The Human Design System cannot tell you what you will become, it can tell you if you are on the right path or not and point you in the right direction for you, your life and the spirit we all have in us.

I recommend to all my clients that they have a Human Design reading, if they can afford it. The information is like being given an instruction book that is unique to you as a person. This book explains what will make you happy and what frustrates, angers or hinders you in being you. Most individuals become ill because they are doing what they should not be doing, doing something they are not designed to do. As an example in my own life, as a Projector I can become a slave to other peoples' personalities. Working myself to the bone riding on the energy of Generators. This was my life until very recently. Most of my diseases come from feeling bitter because these people have not recognised my talents. I store this bitterness in my muscles and I can now attribute my back issue to me acting and being someone I am not. What astounds me is the accuracy of these readings. I have looked at astrology before and been mildly interested but this is in a completely different league.

A human design reader takes your birth date information and puts it into a computer which produces a bodygraph which they can analyse. The information has a solid, verified scientific basis to it.

I have recently been working with the Human Design System and along with Tim Harnden, who I have mentioned earlier, we have developed a very simple but direct form of therapy that speaks to the core of a person. When I was studying hypnotherapy, Dr Tad James, the developer of Time Line Therapy® spoke of the fact that to heal, we just need a good connection with the client's unconscious mind. However this requires hypnosis. He had no waking conversational way of making this connection. The process we have developed does not require hypnosis, therefore the client is awake during the therapy.

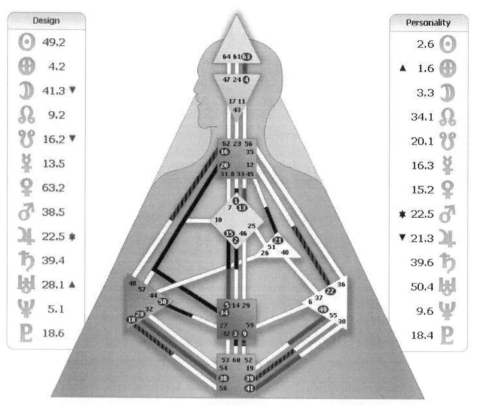

This bodygraph shows us someone who has three disconnected flows of energy and awareness going on at the same time. This can be very confusing for the person concerned and those around them. They are under constant mental pressure (the two linked triangles at the top of the chart) and their intuition centre (the dark triangle of the left) is also pressurized making them continually on the look-out for their true purpose in life. The type is a Manifesting Generator, the most powerful of all types, with fast, and often extreme, energy that will make them want to rush into decisions that will not be productive, unless they wait

to respond to what comes towards them in life. The not-self (open white areas) amplify the emotional energy and will power of those around them, which, if they are not operating correctly can tend to draw them away from living their own potential and instead become a slave to proving themselves and pleasing others. Their inherent gift is to bring a new creative direction to others. If they follow their strategy and inner authority they would stand out as a living example of a uniquely gifted and creative individual, who reaches their height of wisdom and influence after the age of 54.

There are four types of personality

At its most basic level, the Human Design System shows us that there are just four distinct types of human beings.

There are two energy types – The Manifestor and The Generator (there is also a combination called the Manifesting Generator - see later).

There are two non-energy types – The Projector and The Reflector.

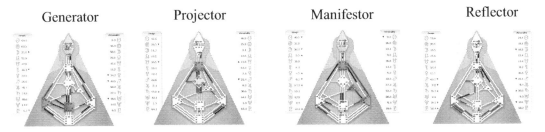

Generator   Projector   Manifestor   Reflector

The Manifestor

Surprisingly small fractions of the world's population (only 8%) are manifestors. Manifestors are pure energy beings. They are specifically designed not to be controlled by anyone. They are the only true initiators. They simply act or put things directly into action. But they need to inform those who will be affected by their actions of what they are about to do before they act. When they act without informing, they meet resistance, because the people involved in the consequences of their actions can feel ignored, or feel as if they have been run over by a lorry! As a result Manifestors can end up feeling very cut off from people.

Predominant negative feeling: Anger.

Strategy: Inform before acting.

Famous Manifestors: Vanessa Redgrave, J. Edgar Hoover, Hermann Hesse, Helmut Kohl, Richard Burton, J.Krishnamurti , Johnny Depp, Jerry Seinfeld, Yogananda Paramahansa.

The Generator

The majority of the population (about 70%) are generators. They are designed to respond to life. Unlike manifestors they have no idea of where they are going until they respond. Therefore they have to wait until life initiates them first. Generators are potentially the most powerful of all the types, but unless they understand how they work, they are the most frustrated people alive. They only know what is right for them to do or say by their response to something. Their response comes from deep in their abdomen and is most often in non-verbal sounds: "unun", "ahunh", "mmmmm", "ahhhhhh" etc. If they do something spontaneously, they often get involved in the wrong things, meet resistance, get frustrated and quit.

Predominant negative feeling and Strategy is the same as for the Manifesting Generator

Famous Generators: Elvis Presley, The Queen Mother, Margaret Thatcher, B.F. Skinner, Susan Sarandan, Orson Welles, Albert Einstein, Dalai Lama, Bill Clinton, Mozart, Prince Charles, Madonna, Meryl Streep, George Harrison, James Dean, Vladimir Lenin, Thomas Mann, Carl Jung, Judy Garland, Timothy Leary, Oprah Winfrey, Meg Ryan, Greta Garbo, Richard Branson.

The Manifesting Generator

There are two subcategories of generators, pure generators and manifesting generators, both comprising of about 35% of the world population. The main difference between them is that, after responding to something, manifesting generators can act more quickly than pure generators.

Manifesting Generators are Manifestors with a Generator strategy. They have an endless resource of energy. Generally they love to be in the thick of life. Their greatest dilemma is to learn that their true power lies in waiting for opportunities to come to them. If they actively try to pursue their goals and dreams they will encounter only resistance and pain. When they relax, then their lives can be poetry in motion.

Predominant negative feeling: Frustration in the pure generator and frustration combined with anger in the manifesting generator.

Strategy: Wait to act until you are clear about your response. Do not initiate.

Famous Manifesting Generators: DH Lawence, Indira Gandhi, Jackie Onassis, Prince William, Sean Connery, Frederic Chopin, Marie Curie, Hillary Clinton, Clint Eastwood, Sigmund Freud, Mahatma Gandhi, Steffi Graf, Marie Antoinette, Mikhail Gorbochev, Jimi Hendrix, Pope John Paul II, Janis Joplin, Friedrich Nietzsche, Richard Nixon, Yoko Ono, Prince.

Projectors

Projectors (about 21% of the population) are naturally able to work with and guide the energy of others, but only when they are recognized for their unique abilities and traits. Projectors know that they are recognized and appreciated when they receive an appropriate invitation. Without an invitation, the projector does not know if they will be able to put their talents and abilities to use in any way that is natural or healthy for them. They are people whose specific gift is to work with and guide the energy of others. They alone can understand both manifestors and generators. They also have a design to wait, and the key that unlocks their power is recognition. Unless they are recognised, they are powerless. Once they are recognised, they can achieve almost anything.

Projectors need more knowledge of their own inner design than manifestors and generators in order to know what invitations are good for them. When they are recognized for who they really are according to their specific design, they come into their true power. If they attempt to act or to join in without an invitation, they meet resistance and are not recognized by others.

Predominant negative feeling: Bitterness.

Strategy: Wait for all special invitations in life: marriage, career, family, love, etc. Do not pursue or initiate.

Famous Projectors: Princess Diana, Tony Blair, Virginia Woolf, Queen Elisabeth II, Princess Diana, Karl Marx, Ramana Maharshi, Mick Jagger, Joseph Stalin, Paul McCartney,

Ringo Starr, Osho, Napoleon, Woody Allen, Salvador Dali, Rudolph Nureyev, Elizabeth Taylor, Fidel Castro, James Joyce, Barbra Streisand, Ulysses S. Grant, Henry Miller, Douglas MacArthur, Demi Moore, Nastasia Kinski, Courtney Love, Shirley MacLaine.

Reflectors

The most rare of the four types, Reflectors (less than 2% of the population) are open to the world in every way, since they have nothing fixed in their nature to rely upon. If they do not understand how their design works and they can feel deeply lost and overwhelmed by life. They take others in very deeply. Reflectors are often deeply disturbed due to lack of self-knowledge and adverse conditioning, but they can become very wise if they understand their openness and how to work with it.

Reflectors that do not truly know themselves can be deeply disappointed in life. Before making major decisions, they need to wait out the cycle of the moon (approximately 28 days) because the movement of the moon through the wheel of the zodiac gives the Reflector access to his or her own inner wisdom over time. They have a fixed lunar pattern that repeats every month. Sometimes they are a projector, a Manifestor and even a generator. Reflectors need to understand more about their design and the Human Design System than anyone else to be able to successfully apply their strategy.

Predominant negative feeling: Disappointment

Strategy: Wait out the moon cycle (28.5 days) before making major decisions

Famous Reflectors: Michael Jackson, Graham Greene, Mendelssohn, Uri Geller, Rosalyn Carter (wife of Jimmy Carter), Eduard Mrike (a German poet), Thorwald Detlefsen (a German psychologist and author of esoteric literature).

For more information on Human Design System please go to www.humandesign.info. If you request a design reading, tell Richard Beaumont that you have read this book and he will assist you in looking for the right reader for you.

Following a reading, if you decide to study Human Design System in more detail please do so with caution. I mention this because Birgitte, Lucille and Tim all persuaded me to research into this work. This involved doing what Human Design call 'The Experiment' and I personally found this extremely challenging. I believe myself to be quite enlightened, however it was a very difficult 'experiment' to do. Coming from a background of linguistics, I found much of the literature that supports Human Design System has a lot of negative suggestion. Filtering out this is not easy. Human Design System does not have or suggest doing any form of therapy; I believe this to be wrong and if you decide to go down this road please have the support of an excellent therapist, who can work with you to resolve any deep seated issues that may appear. I know Richard Beaumont has a similar opinion to me but I cannot speak for any other readers.

Ozone and other therapies and interventions

Other amazing therapies include Ozone therapy. This baths each cell in the body with oxygen. It's claimed results are incredible; brain tumours disappearing, diabetes being cured and other changes that are wonderful. My friend and colleague Tremayne Reiss www.phytoplasm.co.uk has literature on this therapy plus other interventions for cancer, which are worth looking at.

I believe that in the future as soon as a person is diagnosed, they will have to go to a practitioner in emotional clearing. It will take time for this to happen but as the general public becomes aware of the direct link between disease and stressful events and the fact that clearing emotions is fast and simple, plus being inexpensive in comparison to pharmaceutical drugs, they will opt for this option. It will take time but the media and the medical profession will be key players in creating this change in attitude. However, the force to change will come from the clients themselves who will demand that such interventions are standard practice.

As for the pharmaceutical industry, like any business they will change or see their profits decrease. They will fight at the start to protect their business, but I am certain they will see the potential and develop new drugs that work with the two phases that support the body in the way of quantum physics. Certain interventions will become a thing of the past (such as chemotherapy and radiotherapy), as soon as the industry sees the potential to develop interventions that the public want and that they can make money from positive change will happen. The truth is we cannot deny the fact that many people will still want to 'pop a pill' to heal themselves - our lives are so busy that pill popping has its uses. It will take a few generations to change attitudes and make the pill popping public address their issues by other means. NES fulfils the pill popping nature and approaches to the quantum field principles at the same time.

I believe that a META-Medicine® Diagnosis will also become the norm, alongside what we know as a traditional medical diagnosis. Training in META-Medicine® does not take as long as it takes to train to be a doctor. Doctors spend five years training and two to three years specialising. They are very knowledgeable and very skilled in diagnosis, which is why we insist that a client has a medical diagnosis before a META-Medicine® diagnosis. Licensed META-Medicine® Health Coaches have to have this medical information before they can do their stress-based diagnosis. The therapy then works alongside the medical therapy. The interventions called a META-Medicine® Therapy plan include changes to the mind, body, spirit, social and environment.

Training to become a Licensed META-Medicine® Health Coach requires pre-study; taking a course that approximates to 10 days, completing an open book exam, doing thirty 'case studies' and attending a live examination where the student has to complete an entire META-Medicine® stress-based diagnosis with a client, including a META-Medicine® Therapy plan. This is open to anyone interested in health and disease and who is not necessarily a health practitioner. Many people also attend the training just to resolve a personal issue, get the information and are not necessarily interested in becoming licensed.

Why we get disease is fascinating, and the META-Medicine Certification course answers many questions, each trainer has specific specialities that they like to talk about. All of them have to cover the META-Medicine® criteria, which I have listed in the back of the book.

Energy and energetic medicine is definitely on the increase. The Russians have been actively involved in producing amazing machines that can measure many different things in the body. Birgitte recently had a treatment for her blood by Richard Beaumont (Human Design). She told me that the effects were immediate; she felt energised after previously having lost a lot of power in her muscles as I described earlier. I have since found out that this was one of the early Scenar devices, In chapter 15 I mention how NES Health have developed this further into a device called the Mi-Health. Likewise I have personally had a full body reading by a machine called the Valeom machine by my friend and colleague Dr Kwesi Anan Odum. Scenar and the Prognos machines are also incredible devices that work on energetic principle. Many of these machines are very pragmatic, which is very Russian. Dr Kwesi told me that the Americans spent a million dollars developing a pen that could write in space. The Russian use a pencil.

The Russians were instrumental in mapping the brain. I have heard of brain scanners that can identify the relays with even more accuracy and depth than we presently have. I have not been able to find any literature to back this up. The Russians are definitely going to play a significant part in the change of medicine in the future and I for one will be exploring these options as and when I find them and I will report on them on my websites.

Of course, the medical profession will develop new strategies for drug interventions, such as tailoring drugs based on DNA.[128]

But this book is not about that; there is plenty of reporting about medical interventions in the media. A colleague of mine, Robert Davidson, had a lot to do with introducing Homeopathy into the UK. He said to me that, in his opinion more and more people are showing up with chronic diseases that are very challenging to heal even with homeopathy. There is definitely a change in disease and our awareness of them and how we treat them. However the future is bright and there is still so much more to learn. At least with META-Medicine® we have a road map that explains so much. There will be more to come and as I mentioned at the start of this book, META-Medicine® is a great system but it is not the only one, there will be something else that supersedes it in the future. For the moment it is a brilliant system that I firmly believe will change the face of medicine in the world today.

Conclusion of some stories
Birgitte's ongoing transformation
Birgitte Bakke is changing her life as I mentioned earlier. Her paralysis has completely disappeared. Recently I caught up with her in Bergen, Norway in mid 2009 and she told me since the paralysis she has changed her career and is no longer working in the health arena, instead she is focussed on being a musician and creative activities. Knowing her this is definitely what she should be doing in her life. She told me that she has more strength in her body than she has ever had. I am proud of her. I know how deep she has had to dig in order to achieve this transformation. She is an inspiring person. She still applies what she knows to her life and she stopped doing the things she thought she should do; the NOT self. The combination of her many years of training and being qualified as a Health Practitioner plus her personal development training through NLP, Time Line Therapy and Hypnotherapy, her study of META-Medicine® and recently her acknowledgement of her personality and design as a person through the Human Design System has transformed her. She has grown massively as a person and turned from a troubled person whose life was challenged by illnesses, depression and lack of energy into a grounded, happy healthy woman.

Georgie and her breast cancer
Georgie Atkinson is now on a completely different path in her life. The pH balancing has got rid of the tumour in the dermis and the lymph glands have healed. She underwent hypothermia and low dose chemotherapy to get rid of multiple lymph cancers that had grown in the chest. Something she attributed to the constant barrage of abuse she received from the PDT scientist she was working with. She is an inspiration to any woman who has had breast cancer. She tells me she will be writing a book about her journey. I am sure that it will be a great read.

The META-Medicine® breast cancer story
You may remember the story from the start about the woman whose child went into a coma after an accident involving a car; the consultant tells her that her child is going to be fine - after that she discovered a lump in her left breast, she feels terrible, tired and she has no energy. She goes to the doctor and is diagnosed with breast cancer. What happens now?

243

The present system - after the medical diagnosis - she develops metastasis, lymph, liver and bone – she has chemotherapy, radiotherapy and a mastectomy with the lymph glands also removed in the same operation. She survives this but later on they find liver cancer. She is also found to have leukaemia. She has a further bout of experimental chemotherapy, which seems to shrink the liver cancer and the leukaemia cell count changes for the better. Then the bad news; the liver and bone cancer comes back and she eventually dies in a hospice heavily sedated with morphine, due to the pain of all the cancers.

The META-Medicine® Integrative approach - she finds a lump in her breast, she goes to the doctor, immediately has a brain CT which confirms that the breast cancer is in resolution. She is then immediately counselled by a licensed META-Medicine® Health Coach whose diagnosis is that the 'Glandular' breast cancer was from a deep worry conflict with her son six months earlier. Together, the META-Medicine® Health Coach and the woman develop a therapy plan. She clears out the emotion of the conflict shock of the child being hit and the shocks from the medical diagnosis. She changes her diet and is paid (via government funded health insurance) to recoup at home. Her business is taken care of in the meantime. Her family and friends all support her and are coached in how to assist her to making a full recovery. The META-Medicine® Health Coach works with her throughout the whole plan. She has no metastasis, the tumour is left alone and becomes encapsulated; it stays and she lives with it. She carries on with a normal productive life.

Adam and his Achilles heel

Adam Sprackling is now happily married and running a successful business in the personal development and business coaching field in Brighton UK. His leg and skin are completely healed and his life is amazing. I went to his wedding and I was so happy to see him enjoying life to the absolute full. I know he worked and worked on himself to really change his life. The issue with his leg was certainly a turning point.

Every illness has a meaning; even a herniated disc can change a life.

I learnt from the issue with my back, and my attitude now to life has dramatically changed for the better, and I am doing what I am destined to do. I know I did not have a cancer, but the effects made me almost lose everything I had worked for in my life. I now have no pain; I jog, run, walk and live a completely normal life. I have had another MRI and it shows that the cartilage is not pressing up against the nerves anymore. It was a long journey, one which I would never wish upon my worst enemy. However, I have learnt so much during this time and have completed the promise I made to myself back when I was walking up that hill to school, which was to find out why debilitating diseases happen. I believe I have done that, and gone way beyond what I thought I would discover, and if my mother was still alive today, I hope that she would be proud of me, proud of my spreading the word of this incredible information.

The real reason I wrote this book.

I left Kim's house and as I drove home something amazing happened to me a few miles into the journey; I had to pull the car over. A massive wave of intense emotion came over me. The feelings you get when something spiritual has just happened. Kim had a son. He was now eighteen. His mum was alive because of the work that I did with her. I wish there had been people like me in the world when my mother had breast cancer so that perhaps she would still be alive to see my son grow up. This was the real reason I wrote this book. Please tell others about META-Medicine® and together we can make sure that many more lives are healed by this incredible information.

INDEX

Nimustine (ACNU) · 218
Nitrogen yperite' · 218
NLP · iv, vi, 9, 19, 20, 21, 22, 41, 42, 44, 52, 64,
    73, 77, 99, 101, 103, 122, 125, 172, 199, 203,
    227, 234, 236, 242
NLP trainer · 20, 21, 52, 77
Non-Hodgkin's lymphoma · 217
Nut and Seeds · 171
Nutri Energetics System · 2, 29, 120, 121, 122, 228,
    232, 233, 234, 235, 236, 241
Nutrition · 168, 236, 248
Nutritionist · 171

O

Obsessive thinking · 53, 57
Oral poliomyelitis vaccine · 146
Ovarian cyst · 8, 189
Ozone therapy · 241

P

Part A Disease cycle · 96
Part B Disease cycle · 88, 96, 97
Parts · 70, 77
Paul Gallo · 140
PDT · 52, 64, 214
Penny Brohn Cancer Care · 26
People Against Cancer · 214
Pertusis · 146
Pertussis · 149, 150, 151
Peter Fraser · v, 3, 29, 38, 69, 104, 121, 122, 228,
    233, 234
Petter Boeckman · 198
PH · 165
Pharmaceutical industry · 2, 3, 15, 16, 17, 18, 28,
    47, 139, 145, 147, 162, 218, 223, 226, 232, 233,
    241
Pneumococcus · 148
Pneumonia · 133
Poisoning · 27, 39, 92, 126, 133, 158
Potassium · 168, 219
Prednisolone · 111
Pro-biotic · 27, 124, 127, 129, 143, 154
Professor Raef · 212
Professor Wolf Reik · 5
Progestagens · 179
Prognos · 242
Programming conflict · 79
Projector · 237, 238
Prozac · 103
Psycho-genealogy · 79, 80

Q

Quantum · 4, 5, 15, 47
Quantum mechanics · 4

R

Radiologist · 115
Radiotherapy · 87, 188, 189, 220
Ralph Moss PhD · 3
Reflector · 238, 240
Regeneration phase · 58, 59, 128
Reiki · 222, 232
Religion · 197
Removal of ovaries · 189
Reproductive system · 106
Response rates · 227
Retina · 109
Richard Beaumont · 237, 241, 242
Robert Waghmare · v, 14, 111
Ronald Gdanski · 248
Rubella · 146, 155, 157, 158
Rudolph Steiner · 26, 154
Rupert Sheldrake · 137
Rose Hayman - 236

S

Salmonella · 127
Scenar · 242
Schizophrenia · 200
Screening · 216
Screening for cancer · 216
Second phase · 55, 59, 60, 61, 74, 86, 92, 93, 94,
    95, 97, 98, 102, 103, 110, 117, 121, 128, 131,
    132, 134, 143, 147, 148, 151, 154, 159, 162,
    164, 165, 166, 172, 173, 212, 221, 222, 223,
    224, 229
Segerstrom and Miller · 15, 35, 248
Septicaemia · 132, 133
Sexual conflicts · 191
Sexuality · 196, 197
Shock · 1, 10, 12, 19, 29, 30, 35, 36, 37, 38, 39, 40,
    43, 44, 45, 48, 49, 50, 51, 52, 54, 56, 58, 63, 64,
    65, 69, 72, 74, 77, 79, 80, 81, 95, 96, 100, 101,
    102, 104, 111, 113, 115, 119, 124, 125, 126,
    131, 134, 137, 147, 157, 166, 180, 194, 195,
    196, 200, 205,   211, 213, 223, 224
Side effects · 147
Sir Gerry Robinson · 12, 13
Smallpox · 126, 133
Smell · 39, 51, 56, 69, 105, 108, 132, 138, 140,
    156, 157
Social identity conflicts · 182
Sodium · 168, 219

About the Authors
Richard Flook

Richard heads up the international training of META-Medicine®. Since early childhood, after the divorce of his parents and subsequent death of his mother from metastasised breast cancer, he has felt a deep compulsion to find an answer as to why this disease struck down the most important person in his life.

After the divorce, Richard and his two brothers were cared for by their father in the family home some 400 miles (600km) away from where their mother lived. He was only twelve years old when he experienced the horror of losing his mother and even though at a distance, he lived through the trauma of her struggle, seeing her endure a mastectomy, chemotherapy, radiotherapy, secondary tumours and then her eventual acceptance of death.

It was on the day she died that he made the decision to try to discover a better way to assist people to heal. He knew intuitively that there was a connection between his parent's divorce, the massive distance separating his mother from her three boys, and the breast cancer. He decided to study psychotherapy at university but instead, through challenging circumstances, he found himself working and then running the family wine and spirit business.

Although successful in business, the decision he made when he was twelve years old was still burning in the back of his mind. Some twelve years later on in life at the age of thirty, he was able to follow his dream and through the intensive study of Neuro Linguistic Programming (NLP - an advanced form of psychotherapy) while successfully running the family business, he eventually became a master and qualified trainer of NLP, hypnotherapy and Time Line Therapy® - (an incredible system that, at lighting speed, releases emotions and negative decisions.)

It was at that time he came across the work of the doctor whose basic theories form the foundation of META-Medicine®. He wanted to learn more but at that time could not train or find other information regarding these theories because they were hidden and also only available in German. However, hungry to share what he knew about META-Medicine® and to impart the knowledge of how the mind and body work as one in creating and healing a disease, he approached some of the medical leaders in the field of cancer care. He was told by the medical fraternity that there was no mind-body connection and medical science would eventually find a cure for all diseases. The conclusion he was forced to make was to leave this field alone until such a time that the undeniable truth of a psychological link to disease was proven and the information he knew was out there could become more freely available.

Confused and disheartened by people who were later to become his peers, and because of his successful background in business, he became a trainer in NLP communication techniques in major blue chip organisations: J.P. Morgan, Chase Manhattan Bank, Samsung, Sony Eriksson were among his clients.

Richard met Johannes Fisslinger, the president of the International META-Medicine® Association at a chance meeting in 2004. Johannes, a native of Germany living in Los Angeles, California, wanted to spread word of the amazing discoveries of META-Medicine®

and, with a skilled team of medical doctors and experts including Richard, they brought META-Medicine® out of secrecy and into the international arena by making the information more easily accessible. Richard brought to the association his skills in training and education and is an active, integral member of the IMMA board. Since that time Richard has been involved in developing META-Medicine® worldwide, including introducing this groundbreaking material to Australasia, Europe, Scandinavia, North America, Iceland, Czech Republic, Japan, China, Russia and the Middle East.

Richard is a pioneer of accelerated and advanced learning techniques producing some of the best practitioners of any discipline he decides to teach. Not only is he one of the most skilled practitioners of META-Medicine® and NLP, getting incredible results with terminal cancer clients, he also works with everyday people, assisting them in transforming their lives at the deepest level. He is renowned for teaching these complex skills with ease to new practitioners and potential trainers, so that they too can get the same miraculous results he does. Richard is a native of the UK lives in Canada, near Toronto with his lovely wife Kristin and his newly born son Oliver. You can contact Richard through www.meta-medicine.com or www.whyamisick.org.

Rob van Overbruggen Ph.D

Rob van Overbruggen PhD, uses his expert knowledge of Neurolinguistic Programming (NLP), Timeline procedures and Hypnotherapy to help clients use their minds to influence their disease process.

Rob was born in 1972, in a small town in the south of The Netherlands. His early education was in the field of Software Engineering, where he learned to identify patterns and understand and incorporate common links from different viewpoints.

To satisfy his desire to understand the mind, he began studying Neuro Linguistic Programming, working with timelines, and Hypnotherapy in 1993.

A year later, he decided to study psychological influences on the cancer process, which later on became his mission in life. In 1995 he was introduced to the basics of META-Medicine®. The patterns that emerged from these were profound, clear, understandable and reproducible, however they were far from accepted by the medical community.

Based on his 12 year study into this field he wrote the book: Healing Psyche - Patterns and Structure of Complementary Psychological Cancer Treatment (CPCT). In his book, he identified overlapping patterns from different psychological approaches to cancer therapy. From this he was able to identify the psychological patterns that influence the cancer process.

This book received great reviews from pioneering icons in the field, such as Carl Simonton MD, Christiane Northrup MD and Hendrik Treugut MD.

Rob holds a Doctorate in Clinical Hypnotherapy, and is an internationally licensed Hypnotherapist, NLP, and Timeline trainer. He is the founder and director of Mexion, a company specializing in therapy and training. He is the director of therapeutic research for Healing Psyche, and is responsible for maintaining the quality of licensed hypnotherapists in The Netherlands. You can contact Rob through www.healingpsyche.com or www.metamedicine.com.

Endnotes

1 Extreme Drug Resistance Assay test. The EDR Assay provides information that can be critical to your care, by identifying chemotherapy drugs that are unlikely to be effective. The Extreme Drug Resistance (EDR) Assay is an advanced laboratory test for cancer, also known as a "chemotherapy drug resistance test." This test is performed by growing a portion of the cancer tumour in the presence of different chemotherapy drugs in the laboratory. If the cancer cells grow in the presence of a very high (extreme) dosage of a chemotherapy drug, studies have shown that the cancer is unlikely to respond to that drug in the patient's body. The test results are usually released to the treating physician within 10 days of specimen receipt, so that the physician can select the best chemotherapy regimen for the patient, without wasting valuable treatment time. Source: - www.virtualtrials.com

2 Lancet, 1999; 353: 1437-8

3 'The Ghost in your Genes' - Horizon BBC Science. Epigenetics adds a whole new layer to genes beyond the DNA. It proposes a control system of 'switches' that turn genes on or off – and suggests that things people experience, like nutrition and stress, can control these switches and cause heritable effects in humans. Source: - 'The Ghost in your Genes' Horizon BBC Science

4 Genomic Imprinting (Frontiers in Molecular Biology) by Wolf Reik and Azin Surani ISBN-13: 978-0199636259

5 Lipton & Bensch 1991) Microvessel Endothelial Cell trans-differentiation (BL p72/3)

6 A placebo is a sham medical intervention intended to lead the recipient to believe that it may improve his/her condition. In one common placebo procedure, a patient is given an inert sugar pill, told that it may improve his/her condition, but not told that it is in fact inert. Such an intervention may cause the patient to believe the treatment will change his/her condition; and this belief does indeed sometimes cause the patient's condition to improve. This phenomenon is known as the placebo effect. Source: - Wikipedia

7 3 April 2003 | GENEVA -- Cancer rates could further increase by 50% to 15 million new cases in the year 2020, according to the World Cancer Report, the most comprehensive global examination of the disease to date. However, the report also provides clear evidence that healthy lifestyles and public health action by governments and health practitioners could stem this trend, and prevent as many as one third of cancers worldwide. Source: - World Health Organisation Website - www.who.in

8 Death by Medicine: Article by Gary Null PhD, Carolyn Dean MD ND, Martin Feldman MD Debora Rasio MD, Dorothy Smith PhD - October 2003 - "A definitive review and close reading of medical peer-review journals, and government health statistics shows that American medicine frequently causes more harm than good. The number of people having in-hospital, adverse drug reactions (ADR) to prescribed medicine is 2.2 million.1 Dr. Richard Besser, of the CDC, in 1995, said the number of unnecessary antibiotics prescribed annually for viral infections was 20 million. Dr. Besser, in 2003, now refers to tens of millions of unnecessary antibiotics.2, 2a The number of unnecessary medical and surgical procedures performed annually is 7.5 million.3 The number of people exposed to unnecessary hospitalization annually is 8.9 million.4 The total number of iatrogenic deaths shown in the following table is 783,936. It is evident that the American medical system is the leading cause of death and injury in the United States. The 2001 heart disease annual death rate is 699,697; the annual cancer death rate, 553,251." Source: www.newmediaexplorer.org

9 NHS employees at record level - The number of people employed by the NHS has risen, recent figures show. The NHS workforce has grown by 30%, new figures show, with 1.3 million people employed last year, up from one million the decade previously. Published by the Information Centre for Health and Social Care, the annual NHS census shows that NHS employees now stand at record levels, with an increase in the number of doctors and nurses coupled with a rise in managerial positions. In total, 34,301 extra people were working for the health service in 2005 compared with previous years, including 5,309 doctors and 6,646 nurses. The number of managers increased by 1,665 to 39,391, almost double the 20,842 charged with running the health service in 1995. Source: netdoctor.co.uk

10 Junior doctors earn from £44,117 to £69,369. Doctors in the new specialty doctor grade earn between £36,443and £67,959. Consultants can earn between £74,504 to £176,242, dependent on length of service and payment of additional performance related awards. Many general practitioners (GPs) are self employed and hold contracts, either on their own or as part of a partnership, with their local primary care trust (PCT). Salaried GPs employed directly by PCTs earn between £53,249 to 80,354. Summarised from:- www.nhscareers.nhs.uk

11 National Average Salary for a plastic surgeon is $298,000 based on collective figures from around the USA in 2008/2009. Some make as much as $4million and pay as much as $50,000 in insurance. Source:- http://mdsalaries.blogspot.com

12 Can Gerry Robinson fix the NHS. Management guru Gerry Robinson faces his biggest challenge - to reduce hospital waiting lists.. An Open University programme for the BBC. Source:- www.open2.net

13 The results of the 2008 ASHE show that median weekly pay for full-time employees in the UK grew by 4.6 per cent in the year to April 2008 to reach £479. Median earnings of full-time male employees was £521 per week in April 2008; for women the median was £412. Source :- www.statistics.gov.uk

14 Conclusion of papers on stress and disease. Segerstrom and Miller 2004, Kopp and Rethelyi 2004, McEwen and Lasky 2002, Mcewen and Seeman 1999.

15 Controversial EU vitamins ban to go ahead - By Sam Knight, Times Online. A controversial new EU regulation that has threatened to outlaw thousands of mineral supplements and bankrupt health food stores across Britain was upheld this morning. The European Court of Justice approved the Food Supplements Directive even though the court's own Advocate-General advised that the Directive was invalid under EU law. Source: - www.timesonline.co.uk

16 Harvard Study Effect of Oral administration of Type II Collagen on rheumatoid arthritis – Published in Science September 1993. Abstract - Rheumatoid arthritis is an inflammatory synovial disease thought to involve T cells reacting to an antigen within the joint. Type II collagen is the major protein in articular cartilage and is a potential autoantigen in this disease. Oral tolerization to autoantigens suppresses animal models of T cell-mediated autoimmune disease, including two models of rheumatoid arthritis. In this randomized, double-blind trial involving 60 patients with severe, active rheumatoid arthritis, a decrease in the number of swollen joints and tender joints occurred in subjects fed chicken type II collagen for 3 months but not in those that received a placebo. Four patients in the collagen group had complete remission of the disease. No side effects were evident. These data demonstrate clinical efficacy of an oral tolerization approach for rheumatoid arthritis. Source: - www.healingwithnutrition.com

17 UK doctors concerned about motives for making statins non-prescription drugs. May 2004. After the UK government announced it was to make statins OTC (over the counter) drugs, some doctors and consumer groups wonder whether the UK population is being used as guinea pigs. Some statins have been found to have side-effects. These are rare, but can be serious. The problem is there are no huge studies to measure how widespread the side-effects are. Some doctors are concerned about this. Others say that the best way to protect yourself from the effects of high cholesterol is through diet and exercise. Source: - www.medicalnewstoday.com

18 What doctors don't tell you – Lynne McTaggart P95-102.

19 Lipitor - Reports of Neuromuscular Degeneration by Jonathan Campbell, March 16, 2004. Numerous adverse side effect reports have implicated Lipitor as a possible cause for severe neuromuscular degeneration. Some people who have been using Lipitor for two years or more report symptoms similar to multiple sclerosis or ALS - Lou Gehrig's Disease - in which they are losing neuromuscular control of their bodies. Source: - www.newmediaexplorer.org

20 An estimated 5 percent to 10 percent of all breast cancers are hereditary. Particular mutations in genes associated with breast cancer are more common among certain geographic or ethnic groups, such as people of Ashkenazi (central or eastern European) Jewish heritage and people of Norwegian, Icelandic, or Dutch ancestry. Particular genetic changes occur more frequently in these groups because they have a shared ancestry over many generations. Source: - Genetics home reference US National Library of Medicine http://ghr.nlm.nih.gov

21 Most cases of breast cancer, about 90%, result from one or more mutations, mistakes made while the cells are dividing in the breast tissue. We're not sure what causes these body cell ("somatic") changes -- what you eat, where you live, passing cosmic rays have all been suggested as culprits. Another 10% of breast cancer is associated with specific inherited mutations. So far, we've identified two genes, the BRCA1 or the BRCA2, which are passed from generation to generation with mutations for breast cancer already in them. Source: - www.thedoctorwillseeyounow.com

22 Lipton & Bensch 1991- Microvessel Endothelial Cell transdifferentiation (BL p72/3)

23 Darwin F 1888 Letter to Moritz Wagner (BL 50)c

24 Environmental pollution and the global burden of disease (David Briggs Br. Med. Bull. 2003; 68: 1-24.) The impact of environmental pollution on congenital anomalies (Helen Dolk and Martine Vrijheid Br. Med. Bull. 2003; 68: 25-45.) Infertility and environmental pollutants (Michael Joffe Br. Med. Bull. 2003; 68: 47-70.) Contribution of environmental factors to cancer risk (Paolo Boffetta and Fredrik Nyberg Br. Med. Bull. 2003; 68: 71-94.) Air pollution and infection in respiratory illness (Anoop J Chauhan and Sebastian L Johnston Br. Med. Bull. 2003; 68: 95-112.) Evaluating evidence on environmental health risks (Lesley Rushton and Paul Elliott Br. Med. Bull. 2003; 68: 113-128.) Environmental effects and skin disease (JSC English, RS Dawe, and J Ferguson Br. Med. Bull. 2003; 68: 129-142.) Ambient air pollution and health (Klea Katsouyanni Br. Med. Bull. 2003; 68: 143-156.) Electromagnetic radiation: Environmental pollution and health (Anders Ahlbom and Maria Feychting Br. Med. Bull. 2003; 68: 157-165.) Hazards of heavy metal contamination (Lars Järup Br. Med. Bull. 2003; 68: 167-182.) Health hazards and waste management (Lesley Rushton Br. Med. Bull. 2003; 68: 183-197.) Contaminants in drinking water: Environmental pollution and health (John Fawell and Mark J Nieuwenhuijsen Br. Med. Bull. 2003; 68: 199-208.) Indoor air pollution: a global health concern (Junfeng Zhang and Kirk R Smith Br. Med. Bull. 2003; 68: 209-225.) Asthma: environmental and occupational factors (Paul Cullinan and Anthony Newman Taylor Br. Med. Bull. 2003; 68: 227-242.) Noise pollution: non-auditory effects on health (Stephen A Stansfeld and Mark P Matheson Br. Med. Bull. 2003; 68: 243-257.) Risks associated with ionizing radiation: Environmental pollution and health (MP Little Br. Med. Bull. 2003; 68: 259-275.) Source British Medical Bulletin – Oxford Journals - http://bmb.oxfordjournals.org

25 Willett 2002) (BL p72).

26 HF Nijhout (Nijhout 1990) 'Biology of Belief' p.41.

27 28   Reference the website of Association of cancer research and their current projects list. Source: - www.airc.org.uk

28 Ronald Gdanski, Author of the book CANCER, Cause, Cure and Cover-up Extract According to mainstream medicine, defective genes sending the wrong signals cause production of too many growth hormone receptors in the cell walls and cause about 35 per cent of breast cancers. Women with a family history of cancer who think they have defective genes are having

their healthy breasts removed to prevent cancer. Others live in great fear of the disease. They have been deceived. "Defective" genes have nothing to do with the rapid growth of breast or any cancer. In breast cancer, "bad" genes are described by disrupted growth factor functions, yet no research has identified the source of the dysfunction. The normal way to designate genes is by chromosome "number" and "arm": so-called "defective" breast cancer genes do not have these proper designations and are just theoretical. They have never been located and identified according to the combination of genetic bases and amino acid fault. Nor have any other "cancer genes." Source: - www.alive.com

29 Kling 2003; Jones 2001; Seppa 2000; Baylin 1997) (BL p72)

30 Waging a War Against Cancer Versus Healing Your Life by Bernie Siegel, MD source: - www.berniesiegelmd.com

31 Rudolf Steiner (25 or 27 February 1861[1] – 30 March 1925) was an Austrian philosopher, literary scholar, educator, architect, social thinker, playwright and esotericist.[2][3] He gained initial recognition as a literary critic and cultural philosopher. At the beginning of the twentieth century he founded a new spiritual movement, Anthroposophy, as an esoteric philosophy growing out of European transcendentalist roots with links to Theosophy. Source: - Wikipedia

32 Greenberg 2003 Bruce Lipton page 138.

33 Bruce Lipton p139 - Baylor school of surgery New England journal of medicine 2002.

34 Reference the University of South Carolina Chernobyl research initiative. Source: - http://cricket.biol.sc.edu/Chernobyl.htm

35 Drinking too much water can lead to a condition known as water intoxication and to a related problem resulting from the dilution of sodium in the body, hyponatremia. Water intoxication is most commonly seen in infants under six months of age and sometimes in athletes. A baby can get water intoxication as a result of drinking several bottles of water a day or from drinking infant formula that has been diluted too much. Athletes can also suffer from water intoxication. Athletes sweat heavily, losing both water and electrolytes. Water intoxication and hyponatremia result when a dehydrated person drinks too much water without the accompanying electrolytes. Source: - www.about.com

36 An air embolism, or more generally gas embolism, is a physiological condition caused by gas bubbles in a vascular system. For very large venous air embolisms, death may occur if a large bubble of gas (centimetres) becomes lodged in the heart, stopping blood from flowing from the right ventricle to the lungs (this is similar to vapor lock in engine fuel systems). Source: - Wikipedia

37 Shocking statistical evidence is cited by Gary Null PhD, Caroly Dean MD ND, Martin Feldman MD, Debora Rasio MD and Dorothy Smith PhD in their recent paper Death by Medicine - October 2003, released by the Nutrition Institute of America. Source: www.newmediaexplorer.org

38 The complete list of things that give you cancer according to epidemiologists Source: - www.numberwatch.co.uk

39 Ovarian cysts causes Source: - www.mayoclinic.com

40 What causes prostate cancer? Source: - www.ehealthmd.com

41 Type II Diabetes : Cause and Risk factors Source : - ww.dlife.com

42 Segerstrom and Miller 2004, Kopp and Rethelyi 2004, McEwen and Lasky 2002, McEwen and Seeman 1999

43 Bruce Lipton p.146 Lipton et al 1991.

44 Bruce Lipton – Biology of belief p104

45 The Sympathetic Nervous System - Source //home.swipnet.se/sympatiska/nervous.htm

46 Lipton & Bensch 1991- Microvessel Endothelial Cell transdifferentiation (BL p72/3)

47 Lipton et al 1999 - BLp146

48 Science Daily Stress may help cancers cells resist treatment Extract "Scientists from Wake Forest University School of Medicine are the first to report that the stress hormone epinephrine causes changes in prostate and breast cancer cells that may make them resistant to cell death." Source: -www.renegadeneurologist.com

49 Van der Kolk et Alia, 1996, p291-292.

50 Parts Integration and Psychotherapy by Richard Bolstad. A neurological Model for understanding the task of therapy. Source : - www.transformations.net.nz/trancescript

51 A new understanding on spontaneous remissions of cancer Extract: "There are many documented cases of cancer that underwent spontaneous regression after acute bacterial infections e.g. streptococcal or staphylococcal infections. A study carried out by Kleef et al for the office of Complementary and Alternative Medicine [NIH, Bethseda] concluded that the

occurrence of fever in childhood protected against the later onset of malignant disease and that spontaneous remission is often preceded by febrile infections." Source www.second-opinions.co.uk

52 The Healing Crisis 'What is it?' AKA: The Cleansing Reaction, The Detox Reaction, and The Herxheimer Reaction. Source: - www.falconblanco.com

53 Brain Electrical Activity In Epilepsy: Characterization Of The Spatio-Temporal Dynamics With Cellular Neural Networks Based On A Correlation Dimension Analysis (2000) by R. Kunz, R.Tetzlaff, D. Wolf Source www.citeseerx.ist.edu

54 Understanding Depression, signs, symptoms, causes and help. Extract: - "Some people describe depression as "living in a black hole" or having a feeling of impending doom. However, some depressed people don't feel sad at all — instead, they feel lifeless, empty, and apathetic. Whatever the symptoms, depression is different from normal sadness in that it engulfs your day-to-day life, interfering with your ability to work, study, eat, sleep, and have fun. The feelings of helplessness, hopelessness, and worthlessness are intense and unrelenting, with little, if any, relief." Source: - www.helpguide.org

55 Brainwave cap controls computer "A team of US researchers has shown that controlling devices with the brain is a step closer. Four people, two of them partly paralysed wheelchair users, successfully moved a computer cursor while wearing a cap with 64 electrodes. Previous research has shown that monkeys can control a computer with electrodes implanted into their brain. The New York team reported their findings in the Proceedings of the National Academy of Sciences." Source: www.bbc.co.uk

56 Decoding the Human body field Fraser, Massey and Parisi Wilcox p239

57 Side effects of cancer drugs. Source: - www.cancerhelp.org.uk

58 Emotional memory study reveals evidence for a self-reinforcing loop. Durham N.C.. -- Researchers exploring the brain structures involved in recalling an emotional memory a year later have found evidence for a self-reinforcing "memory loop" -- in which the brain's emotional center triggers the memory center, which in turn further enhances activity in the emotional center. Source : - www.eurekalert.org

59 PTSD and Physical health "People with post-traumatic stress disorder (PTSD) often experience a number of psychological difficulties such as depression, other anxiety disorders, and substance use-related problems; however, in addition to these psychological difficulties, individuals with PTSD may also be more likely to experience physical health problems." Source http://ptsd.about.com

60 Contributions of functional imaging to understanding Parkinsonian symptoms. Current Opinion in Neurobiology, Volume 14, Issue 6, December 2004, Pages 715-719. Scott T. Grafton. Source: - www.sciencedirect.com

61 Comparison of neuronal activity in the supplementary motor area and primary motor cortex. Cognitive Brain Research, Volume 3, Issue 2, March 1996, Pages 143-150. Jun Tanji and Hajime Mushiake. Source: - www.sciencedirect.com

62 Death toll linked to Gardasil vaccine rises - Complications include shock, 'foaming at mouth,' convulsions, coma. www.worldnetdaily.com

63 Udo Pollmer (b. 1954) is a food chemist. Since 1995 he has been director of the European Institute of Food and Nutrition Sciences (EU.L.E), in which scientists and doctors have joined forces to educate the public based on international specialist literature on nutrition, foodstuffs and health. In a great many publications and Interviews Udo Pollmer has harshly criticized nutritional campaigns and recommendations such as Deutsche Gesellschaft für Ernährung (DGE, German Nutrition Society).

64 Quote taken from a talk by Michael D. Gershon: "The Second Brain". Source www.media.mit.edu

65 From Chest. The official publication of the American College of Chest Physicians. Tuberculosis Veterans of World War II. Roy A Wolford 1945 Source: - www.chestjournal.org

66 Region of Peel, BCG Vaccination document – extract "Although BCG has been used widely for a long time the rates of TB in countries that use BCG have not changed. One third of the world's population has TB infection and two million people a year dies of TB. BCG alone is not enough to stop the spread of TB. Source: - www.region.peel.on.ca.

67 Graph has been redrawn - England 1855-1964 Decennial Death Rates from respiratory Tuberculosis. Source: - www.whale.to

68 Tuberculosis in the United States 2004 TB at all-time low, but decline is slowing and racial disparities persist. Source: Office of enterprise communication Media relations CDC - www.cdc.gov

69 Tuberculosis in Canada Community Prevention and Control Public Health Agency Canada – Ottawa Prepared by Edward Ellis MD, MPH, FRCPC Source: www.phac-aspc.gc.ca

70 Luc Antoine Montagnier (born 18 August 1932 in Chabris, France) is a French virologist and joint recipient with Françoise Barré-Sinoussi and Harald zur Hausen of the 2008 Nobel Prize in Physiology or Medicine, for his co-discovery of the Human Immunodeficiency Virus (HIV). Source: - Wikipedia

71 Interview with Luc Montanier – Did lUc Montainer discover HIV? Text of a videotape interview performed at the Pasteur Institute, July 1997. By Djamel Tahi. Source www.virusmyth.com

72 Smegma (Greek smēgma, "soap") is a combination of exfoliated (shed) epithelial cells, transudated skin oils, and moisture. It occurs in both male and female genitalia. In males, smegma helps keep the glands moist and facilitates sexual intercourse by acting as a lubricant. Source: - Wikipedia

73 Aids Info, Preventive HIV Vaccine – a service of the US Dept of Health and Human services. – Extract – 'The experimental HIV vaccines currently being studied in clinical trials do not contain any "real" HIV, and therefore cannot cause HIV or AIDS. However, some HIV vaccines in trials could prompt your body to produce antibodies against HIV. These HIV antibodies could cause you to test "positive" on a standard HIV test, even if you don't actually have HIV.' Source http://aidsinfo.nih.gov

74 Lynne McTaggart: 'What Doctors Don't Tell you' - p154.

75 Interview Stefan Lanka - Challenging BOTH Mainstream and Alternative AIDS Views - By Mark Gabrish Conlan Dec. 1998 Source www.viusmyth.com

76 'What Doctors Don't Tell You' p. 200, the lancet 1994; 343: 871-81

77 Medical consequences of what homosexuals do by Dr Paul Cameron, Ph.D. Source: - www.familyresearchinst.org

78 Number of partners doesn't explain gay HIV rate. By Steven Reinberg Health Day Reporter – The HIV epidemic among gay men can't be explained by their number of sexual partners, U.S. researchers report. More than half the new HIV infections diagnosed in the United States in 2005 were among gay men, a team at the University of Washington, Seattle, noted. In addition, as many as one in five gay men living in cities may be HIV-positive. But the sexual behaviours of gay and heterosexual men in the United States may not be as different as most people think, the researchers said. In fact, two surveys found that most gay men have a similar rate of sex with unprotected partners compared to straight men or women. Source: - The sexual health Network. http://sexualhealth.e-healthsource.com

79 Treating Bladder cancer. Extract "Chemotherapy drugs such as thiotepa and doxorubicin appear less effective than the immunization used against tuberculosis (TB). This modified TB germ, known as bacillus Calmette-Guerin (BCG), creates an immune response that spills over and attacks the cancer cells as well. The mode of treatment is called immunotherapy. BCG is completely effective in more than 70 percent of superficial tumors and carcinoma in situ (a very early stage of cancer). It reduces cancer recurrence by 40 percent to 45 percent, whereas chemotherapy produces only an 8 percent to 18 percent reduced rate. Each agent has its occasional side effects that must be anticipated and addressed". Source: - www.myoptimumhealth.com

80 Treating Group B Strep: Are Antibiotics Necessary? By Christa Novelli - Most women who have been pregnant in the last few years are familiar with the terms Group B Strep (for Group B Streptococcus), or GBS. The US Centers for Disease Control and Prevention (CDC) and the American College of Obstetricians and Gynaecologists (ACOG) recommend that all pregnant women be screened between weeks 35 and 37 of their pregnancies to determine if they are carriers of GBS. This is done by taking a swab of the pregnant woman's vaginal and rectal areas. Studies show that approximately 30 percent of pregnant women are found to be colonized with GBS in one or both areas. Source: - www.healthychild.com

81 Adapted from BBC News Health MRSA Superbugs. Feb 2005. Source: - www.bbc.co.uk

82 Adapted from various articles by Stephan Lanka. Source: - www.virusmyth.com

83 Preface Dr Sears - The Vaccine book xv.

84 Lynne McTaggart What doctors don't tell you p138.

85 Lancet, 1998; 351: 398-403.

86 Tetanus Vaccination by Jason Sanders. Article : In the USA, with an average of seven to ten deaths a year from Tetanus, there's a 180-260 times greater chance of dying from Tuberculosis. Source: - www.wellbeing.com.au

87 Dr Sears - The Vaccine Book, p.264.

88 Dr Sears - The Vaccine Book, p.49.

89 French ban hepatitis b jab in schools Dec 1998. The potential link between the hepatitis B vaccine and multiple sclerosis has led the French government to suspend vaccinations in schools, much to the consternation of pro vaccination groups. Critics of the decision, including the National Union of Paediatricians and the World Health Organisation, argue that the decision may lead to a public loss of confidence in the vaccine and the risk of other countries following suit. Source: - www.wddty.com

90 Figures taken from Ca immunisation guide, 7th edition 2006. A graph (fig5) Hepatitis B – Trends in reported incidence by age group, Canada 1990 – 2004. Source: - www.phac-aspc.gc.ca

91 Hepatitis B control in Europe by universal vaccination programmes: the situation in 2001. Source Pub Med - US Library of Medicine and the National Institute of health. www.pubmed.gov

92 Lynne McTaggart What doctors don't tell you p.124

93 Quote from Edna West referring to the Polio vaccine in her article Polio perspective. Source: - www.whale.to

94 MMWR, Mumps - United States, 1985-1988. 1989; 38: 101-105.

95 Study dispels link between Autism and Measles vaccine. By Serena Gordon September 2008. Extract "We are certain that there's no link between autism and the MMR," Dr. W. Ian Lipkin, director of the Mailman School of Public Health Center for Infection and Immunity at Columbia University College of Physicians and Surgeons, said at a Wednesday teleconference." Source : - www.health.usnews.com

96 Extract: "The largest reason for launching the (Chicken Pox) jab appears to be economics. Because the medical costs of chickenpox cases are low, it is more expensive to immunize, which costs $39 per dose, than it is to treat chickenpox. In fact, the entire vaccine programme would cost $162 million a year in the US. But to make the cost-benefit equation add up, the authorities have thrown in as a cost the amount of parental income or work time lost because a child had to stay home with chickenpox. Several researchers have attempted to quantify this loss as equalling $293 per family, or $183 per chickenpox cases (Pediatr Infect Dis J, 1994; 13: 173-7). The days lost are often more than the child actually needs because many schools have policies forcing children to stay at home well past the communicable stage. Therefore, the net theoretical benefit of this vaccination is to save some $6.6 million of lost income in the US alone (J Pediatr, June 1994). Other journals have somehow blown this into a $400 million savings (The Lancet, April 16,1994). Source: - www.wddty.com

97 Why isn't the chicken pox vaccine available in the UK? The chickenpox vaccine is now licensed in the UK but it is not part of routine childhood vaccinations. The vaccine against the varicella virus (which causes chickenpox) is not currently recommended for standard use in children. In most cases it is a mild illness and around 89% of adults in the UK will develop immunity to the illness. If the chickenpox vaccine were to be added to the list of childhood vaccinations, it is feared that there would be a greater number of cases of shingles in adults, until the vaccination was given to the entire population. This is because adults who have had chickenpox as a child are less likely to have shingles in later life if they have been exposed occasionally to the chickenpox virus (for example by their children). This is because the exposure acts as a booster vaccine. Source: - www.nhs.uk

98 What doctors do know about Chicken Pox Jabs, June 1999. Source: - www.wddty.com

99 Dr Sears – The Vaccine book. p122

100 The flu vaccine a shot in the dark. April 1990 Source: - www.wddty.com

101 Flu Vaccine may make Asthma worse March 1998 Source: - www.wddty.com

102 JAMA, 1988, Osterholm et al., 260: 1423-1428.]102

103 Super Size Me is an Academy Award-nominated 2004 documentary film, directed by and starring Morgan Spurlock, an American independent filmmaker. It follows a 30-day time period (February 2003) during which Spurlock subsists exclusively on McDonald's fast food and stops exercising regularly. The film documents this lifestyle's drastic effects on Spurlock's physical and psychological well-being and explores the fast food industry's corporate influence, including how it encourages poor nutrition for its own profit. During the filming, Spurlock dined at McDonald's restaurants three times per day, sampling every item on the chain's menu at least once. He consumed an average of 5,000 calories (the equivalent of 9.26 Big Macs) per day during the experiment. In February 2005, Super Size Me Educationally Enhanced DVD edition was released. It is an edited version of the film designed to be integrated into a high school health curriculum. MSNBC has also broadcast an hour long version of the film, in addition to the regular version. Source: - http://video.google.com

104 How Is Sex Determined? by Rick Groleau. Extract "Most of the time, an embryo growing in the womb fully develops into either a male or a female with all the appropriate body parts and, many scientists believe, a mindset programmed according to its gender. What determines its gender—in most cases—are its sex chromosomes: two X chromosomes in the nucleus of its original egg cell and it will become a female; a Y and an X chromosome and it will become a male. But exactly what happens in the womb to make a boy or a girl? This interactive feature illustrates the astonishing changes that occur during the first 16 weeks of development." Source: - www.pbs.org

105 Women's Organising and Public Policy in Canada and Sweden p.310-312. Source: - http://books.google.com
106 In Africa, cultural taboos against homosexuality that were imported by white missionaries are now helping the spread of HIV. This report from the UN goes into some detail, but to summarise. Infection rates among men who have sex with men (MSM) are many times higher than among men who don't. Not because of promiscuity, higher susceptibility, but because of prejudice and ignorance that mean AIDS programs don't address them or reach them. Most MSM are either bisexual, married, or closeted, because it's dangerous to be otherwise in countries where homosexuality is an offence, punishable by sentences ranging in severity up to imprisonment and even death. Source: - www.rainbowreporter.com

107 Reference graph in Wikipedia (same sex relationships, which shows where Homosexuality is illegal Source: - Wikipedia.

108 The medical news from around the world 1,500 animal species practice homosexuality. Homosexuality is quite common in the animal kingdom, especially among herding animals. Many animals solve conflicts by practicing same gender sex. Source: - www.news-medical.net

109 Wolf behaviour – All you need to know about Wolves. (alpha wolf). Social order and visual communication (Mech 1999) Source; - www.freewebs.com

110 Animals and human sexuality: is biology the missing link to our future? By Ali the Sexpert - January 2008. Source: - www.pastthepages.ca

111 Catholic education resource centre - The Health Risks of Gay Sex by John R Diggs Jr., MD. As a physician, it is my duty to assess behaviours for their impact on health and wellbeing. When something is beneficial, such as exercise, good nutrition, or adequate sleep, it is my duty to recommend it. Likewise, when something is harmful, such as smoking, overeating, alcohol or drug abuse, and homosexual sex, it is my duty to discourage it. Source: - www.catholiceducation.org

112 Sexual Partners - Men more likely to have more than one. During 2004/05 men were more likely than women to have had more than one sexual partner in Great Britain during in the previous year. Thirteen per cent of men aged 16-69 had multiple sex partners compared with 9 per cent of women aged 16-49. For both sexes, multiple sexual partners were most common among those aged below 25. Over a third of men aged under 25, a fifth of women aged 16 to 19 and a quarter of women aged 20 to 24 reported having more than one sexual partner in the previous year. Men and women aged 25 to 49 were most likely to have only one sexual partner and also least likely to have none. The proportion of both men and women who had not had a sexual partner was highest among those aged under 20. Among adults that were married or cohabiting, 5 per cent of men and 1 per cent of women had not had a sexual partner in the last year. Source: - www.statistics.gov.uk

113 Bruce Lipton, Biology of Belief, Chapter 2.

114 Cancer. As Eaton et al. [1994, p. 361] note: Medical anthropologists have found little cancer in their studies of technologically primitive people, and paleopathologists believe that the prevalence of malignancy was low in the past, even when differences in population age structure are taken into account (Rowling, 1961; Hildes and Schaefer, 1984; Micozzi, 1991). Source: - www.beyondveg.com

115 People Against Cancer – The failed war on Cancer. Editorial. Source: - www.peopleagainstcancer.net

116 Chemotherapy Heal Cancer and the world is Flat - Lothar p112.

117 Chemotherapy Heal Cancer and the world is Flat -Lothar p113.

118 Archives of Internal Medicine, 2008; 168: 2311-2316

119 Breast cancer: It can disappear without treatment, researchers find - Nov 2008. Breast cancer may spontaneously regress if left alone, researchers suspect. They have found that even advanced, aggressive breast tumours have disappeared after six years or so without any treatment or medical intervention. Source: - www.wddty.com

120 Chemotherapy Heal Cancer and the world is Flat - Lothar p113.

121 History of cancer chemotherapy. Source: - Wikipedia

122 Goodman *et al* 1946.

123 Chemotherapy and the world if flat - Lothar P157

124 Wenzel-Seifert and Lentzen. Chemotherapy and the world if flat Lothar p158.

125 Chemotherapy Heal Cancer and the world is Flat - Lothar p158.

126 Chemotherapy Heal Cancer and the world is Flat - Lothar p68.

127 Summarised from Chemotherapy heals cancer and the world is flat - Lothar Hirneise p.71.

128 The New York times - Patient's DNA May Be Signal to Tailor Medication by Andrew Pollock. Extract: - "For more than two years, Jody Uslan had been taking the drug tamoxifen in hopes of preventing a recurrence of breast cancer. Then a new test suggested that because of her genetic makeup, the drug was not doing her any good." Source www.nytimes.com